Western warfare in the age of the Crusades,
1000–1300

# Warfare and History

General Editor
**Jeremy Black**
*Professor of History, University of Exeter*

## Published

*European warfare, 1660–1815*
Jeremy Black

*The Great War, 1914–18*
Spencer C. Tucker

*Wars of imperial conquest in Africa, 1830–1914*
Bruce Vandervort

*German armies: war and German politics, 1648–1806*
Peter H. Wilson

*Air power in the age of total war*
John Buckley

*Ottoman warfare, 1500–1700*
Rhoads Murphey

*European and Native American warfare, 1675–1795*
Armstrong Starkey

*Vietnam*
Spencer C. Tucker

*Western warfare in the age of the Crusades, 1000–1300*
John France

## Forthcoming titles include:

*English warfare, 1511–1641*
Mark Charles Fissel

*Seapower and naval warfare*
Richard Harding

*The Korean War*
Stanley Sandler

*Frontiersmen: warfare in Africa since 1950*
Anthony Clayton

# Western warfare in the age of the Crusades, 1000–1300

John France

*University of Wales, Swansea*

First published in 1999 by UCL Press

UCL Press Limited
1 Gunpowder Square
London EC4A 3DE
UK

The name of University College London (UCL) is a registered trade mark
used by UCL Press with the consent of the owner.


**British Library Cataloguing-in-Publication Data**
A CIP catalogue record for this book is available from the British Library.


**Library of Congress Cataloging-in-Publication Data are available**

ISBNs: 1-85728-466-6 HB
       1-85728-467-4 PB

Typeset by Best-set Typesetter Ltd., Hong Kong.
Printed by T. J. International, Padstow, UK.

# Contents

# CONTENTS

To my wife, Angela, a veteran of many muddy fields.

# Acknowledgements

I am deeply indebted to an enormous number of people who have helped me in the writing of this book. In 1995 I was able, through the generosity of the British Academy, to travel in Italy and much of the Middle East. Subsequently, with help from the University of Wales, Swansea, I went to the Lebanon and revisited Syria. During these travels a large number of people provided a lot of practical help. In Italy, I would like, in particular, to thank the local authorities at Manerbio and Frascati, whose officers went out of their way to put their local knowledge at my disposal, and the librarians at Avezzano who took so much trouble over my queries. Peter Clark and his colleague, Hadeel Alahmad, at the British Council in Damascus were immensely helpful. Dr Alison McQuitty, Director of the British School at Amman, provided hospitality and helpful advice, as did Dr R. Harper, Director of the British School at Jerusalem, who also laid on a memorable tour of castles. Dr Mohammed Moain Sadek, Director of Tourism and Antiquities for the Palestinian National Authority, was kind enough to escort me around some fascinating sites in Gaza. In all these countries and others I was received with great kindness, for which I offer thanks.

I must acknowledge great debts in terms of ideas. Professor J. C. Holt, though writing in a different context, first fixed my mind on the importance of landed property. I owe a great deal to the ideas of Professor John Gillingham, whose work on war has been so influential. It was thanks to Professor Bernie Bachrach that I was invited to address the Haskins Society at Houston, providing me with an opportunity to sharpen my ideas at a critical time: as a result of these discussions I owe a particular debt to Professor Richard Abels and Dr David Crouch. Kelly de Vries is a splendidly robust person to try ideas out on. Ronnie Ellenblum of Hebrew University was kind enough to share with me his enormous knowledge of crusader archaeology, while Denys Pringle has generously provided much knowledge and assistance on crusader castles. On Middle Eastern warfare I owe a great deal to Yaacov Lev of Bar Ilan University. Valerie Eads was extraordinarily generous with her research on the wars of the Countess Mathilda of Tuscany and I look forward to it coming to fruition. I have been able to draw upon Matthew Strickland's profound knowledge of the Anglo-Norman world. Numerous discussions with Matthew Bennett of the Royal Military Academy, Sandhurst have contributed greatly to my knowledge of the nitty-gritty of medieval warfare. Dr David French, former Director of the British Institute of Archaeology at Ankara, fixed the importance of roads in my mind, while Peter Edbury and Helen Nicholson of University of Wales, Cardiff have been extraordinarily helpful. Professor Malcolm Barber of Reading University and his colleague, Tom Asbridge, have both provided much stimulation. I owe a great debt to Jonathon Phillips of Royal Holloway who runs the Crusades Seminar so well. Susan Edgington kindly allowed me to use her forthcoming edition of Albert of Aachen and provided many references. A. V. Murray of the University of Leeds was relentless in the pursuit of bibliography on my behalf. Andrew Lambert of King's College stimulated my interest in the Lebanon. Professor Gerrit Schutten of Groningen was kind enough to provide assistance on maritime history.

I owe special thanks to Professor Bernard Hamilton who read Chapter 1 and improved it enormously, and to my colleagues Bill Zajac and I. W. Rowlands who looked at many parts of the text and were generous with their time and knowledge. I must thank Professor Jean Richard, Professor Michel Balard, Professor J. Riley-Smith and Professor Gérard Dédéyan, for their kindness and encouragement at various times. Professor David Eastwood and my colleagues in the History Department of University of Wales, Swansea deserve thanks for putting up with my enthusiasms. For all these ideas and advice I am enormously grateful, but of course responsibility for the material is mine alone.

All scholars rely heavily on learned institutions and libraries. The staff of the University of Wales, Swansea library, Cambridge University Library and the Institute of Historical Research have been extraordinarily helpful, but I must also thank those who work at the British Library and the National Library of Wales.

The staff of UCL Press have given me considerable and useful guidance, and the General Editor of this series, Professor Jeremy Black, has been a great inspiration.

*Plate 1    The equipment of a late-eleventh-century knight as portrayed in the Bayeux Tapestry scene of William's preparations for the invasion of England. By special permission of the City of Bayeux.*

*Plate 2    Note the traction-trebuchets and the difference in equipment between the crossbowman and the simple bowmen. By kind permission of the Burgerbibliothek of Bern.*

*Plate 3    The protective armour and helm of this thirteenth century knight show marked development from those worn by the figures in the Bayeux Tapestry. By kind permission of the Trustees of the British Library.*

*Plate 4  A thirteenth-century transport-wagon. Note that it is four-wheeled and has a team of two horses. By kind permission of the Trustees of the Pierpoint Morgan Library, New York.*

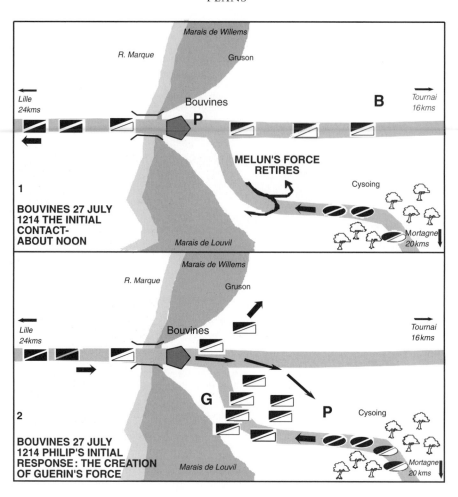

**1**

**BOUVINES 27 JULY 1214 THE INITIAL CONTACT-ABOUT NOON**

**MELUN'S FORCE RETIRES**

**2**

**BOUVINES 27 JULY 1214 PHILIP'S INITIAL RESPONSE: THE CREATION OF GUERIN'S FORCE**

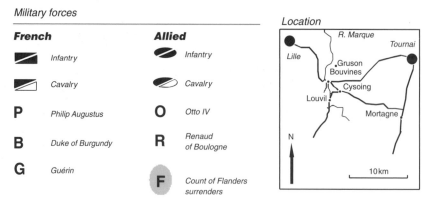

**Military forces**

**French**

▨ Infantry

▨ Cavalry

**P** Philip Augustus

**B** Duke of Burgundy

**G** Guérin

**Allied**

◗ Infantry

◗ Cavalry

**O** Otto IV

**R** Renaud of Boulogne

**F** Count of Flanders surrenders

**Location**

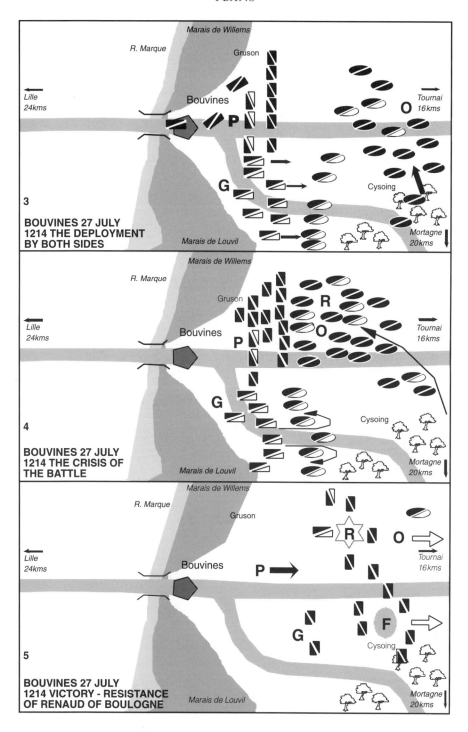

Marais de Willems

R. Marque

Gruson

Bouvines

Lille
24kms

**P**

Tournai
16kms

**O**

**G**

Cysoing

Mortagne
20kms

Marais de Louvil

3

**BOUVINES 27 JULY
1214 THE DEPLOYMENT
BY BOTH SIDES**

Marais de Willems

R. Marque

Gruson

Bouvines

Lille
24kms

**P**

**R**

**O**

Tournai
16kms

**G**

Cysoing

Mortagne
20kms

Marais de Louvil

4

**BOUVINES 27 JULY
1214 THE CRISIS OF
THE BATTLE**

Marais de Willems

R. Marque

Gruson

Bouvines

Lille
24kms

**P**

**R**

**O**

Tournai
16kms

**G**

**F**

Cysoing

Mortagne
20kms

Marais de Louvil

5

**BOUVINES 27 JULY
1214 VICTORY - RESISTANCE
OF RENAUD OF BOULOGNE**

# Chapter One

## *Proprietorial warfare*

This book examines the history of war in what are usually called the "High Middle Ages". At the beginning of the second millennium, Europe was no longer threatened by external attack and it was clearly set on a course of remarkable economic, social and political development. In 1095 the First Crusade was launched, establishing a great military endeavour that was a central preoccupation of Europeans until the end of the thirteenth century. The fourteenth century ushered in great changes in war and society under the influence of economic change, the Black Death and the invention of gunpowder. This is not to say that in the period 1000–1300 warfare was unchanging. But change was subtle, and across this period armies and warfare bore a common stamp which was different from what had gone before and certainly different from what came after.

It is a truth barely worth labouring that an army will reflect closely the nature of the society that produces it. The writer of military history, therefore, is not concerned with some discrete and separate corner of history which can be written about on its own, but must consider the whole political, social and economic development of the age in order to understand the nature of war and the changes that occurred in it. In this period, warfare was shaped by four main factors:

(a) the dominance of land as a form of wealth;
(b) the limited competence of government;
(c) the state of technology which, broadly, favoured defence over attack;
(d) the geography and climate of the West.

Landownership was the distinguishing characteristic of the ruling elites of western Europe. In itself it conferred power, as it always had. Kings claimed an overarching sovereignty and proclaimed that others exercised

1

governmental power only as their delegates. But in practice they were not sharply distinguished from other landowners, who shared their authority rather than acted as its agents. Nor was the pattern of royal ownership in any way different from that of other powerful men and women. In the nature of things, landownership was dispersed, for estates were gathered into families by random means – the accidents of birth, death, marriage and political patronage. A landholding was normally made up of packets of land, often very small individually, scattered amongst the similar holdings of others. The power of sovereign authority over these agglomerations was limited, because communications were poor, and the king could only make real his authority where he or some close delegate resided – on his own demesne. Given this weakness, war was essential to defending and expanding lands and rights because – in the absence, or at least relative weakness, of superior authority – it was, if not the only, then at least the ultimate, means of settling disputes.[1]

Warfare in this period was, therefore, nearly always proprietorial, or at the very least influenced by proprietorial considerations. This is not to say that warfare was always and only about landed possession; but merely that it was a powerful influence that was always taken into account. The outstanding characteristics of medieval warfare, the castle and the armoured knight, arose from the dominance of proprietorial power. Because land transport was poor and expensive, it was cheaper for landowners to travel around their estates eating up the renders of scattered lands. This meant that they needed collecting points with comfortable accommodation, which were strong enough to resist a degree of attack – in short, castles. But, in the end, strength rests in men, so easily raised mobile local forces were needed that could gather at the lord's command. In this sense, the armoured, mounted knight is a response to the needs of proprietors. Some were mere hirelings, sharing the lord's table, but this proximity gave them ambitions and a commonality of interest with their masters. Knights were the most important element in the armies of the age, but everywhere they needed infantry. The knight was very mobile, but the landscape of western Europe is highly variegated and does not always favour mounted warfare. Indeed, although there was much open land, hedges, thickets and woodland were common and could shelter infantry, especially archers. Even in armies of modest size, therefore, the knight was never alone. Moreover, medieval society changed and the make-up of the people who went to war changed with it, although this was to some extent disguised by very obvious elements of continuity. In fact, so deep-seated in the minds of western Europeans were the economic, social, political and geographical forces which shaped warfare that they proved singularly reluctant to change their style of warfare when they came into contact with other civilizations.

The fact that land was the dominant form of wealth and that liquidity was very limited was a major reason why armies were small. Even kings could not afford to maintain standing armies or large arsenals. War is an expensive business: in 1091, King Philip I of France was happy to defray the costs of supporting his bodyguard by hiring them out.[2] As a result, soldiers were expected to equip themselves from the proceeds of their landed holdings – often provided for them by the lord for this very purpose – and from the fruits of pillage. Even so, soldiers always expected cash payments, not least if they served beyond customary limits, and commanders preferred to engage them on flexible terms. As liquidity increased in the twelfth century, the "cash nexus" became ever more important. However, because this remained a relatively poor society, dependent on exploiting the peasant surplus, armies remained *ad hoc* bodies, kept together only for as long as necessity demanded. Professional soldiers did emerge, but commanders dismissed them as soon as possible because of the enormous drain on resources.

This had a considerable effect on military technology. Without an infrastructure of war there could be no systematic development. The only repository of military memory, beyond that of individuals, lay in the households of major rulers, but these were very few and far between and their members never wholly military in their concerns. Therefore, it is not surprising that there was never a great leap forward. Throughout the period, the killing-ground was always very largely limited by the range of the bow and the length of sword or spear, and of the right arm that wielded it. There was change, because the general economic growth of Europe allowed a wider use of metal and individual ingenuity produced some diversification of weapons. But, in general, because provision of weapons was the obligation of the individual, the wealth and skill generated by economic expansion was diverted into the weapons and protection of the wealthy. The most obvious technical improvements were in fortifications. The wooden tower built at Montargis in 1056 by the Lord Seguin could hardly be compared with the huge stone mass of Caerphilly constructed 200 years later. But the development of military architecture and of siege-machinery, which occurred in the late twelfth and thirteenth centuries, depended on civilian innovation and arose from the hiring of specialists from outside the military sphere. In the earlier part of our period, the principles of siege-engines seem to have been well known, but actually building them was difficult and subject to frequent failure.[3] Improvements in siege-technique seem to have sprung from better general organization rather than advances in technology.

Medieval warfare was, in some very important respects, markedly different from that of the modern era. Most fundamentally, war was not solely the prerogative of government. The notion of sovereignty survived from the Roman Empire and helped to give the royal office its special prestige.

3

However, there was a skein of competing forces that pretended to aspects of sovereignty or rivalled and paralleled what we would recognise as its proper competence. Throughout our period the primary form of wealth was land, and everywhere its ownership on any scale gave quasi-governmental powers. Landed property was seen in a very absolute sense and its very concrete nature tended to overshadow sovereignty, for power sprang from possession of land. To be a king was of necessity to be first landlord of the realm, a position which merged into that of other landlords and blurred the distinction between the king and others, and that between sovereignty and ownership. The prestige of monarchy in medieval times was enormous and its position unique, but its uniqueness could be very narrowly interpreted and it could certainly be seen as excluding a commanding authority.[4]

"Private war" has been excoriated by modern historians and regarded as the scourge of the medieval world, but government was so limited, and its competence so narrow, that the struggle for power and influence amongst the elite could often only be conducted by war. We call the men against whom Louis VI of France fought in the early twelfth century "robber barons", but it is a description that they would hardly recognize. It was their misfortune to be survivors of an older genre of behaviour in a new age with new ideas. At the beginning of this period, medieval states lacked any clear definition or firm structure: these emerged only in the second half of the twelfth century, but even then their position was not unchallenged. In the eleventh century the very existence of monarchy was threatened, and one writer has remarked that at that time "the age of kings seemed to have passed and that of princes to be the future".[5] The notion of the state and the remains of such an organization had decayed, and had largely been usurped by an aristocracy whose strength was built on its special position in the European countryside, a strength buttressed greatly by castles. Kings always had to rely on the powerful to support them and raise troops. In the monarchies of Germany and France, sheer distance, poor communications and the rivalries of royal houses enabled nobles and local authorities to take power and hold it. Even in England, which is usually regarded as a small and tightly ruled land, the North was almost another country, and the lords of the Welsh March were largely left to their own devices by the Norman kings.

In fact, there was a deep confusion of what for us are two separate concepts – sovereignty and ownership. Every kingdom was a lordship and every king had the preoccupations of a landowner: every lordship resembled a kingdom and its holders felt entitled to some of the perquisites of a king. Both can best be seen as *mouvances*, circles of influence based on landownership which rarely coincided with the geographical area of settlement of any nation or any particular geographical unity. Moreover, these circles of influence overlapped

4

heavily. Otto-William, Count of Mâcon (982–1026), was the son of a king of Italy; he held Mâcon of the Duke of Burgundy who was a vassal of the Capetian king of France. He was also related to the old Carolingian ruling house, whom the Capetian kings had displaced and held land of the Empire east of the Saône. A very important group of lords, the Count of Flanders, the Duke of Louvain and the Count of Hainaut, were vassals of both the Empire and the Capetian monarch. In conflicts between *mouvances* this gave scope for vassals to change sides: in 1185 the castellan of Péronne, a vassal of the Count of Flanders, defected from his lord and received his castle of Braine as a fief of Philip of France.[6]

Although the history of war is primarily that of war between the *mouvances*, it must be remembered that there was another dimension to medieval warfare. The holders of power were a tiny minority in an armed or potentially armed society. Force of arms was the final sanction of the elite, and thinkers would soon seize upon it as the justification of their power and privileges. So the apparatus of war in the widest sense was also intended to enforce the social order. The castle and the armed band were not merely a defence against other *mouvances* but also the means by which the lord exploited the peasantry. It is no accident, as we shall see, that military terminology and practice were deeply infused with considerations of status. Moreover, the threat of social war was present in the minds of the elite and informed the way in which they treated their necessary allies, the footsoldiers and other socially inferior troops. Kings and magnates claimed a monopoly of war and in time generated a military ethos, chivalry, which glorified their role. Because the great magnates had colonized the Church, which produced most of the written records, these focus on their role, but war was not an entirely aristocratic business and it involved very directly considerable sections of the populace. The basis of their involvement is a complicated matter. It has often been assumed that all freemen were obliged to provide military service to the Crown, and there were certainly occasions in the life of any group or nation when all able-bodied men would wish to rally to the support of the authorities, but the evidence for an actual obligation owed to a sovereign authority is vague. Only in areas under special threat – Christian Spain being an obvious example – or in moments of crisis, was the *levée-en-masse* a reality. Indeed, the whole notion of a "nation in arms" was inimical and dangerous to an elite that claimed a monopoly of war.[7]

Kings and great princes looked first and foremost to their own lands to raise troops. Their lands, like those of all the great men, were scattered, which made the process difficult. If they wanted to raise a large force, or even a relatively small force whose raising did not strip all their lands of troops, they had to persuade others to join them. Hence armies tended to be small and took time to gather. Hence, too, they were always *ad hoc* gatherings, for there were no barracks, no regulars, no infrastructure of war such as Rome had enjoyed or we have developed in the modern age; persuasion was always political in its nature, producing inconsistent results. In fact, the gathering of anything that we might call a large army was a relatively rare act, for few great lords or even kings had a single interest that compelled concentration of forces – rather, they had many local enemies and friends in the various zones of their activity, and thus many objectives, and so the raising of limited resources for limited ends was for a long time the norm.

This situation legitimized what we tend to see as private military followings: hence that special characteristic of medieval society – the lack of a distinction between public and private war. All kings, until the very end of our period and beyond, had great subjects who were capable of waging war on their own account. Therefore, they had to be satisfied by successful war, and the need to plunder was often paramount in the minds of contemporaries – even kings. The successful leader was one who rewarded his followers – in early medieval times gold rings were traditional – or who gave them an opportunity to reward themselves. Charlemagne's great attack upon the Avar kingdom may have had other objectives, but it yielded an enormous booty of significant economic importance, while the fruits of Christian victory in Spain made possible the building of the huge abbey of Cluny in the late eleventh century. At the end of the twelfth century, it was widely believed that Richard I of England was killed in a dispute over plunder.[8] This essentially private motive powerfully influenced decisions about war and peace, and continued even down into the early modern period, for kings were long expected to wage war for a profit.

War, therefore, was not simply a public function. Even the Church, which had inherited Roman notions of sovereignty, had ambivalent attitudes. For contemporaries, private war was not a contradiction, but simply an extension of legitimate self-interest which was not wholly differentiated from sovereign power, itself always deeply personal in nature. Indeed, it is often difficult to see much sense of public good, clear and distinct from private aggrandizement, in the decisions of monarchs about peace and war. This is hardly surprising. There was a notion of sovereignty and of the king's duty to all his people, but until the end of our period no sense of separation between the person of the king and his office. The king was many persons and presided over a society in which some kinds of governmental power had become mere property, so his war-making was conditioned by a variety of forces, notably a deep concern for his property and that of his family.[9]

By the beginning of our period, in most parts of Europe, private arrangements between king and magnates, and magnates and their greater followers, were the main way in which kings supplemented the military resources of their own demesnes. Magnates acknowledged themselves as vassals of the king, owing him homage for their lands and in turn demanding service from those who held of them. This system was not purely military: it arose from the problem of delegation in an age of dispersed holdings and poor communications. But holding land inevitably involved protecting it, so that the system was militarized, although to an extent that varied from time to time and place to place. This military–tenurial system, which we often call "feudal", provided the best-equipped soldier of the age, the heavily armoured cavalryman. However, what a magnate or a knight was prepared to concede to an overlord in military service depended on particular circumstances. A knight holding a single fief was not in a strong position to resist his lord, although custom and practice might limit his service to 30 or 40 days, and he might even modify this if he owed service to another lord. When the Count of Anjou wished to join with King Philip of France in attacks on Normandy in the mid-eleventh century, he raised great numbers of troops, but never acknowledged a formal obligation. Within duchies, counties and lordships, *servitium debitum*, the military service owed by landowners to their lords, only became fixed very slowly. These substantial men, the dukes, counts, vicecounts and *domini*, held castles that were the guarantors of their land; near his castle a man was strong, beyond it his power shaded away into the power of others. All of these men, from the king to the most minor castellan, employed others – soldiers who garrisoned their castles and served them in arms – some of whom held land and some of whom did not. Multiple homage was common, so there was no tidy feudal pyramid, and this increased the basic confusion created by the fragmentation of landholdings. The oath that we call feudal, essentially not to harm, but to aid and counsel one's lord, might be taken simply as a means of making peace between men, implying no subordination; this was even the case when an act of homage for land was involved. What mattered was that the lord was the predominant power who could enforce his authority and prevent his vassals moving to somebody else. The king, the dukes and the counts of France predominated within their areas, which is not necessarily to say dominated. A magnate of forceful character with extensive lands, such as Duke William of Normandy, could dominate, but a succession problem could weaken even a strong unit – such as the county of Anjou in the 1060s. Every great magnate had to watch his *mouvance* lest it fray at the edges or be encroached upon by others. The result was a pattern of constant petty war, in which feuds and personal quarrels were commonplace. The weakness of sovereign authority in most of Europe meant that war was a frequent means of settling disputes between great men.

German magnates acknowledged that their offices and fiefs were held of

7

the king and performed homage. But in practice they held autogenous jurisdiction based on huge allodial holdings. The monarch had extensive lands and, by successful war leadership in Italy and on the eastern frontier, drew others into his service. In a real sense, "Emperor" was a military title. Royal power over the Church enabled kings to fix quotas for the military service of the great bishoprics and monasteries, but even this was not something that could be automatically called upon. The autonomy of the German princes was such that feud and war were normal methods of settling quarrels. It was the obligation of all of the German king's vassals to join the expedition for his coronation at Rome, but in the case of Frederick I, preparations and internal problems meant that he departed in October 1154 "almost two years having elapsed since the expedition had first been vowed" and was crowned only in June 1155.[10] In Italy, the German monarch was king, but there were relatively few great magnates. For the most part, the economic power of the cities drew the local nobles into their orbit, and it is impossible to differentiate between them and the urban mercantile patriciate. The cities exercised a kind of collective lordship over the surrounding *contado*. In defence of their privileges, strong city militias arose which could be supplemented from the rich revenues of mercenaries. These city–states were valuable but undependable allies and dangerous enemies.

From our perspective, much medieval warfare seems very small-scale. This tended to change because the greatest of the lords – the king, dukes and great counts – profited from the economic expansion of the twelfth century, and this facilitated the raising of troops, amongst whom mercenaries became more common, while credit transactions made possible ambitious fortress construction. Competition amongst feudal lords led to the rise of larger units of control and conflict developed on a greater scale, but it was essentially about the same thing – keeping the *mouvance* together, exploiting family claims and defending the patrimony – and fought by the same means of ravaging and destruction. Even when armies of considerable size were raised, major engagements were rare. The leaders who gathered armies had to invest enormous resources of their own and to persuade others, many of whom might be doubtful adherents, to do likewise. Weapons, warhorses, means of transport, the paraphernalia of war – all of these represented a huge investment of resources and political credibility which could only in extreme circumstances be exposed to the risks of battle.

Succession disputes in which both sides had claims that commanded respect, rendering compromise difficult, often produced battle: in April 1068, Fulk Requin defeated his brother at the Battle of Brissac and succeeded to the county; at Cassel in 1071, Robert the Frisian fought Arnulf III for the county of Flanders; the Anglo-Norman succession dispute was settled in favour of

Henry I by his victory over Robert Curthose at Tinchebrai in 1106 and in 1141 Stephen was defeated at the battle of Lincoln. The inconclusive nature of some of these encounters is a good indication as to why battle was often avoided: at Cassel, Robert was captured but Arnulf killed – political negotiation then decided the outcome of the succession dispute. And Stephen's defeat at Lincoln had little effect on the long civil war in England. The highly conclusive results of Hastings and Tinchebrai, however, provide another very good reason for avoiding battle – it could be conclusive in entirely the wrong way for those who sought it, as Harold did in 1066. Medieval commanders were perfectly aware that in battle, as Vegetius said, "fortune tends to have more influence than bravery". At Conquereuil in 992, Conan of Brittany was in hot pursuit of his defeated Angevin foes when he paused to strip off his armour because of the heat, and was promptly killed by some Angevins who had fled into the thickets where he halted – and so the verdict of battle was reversed. At Tagliacozzo on 23 August 1268, the victorious Germans seem to have scattered to pillage and were surprised by a rally of the fleeing French.[11] Battle was often the outcome of extreme situations when the very existence of one side or another was threatened, as in the Crusades, but it was not always open to commanders to avoid it.

Nor were major sieges lightly entered into. The garrison of a castle or fortified town, if well prepared, could strip the surrounding country, exposing the besieger to starvation. A sally, such as that when Robert Curthose unhorsed his father, whose forces then scattered at Gerberoi in 1079, could catch them unawares. Allies could harass them in their camp. In any case, stripping other lands to mount a long expedition might expose you to attack elsewhere. Philip I of France was defied by so many of his vassals from behind the walls of their castles that he spent his life rushing from one siege to another, and on his deathbed confessed that the resistance of Montlhéry had made him old before his time.[12] By the later twelfth century, better organized armies could make short work of all but the strongest castles with elaborate fortifications that few could afford. The increasing numbers of castles which are apparent by the late eleventh and early twelfth centuries is a tribute to growing wealth and new standards of ostentation amongst the aristocracy. But the very existence of castles from the early eleventh century had the effect of intensifying the fundamental nature of medieval war.

The sheer expense of raising an army and the technical limitations that made it difficult for an army to feed itself tended to limit the size of armies. It was also a powerful influence on tactics. Because of the need for food and the fact that plunder was part of the soldier's pay, ravaging was an integral part of the business of managing an army. And this could be made to serve a military purpose – destroying the countryside of your enemy would impoverish him, shake the loyalty of his vassals, who it was his duty to protect, and make him and them question the point of fighting on if a settlement was possible. By the standards of the twentieth century, medieval man's capacity for destruction was limited. Few armies would have bothered to uproot an olive grove, or totally burn damp corn, but then they did not need to. When yields were so small, the destruction of any significant part of a crop could reduce a whole community to beggary, or its lord to borrowing. Mills, ovens and presses could be wrecked with long-term consequences. If stored food, especially grain, was plundered and spoiled, the whole village would starve in the winter. This would be a terrible injury to inflict on a rural society and it would have a direct effect on the lords who dominated it – for the great took their renders largely in kind, although this changed somewhat in the course of the twelfth century. No wonder that Duke William of Normandy "sowed terror in the land" when he made war. The cushion between society and starvation was very small.

The multiplication of strongholds increased the attractions of this strategy. Moreover, destroying the land about a castle might make the garrison, apprehensive of starvation when military operations ceased, come to terms. Living off the land imposed further problems: it was only really possible in summer and autumn, and hence war tended to be episodic, with a well defined "campaigning season". The need to feed an army's horses reinforced this, for they needed such vast quantities of food that it was possible only when there was plenty of grazing. Moreover, it created a tactical problem. An invading army that spread out to ravage could be defeated in detail – this happened to Saladin at Montgisard in 1177. But if the army stayed together it would starve, not least because it needed to disperse to feed its horses. It was not for nothing that Vegetius was admired at this time, for he understood the very essence of the military problem, feeding an army: "A great strategy is to press the enemy more with famine than with the sword". It was, therefore, a good tactic for a defending army to stand off and refuse battle, while staying in the presence of the enemy – a frequent pattern of war throughout our period. Border areas between substantial rival powers, such as the Norman Vexin or the Welsh March, were particularly exposed to the war of ravaging which was the invariable accompaniment even of larger-scale operations, and as a result were studded with fortifications that acted as places of refuge and centres of defence.[13]

Brutal though it was, war as fought within western Europe was not without restraints, which resulted largely from its proprietorial nature. Its leading combatants were landowners who were commonly neighbours and kin. In a situation of frequent conflict, the victor of today might be the vanquished of tomorrow, so self-preservation inclined men to mercy. Moreover, the possibility of ransoming prisoners offered rich rewards. The economic motivation for such clemency is indicated by the brute fact that infantry on the losing side in a conflict were generally massacred. The complexity of landed relationships blurred allegiances and made it difficult to define treason to a ruler, hence the obvious fact that there were very few political executions in this period. The obvious victims of war were the peasants, but even they were spared the worst horrors because conflicts were usually about control of land and the people on it, and nobody wanted to rule over a desert. Furthermore, by the eleventh century, slavery – such a scourge of peaceful populations in the past – was uneconomic. The Church inveighed against the horrors of war, and doubtless this had some influence, but it was the economics of landowning that really mitigated the horrors of war.[14]

War had its ethics, and these were grafted on to the warrior ethos which infused the upper ranks of society and exalted the military virtues of bravery and loyalty to form what we call chivalry, the "Code of Conduct" of the European upper class. But ethical considerations had only a limited influence on the conduct of war, and when great issues were at stake horrific behaviour was not uncommon. Wars between Christians might be loosely governed by rules, but these did not apply when Christian fought pagan. For many years, Charlemagne's armies ravaged Saxony with great brutality, but he was careful to persuade the Church to agree to his conquest of Christian Bavaria in 787. In principle, Christians felt that they could behave much as they pleased in war with non-Christians, and something approaching total war did sometimes occur in such circumstances. However, in practice, unless they could conquer their enemy in one fell swoop, Christians were obliged, at least for some of the time, to treat them as neighbours and thus some of the ethics of war came to apply. The case of those Christian peoples whose economic and social structures, and therefore ethical behaviour, was different from that of mainstream Europe was more complex. Here again, a predisposition to total war had to be mitigated.[15] The ethics of war arose from and were limited by the central concerns of a landowning group – they were an aspect of proprietorial warfare.

Our understanding of medieval war has changed radically in recent years. To an older generation of historians, war was battle. The most important modern writer on warfare was Clausewitz. At Jena in 1806, Clausewitz witnessed Napoleon's destruction of the Prussian army in which he served. Drawing on this experience, Clausewitz rejected the ideas of the eighteenth-century school of warfare, which emphasized manoeuvre and position, and argued that the real point of war was to destroy the enemy in battle. His ideas were popularized when von Moltke the Elder, asked to account for his startling victories, attributed them to Clausewitz's ideas. Clausewitz never wrote about medieval warfare, but his ideas influenced those who did. Hans Delbrück (1848–1929) wrote a monumental *History of the Art of War within the Framework of Political History*, whose third volume, appearing in 1923, dealt with the Middle Ages. The impact of Clausewitz is apparent in the heavy emphasis that he places on battle. The same can be said of Sir C. W. C. Oman's *History of the Art of War in the Middle Ages*, whose two volumes were published in London in 1924.

Recently, historians have emphasized the infrequency of battle and the relatively small size of medieval armies. They have noted the strength of fortifications and observed that the technology of the age made assault on them difficult. Because of the difficulties of maintaining forces, war was frequently fought for limited ends and interrupted by periods of truce. It has seemed to recent writers that the sources, when carefully examined, suggest that the staple of war was the raid – a cheap and expedient way of undermining the economy and willpower of your enemy. Even when a larger force was gathered, its primary function was to destroy, and in so doing feed itself – ravaging was integral to the business of feeding an army and therefore an essential part of war. In the words of Vegetius: "It is preferable to subdue an enemy by famine, raids and terror, than in battle where fortune tends to have more influence than bravery". Thus modern writers on medieval war emphasize what might be called "Vegetian warfare", centred on raids and destruction, rather than battle or even siege.[16]

This may be a general picture of war in this period, but it is not a complete one. This pattern of war involved a tremendous commitment of resources in terms of the capacities of the competing forces and it could have terrible consequences for the parties to it. The Giroie were a prosperous Norman family, patrons of the abbey of Évreux, but when Robert found that his castle had been burnt during his absence on a raid, Ordericus comments: "So at one blow the noble knight was utterly disinherited and forced to live in exile in the houses of strangers". The perspective of the combatants has to be considered, therefore, when we make judgements about warfare. Even a major power such as the King of France might find himself with very limited resources in a particular area, where a defeat might have major consequences. In the 1030s, Odo II of Blois, a mere count, had challenged the might of both the King of France and the German Emperor in an effort to gain the throne of Burgundy: their extended responsibilities laid them open to his localized challenge. The savagery of war and the destruction that it wrought was a frequent cause of ecclesiastical criticism. Evidence of such horrors is not confined to churchmen: "He does not leave a good knight alive as far as Baiol, nor treasure nor monastery, nor church nor shrine nor censer nor cross nor sacred vase: anything he seizes he gives to his companions. He makes so cruel a war that he does not lay hands on a man without killing, hanging and mutilating him." We need to recognize the brutality and destructiveness as they appeared to contemporaries. William the Marshal distinguished himself in his first action, when the knights of Philip of Flanders and Matthew of Boulogne tried to break into the town of Neufchâtel. In a nasty scrum of armed men in the narrow streets of the town, William's horse was killed and he was almost captured by enemy foot who cast an iron hook about his shoulders.[17]

Nor should we fail to recognize that throughout this period there was much large-scale warfare. At the beginning of the period Fulk Nerra, Count of Anjou (987–1040), was prepared to hazard battle and to build some of the most formidable fortresses of his age in a sustained effort to extend his county. The Norman army that conquered England in 1066 mobilized in all some 14,000 men, including 7,000 effectives, of whom about 3,000 were cavalry. Guiscard's army, which attacked the Byzantine Empire in 1081, numbered some 15,000, supported by a fleet. The Crusades to the Holy Land raised armies of quite exceptional size. At Hattin in 1187, 20,000 troops of the Latin Kingdom of Jerusalem faced 30,000 of their Islamic enemies, while large French and German armies clashed at Bouvines in 1214.[18] In the thirteenth century, armies of up to 20,000 were raised in Italy. Raising and equipping such forces was an enormous investment in terms of the resources of the age.

It is, therefore, remarkable that armies were sometimes sent and sustained far from their own homes. The Crusades have always attracted historians, but the expeditions of the German emperors to Italy were remarkable efforts that called for tremendous exertions, and they have been neglected of late. Much recent writing has been about the Anglo-Norman world, whose warfare has sometimes been spoken of as though it typifies that of western Europe. In fact, special conditions in every part of the world had their effect on the conduct of war, and this is a false perspective.

Medieval commanders were cautious about hazarding their armies in major confrontation, but they were not entirely unwilling, nor were they fully in control of any given situation. In 1054, Philip of France struck into Normandy with two armies, and as the royal forces spread out to ravage, Duke William of Normandy's forces fell upon some of them at Mortemer, inflicting losses significant enough to force a withdrawal. In 1057, another French invasion army was attacked as it crossed the river at Varaville, with heavy losses to its rearguard. To those who took part in them, these were real battles. This was the obvious response to the entry of a ravaging enemy army – to shadow it, restricting its foragers – but in the course of such a campaign running fights would develop to a greater or lesser degree of intensity. In 1188, Philip Augustus raided Gisors and was repulsed: Henry II, acting on the advice of William Marshal, pretended to have dispersed his troops and then fell upon his enemy's unprepared army and routed them. The sharpness and sustained nature of fighting needs to be recognized: after his victory in 1188, Henry II devastated Montmirail in a winter campaign whose savagery recalled the Conqueror's notorious harrying of northern England a century before. The common experience of medieval warfare – raid and counter-raid – could merge easily into battle. At Carcano on 9 August 1160, Frederick I's infantry were caught napping and a major battle ensued. At Brémule in 1119, the King of France seems simply to have lost patience and launched a disastrous charge.[19]

Moreover, when the prize was right, commanders were perfectly prepared to fight pitched battles. The Hohenstaufen wars in Italy produced many battles – the city–states of northern Italy were highly aggressive in defence of their autonomy and were quite ready to fight. It is notable that sieges of their cities are marked by very frequent sallies: one by the citizens of Parma defeated Frederick II at Vittoria on 18 February 1248. And here perhaps is another perspective: we make a clear distinction between field-warfare and siege. But in reality this is a false distinction. Every commander has to decide how best to strike at his enemy. An attack on any fortress required considerable resources and organization. To attack a city was a huge undertaking. Frederick Barbarossa besieged Crema from July 1159 to June 1160 and Milan from May 1161 to March 1162. These sieges triggered a whole series of military engagements. This warfare was especially bitter because, in a sense, it was also social war: Barbarossa and his barons saw the city people as different and inferior. By contrast, Anglo-Norman warfare was between people of essentially similar social backgrounds and outlook. Moreover, it is much easier to dismiss sieges from an Anglo-French perspective, for in this theatre of war there were no major cities. Even so, the siege of Château Gaillard lasted for five months and had a decisive effect on the war between John of England and Philip of France.[20] Sieges were simply a specialized form of battle. The methods of attack and the devices of defence became ever more elaborate, but the risks remained as great to both sides. Milan was razed in 1162 and Frederick II's army was destroyed at Vittoria in 1248.

Battles and major sieges were not common in European warfare, but nor were they so rare that they can be set aside as exotic events – for the reality is that they were the ultimate tests of war, and examination of them tells us a lot about medieval armies. The common experience of war was ravaging and destruction, but when great issues were at stake there was a readiness to accept battle, and enormous efforts were made to raise large forces and sustain campaigns, many fought over long distances. Large-scale military activity became more common as feudal regimes consolidated and articulated. Even so, campaigns often did little more than ravage; but we need to remember how effective that could be, what a vast effort the maintenance of an army over a period of time was, and what an enormous risk was involved in taking it into the presence of the enemy.

# Chapter Two

# *The weapons of war*

Contemporary descriptions of armies always distinguish between cavalry, the knights and infantry. The equipment with which they fought was appropriately different, but the differences were not merely functional. All who came to war brought their own equipment: the rich, the proprietors and their immediate supporters, could afford the best weapons and defensive equipment. Even when they fought on foot, knights were distinguished by superior equipment. The limitations and possibilities offered by weapons exerted a powerful influence on the conduct of war.

There is an unchanging quality about the appearance of war in the period 1000–1300. The mail-clad knight on horseback of the eleventh century, familiar from the Bayeux Tapestry, appears to differ only in small ways from, for example, the celebrated crusader portrayed in the Westminster Psalter. The most obvious difference is that the latter wore a great helm, or pot helm, which protected the whole head, neck and face, rather than the simple pointed iron cap of the Norman knight of 1066. This simple cap continued to be used throughout the period, although it had many variations. Sculpture on Angoulême cathedral shows a fluted helmet and another with a pointed rear drawn out into a neckguard. Cavalry in the Maciejowski Bible of the mid-thirteenth century wear a rather rounded form, also found in twelfth-century examples, but they have nasal guards, which seem generally to have fallen out of fashion before the end of the twelfth century, allegedly because an enemy at close quarters could seize the guard and blind its wearer. A variant type with a point inclined forward may have come from the East. Domed and flat-topped steel caps appeared in the twelfth century. All of these helmets were secured with a leather strap tied under the chin, and were worn over a coif of mail which formed part of the mail shirt, the hauberk.[1]

Pointed, domed and flat-topped helmets were sometimes fitted with face masks, leaving the back of the head protected by nothing more than the coif. The funerary monument of William Clito, dated 1127, has a masked helm and there are Spanish examples from about the same date. They perhaps represent an extension of the broad nose-piece to protect against arrows. Russian helmets, which generally are conical, have a rather similar kind of protection for the eyes built into the structure of the helm itself.[2] Between 1160 and 1171, the Count of Loos wrote to Louis VII of France asking for a masked helm, which suggests that they were then a novelty. A German manuscript and a Flemish funerary plaque, both of about 1175, show masked helms in a developed form. By about 1220, the fully enclosed form is illustrated. They were leather-lined, tied on with leather straps and worn over the coif on a steel arming cap, wound with fabric, which formed a base.[3] The great helm continued to be important well beyond our period, and developed conical and rounded forms which made it less vulnerable to down-strokes.

By the late thirteenth century, the bascinet, a deep one-piece pointed helmet with protection for the ears, cheeks and neck, appeared. It was worn over the mail coif.[4] The kettle-hat, first illustrated in the mid-thirteenth century, had a deep bowl which sat low on the head and a broad brim which protected the face from blows, but allowed all-round visibility. A variant form had a flat top and sloping brim. Because it continued to be used by both cavalry and infantry throughout the Middle Ages, we can assume that it was highly effective. The cervellière was a bowl-shaped cap that lacked a brim, a form intermediary between the kettle-hat and the bascinet. All of these styles could be worn over the mail coif, but there are illustrations of flat steel caps worn under the coif. By the later thirteenth century, knights could reinforce the neck protection afforded by the coif with the bevor, a steel collar, and some helmets were being fitted with visors. Helmets changed across this period, but there is no clear line of development, and this is true of other aspects of a knight's equipment.[5]

The main body protection was the shirt of rivetted metal rings, the hauberk, which is very clearly illustrated in the Bayeux Tapestry. Its form was a long mail shirt split at the groin, with flaps hanging down from the thighs to about the knees. These could be tied around the leg like a cowboy's chaps, or, more commonly, left to hang as a kind of split skirt. The mail coif was usually integral with this garment, although by the end of the thirteenth century it was sometimes separate. A mail flap or ventail, to protect the lower part of the face, became common in the twelfth century. Throughout our period, this mail cover would have been worn over a long undershirt, which eventually became the padded aketon. Generally, the hauberk of the Bayeux Tapestry had short sleeves, but in a few cases a separate mail forearm protection is shown, extending from under the hauberk sleeve down to the wrist. Some of the figures also wear mail leggings, *chausses*, which cover the leg from below the hauberk's flaps down to but not covering the shoe, although most wear only cloth on the legs.[6] None of the figures of the Bayeux Tapestry has mail protection for the feet or hands. In the twelfth century three-quarter length sleeves, loose at the ends and sewn with a band of leather or fabric to protect the skin from rubbing, are very common in illustrations such as that of an English manuscript figure, reputedly of Robert Earl of Gloucester and dating from *c.* 1150, although he also had cloth padding extending to the wrist. His hauberk ends at the knee, below which hangs what appear to be the ends of a long and flowing shirt. One might dismiss this last as artistic licence, but for its recurrence in French and English art of the period. By the end of the century, the more close fitting kind of long hauberk sleeve is much more common in illustrations, and is often shown with integral mailed mittens or mufflers with leather palms, which continued until plate gauntlets were developed in the later thirteeth century. By the thirteenth century, mail or padded *cuisses* protected the area from the thigh to the knee. The lower leg was protected by *chausses* of mail or metal scales or greaves of plate.[7] Leather armour, usually made of boiled and cured leather, *cuir bouilli*, was sometimes worn over mail. By the mid-thirteenth century this had evolved into shaped leather plates, the *paires de cuiraces*, tied front and back over the hauberk. By about the same time, *poleyns* of leather or metal protected the knee: they are very evident in the Canterbury Apocalypse.[8] Surcoats were a fashion that seems to have come from the East, where such garments offered protection from the heat of the Sun, but they could be padded for additional protection.

In the *Song of Roland* there are references to "double mail" and "triple mail", while in his account of the fight between Richard of England and William of Barres, the poet Guillaume le Breton refers to the "thrice-woven hauberk" of the combatants. In terms of the usual way of making mail, in which each ring was threaded with four others, this is a nonsense. It is equally unlikely that anyone would have worn three full hauberks. It is possible to weave mail very densely so that each ring is interlocked with six others, but no Western example is known: however, that does not mean it did not happen. Perhaps Guillaume meant that these two wealthy and important men had reinforced the chests of their hauberks with additional strips of mail. In this same passage, Guillaume le Breton speaks of plates of steel being inserted under the hauberk and the aketon. This is the earliest evidence for the use of plate armour. Gerald of Wales describes the Norse wearing coats of "iron plates skilfully knitted together" when they attacked Dublin in 1171, but this anticipation of the later medieval "coat of plates" never seems to have become popular. Furthermore, another layer of protection was introduced by the mid-thirteenth century, when the padded surcoat was being replaced by one in which strips of iron were riveted to its inside.[9]

Mail provided protection to the wearer while leaving him freedom to move. Those who have worn modern examples of chain mail stress that a belt helps to redistribute weight and makes the garment more comfortable to wear. No belts are shown in the Bayeux Tapestry, but they do appear in later illustrations. Differential ring sizes were a way of tailoring the hauberk to the contours of the human body, but they may also have served to lighten it – in the St Petersburg armour, heavier rings occur high on the chest and smaller, lighter ones lower down. Even in crusader settlements in the East where heat might have inclined men to lighter forms of protection, the Franks clung to Western mail. They did adopt the *hazagand*, a mail jerkin covered with fabric on the outside and padded within, first mentioned in the *Chanson d'Antioche*, but the general preference for Western armour suggests that it was effective.[10]

Contemporaries, indeed, commented how well knights were protected, although presumably wealthier men had the best armour. At the siege of Falaise in 1106, Robert Fitzhamon received a heavy blow on the helmet which left him an idiot until his death, but Henry I survived a serious strike at Brémule in 1119. In his memoirs, the Arab nobleman Usamah tells us of an encounter with Franks in which his cousin was thrown from his horse and repeatedly stabbed by their footsoldiers before being rescued, and comments that he was saved by his mail. On another occasion, he jabbed his lance at a Frankish knight who seemed to be wearing only a surcoat. The knight was so badly hurt by the blow that he doubled up in the saddle, dropping his shield and helmet. However, the man recovered, because under the coat he was wearing mail. But the mail had to be properly prepared. When Earl Patrick of Salisbury was ambushed and killed in Aquitaine, William Marshal (Guillaume le Maréchal) managed to slip on his hauberk and fight, but this did not protect him from a severe sword-wound in the thigh, for he was not fully equipped. Usamah says that his father was badly injured by an enemy spear because a groom had left undone the fastening of his hauberk.[11]

The constant effort to improve protection which ended with the knight swathed in many layers – steel plates, padded a aketon, mail, perhaps some-times in double or triple layers, a leather breastplate and a padded and later armoured surcoat and coat of plates – is suggestive of the shortcomings of mail. It is difficult to see how any mail could resist a direct hard thrust from a couched spear, backed by the momentum of a mounted man. Guillaume le Breton says that Richard I and William of Barres galloped at each other, spears lowered, and only the plate armour finally stopped the lance, which had pierced the shield, torn the "thrice-woven" hauberk and holed the aketon. The consequences of such a blow could be terrible:

Nought for defence avails the hauberk tough,
he splits his heart, his liver and his lung
And strikes him dead, weep any or weep none.

(Sayers)

Our best evidence of the ferocity of medieval warfare comes from the injuries inflicted on the victims of the Battle of Wisby in 1361. These caused an eminent anatomist to remark: "It is almost incomprehensible that such blows could be struck" and he explained their effectiveness by suggesting that attackers "stepped or jumped forward" as they struck their blow. Wisby was a largely infantry battle, and perhaps a man on horseback could not strike so hard, but cavalry engagements involved extremely close-quarter fighting. Usamah reports how one of his men escaped after his head was caught under the armpit of a Frank in a skirmish. The Bayeux Tapestry shows that arrows could penetrate mail, and crossbow quarrels must have been deadly.[12] The likelihood is that while it could not stop a true blow, mail was very effective against glancing blows which, in the confused hacking-match of battle, must have been far more common.

The shield was essential to turn direct blows, which is why it was only abandoned with the introduction of full plate armour in the late Middle Ages. In the Bayeux Tapestry all of the Normans, and most of the better-armed Saxons, carry slightly concave kite-shaped shields with rounded tops that taper to a point. Such a shield protected a footman from the upper torso to the knee, while a horseman in his crouched position was sheltered from the shoulder to the knee, leaving the lower leg exposed. However, it is clear from the tapestry and other illustrations that as the horseman galloped his shield trailed, leaving his lower body exposed. In the hands of footsoldiers these shields could be overlapped, as they apparently were at Hastings, to form the "linden wall'. It is interesting that on the Saxon side some poorer soldiers with no other armour carry shields which seem to have been less elaborately made. A few on the Saxon side had round, very convex shields, and one figure has a rounded oblong reminiscent of a Roman shield. It has been assumed that these were styles that were going out of favour at the time, but there is an early twelfth century sculpture on Angoulême cathedral of two knights charging into one another, lances couched in the classic style, in which both carry round shields, so we should beware of assuming uniformity in this respect.[13]

Shields were clearly made of wood, for arrows are shown stuck into them, although they usually had an iron boss and were probably bound with metal at the edges. The soldier held on to his shield with a series of straps and handles, but mounted men could hang it from the neck around the left shoulder. The kite-shaped shield remained popular in the twelfth century, although in some examples it became more sharply concave with a cut-off top, perhaps to give a better view. In the thirteenth century the shield retained this shape, although it was less concave, but shrank in size until it covered only the torso, perhaps because leg armour was more effective; in any case, the trailing effect of the long shield had probably left the mounted man vulnerable at this extremity. But there was no even development, and there are French portrayals of enormously wide but short shields being carried by knights.[14] If he survived the charge with lance, the knight was formidably protected against all but the most direct blow in the *mêlée*, although the total weight of his equipment was considerable, and this would have counted against him if he was unhorsed and had to fight on foot. Moreover, the great helm, if he was wearing one, restricted his view, which probably explains the popularity of other styles of helmet.

Forms of armour other than mail were used – leather jackets studded with metal are illustrated. Western sources occasionally seem to show figures clad in scale or lamellar armour. The former is made of metal scales knitted to one another to form a sort of coat of small plates, while scales were sewn on to a leather or material base. It has been suggested that, in the Bayeux Tapestry, Guy of Ponthieu's clothing was scale armour; the present writer thinks that it is not armour at all, but a rather splendid gown worn under a cloak. Two other figures, one of whom is Duke William leading his army to the Mont-St-Michel and the other Odo of Bayeux at Hastings, wear garments that are apparently covered with triangular plates, and a further depiction of William shows his mail in the conventional way, overwoven with a triangular pattern. All of these appear to me to be efforts to pick out distinguished figures in animated scenes, and the suggestion that they are representations of early *jazerans*, a jacket of Eastern origin, seems unlikely at this date.[15]

The scale and lamellar armour shown on some Gothic sculpture was undoubtedly fanciful and self-consciously exotic; the "King of Sodom" on the interior of the west wall of Rheims cathedral is deliberately contrasted with another figure of a Christian knight.[16] These kinds of armour were commonplace in the Byzantine and Islamic lands. In Spain, the two sides of the religious divide seem to have influenced one another considerably; Islamic armour was clearly influenced by Christian forms, while lamellar and scale are found amongst the Christians.[17] In Russia and some of the Balkan states, Byzantine and other Eastern influences also resulted in the use of lamellar and scale armour. Representations of scale and lamellar armour are common in South Italy, and it is tempting to suppose that their light weight suited climatic conditions there, but the artists may have used Byzantine models. By the early fourteenth century, a distinctive hybrid style of armour relying on mail and the extensive use of decorated *cuir-bouillon* had evolved in southern Italy.[18] Heavier forms of scale, lamellar and segmented armour became important in the West in the later Middle Ages, but it is not evident that this was due to southern and Eastern examples.

The personal weapons of offence changed comparatively little across the period. The spear, the weapon of the soldier since time immemorial, changed least of all. Shafts have inevitably perished. In the Bayeux Tapestry all of the spear-shafts appear to be spindly, whereas those in thirteenth-century sources seem more substantial, and this has been connected with the rise of "shock" tactics by cavalry, but it may reflect the limitations of embroidery and the more naturalistic style of thirteenth-century illustration. Surviving spearheads from all periods show a bewildering variation but there is, broadly speaking, a tendency to divide into the narrow penetrative type and the wider leaf-blade with a cutting edge that could be used like a sword. It natural to assume that cavalry spears had longer and heavier shafts and narrow points for penetration, to facilitate the knightly tactic of charging at the enemy with spear couched. The spear-point preserved with the hauberk and other equipment of a mounted warrior, of tenth-century Kievan origin, is round and clearly of the narrow "penetrative" type. Moreover, the broader type lent itself to slashing and cutting, and could well have been useful to infantry. However, in the Maciejowski Bible one knight carries a wide-bladed spear, while infantry would have favoured the penetrative type for use against cavalry.[19] All of this suggests that a simple classification between infantry and cavalry spears is impossible, and that the wide variations reflect local experiments and ideas, and also the growing availability of iron across our period.

Some 14 types of sword have been distinguished in the period 1000–1300. All are, broadly, flat, light-cutting or hacking weapons with relatively blunt points. The sword tended to be 76–83 cm long, and many examples have a shallow valley running down the length, although others have a raised ridge like the "sword of Godfrey de Bouillon" held by the Franciscans in the Church of the Holy Sepulchre at Jerusalem. As time went on, the rather blunt triangular points gave way to a more tapered shape with an acute point; it is assumed that the increasing effectiveness of armour placed a greater emphasis on accurate thrusting with the point rather than cutting or battering with the edge. All of these weapons were individually built by craftsmen and were relatively light, about 1.5 kg, and beautifully balanced. In the thirteenth century very large two-handed swords appeared, presumably to counter the improved armour of the knight. The *falchion* was another response to the same problem. It was a large single-sided sword, which widened towards the point, with a curving cutting edge like a machete: the main weight of such a weapon was close to the point, giving it tremendous cutting power. The *falchion* was used by infantry and cavalry, but it must have been very awkward to handle, which is perhaps why some early examples appear to be two-handed and another has a special handle. The sword was not simply a knightly weapon. The citizens of Bruges who stormed their castle after the murder of Charles the Good in 1127 had swords, while arms legislation in many parts of Europe from the late twelfth century onwards prescribed the sword for wide ranges of society.[20]

The club or mace is not commonly illustrated, although it appears in the Bayeux Tapestry and features in a carving from the Pyrenees: however, it appears frequently in the Maciejowski Bible. The flanged type, which became the norm in the West, had a history in Islam before the Crusades and may well have been copied. At Courtrai in 1302, contemporary sources record the Flemish infantry using a kind of club called the *goededag*, which appears to be pictured on the famous Courtrai chest. It is not mentioned again, so it is possible that this was a reference to the blow struck rather than the weapon itself – the word actually means "good day" – in much the same vein as "Take That!" The long-handled axe is shown frequently in the Bayeux Tapestry and William of Poitiers testified to its effectiveness. Its subsequent history is unclear – it seems to have persisted in Scandinavia, Scotland and Ireland, but elsewhere references or pictures are uncommon in the twelfth century. King Stephen of England wielded one after being unhorsed in 1141 at the battle of Lincoln, and the near-contemporary writer, Wace, seems to regard it as an exotic weapon of the past. This may be very idiosyncratic: one of the knights who murdered the archbishop is shown on the "Becket Casket" bearing an axe, while it was certainly in use in Italy, for at the siege of Crema, Bertolf of Gerach was killed by one. By the thirteenth century, a short-handled version was in use amongst knights and a long-handled one amongst infantry, which makes it probable that it never disappeared. A variant form of axe, or perhaps of mace, illustrated from the thirteenth century onwards, has a sharp beak: presumably its emergence, like that of the ordinary axe and mace and the increasingly sharp point of the sword, was due to the greater use of plate armour, which it would have been meant to pierce.[21]

One item of the knight's equipment which changed considerably by the thirteenth century was the horse. The eleventh-century horse seems not to have been bigger than 12 hands, rising exceptionally to 14 or 15: to put this into perspective, a modern Shetland pony is 10 hands, an animal of 12 would still be regarded as a pony, while 14 would be a small hunter. These are, of course, estimates and much weight is placed on contemporary illustrations which all show riders riding "long" with their feet well below the horse's belly. Then there are anecdotes, such as the story of Richard, son of Ascletin of Aversa, who liked to ride a horse that was so small that his feet touched the ground. It is hardly surprising, in view of this, that Eastern heavy cavalry with horse-armour came as a surprise to the soldiers of the First Crusade, for their horses could not possibly have carried such weight. In fact, Islamic armies had used horse-armour since early times, although sometimes it was of felt. By the end of the twelfth century, this kind of equipment was known in the West. Horses covered in iron are attested to as early as 1187. After his victory over the French at Gisors in September 1198, Richard I of England anounced his capture of 200 horses "covered in iron". At the Battle of Steppes in 1213, the victors, knights and other mounted men, had horses covered with iron. A manuscript of Girard de Roussillon of about the same date shows characters from the Roland cycle fighting on armoured horses, but the shading to show their mail hauberks is quite different from that used on the horse-covers, which suggests that this was quilted armour like that used by modern picadors in the bullfight. The use of cloth caparisons to cover horses in the thirteenth century became a commonplace, and it is difficult to envisage what was under them, but there are clear pictures of horses clad in mail.[22]

Such equipment must have demanded a stronger, heavier and bigger horse to carry it, especially as – quite evidently – developments in armour made the knight heavier. The total weight carried into battle by the eleventh-century knight was of the order of 32 kg: a late medieval suit of plate armour weighed about a third more than this, and the knight of that period probably carried rather heavier equipment to cope with his heavily carapaced foe, giving a total of about 45 kg. We can, therefore, guess that the thirteenth-century knight's equipment was of the order of 8–10 kg heavier than that of his predecessor of the eleventh century – and this might be much more if he wore all possible reinforcements. It is not surprising that at the end of the thirteenth century the phrase "great horse" became a technical term. Such animals were costly to buy and expensive to maintain: at Florence in the thirteenth-century, the annual upkeep of a warhorse was 40 florins, twice the sum for a footman. We can deduce something of the size of thirteenth century horses from the known dimensions of horse transport ships used in the Crusades. These suggest warhorses of the order of 15–16 hands, probably of a stocky build like a modern hunter. In 1993, a major horse burial in two pits was discovered close to the old Palace of Westminster. The animals appeared to have died in the early fourteenth century, and were of the order of 15 hands and upwards. These may not have been warhorses, but they suggest a horse population in which individuals could achieve formidable size and which would have served as a strong breeding base.[23]

One effect of the growing complexity of the knight's equipment was to make it ever more expensive. The cavalry of an army in the eleventh century were simply described as *milites* to distinguish them from the foot, *pedites*. By the thirteenth century there were clear gradations: most notably *serjans à cheval*, who were not as well equipped as the knights proper, were a major element of cavalry by the thirteenth century when they fought at Bouvines. This development was partly a result of social changes which are discussed below. The problem that arises is that although thirteenth-century written sources pick out such people, illustrations do not. They focus on the knight because, by and large, artists were producing for the aristocracy into whom the knights had become assimilated. It may well be that later thirteenth-century pictures of relatively lightly armed figures represent sergeants, or they may merely be shorthand representations of knights. Gislebert of Mons distinguishes between the knights and the other "armoured cavalrymen" amongst the Flemings who attacked Hainaut in 1184, and says that the 400 knights from Cologne were supported by "60,000 soldiers, some mounted and some on foot". Elsewhere, he refers to "mounted sergeants". Later, he says that in the force that Baldwin of Hainaut led to the aid of Philip of France against the Angevins in 1187, there were sergeants "armed as well as knights", even to the extent of having armoured horses. Clearly, it was unusual for mere sergeants to be as well armed as this: the protection a horseman carried and the quality of his offensive weapons largely reflected his wealth and status. In the thirteenth century sergeants became a normal element in the armies of the West and the crusader states.[24] There is no indication that they were used in any different role from the knightly cavalry. What must be recognized is the importance of status and the protection that it conferred.

The greatest change in status comes when we turn from the mounted man to the footsoldier. Pictorial sources present us with severe problems, because the artists were more interested in the knights, of whom there are a dispropor-tionate number of representations. Not all who appear fighting on foot are "footsoldiers" in the simple sense of the word – they may be dismounted knights, as is the case in the twelfth-century German "Victory of Humility over Pride" or an illustration in the "Psalter of St Louis" from the thirteenth century.[25] Moreover, those who produced written sources were also more interested in the knights than those of lower status.

Archers generally stand out clearly in pictures, although not always in chronicles. In the Bayeux Tapestry the Normans are divided between knights and archers who wear no metal armour. Apart from a solitary Anglo-Saxon, all of the archers are Norman. In the main panel there is a group of six. It has been suggested that these are professionals, because they seem to wear quilted armour, in contrast to the smaller figures of archers in the lower border, who may be levies or sailors, but this is uncertain. Only one archer is portrayed wearing armour, the mail-clad bowman of Pl. 60. Archers, like the armoured foot who were very numerous in William's army, are grossly under-represented in the Bayeux Tapestry – only 29 are shown – because its account centred on the Norman knights, who were the kind of people who would have formed its audience. The single armoured bowman might represent some well known person who specialized in archery; weaponry was not yet a matter of status and both the Conqueror and Curthose, his son, were famous bowmen. But aside from this odd figure, if we look at the innumerable illustrations of bowmen through to the Maciejowski Bible and beyond, it is quite evident that those who bore the simple bow had no protection and little other armament, and this is also true of late medieval illustrations. Their weapon was a stave, round in section with nocks at each end to hold the string, and it was fabricated with sapwood on the outside of the bend and heartwood on the inside to maximize spring. In the course of our period, bows always seem to have been about 1.82 m long. Range depended on length and strength expressed as poundage, but anything up to 365 m was possible and they could be very effective against chainmail. Composite bows of horn, sinew and wood were known in the West, for Gerald of Wales commented on them and illustrations occasionally appear to show them. The sheer power of the composite design meant that the bow could be quite short, making it ideal for use on horseback, and in the hands of skilled horsemen such as the Turks it was a deadly weapon. However, it was never popular in the West, probably because in damp conditions its glue dissolved and the whole thing fell apart.[26]

Crossbowmen seem to have enjoyed a quite different status. The crossbow had been used at least since the ninth century. In its simple form it consisted of no more than a very strong short stave-bow set on a stock and equipped with a trigger. It took time to load because of the rigidity of the bow, but it fired a short missile – the quarrel – in a flat trajectory with a higher velocity than conventional bows. The maximum range may have been as great as 200 m, but the effective range was about half that, and it was capable of penetrating 7 cm of wood. By 1300, crossbows were made with a stirrup at the front end of the stock and this allowed the operator to use his leg-power to draw the string. The actual bow was now often composite, of some combination of wood, horn and sinew, which gave it more power. Sometimes a goat's foot lever was fitted; this pivoted on a pin and drew back the string in a claw, thus increasing its rate of fire and allowing more power. Arrowheads were often narrower, designed to pierce armour.[27]

Richard I was a great master of crossbowmen, who formed a major component in all of his forces. By this time the Genoese were specialists and Richard often employed them. They represented an elite amongst the infantry, although it should be noted that some of the *balistarii* mentioned in English royal records were probably engineers who made siege equipment. The crossbowman is depicted in mail armour from the end of the twelfth century and occasionally he bears other arms. Moreover, by this time he was certainly often mounted. Philip Augustus maintained 133 foot and 80 mounted crossbowmen in 1202–3, while in 1200 King John sent 84 to France, 26 of whom had three horses and 51 had two, while the rest had only one. In the West and in Outremer they provided mobile fire-power for the armies of the late twelfth and thirteenth centuries. At Arsuf in 1191, Beha ad-Din was deeply impressed by the bowmen of Richard's army, who held off Saladin's horse-archers. He describes them as clad in thick felt and coats of mail, and recalls that he had seen up to ten arrows stuck in a single man. He makes it clear that both crossbowmen and archers were at work, so he may be describing one in terms of the other or he may really mean only the crossbowmen, or perhaps all were equally well equipped on that occasion. In a late twelfth-century manuscript of Peter of Eboli, however, there is a sharp contrast between the crossbowman in his iron cap and hauberk and the simple unprotected bowmen, and this is reproduced in the Maciejowski Bible.[28]

Apart from the archers, all of our sources make it clear that there were other *pedites* at work in medieval armies, and it is particularly difficult to get a view of their weapons and role. It needs to be remembered that even agricultural tools could be useful and that illustrations of slings are not uncommon. William the Conqueror brought large numbers of *pedites loricati* for the attack on England and assigned them an important role at Hastings. The few representations of them in the Bayeux Tapestry show that they were equipped with the same armour as the Norman cavalry and the Anglo-Saxon thegns. It is unlikely that they were all infantrymen in the simple sense of the word, for the capacity of William's ships to carry horses was limited and these may have been dismounted knights. However, they and the Anglo-Saxon thegns can be taken as types of the best-armed foot of the age. The Anglo-Saxons never seem to have taken to fighting on horseback, probably because they did not feel the need. It is notable that the Tapestry shows a large number of unarmoured footmen, presumably peasants pressed into service for the emergency. Anglo-Saxon foot served the Norman kings very effectively – notably at Tinchebrai – but we know nothing of their weapons and equipment. Welsh infantry fought in Anglo-Norman and Angevin armies. Modern writers have tended to see them as lightly armed, for they were used as fast-moving raiders, but at Lincoln in 1141 they stood and fought well, suggesting a rather different kind of armament. In the wars of Frederick Barbarossa in

Italy, both sides used footsoldiers in substantial numbers, but the Italian foot fought especially well at Carcano and Legnano. Infantry were an important element in the armies of the Franks of Outremer.[29]

Depictions of lightly armed men fighting on foot in the twelfth century suggest that cloth armour and an iron cap with a shield were commonly the defences of the better-armoured footman. There is a contemporary description of a Frank at the siege of Acre in 1190, dressed as a footsoldier in an iron cap and a tunic of multi-layered and closely sewn linen. Some of the infantry of the mid-thirteenth century in the Maciejowski Bible are shown in padded knee-length jackets with high-standing collars and steel caps, but a spearman has no more than a steel cap and a slinger only a small round shield. The infantry weapon of offence *par excellence* was the spear, and this is frequently illustrated, but swords and maces do figure in twelfth-century representations.[30]

Infantry weapons became more specialized. At Bouvines, Philip of France was attacked by infantry with long lances and hooks to bring down riders. At Courtrai pikes held off the French cavalry, whose horses were then felled by heavy maces. By the time of the Maciejowski Bible, a wide variety of weapons featuring more metal tips and edges seem to have been in the hands of footsoldiers, including daggers, early forms of the falchion – some with a long handle – a variety of spear-points, axes and clubs.[31] Overall, the infantry are a very variegated group, who may often have been stiffened by dismounted knights. However, at all times there were well armed infantry, and by the end of the period their equipment was improved and becoming more specialized. Their existence reminds us of the mercenaries used, for example, by the Angevin kings and including even Saracens. Many of the exhumed casualties of the Battle of Wisby in 1361 wore mail with coifs and such figures appear in thirteenth-century sources. While the figure in Bodleian Douce 180 is clearly identified as a knight by his shield with arms, other manuscripts show figures who may well be simply well protected foot equipped with hauberks and coifs.[32]

Overall, although there were no great changes, the quality and quantity of offensive weapons and defensive armour seems to have improved in the period 1000–1300. There was a marked diversity of types of equipment: the length of hauberks and the size and quality of rings seem to have varied over the period, and weapons such as swords look different even when they conform to a general common pattern. It is not possible to date the introduction of improvements, such as the stirrup, to the crossbow, or to suggest when daggers became commonplace amongst soldiers. The apparent similarity of knightly armour across Europe probably covers regional differences – such as the fondness of South Italians for leather armour – and we have noted changes over time. This pattern of diversity is hardly surprising. Everywhere, it was the duty of the soldier to provide his own weapons, and as long as they conformed to the broad quality parameters appropriate to his rank, he could have any variation that he wished to pay for. Each soldier would have had his weapons made at a local supplier and each craftsman had his own methods. The ability to pay guaranteed considerable diversity. At the lowest level, peasants would bring agricultural implements – at the highest the great lord trapped himself out with splendid and multi-layered armour.[33] The massive influence of social structure on the conduct of war is very evident in equipment. Important lords always seem to have maintained some household knights whose armour they may have provided: and kings, such as those of England, maintained arsenals that must have been a force for uniformity. However, quite visibly, across Europe there was variation around certain basic patterns in weapons and armour. The reasons for this lay in the technology of the age.

# Chapter Three

# *War, society and technology*

Medieval metallurgy was advancing. Although primitive bloomery hearths, which could only produce a maximum of 40 kg in a session, continued to be used, larger and more advanced furnaces, such as the Corsican and Catalan types, with powerful bellows could smelt up to 150 kg of iron in one process. The *Stückhofen*, which was developed in Germany at the end of our period, was 3–4 m high and capable of producing up to 900 kg in a single operation. None of these furnaces could produce liquid iron except accidentally and under the most favourable conditions, when the subsequent cast iron seems to have been rejected as too brittle to use. They produced a soft malleable mass of iron, the bloom, which could be forged into wrought iron, or, at great trouble and expense, into steel. By the end of the twelfth century there was substantial industrial production of iron in virtually all of the countries of western Europe. Larger furnaces put pressure on wood reserves and as a result coal was used from about 1190, although this was only to bulk out charcoal. Water-driven bellows were employed from the twelfth century, and by the thirteenth century hammer mills using water power are known. The scale of production could be considerable – the great iron forge-building at the Cistercian abbey of Fontenay in Burgundy is testimony to that. Trade in metal was vigorous, with Flanders, for example, importing iron from Spain.[1]

The development of a flourishing iron industry all over Europe was a product of the great European expansion of the period 1000–1300, whose most obvious symptoms were the growth of populations and the flowering of cities. But the demand for arms must have been a powerful stimulant, for by the end of the thirteenth century there was large-scale weapons production in most European countries, with very notable centres in Italy, Flanders and Germany, especially in the Rhineland. The scale of production could be very large: in 1172, the ironworkers of the Forest of Dean sent 100 axes, 1,000 picks, 2,000 shovels and 60,000 nails for Henry II's expedition to Ireland, and 50,000 horseshoes were supplied for Richard I's crusade. More particularly, the demand for weapons must have stimulated production of steel. Since Roman times there had always been an awareness of the superior qualities of steel, and medieval sources distinguish between the two metals.[2]

Since there was no science of metallurgy, the production of weapons and other metal goods was a craft process that was dependent on the skills of the individual smith, whose experience taught him how to create iron with the right qualities. Even large-scale production of arms was essentially craft-based, and remained so through to the nineteenth century. Production methods for many weapons were probably pretty routine, but the production of steel involved great skill. The sword, the finest of all weapons, was created by the pattern-welding of strips of iron, which produced a strong, flexible steel that could take an edge and stand up to the violent hammering on hard surfaces that characterized medieval warfare. Damascus and Toledo blades were much admired in the West, which for a long time did not have access to the Indian crucible steel from which they were forged. But the very high international reputation of German swords shows that even by the eleventh century European techniques were developing.

The hauberk was made of rings, some of which were punched out of carefully flattened steel; mostly, however, they were drawn from wire, shaped on a mandril and the ends and holed for a rivet. Each ring was threaded with four others and the rivets inserted to build up the whole. It was a very slow process that required great patience, an impression well conveyed by a fifteenth-century illustration. Once it was assembled, the whole hauberk was annealed in the forge. Plate armour only began to appear towards the end of the twelfth century and then it seems that small reinforcing pieces were fitted under the hauberk. It is unfortunate that we do not have any early pieces. It was only towards the later thirteenth century that plate armour proper emerged, and we can assume that this was the result of smiths gradually working out how to produce, at reasonable cost, good-quality steel which was light and designed to fit well, yet was strong enough to protect.[3]

It is interesting that manuscript pictures of armourers nearly always include the making of helmets, and this presumably reflects the fact that the fabrication of any kind of large plate involved considerable skill. Sometimes the pointed helmet was made by hammering a single piece of metal: tenth-century examples are the "helmet of St Wenceslaus" in the treasury of Prague cathedral and a Kievan example in the Artillery Museum in St Petersburg. In the form called the *Spangenhelm*, fabrication was by welding together a series of shaped segments on a conical frame. The appearance of these helmets varies considerably in the Bayeux Tapestry, with some seeming to have horizontal or vertical bands and others not: however, this may relate to decoration rather than structure. In an age of artisan production, knowledge of techniques must have spread slowly and unevenly, for there was no real technical literature or tradition of teaching.[4]

Although the level of skill involved in the the production of minor weapons – spear- and arrowheads, for example – was limited, it still involved much time and labour, especially if specific shapes were needed with hardened cutting edges. There were varieties of arrowheads, with long narrow types being used for piercing mail. The basic smelting of the iron was difficult and required careful judgement of times and temperatures, and the whole manufacturing process was a handcraft that was dependent on individual skill and knowledge. These were expensive processes: tools were commonly made largely of wood, and shod with iron only at the cutting edges. A spade of this kind appears in the twelfth-century manuscript illumination of the "Dream of Henry I" and in the Maciejowski Bible, and precisely similar tools dating from the nineteenth century can be found in the Beaune wine museum. It is difficult to establish what costs were in the Middle Ages, not least because of regional variations. In tenth-century France, a mailed coat was valued at 60 sheep or six oxen. In early fourteenth-century England, the price was a sterling pound, the equivalent of about 20 sheep or two oxen, while at the same time in France it was three *livres tournois*.[5] Although there were variations, on the basis of such figures it is possible to postulate a real fall in prices over the period under consideration. But demand for iron was clearly rising and the development of the industry was proceeding apace, even though it remained, broadly, a craft industry.

It was this huge expansion of production, rather than any pattern of innovation, that made possible more and more sophisticated weapons in the thirteenth century. In the early ninth century, Charlemagne demanded that each pair of freemen summoned to the host should bring between them a lance, a shield and a bow with two strings and twelve arrows. This would have involved a very minimal amount of iron. By contrast, vassals were expected to come well armed with a mail shirt and provided with horses. By 1181, iron weapons were evidently more common, because Henry II of England promulgated an Assize of Arms in 1181 requiring all those who possessed £100 Angevin to provide themselves with a horse and full knightly equipment, while those with £20–40 should have a hauberk, iron cap, lance and sword, and even those of lesser status were to have a quilted coat, iron cap and sword, or bow and arrows. The Assize for England commanded that the burgesses and the "whole body of freemen" should have a padded surcoat, an iron cap and a lance, while knights were required to provide themselves with a hauberk, iron helmet, shield, lance and horse. By the time of Edward I's Assize of Winchester in 1285, the regulations demand even more metal weapons. Those with land to the value of £15 and with 40 marks per year must have a full hauberk, helm, sword, knife and horse: lesser men with land worth £10 and incomes of 20 marks can make do with a short-sleeved hauberk, but must have helmet, sword and knife. The 100 shilling freeholder must provide a padded surcoat, iron cap, sword and knife, and a sword is expected even of a 40 shilling freeholder, along with a knife, bow and arrows. Even the 20 shilling man must produce a spear, scythe and knife, and only the poorest are limited to bows and arrows.[6]

Communal charters in the Low Countries tell the same story. In 1244, the better-off amongst the Luxembourg bourgeoisie were expected to serve their lord armoured and on horseback, while at Mortagne in 1251 and at Bruges at about the same time they were required to produce a sword and elaborate equipment. The less well-off in these city ordinances were footsoldiers with a padded surcoat, iron cap and lance. By the end of the thirteenth century in Flanders, weapons were much more common than ever before and the widespread circulation of the short-sword, which was of Italian origin, is particularly indicative of this. In the Italian cities the communes required men to serve well armed either as infantry or, in the case of the wealthy, as cavalry, and laid down minimum specifications. By the mid-thirteenth century, Florence was divided into six quarters (*Sesto*), each of which was responsible for a proportion of the specialized troops required, from heavily armoured cavalry through crossbowmen to *Pavesarii* (shield-bearers) and sappers. Such provisions were commonplace in the cities of Italy.[7] And this new availability of iron, which gave western Europeans a huge advantage over the peoples on their periphery, was a result of the general development of the European economy, which had great influence on the conduct of war.

This is hardly the place to analyze at length the great European expansion of the period 1000–1300. The simplest evidence of it was the growth of cities, which was much commented on by contemporaries. The development of trade produced new classes of people and new kinds of wealth. A major consequence was the burgeoning diversity of European society. The famous characterization of European society as divided between those who fight, those who pray and those who labour was formulated in the early eleventh century and was visibly inadequate by the mid-twelfth century. John of Salisbury described the amazing diversity of his world, which included the townspeople who Henry II's Assize of Arms of 1181 recognized as a distinct social category. What has been called the "monetary explosion" of the eleventh century had a deeply unsettling effect on Western society, creating a new fluidity as society became richer.[8] This enabled those who controlled the new wealth, the kings and nobility, to protect themselves better than ever before. In so far as there was innovation, this was its motor, for the idea of technical innovation was not yet strong enough and the educational under-pinning for it emerged only slowly.

This narrow view of the purpose of technology had profound effects on warfare. The crossbow was an effective weapon but its development seems to have been slow and it was rarely deployed *en masse*. Richard I, quite exceptionally, used large numbers at Arsuf, to deadly effect. Mounting crossbowmen enhanced their mobility and with it the firepower of patrols and strike-forces, and they were commonly used in this role from the time of Philip Augustus onwards. But, generally, the weapon never reached its full potential, and seems to have been most effectively deployed in sieges. This was partly a matter of expense, a reluctance to spend on mere foot. Partly, it was a consequence of ambivalent attitudes: at the siege of Rochester John wanted to hang the garrison but was persuaded to spare all but the crossbowmen. Richard I on his deathbed spared the life of the crossbowman whose quarrel mortally injured him, but his intimates nevertheless butchered him. But there was a further cause of the slow development and deployment of this useful weapon. There was no forum in which to develop weapons. Warfare was episodic and there were no permanent staffs to form intellectual centres: the "Twelfth-century Renaissance" bred no academies of war, for war already had its elite, who felt no need to give way to any new forces. By the end of the twelfth century, powerful monarchies were acquiring arsenals and these must have been busy places in times of war. Their very existence must have stereotyped arms and armour to a degree. But there was no marriage of thought and technology, so that advance remained piecemeal and by individual experiment. In these circumstances, new ideas would have been diffused only slowly and unevenly. In this way, the conservatism of a social elite slowed military development, and it was in areas where expertise was most needed and theirs most lacking that technology made its greatest impact – on military architecture and poliorcetic.[9]

The slow development of technology had other effects on the conduct of war. Supply was always a major constraint on the size and movement of armies. William the Conqueror made a very cautious and entirely unopposed approach to London in 1066, but his army became desperately short of supplies on the way. At Flarchheim on 27 January 1080, Henry IV was victorious in battle, but was unable to follow up his victory because the Saxons had sacked his camp, and he had to retreat. In 1097, William Rufus's attack on Wales was frustrated by guerrilla tactics that prevented his army from foraging and thus forced a retreat, and the same happened to Henry II in 1165. Richard went to great trouble to guard his supply lines during the Third Crusade. St Louis made the most elaborate preparations to feed his army for his attack on Egypt, creating what was virtually a logistic base on the island of Cyprus: ultimately, his army was destroyed not by enemy victory but by the cutting of his communications with Damietta – without food he had to surrender. Philip III was equally careful in stockpiling provisions for his attack on Aragon in 1285, but he faced retreat in desperate conditions of starvation when the enemy cut him off from secure access to his bases.[10]

The basic necessity of an army was food, and in the context of the age this meant bread: even at a moment when the First Crusade was blessed with plentiful supplies of meat, Raymond of Aguilers commented on the lack of bread.[11] The technology of food preservation was not highly advanced: grain would have been the most durable form in which to carry this staple, but that would have meant carrying waste husk and some kind of milling equipment. Flour saved weight but was very liable to go off. In any case, both are bulky and bulk transport was limited by the available technology.

The basic measure of food which we need to take into account is that a man living a fairly active life needs about 1 kg of bread (or the calorific equivalent) to feed him per day. Packhorses could carry 100–150 kg, enough to feed 150 men for a day, so a force of 3,000 would need 140 horses for a single day's food. Each horse takes up about 2.5 m of road, so that in single file they would be strung out along 350 m of road. However, if the 3,000 men included cavalry, the warhorses would need fodder, because except at the most favourable times of the year they could not fend for themselves without losing condition: in the German army of 1914 the ration was 11 kg of grain and fodder per day for a horse. The advantage of pack animals was that they could go almost anywhere: in Byzantine times the road system of Asia Minor included stepped roads which clearly could not carry wheeled vehicles, and it is likely that the preserved stretch of road from Antioch to Aleppo was intended for pack use, because it is not scored by wheels. The army of the First Crusade certainly had carts when it travelled across Europe: Peter the Hermitis force had a train a mile long, but these seem to have been abandoned in Asia Minor. The French army on the Second Crusade was also dependent upon pack animals. Since these were some of the best roads available, the advantages of this form of portage are evident, but so, equally, are the drawbacks. Pack animals cannot carry large or awkward objects, their packs need careful balancing and they must be emptied at night. They also need to be fed, and so consume much of their carrying capacity.[12]

Wagons could carry much more. By the eleventh century, the horseshoe had made the horse a formidably efficient form of traction. Better harnesses and linkages meant that a single horse could pull a load of 900 kg. Moreover, the better harnesses meant that teams could be linked to wagons, with improved results. Wagons themselves developed: pivoted front axles made large four-wheeled types possible, and by the thirteenth century they were replacing two-wheeled ones. But horses were not always available and oxen all too often had to be used. Moreover, even the most efficient wagon was limited by roads and weather, both very uncertain quantities in the medieval West. In the right conditions, good wagons could help an army enormously. When Philip Augustus decided to retreat from Tournai before the Battle of Bouvines, his infantry were able to move very quickly because they put their weapons and equipment in carts which, perhaps, resembled the ladder-sided examples portrayed in the Maciejowski Bible, which were pulled by two horses. At Hattin, Guy was able to carry elaborate tents into battle, and these must have been transported in wagons. In the plain of the Po, armies carried wooden sheds for shelter and we hear of small missile throwers mounted on carts, but this was flat easy country in summer: in winter cartage would have been more difficult. Lack of bridges was another formidable problem for an army that was dependent on wheeled transport – indeed, in Spain the existence of Roman bridges was a major influence on campaigns. On the northeastern frontier of Germany there were virtually no roads, and the German expansion was long confined to the river valleys where supply by ships was possible: on one occasion, scouts blazing a route through virgin territory took nine days to cover less than 70 miles.[13]

Carts of the two-horsed type shown carrying armour and equipment in the Maciejowski Bible must have been able to carry a load of about 450 kg, which would have fed 500 men for a day. But because good carts and good roads did not always coincide, we have to recognize that the transport problem continued. Moreover, many commanders would not have been able to specify what kind of transport they received. The efficiency of carts explains why armies such as that of Frederick I on the Third Crusade could pass through friendly territory without pillaging and still sustain themselves. But there were definite limits to what could be carried, imposed by roads, weather and seasons and by military necessity – for mobility could be compromised by too elaborate a baggage-train. This is why armies often used fleets. Henry II employed ships in his attacks on Wales. Edward I used huge fleets to supply his great armies as they destroyed Welsh resistance. Once the conquest was achieved, he built ports to supply his major strongpoints. Great engineering works were undertaken to straighten the River Clywdd, so that a port could be built by Rhuddlan castle. Edward's elaborate logistic preparations for the Scottish campaigns are well known and always included a major fleet: even so, before the Battle of Falkirk in 1298 his supply situation was so bad that elements of his army were rebellious. The army of the First Crusade enjoyed invaluable naval support, as did Richard I at the Battle of Arsuf.[14]

But naval support was not always available, and the transport problem was one of the factors that limited the size of medieval armies. It was probably not as important in this respect as cost or the need to adjust the force to the scale of the task, but it was a major consideration. In 1066, England was conquered by an army of about 7,000 Normans and allies. Just over 200 years later, the fate of South Italy was decided at Tagliocozzo by armies which, together, numbered only about 10,000. In the light of this, scepticism of the large numbers that chroniclers often attribute to armies is a right and proper reaction: for example, the idea that Frederick Barbarossa mobilized 100,000 for the Third Crusade needs critical examination. In fact, the threat of starvation remained with armies from first to last: Jean le Bel reported his sufferings during a 1327 campaign against the Scots – bread, when there was any, soaked in horses' sweat, foul water and expensive wine. His experience could stand for that of the soldiers across this period and far beyond.[15]

It is very difficult to gain a real impression of what a medieval army on the march looked like. Our illustrations are only occasionally large-scale, but they convey a suspicious uniformity which was probably imposed by the artist on a much more diversified reality. Because weapons and armour changed only slowly, they must have enjoyed very long lives. The sword that Otto IV (1198–1215) bore at the Battle of Bouvines in 1214 was actually made in the eleventh century and redecorated for him in about 1208. Probably only the better-off could afford to be up to date, while the remainder wore what amounted to hand-me-downs, patched, developed and augmented as their pockets made possible. However, the increasing production of iron improved the weapons and protection of even the footsoldiers. In the Maciejowski Bible of c. 1250, many footsoldiers are seen wearing padded aketons and steel caps: this is the kind of equipment that contemporary kingdoms and cities were requiring their poorer citizens to keep for the purposes of war. A minority of the infantry illustrated carry much more elaborate equipment – hauberks and swords. In the case of mounted men, an apparent uniformity probably conceals considerable differences in the quality of protection, but they are almost invisible to us.[16] There must have been enormous diversity, but mainly of variants of basic types. Weapons and armour had advanced somewhat, but the knights and foot of the Bayeux Tapestry would have been able to fight perfectly competently at the end of the thirteenth century, although their equipment would have relegated them to the second or third rank. Better carts and more horses improved supply marginally, but without any dramatic advance. War had changed in the two and a half intervening centuries, but even at the end of the thirteenth century the warriors of the Bayeux Tapestry would not have found their equipment hopelessly obsolete.

# Chapter Four

# *Warfare and authority*

Medieval society was dominated by landed proprietors and it was they who decided upon and directed war. Throughout our period, such people saw in its conduct a guarantee of their position in society. War, therefore, was powerfully influenced by the relationships amongst this elite. Because they were, relatively speaking, a small group, a great deal depended on personal attitudes and relationships, especially as all major landowners enjoyed a high degree of independence. Valour and reputation therefore counted for a great deal. Richard I of England was a great commander, but in his own day it was his bravery as a soldier that men respected. His fatal wounding at the siege of Chalus while exposing himself to the enemy was not a chance and isolated act, but part of the whole logic of his life.[1] Not all kings in this period were good soldiers, but most were at pains to acquire something of a military reputation: Philip Augustus was never in the same league as Richard, but he fought bravely and this same quality was much admired in Louis IX, whose actual conduct of military affairs was deeply flawed. The constituency to which these men had to play was the aristocracy, and while not all of them were committed soldiers, all saw military values as a norm for their caste, a kind of test of belonging. It is notable that the three least soldierly kings in English history in this period, Stephen, John and Henry III, all had grave political difficulties.

The aim in this chapter is to consider how war sprang from the loose nature of the ties that bound this elite, and how it was influenced by this basic condition. For the church, drawing on its Roman inheritance, there was no doubt who ought to control war – the sovereign authority, whom all others should obey. However, this was no longer a simple issue in medieval times, for the Church itself claimed to be able to direct war, although the legal formulation of this was never very satisfactory. Moreover, after 1095 the papacy elaborated the special doctrine of the crusade, which was effectively a war waged at papal command. The heart of the problem, however, was the fragmentation of sovereignty in the Middle Ages. The *princeps* of Roman times was unequivocally the seat of all legitimate authority: to the emperor and his officers, St Augustine entrusted the right to wage war. But the very same word, *princeps*, had a much wider application in the medieval world.

An emperor or a king was undoubtedly a sovereign authority, but the weakness of royal power in many parts of Europe meant that others wielded public authority at a very high level. They might enjoy the title of duke, margrave or even count, and in the German empire they might be archbishops, but they were collectively described as princes, *principes*. Such was their power that the papacy itself gave them considerable recognition. Of 152 lay addressees in the *Register* of Gregory VII, no less than 80 are princes in the sense of ruling persons who are not kings, and the pope speaks of *rex seu secularis princeps, reges aliique principes*. Even in Anglo-Saxon England there were great earls whose power rivalled that of the king, and Northumbria was almost a separate entity. In Germany, the power of the Salian kings served to check the emergence of territorial principalities – although not in marginal areas such as those ruled by the dukes of Bohemia and Poland – until the thirteenth century, when the preoccupations of Frederick II in Italy impelled him to accept the growth and consolidation of the ecclesiastical and secular princes as a result of the *Confoederatio cum principibus ecclesiasticis* and the *Statutum in favorem principum*.[2]

Throughout our period, the *principes* of Germany waged war on their own behalf, with little reference to their king. It has been said that "German bishops and abbots feuded as a matter of course". In Italy, the power of the German monarchs after the year 1000 prevented the emergence of princes with a strong territorial base, but was unable to check the cities whose independence threatened the basis of their power. In France, the eleventh century was the apogee of princely power, when a duke of Aquitaine could think so little of the monarchy as not to bother to attend a royal election. In the Latin Kingdom of Jerusalem in 1187, the lord of Outrejourdain could refuse to obey his king on the grounds "that he was just as much lord in his own land as he (the king) was of his". Such attitudes must have been common, for landholding blurred the distinction between sovereign and subject. Arnulf of Bavaria claimed to be "duke by the grace of God of the Bavarians and adjacent provinces" and a sympathetic writer scorned Henry I's claims to rule there, "where neither he nor his ancestors held a foot of land". Only in Anglo-Norman England were the ambitions of the nobility sharply checked by a highly centralized royal power, supported by an efficient and loyal administration. But even there it required the unremitting attention and manipulation of a strong personality, and control of the peripheries was difficult.[3]

The princes acknowledged that they held their power of a king or emperor, but they often conducted their own local policies quite independently, and this extended to the waging of what we call "private war". Archbishop Adalbero of Trier, in his agreements, specifically provided for the conduct of feud against Prüm, and the Bishop of Liège's capture of Bouillon in 1141 inspired a celebratory work, *Triumphus Sancti Lamberti de castro Bullonio*. The example of Henry the Lion, who ruled a virtual kingdom within a kingdom under Frederick Barbarossa and waged war as he thought fit, is well known, but he was unusual in German history only for the scale of his activities. In France, princes such as the Count of Anjou even used royal formularies in their charters to proclaim their positions. William of Poitiers struggled to define the position of his hero, Duke William of Normandy, and explained that "Normandy, long subject to the king of France was now almost erected into a kingdom". In fact, in the eleventh century the kings of France were drawn into the feuds of the great princes such as the counts of Anjou and the dukes of Normandy virtually as equals.[4] These princes would have claimed to hold power of the king to whom they owed service, but they resisted all definition of their duties and the extent of their actual support for him varied according to circumstances.

Below the level of the princes was a host of major lords, whose acquisition of elements of royal power was almost unstoppable in the tenth and eleventh centuries. The principalities were unstable: in West Francia in the ninth century, men had been appointed as marquises to control the counts in important border areas and it was they who later became the princes. As the monarchy weakened, they exercised control in their own interests, expanding wherever possible at the expense of their neighbours. But these entities were not institutionalized and their strength depended on an unbroken succession of strong rulers. Burgundy under Richard the Justiciar (ob. 921) stretched from Lyons to the borders of the Ile-de-France, but involvement in the high politics of Europe and succession disputes meant that its rulers lost Champagne in the north and Lyons in the south, and much else besides, by the early eleventh century. Problems of succession created weaknesses. The rule of partition of the father's wealth amongst his heirs enabled the Ottonian monarchs of Germany to extend their power over the great dukes in the tenth century. But even where division was superseded by forms tending to primogeniture, the need to provide for younger children remained. If there was no obvious and able adult son, ambition was bound to play a role in transmitting power. In 1070, Baldwin VI of Flanders died and his 15-year-old son Arnulf was killed in battle by his brother, Robert the Frisian, who succeeded. The princes were caught up in a web of high politics, often with the widest ramifications, and this produced internal problems. In the tenth century the vicecounts, later counts, of Anjou were vassals of the Capetian dukes of Francia, but they profited from the feud of Caroling and Capet to seize Anjou and a whole group of lordships, themselves becoming princes and cultivating a royal style of government.[5]

But there was no reason why this centrifugal process should halt at this level. Anjou was desperately weakened by the succession dispute that broke out on the death of Charles Martel in 1060: by 1067, Fulk Réquin had overthrown his elder brother, but at the price of great concessions to interested outside powers and a considerable loosening of control over the castellans within. Bouchard of l'Ile Bouchard, as a child deprived of his lands in 1044 by Geoffrey Martel, took advantage of this weakness and the support of the Count of Blois to fight the Fouel family for the restitution of his lands. This was an unusual situation in the tightly governed Angevin lands, but in many regions a commonplace. The causes of the weakness of royal power in its very homeland, the Ile-de-France, have been much explored, and their consequences – internal war, which continued until deep into the twelfth century – well described, largely because they are the main theme of Suger's famous life of his master Louis VI. In Mâcon the accession of Otto-William (982–1026) marked a decisive stage in the history of the county. He was the son of Adalbert of Ivrea, king of Italy, deposed by Otto I in 968, and had acquired the county through marriage. As a result he was not known in the area, and was preoccupied by considerable lands east of the Saône and involvement in politics at the highest level. By about 1000 he had handed effective rule in the county over to his 17-year-old son Guy, on whose death in 1005 the title passed to the child Odo. During this vacuum of power, the vicecounts of Mâcon became very influential, while Otto-William's great rival, Hugh of Chalon, encroached to the extent that by 1035 he was holding assemblies of notables around Cluny. The churches of the area resorted to protecting themselves by the Peace of God. Many of the castellans ceased to attend the count's court and attached their castles to their allodial territories, exercising public authority for their own benefit, while others drifted away into the orbit of neighbouring powers, through the agency of multiple homage. The great duchies and counties of France – and this included the Capetian principality – ebbed and flowed, torn by tensions and conflicts which might erupt at any favourable moment. Robert the Frisian had triumphed in 1070 as count of Flanders, but nearly a century and a half later a chronicler could rehearse in detail the claims of the counts of Hainaut whom he had dispossessed. This kind of thing did not happen to every powerful duchy or county, but it could always happen, and the pattern of piecemeal landholding to which governmental rights tended to become attached made it all the more disastrous. The death of Robert the Magnificent and the accession of the child William in 1037 ushered in a difficult period for the Norman duchy, while the distant entanglements of William IX of Aquitaine led to a weakening of that duchy.[6]

The aristocracy were of necessity militarized, for in a world where public authority lacked the means to control the land, it was essential that the landowner defend it. Since Roman times, Europe had been dominated by great men with their armed retinues. And given this weakness of government and its relative poverty, it was upon such men that the public authority leaned to provide soldiers. The central principle of their lives was personal and dynastic ambition. Inheritance gave them rights which they needed to defend and claims which they needed to prosecute – war-making was an essential part of either process. Power was deeply personal, and kings and great lords pursued claims and defended rights in the name of themselves and their families, not in the name of the state.[7] We are mesmerized by the "Empires" of the Angevins, and the Hohenstaufen, but these kings were essentially aristocratic landowners writ large, masters of vast and often uncertainly defined *mouvances* rather than sovereigns of states in our sense, and an understanding of this is fundamental to an understanding of the nature of war in this period.

The military consequences of the dynastic principle can be illustrated by the history of the Angevin counts. They were by origin a Breton family from the marches of that duchy, who seem to have risen in the service of Charles the Bald and then the Capetian dukes, becoming counts of Nantes and vicecounts of Angers. By 929, Fulk the Good was calling himself Count of Anjou. His son, Geoffrey Greycloak (*c.* 960–987), pursued family claims in Poitou, and as a result, although he remained a vassal of the Capetians he now paid homage to the Duke of Aquitaine. By the time of his death and the accession of the Capetian house to the kingdom of France, the chances of inheritance and the thrust of dynastic policy meant that his successor, Fulk Nerra (987–1040), had lands as far east as Orléans, sizeable holdings of the Archbishop of Tours in the Touraine, more land held of the dukes of Aquitaine in the general area of Niort, especially the castle of Loudon, and a strong claim to the county of Nantes. But this was not actually a territorial unity: rather, the family ruled a chain of lands and asserted a series of claims to land and rights, strung out across a vast area, and intersected by the lands and claims of other powerful families, notably the counts of Blois, whose great centres were Tours and Saumur, and the dukes of Aquitaine to the south of the Loire.[8]

Fulk's essential problem was how to tie these far-flung lands together, and the means that he chose was the establishment of lines of fortresses guarding the roads. It has been suggested that these were carefully built about 35 km apart – the distance a group of horsemen could easily travel in a day without overly tiring their horses. The establishment of strong fortresses was not merely a defensive process: it guaranteed the land but also created opportunities for exploiting the problems of others. In 996, Odo I of Blois and Chartres died, leaving a child as his heir, and Fulk joined Aldebert of La Marche in the capture of Tours, but King Robert intervened on behalf of the child Odo II and Aldebert was killed, forcing Fulk to abandon Tours. However, in 1026 he was able to seize Saumur by a surprise attack after Odo II of Blois became absorbed in attacking Fulk's castle at Montboyau, which was dangerously close to the Blésois city of Tours. The claims of Fulk backed up by his determined castle-building created conflicts – in 994 Aimery, Vicecount of Thouars, quarrelled with Fulk over the county of Nantes. On the other hand, the dominating ambition of the house of Blois led to an Angevin alliance with the counts of Vendôme, which began under Geoffrey Greycloak and reached fruition under Geoffrey Martel. The extension of Angevin power along the lower Loire under Fulk Nerra is a remarkable phenomenon which has attracted much attention. It used to be seen as part of a great drive to seize Tours, which eventually fell to Fulk's successor, Geoffrey Martel, in 1044. However, recent work suggests that a much more complex interaction between defence and ambition underlay Fulk's castle-building programme.[9] The point made here is that the very nature of contemporary landholding, and the means available to protect it, produced war.

What is unusual about the conflict between the houses of Blois and Anjou was that it was especially bitter and long-lasting. Fulk fought pitched battles at Conquereuil in 992 and Pontlevoy in 1016, and built at least 13 stone castles. This bitterness perhaps arose in part from the personalities of Odo II of Blois and Fulk of Anjou. It was certainly fanned by their rivalry at the royal court, and by the careful intervention of the kings of France, which encouraged first one side then the other. More fundamentally, each of these dynasties had a strong landed base from which it might hope to dominate the lower Loire. But their main properties were notably interpenetrating. Any serious military act by one party – especially the building of a castle – could threaten the other in a very fundamental way. In the end, the Angevins were more successful because the counts of Blois were distracted by ambitions in Champagne and in Burgundy. The long conflict on the lower Loire reveals to us what enormous resources the feudal principalities could mobilize and how the scale of their conflict could escalate into major warfare sustained over a long period of time. We should not exaggerate the ferocity of the wars of Anjou and Blois. There were long periods of peace, and for much of the time ravaging and raiding were the staples. But at Pontlevoy in 1016 between 3,000 and 6,000 are said to have died on the field, and the notoriety of the event spread even to Germany. In 1044, Geoffrey Martel is said to have captured 1,700 men at the Battle of Nouy, which precipitated the fall of Tours to the Angevins.[10]

Such conflicts were not simply wars over real estate. They were also fought for dominion over men, and most particularly the local rich and powerful. Fulk of Anjou seized Saumur in 1026 and expelled the senior followers of the Count of Blois, but the lesser men were allowed to retain their lands unless they had showed special loyalty to their former lord. Moreover, the descendants of at least some of the expellees later enjoyed partial restitution. After his capture of Tours, Geoffrey Martel received the submission of many of the lords of the Touraine, amongst whom was Geldouin of Chaumont-sur-Loire, who retained his lordship. Others, such as Guicher of Châteaurenault, were deprived of their lands because of their loyalty to the house of Blois. The purpose of ravaging in war was partly to shake followers in their loyalty to their lords. The prevalence of multiple homage and the strength of family ties and personal relationships meant that changes of loyalty could occur. In time of war, every vassal had to consider the worth of his homage. Coercion of and negotiation with such people were both weapons of war and partly explain why it was often so episodic.

We think of conquest as an absolute process, but those who sought to conquer were usually anxious to annex the locally powerful. This was undoubtedly the intention of William the Conqueror in 1066. The heavy losses of the native lords at Stamford Bridge and Hastings enabled him to implant many of his Norman followers, but it was only after the early revolts that he set himself to destroy the Anglo-Saxon upper class as a whole, and even then there were survivors. Frederick I depended heavily on allies in Lombardy to provide bases and the means of conquest, as did his grandson Frederick II, and this affected considerably the way in which they waged war. William Rufus waged war against his brother Robert Curthose almost entirely by bribing over his vassals, and Henry I followed suit. King John alienated many of his vassals by mistreating the prisoners that he captured at Mirebeau, while Philip Augustus's constant pressure eroded Norman loyalty to John, leading to the final collapse of the Angevin lands in 1204. When most of the Angevin lands were lost, Philip Augustus was perfectly happy to accept the homage of all the vassals of the area, although lords who held land in England and Normandy were forced to choose and suffered expropriation in one or the other.[11] Seduction and subversion were a powerful element in the warfare of the Middle Ages, and the prevalence of multiple homage and the ambiguities resulting from splintered holdings could give it respectability. And since this was a less expensive and bloodless way of waging war, it was always popular, although its needs might well restrain the military methods of a commander.

The conflict of Blois and Anjou was unusually ferocious. Commonly, conflict arose for much the same reasons but was fought in a much milder way. Early in the twelfth century, even before his father's death, Louis VI supported Hugh of Clermont against his troublesome son-in-law Matthew of Clermont, ravaging his lands and seizing the castle of Lazarches. However, his forces were either panicked or tricked before Chambly castle and this produced a compromise settlement between the parties. Examples of this kind of limited conflict, in which each side was seeking an adjustment, can be multiplied throughout our period. Ordericus is a great chronicler of such occasions – the war over Brévol is only one notable example of a conflict that did not threaten anybody's existence and was fought at a relatively low intensity. Such conflicts underlay the treaty between Robert Earl of Leicester and Ranulf Earl of Chester in the late 1140s, when Robert almost certainly made similar agreements with the earls of Hereford and Gloucester. Moments of governmental weakness opened the way for the settling of old scores, as in 1229 when Theobald IV of Champagne's attack on the Count of Nevers provoked a powerful alliance of barons against him, prompting the intervention of a royal army under the Regent Blanche of Castille, which imposed a peace. Hugh IV, Duke of Burgundy (1218–72), took advantage of the weakness of the thirteenth-century county of Burgundy to expand his power there by a process of raid and siege across many years, which weakened the attachment of these lands to the Empire. The house of Hapsburg sought to unite its territories in Alsace and Burgundy by an unremitting feud against the Bishop of Basel. Such low-intensity war could be locally destructive. Geoffrey of Anjou conquered Normandy during the reign of Stephen without, as has often been remarked, a single major battle: rather, a painstaking mixture of threats and diplomacy won him support, but at Rouen the determined resistance of Warenne produced a different outcome. Geoffrey ordered his ally, Waleran of Beaumont, to destroy the suburb of Emendreville, which was burned in its entirety, along with many men, women and children who had taken refuge in the church of St Sever.[12]

Moreover, local war and the settling of scores could have much wider implications and could lead to an escalation of military activity. In the reign of Louis VII, some of the Burgundian barons, led by the Count of Mâcon, appealed to the Emperor Frederick Barbarossa for aid against their local enemies. The prospect of a shift in allegiance led to conflict between Frederick and Louis VII of France, and to a French royal expedition to the area in 1166. Because Frederick championed an anti-pope, the much wider conflict over the future of the papacy was involved. Blanche of Castille, the regent for Louis IX, was particularly anxious to settle the Champagne war because Theobald IV was her ally. So there is no simple form of war – that which begins as limited can escalate, the more so when personal feuds are involved. Feud, and the personal bitterness that it engendered, was a powerful influence on medieval warfare. Geoffrey de Mandeville's ravaging in East Anglia inspired real horror, while Frederick II's alliance with Ezzelino of Romano turned Cremona and its allies away from the imperial cause.[13] All of these influences affected the decision for and the means of making war, and the size and importance of the combatants cannot be taken as an indication of the nature of any particular outbreak.

Warfare which was about feudal adjustments, at whatever level, was almost bound to be limited and hardly worth the risks of battle and sustained major conflict. At the same time, however, an apparently small-scale quarrel could escalate and destabilize even the mightiest of feudal agglomerations. This was very much the position in which Fulk's great successor, Henry II, found himself. The building of the Angevin "Empire" was in many ways a case study in feudal politics. Marriage and other relationships created claims that were skilfully exploited with a judicious use of force. Geoffrey le Bel, Count of Anjou (1128–51), had a claim to the English throne and the Norman duchy through his wife Mathilda, daughter of Henry I. This gave legitimacy to his conquest of Normandy, while he supported his wife's and later their son Henry's claim to England, against their rival, Stephen of Blois. Stephen of Blois and his son Eustace fought off the Angevin claim to England, and by 1151 could look forward to an alliance with Louis VII to recover Normandy, but a series of accidents intervened. In September 1151, Geoffrey le Bel died, leaving all of his lands to Henry, perhaps with the reversion of Anjou to the younger son Geoffrey of Anjou when England had been conquered. Then, in 1152, the young Henry married Louis VII's divorced wife, Eleanor of Aquitaine, acquiring a title to that great duchy. Louis VII attacked in alliance with the discontented Geoffrey of Anjou, but Henry was strong enough to fight off Louis VII and to support his allies in England, where the death of Stephen's son Eustace in August 1153 opened the way for a settlement whereby he was recognized as Stephen's heir and duly succeeded in 1154. In that year, he ruthlessly deprived Geoffrey of his claims to Anjou and exploited a rebellion against the Breton duke to make him Count of Nantes.

A bewildering series of chance events in the years 1151–3 had made possible the elevation of Henry II to enormous power. The rapidity of these events and his reaction to them wrong-footed Louis VII at every turn. Henry, like his father, used force when appropriate, but only in the name of what could be presented as a legitimate pretension. By 1154, Louis VII was in no position to threaten such a powerful vassal. Henry had no wish to undermine his overlord, whom he acknowledged as such for all his continental lands in 1154. This was a remarkable concession for Henry to make, and of the highest importance both for Louis and himself: the counts of Blois-Champagne did not make such an explicit oath until 1198. Despite their subsequent quarrels, at Montmirail in 1169 Henry sought Louis's consent to his succession arrangements, which divided his dominions between his sons.[14] This clearly demonstrated acceptance of royal superiority seems to have conditioned the whole relationship between the two rulers, and must be seen as balancing the undoubted material preponderance of Henry II.

The conflicts of Angevin and Capetian were enormously important; yet the fighting was relatively small-scale and battle was rare. This was the result of the situation in which the protagonists found themselves. The French royal demesne was rich, and this made Louis VII a formidable enemy – but he was not as rich as Henry II, who now ruled England and the western half of France. Louis's best hope was to foment discontent in the Angevin dominions, and the instability of even the greatest of lordships made this possible. In 1151 many thought that Henry of Anjou would be ejected from Normandy by an alliance of Louis VII and Stephen, and the Norman lords were preparing to change sides. It was just this unravelling effect that Henry must have feared. But this had consequences for his general conduct of government. He was anxiously insisting on the duties and obligations of his vassals, so he could hardly deny that he had such duties and obligations to his own overlord, Louis VII. This is why Henry II remained essentially on the defensive and pressed forward only where he had manifestly good claims – for the precarious nature of loyalty in his many and diverse lands meant that subversion was to be feared.

Even before Henry had gained England, Louis VII attacked Normandy and supported the revolt of Geoffrey of Anjou. But Henry quickly strengthened his frontier, and by 1154 Louis VII agreed to allow Henry to buy back what he had captured. More importantly for Louis VII, in 1156 Henry did homage for Normandy, Anjou and Aquitaine. It is a sign of his good will that Louis did not support Geoffrey's second revolt in 1156, and by the treaty of 1158 the two kings settled the difficult question of the Norman Vexin, leaving Henry free to deal with Breton problems.[15] In general, Louis had always adopted a policy of peaceful dealing with his great princes, but the sheer power of Henry made the continuation of such a policy difficult. Two such powers side by side would inevitably quarrel, just as neighbouring landowners inevitably raise lawsuits against one another. For the most part, bickering of this kind was the substance of wars, but Louis VII was in a difficult position, while the sheer incoherence of his dominions kept Henry was on the defensive.

In 1159, Henry II attacked Toulouse. This was a very large military effort, in which he was supported by Malcolm, King of Scotland, Raymond-Berengar of Barcelona and Raymond Trencavel of Béziers, causing Louis VII to ally with the Count of Toulouse. But it was far from a simple act of aggression, because the dukes of Aquitaine had an ancient claim to the overlordship of Toulouse, which was eventually acknowledged in 1172 and again in 1198. Bickering between Louis and Henry continued. It was not usually Henry who held the initiative and treaties, such as the peace of Vendôme in 1170, were common. Louis began intervention in the Auvergne where both sides had ill-defined claims, but these were settled in Henry's favour by an arbitration which led to a lasting peace with Louis VII.[16]

Henry II's primary interest was maintenance of the *mouvance*. Internal rebellion was his greatest fear. The revolt of his sons, Henry FitzHenry and Richard, in 1173–4, was a terrible blow, because they acted as foci for all the discontented barons of his lands and could look to Louis VII for support. By 1174, William of Newburgh recorded: "there were only a few barons at that time in England who were not wavering in their allegiance to the king and ready to defect". Henry's skill and determination defeated the rebels and rallied the waverers in the crucial areas of Normandy and England, but he was forced to exert himself astonishingly. However, once he had made peace with Louis VII he was able to leave the pacification of Aquitaine to his son, Richard, who certainly won his spurs there.[17]

Henry was not aggressive. The huge scale and the nature of his empire meant that collisions with Louis VII and other peripheral powers, such as Flanders, were inevitable. Areas of dubious loyalty, such as Brittany and the Auvergne, were dangerous. Disloyalty was a contagion that could spread quickly in an age in which alliances, feuds and family relationships counted for so much. Henry II was an anxious landlord who spent his reign rushing round his dominions, shoring them up, and occasionally exploiting new claims. He avoided open and direct attack on his overlord and showed a remarkable readiness to come to terms, because to do otherwise could provoke problems with his own vassals. Louis VII was the weaker of the two rulers, but his lands were nothing like as exposed or as potentially unstable as those of the Angevins: he could rarely resist the temptation to stir up trouble and for the most part kept Henry on the defensive. But he lacked the power, and perhaps the will, to push matters to conclusions, which is why fighting remained so small-scale except in the great revolt.

It is instructive to compare Henry II's position to that of his grandfather,

Henry I, who also stood on the defensive throughout his reign. Henry I faced a permanent successions crisis. The claims to the English throne of his nephew, William Clito, were a challenge to his whole position. They provided a pretext for Norman rebels, who could count on substantial help from Louis VI of France (1108–37) in alliance with Flanders and Anjou. With so much at stake and such a balance of power between the opposing forces, it is hardly surprising that violent confrontation was common. There were four major battles and two substantial skirmishes in Normandy during Henry I's reign, as well as a large number of sieges and much border ravaging. By contrast, Henry II never seems to have been present at a battle, unless we include the fighting around Rouen, when he relieved the city from French attack in 1174. It was during this period of the great revolt that three other battles were fought in his name.[18] It was not until the very end of his reign, when Henry faced the aggressive Philip Augustus and the revolts of his sons, that fighting on such a scale erupted again. In general, Henry II was concerned to hold down his enormous lands in the face of inevitable hostility from Louis VII. Since the French king could not destroy Henry, who had no will to destroy his overlord, conflict *à l'outrance* was not in anybody's interests. Henry was a dogged and persistent soldier, a good organizer rather than a brilliant general. But he was, above all, a skilful politician. By contrast, his son, John, misjudged the entire Aquitanian situation in 1201–2, and what should have been a limited squabble with Hugh the Brown escalated beyond control. The limited war that characterized the reign of Henry II was the product of his determination to exploit every opportunity to control events and to ensure that limited ends necessitated limited means.

At much the same time, war in the Lombard plain, between the cities of the area and Frederick I Barbarossa, produced a radically different situation, for this was not about feudal adjustments – rather, it was a collision of different societies, in which each believed that it was radically threatened by the other. By Barbarossa's accession to the Empire in 1152, a very special political situation had evolved in Lombardy. The old Lombard kingdom, which formed part of the German empire, had always been more urban than other parts of Europe. The emperors had restricted the growth of powerful magnates in the region, so that the lesser nobility were drawn into the cities. The cities had profited from the Investiture Contest and the subsequent dynastic changes in Germany, which had weakened its monarchy to achieve effective independence. By 1152, the cities were used to ruling themselves and had developed their own organs of government. In Germany, Frederick accepted the shift in the balance of power in favour of the nobility, that was caused by the long period of royal weakness. In Italy, the evidence suggests, he was only grudgingly prepared to accept the autonomy of the cities provided that they acknowledged his authority and his right to extensive payments. There was in fact a social dimension to the Italian wars that was entirely lacking in the Angevin–Capetian rivalry, which was, for the most part, fought out by people of fundamentally similar outlook for fairly limited ends. The rise of cities, and with it new social groups, must have been familiar to Barbarossa from his own German experience, but for them to insist on high status for their citizens and the exercise of political power was a clear breach of the social order. This was truly the world turned upside down, for the cities claimed a kind of collective lordship over all others in their *contado* – hence Otto of Freising's hostile description of the cities, with their wicked domination over the country nobility, and their habit of conferring knighthood on mere tradesmen.[19] In the end, this hatred and contempt underlay the savagely fought war in the Lombard Plain.

Moreover, the situation in Lombardy offered Frederick rich possibilities. When he first appeared there, many of the smaller cities complained about the domination of Milan. At first, he was not strong enough to achieve anything decisive, but in 1158 he besieged Milan, which capitulated on terms. By the Roncaglia decrees of November 1158, Frederick outlined a schema of government that apparently respected the autonomy of the cities within a framework of royal power. But Frederick's resources in Germany were limited and the nobility were not always amenable to providing him with troops, so he relied heavily on his Italian allies. The need for their support meant that he could not administer the Roncaglia decrees in an even-handed manner. His agreement to the Cremonan demand for the destruction of the fortifications of the Milanese fortress-city of Crema precipitated the rebellion of Milan and her allies. Almost the first significant military act of the war was the Milanese capture of Trezzo, after which the Italians in the garrison were massacred, although the Germans were imprisoned. Shortly after, German prisoners at the siege of Crema were hanged. In effect, Frederick was party to a civil war between the cities of the Lombard plain, and the result was sustained and savage fighting over a very long period of time – it is hardly surprising that the author of the *Annales Egmundani*, writing some 30 years after the event, compressed the two sieges of Milan into one that was five years long.[20]

Frederick, fundamentally contemptuous and uncomprehending of the Lombard cities, was plunged into a civil war with heavy social overtones, in which some of the cities felt that their liberties, and even their basic existence, were at stake. Fear of imperial domination meant that they enjoyed the support of the papacy and the Normans of South Italy, which sustained the Milanese party and prolonged the war beyond all expectation. It is hardly surprising that the result was a war of great length, remarkable intensity and

appalling atrocity. The pattern of savagery set under Frederick I was continued in the reign of his grandson, Frederick II. Frederick II was as much of
a dynast as his grandfather, but he lived at a time when notions of the state
and supreme power were beginning to crystallize. Frederick I's claims to
Lombardy were based on his notion of dynastic supremacy, buttressed somewhat by new notions of Roman law and the power of the prince. He found
it difficult to take into account the self-government of cities and their
communal organization. His grandson, Frederick II, had a highly developed
conception of royal power which inspired his assault on the freedoms of the
Lombard cities, and provoked equally barbaric and sustained warfare.[21]

Kings claimed a sovereignty, but in practice they had, to a greater or lesser
degree, to share power with others whose allegiances were uncertain and
could easily – and with every appearance of legitimacy – be transferred to
other lords. Power rested on possession of land and the king had to struggle
to hold and expand his, just like any other landlord. This meant that his claims
came into conflict with those of his vassals and other kings. War over limited
objectives, therefore, could erupt at any time, and for the most part would be
pursued with limited means. But the skein of relationships between a lord –
even a king – and his tenants could unpick with alarming rapidity, and so a
war over territorial adjustment could escalate to a war for survival. And wars
in which one side or another conceived of their survival as being at stake
produced savage and sustained warfare, limited only by the resources of the
parties and the technology of the age. The same brutality prevailed where
leaders of radically different societies confronted one another, as on the
Crusades, or when the social order was threatened.

# Chapter Five

# *Men of war: cavalry*

Medieval warfare was dominated by the great proprietors. In the *Chansons de Geste* the king and his followers, the great lords and their honourable companions, ride out into battle. They are collectively the "chivalry"; a complex word whose meaning encompasses the notion of an armed elite, a style of war and a code of military behaviour in which personal honour is paramount. Within the chivalrous society there were evident differences of status, and the lesser did honourable service to the greater, yet there was a community of shared values. All members of this community rejoiced in the title of "knight", as a kind of token of membership. To understand medieval warfare, it is vital to understand what the knight was.

The Latin word *miles* (plural *milites*) originally meant nothing more than a soldier of any sort; in the words of Justinian's Code, "*Quantos autem milites, sive pedites sive equites*".[1] This meaning continued to be attached to it throughout the Middle Ages. However, from the late tenth century contemporary writers began to use *miles* in a much more specific way. In describing groups of armed men they refer to *milites et pedites*, with the implication that the former have usurped the meaning of the word in some special sense: it is clear from the context that the word *miles* usually meant a soldier on horseback, a cavalryman. Often, the word *eques* is used instead, sometimes by the same writer, and this underlines the point that there was a functional difference between two kinds of soldier, either or both of whom, however, could still simply be described by the term *miles*. But the fact that horses were expensive meant that there was a social overtone to any word applied to a cavalryman; this is evident even from early source material.

The act by which arms were bestowed on a young man for the first time had long been an important "rite of passage". In the eleventh century, it became a distinct Christian ritual for the making of a knight. In the first third

53

of the twelfth century this ceremony took on a much wider significance, as the moment of promotion into a self-conscious group with a special status and particular values, and this became highly developed in the thirteenth century. The Church spoke of such people as an "order of knighthood" with a specific function in the divine economy. By about 1100, substantial noblemen of the Mâcon area are referring to themselves as knights, and as time went on this became increasingly common across the face of Europe, although the process of adopting this title was not accepted everywhere before the end of the twelfth century. In 1167 Peter, bishop-elect of Cambrai and brother of the Count of Flanders, left the Church "and assumed the office of soldier", and in the following year Baldwin of Hainaut's son was "ordained into knighthood with great honour and rejoicing". By the twelfth century the German *ministerialis*, who was a cavalryman of servile origins, was generally thought of as belonging to the same social community as the free knight and soon entered into nobility. The fusion, or at least near-fusion, of knight and nobility is a complex phenomenon that occurred at different times in different parts of Europe, but by the end of the twelfth century knighthood is clearly a social status assimilated to nobility.[2]

Yet in the eleventh century and before, knighthood was certainly not aristocratic. The English word *cnicht* has heavy overtones of servility, and the alleged servility of knights in Flanders engendered bitter quarrels. In 987, Charles of Lorraine's marriage to a woman of knightly rank was held against him in his bid for the French crown. In eleventh-century France, knights were sometimes classified with other household servants of great lords. William of Jumièges tells the story of a smith of Beauvais whose sons seem to have become "knights" of Duke William of Normandy. Ordericus underlines the greed and brutality of the knights, and by implication their limited background, when he tells us of a young man who, once made a knight, went out and robbed a monk – a story with numerous parallels. In Spain, continuous war with Islam created a desperate need for cavalry. There, *caballeros villanos* were carefully distinguished from *caballeros hidalgos*. In Poitou and elsewhere there were *milites ignobiles*, and in England *agrarii milites*. The controversy over the status of the Norman knight has revealed how relatively poor some were. In the late eleventh century the abbot of Peterborough established a sergeancy for one Vivian, but the service that he owed for it was that of one knight.[3] All of this suggests that knights were a very diverse group, and this would not be surprising, because in the eleventh and twelfth centuries, from the cities of Italy to the plains of Flanders, social mobility was a commonplace.

In his masterly analysis of the Capetian charters of the eleventh century, Lemarignier remarked upon the humbleness of the testors as evidence of the declining importance of the royal dynasty, but this could be interpreted differently – as evidence of the king's being in touch with new and developing forces in a realm where men could profit from social mobility to rise. Even in the early eleventh century, writers had bemoaned both the new fluidity of society and the ambition that inspired men, appealing to the notion of the *Three Orders* as a defensive concept which would justify keeping people in general, and not merely the poor, in their appointed places. Glaber, writing in the 1020s, believed that the invading Normans of the ninth century had been led by an apostate Frank, who, he stresses, "rejected the station of his poor parents". The case of Stabilis, who was allegedly a villein of Fleury, reveals how difficult it was to prove status. In northern France, the family of the Wattrelos, who are first heard of as knights of the Bishop of Cambrai, almost reached nobility. The murder of Charles the Good of Flanders in 1127 arose from an attempt to reassert the unfree status of the clan of the Erembald, who had risen to great power within the county of Flanders. Medieval society was not ossified and men could rise, in the Church and in the service, civil or military, of great lords. The members of the militarized household of Henry I, and the mercenary captains of Stephen and King John, are obvious examples. The leading members of the house of Hauteville later took considerable pride in their early history, when they consorted with brigands and robbers.[4] The eleventh century was an age of great social mobility, when the growing wealth of Europe was opening up new horizons and providing new opportunities. This was a society in which there was social movement, especially at the level which concerns us, just below the nobility; knighthood and the profession of arms offered an upward path for men who were clearly of less than aristocratic origins.

The question which arises is why, in the twelfth century, the term *miles* should have become virtually synonymous with noble. It was hardly that the leaders of society had a greater need to become more militarized than they had been in earlier centuries. The collapse of Carolingian dominance created difficult conditions, but these were no worse than those attending the collapse of Merovingian power. There was the same tendency for whole areas to spin away from royal authority while the local powerful usurped power. Viking invasions only exacerbated the general breakdown of public authority. That war or the threat of it became the way of settling disputes was not new, because to a degree medieval sovereigns had always been obliged to leave local powers to solve their disputes by force. Even in England, where there was great respect for the monarchy, militarization had taken place, although it was not so systematic as in the French lands.[5]

The great difference was that the Carolingians had created a layer of powerful families who held positions of trust as counts. The Carolingian collapse was the result of short-lived kings and constant changes of allegiance. In these circumstances, great families abandoned the traditional path to greatness, proximity to the king, in favour of consolidating their local lands and influence. In this way, they concentrated in their hands sufficient wealth to be able to create military establishments of their own. As early as the edict of Pîtres of 863, private fortifications were prohibited – but in vain. The nobility had the means to exploit the peasantry, but saw little need to acknowledge obligation to overlords whose "subjects" they were in some sense of the word. In France, great magnates such as Fulk of Anjou appear as allies rather than vassals of the French king, while Barbarossa was quite legally refused military aid for his Italian campaigns by Henry the Lion. It was the ascent to power of some, but not all, monarchies which enabled them to reverse this process and to establish military obligation upon the great.[6]

As we have seen, the great princes were not able to maintain a monopoly of the royal power, which came to be shared by a whole host of lesser magnates. Lords had always been able to afford the best military equipment for themselves, and by the end of the ninth century the diffusion of the stirrup and the development of the saddle meant that they adopted the style of the heavy cavalryman. But the competitive consequences of the dissolution of power, and the fact that estates were interpenetrating, meant that they were prepared to arm followers in a similar style. The expense and efficiency of this equipment sharply differentiated those who could afford it from the rest of the population. Thus, by about the year 1000, a common style of war and equipment united all who played a major part in war. As early as the late ninth century, the impact of all this in the sharing of a warrior ethic was evident.[7] The retinue of bully-boys formed only part of the *mouvance* of a great man. Important local nobles had to be conciliated and given status, preferably by association. Offspring needed to be endowed with worthy settlements. Out of this situation sprang the rash of fortifications and the networks of *mouvances* built around them.

The bonds that tied these *mouvances* together were what we call feudal oaths. But the oath in itself did little – what mattered was who had real power in a relationship. The situation was further complicated because at all levels there was multiple homage – even knights might have more than one lord. There were, therefore, no clear lines of command, and the fragmentation of landholding was mirrored by the fragmentation of authority across the face of France. The leaders of society were the upper aristocracy, the wealthiest of all with great landholdings, castles and large *mouvances*. It was they who gathered knights and led them to war, often in no cause but their own: in the context of strong monarchy they would serve to win influence with the king. It was only in the later twelfth century that monarchy began to define the bonds of society and to insist that such men were obliged to serve in respect of landholdings and to send contingents to the king. But the basis of service was always fluid.[8] The castle and the retinue formed a theatre for relations between these important aristocrats, the castle-holders who by the early eleventh century were very numerous, and their humbler followers to whom we give the title of knights. This was the foundation of the fusion of knighthood and nobility.

The attitude of the Church also had its influence. By the millennium, the Church was anxious to influence and moderate the behaviour of the warriors. Clergy began to speak of them as a distinct order in Christian society and sought to direct and control their aggressive instinct, a process which culminated in the crusading movement. This ideological pressure enjoyed an increasing, if limited, success amongst the European elite: if their behaviour fell short of the Church's aspirations, then at least they imbibed some sense of moral purpose.[9]

Another factor which facilitated the fusion was that many knights were from noble houses. As laws of inheritance tightened, younger sons or members of impoverished lines, enjoying at best limited land tenure, had to make their way in association with armed bully-boys of humble origins. Landless household knights continued to be common, but land was their aspiration and in the milieu of the castle and the retinue they profited from association with their betters. It was natural for such men, once they had become landowners, to ensure the protection of status by rules of lineage that imitated those of the nobility. Therefore, a whole shared experience tended to turn the more successful of the hired bully-boys of the lords into a kind of lower rank of the aristocracy. The distinctiveness of the military lifestyle and the need for military solidarity stamped all its participants and created shared values. The fluidity of this social milieu enabled some young men to rise in the social scale by military prowess. Noble families began to rewrite their genealogies, pretending that they had descended from such admirable figures rather than ancient noble lineages – to establish the worth of their position in terms of the new *desiderata*.[10] Thus, by the end of the eleventh century, the cavalry were a very mixed group, combining the greatest aristocrats with petty landholders and social climbers who could barely afford the equipment of a mounted soldier. Few were military professionals: the endowed knight was a soldier, but he was also a trusted administrator, while even household men could be confused with other servants. The word designated their military function, but it always had heavy social overtones of "the leaders of society".

By the late twelfth century, the *miles* was a man of elevated quasi-noble and heritable status. Those who described themselves in this way were expected to be men of substance with land. At the siege of Tortona in 1157 Frederick I

Barbarossa was impressed by the valour of a sergeant (*strator*) who killed a fully armed knight while storming the citadel single-handed, and offered him the belt of knighthood, but he refused, preferring his humble status and a rich reward. The assumption has been that such a status needed wealth to maintain it, although the passage is susceptible to other interpretations. Gislebert of Mons speaks of *pedites et milites*, but he also mentions sergeants (*servientes*) often mounted. The *milites* are always carefully distinguished from sergeants, even when, as in 1187, it is explicitly stated that they were cavalrymen and just as well armed as the knights – this clearly implies a social rather than a military distinction. At Bouvines in 1214, the Flemish knights disdained the mere sergeants first sent against them by the French.[11] Undoubtedly, there was some military reason for this sense of superiority: the better-off could afford the improved and increasingly elaborate defences that had been developed.

The growing distinction between knights and others amongst the cavalry was, above all, social, for the landed knights formed a gentry, a kind of subgroup of the nobility. Before the mid-twelfth century, all cavalrymen were called *milites*, but thereafter the consolidation of the better-off and their close association with the nobility produced a powerful new and highly exclusive chivalric ethos. In England and France this coincided with a period when the number of knights shrank drastically. There had always been some reluctance to serve: St Anselm was criticized for producing poor knights for the royal army; and St Hugh of Lincoln tried to claim that his knights owed service only in England – an idea which gained support during the troubles of King John. The French monarchs had to fight similar restrictions. Conscious resistance was reinforced by the chances of inheritance and division of estates, which made enforcement difficult. By the time of Henry II, although many knights still served personally, the vast majority preferred to pay scutage, and the signs are that the king too preferred this, for it enabled him to hire effective soldiers. Richard I proposed to levy money to support a permanent paid force of 300 knights.[12]

The rising cost of military equipment may well have contributed to this reluctance. Moreover, in the second half of the twelfth century there was a new extravagance in aristocratic life which may have deterred many. English knights were also expected to carry civil burdens and some may have wished to avoid them. Many families marginal to knighthood must have been deterred from claiming it because of these factors, and an anxiety to exploit new opportunities for gaining wealth in an expanding economy. From 1224 onwards, the English Crown resorted to forcing knightly status on the basis of a property franchise, although this was not simply for military reasons. In Angevin times the king was owed the service of 5,000 knights, but by the end of the thirteenth century no more than 1,500 could be called to a feudal summons – and then only with difficulty. But it is interesting that, despite this, when the Crown insisted, personal service was often performed, and leading magnates brought satisfactory soldiers with them to muster. There was no demilitarization of the aristocracy and knights, even in relatively peaceful England, for military capacity was a sign of social status. However, war was less common in England than elsewhere so it is not surprising that by the early fourteenth century much English armour was seen as generally old-fashioned. The same reluctance to take up knighthood is found in France.[13]

In both countries, what followed was the creation of the courtesy titles; *armiger*, which gives *écuyer* in French and *squire* in English, and *scutifer*, meaning shield-bearer. These would have a long history as gentry titles, especially in England. In fact, the term *armiger* had long had a gentle connotation: Galbert of Bruges shows them carefully distinguished from the mere foot, companions of notables and clearly mounted. Hugh Magnus served Louis IV in this capacity. Liudprand uses the term to describe a companion of the Byzantine emperor. Ordericus Vitalis says that Robert of Grandmesnil served as *armiger* of the Duke of Normandy for five years before he was knighted, and mentions William, *armiger* of Philip I of France, who the king raised to knighthood. In a letter, St Bernard refers to a young *armiger* who Thomas of Marles wished to make a knight until he fled to Cîteaux. *Scutifer*, shield-bearer, is a less exalted term, but two captured twelfth-century *scutiferi* of Laon who appear in the miracles of Our Lady of Soissons seem to have been of good background.[14] These terms originated amongst the gentle; hence their ultimate social rather than military importance. Their use to describe honourable soldiers points to the importance of the gentry and nobility as the major, but never sole, recruiting source for cavalry.

Throughout this period, the term *miles* denoted a general function, that of soldier, a specific function, that of mounted soldier, and a social eminence attached to a bottom layer of the aristocracy. From the last quarter of the twelfth century, the cavalry appears to be more variegated than ever before, with sergeants and squires joining the ranks. In reality, the new prosperity of the twelfth and thirteenth centuries was probably only making more apparent divisions that had long existed. Moreover, the evidence suggests that as career choice widened for the gentry, so the career soldier emerged. The model of the man who rose by war is William Marshal, but it was a long time before he reached the ranks of the landowners. For much of his career, he was a paid household knight. In the eleventh century there is some evidence that household and landed followers normally accompanied great men to war, and this tenurial solidarity has been seen as important for the success of the Normans in England. The retinues of great men continued to be the most important unit of cavalrymen: rank dominated the military hierarchy. But the very limited English evidence, on the retinues of William Marshal and Peter des Roches, Bishop of Winchester, suggests that followers who served by reason of tenure were not very important or very common. Rather, lords recruited paid men, presumably the kind of young soldiers found regularly at tournaments and in the king's military household.[15] The rise of professional cavalrymen did not end the military function of the knights as a whole, even in relatively peaceful England, because wealth continued to need a military function.

The German *ministeriales*, although divided between rich and poor, also continued to be very obviously highly militarized – in part, a consequence of the relatively weak government of medieval Germany. Their military prowess enabled them also to assert themselves against their masters: many important German prelates were assassinated by their own *ministeriales*. However, they were never the sole element in German military retinues amongst which there were paid men. In Italy, where the rivalries of the northern cities were exacerbated by the ambitions of the Hohenstaufen emperors, city militias led by urban patricians, who were mounted with all the trappings of the traditional aristocracy, continued to be very important. Much has been made of the use of mercenaries in thirteenth-century Italy, but in practice Italian cities were supplementing native forces with men hired from afar rather than replacing them.[16]

The constant warfare of the small principalities of the Low Countries between France and Germany maintained the military function of all who could be described as gentle. War-leaders could draw on a "cloud" of retainers who formed a kind of social interface between the peasantry and the noble knights; they might not be landowners but they were predominantly drawn from the landowning milieu, at least by the thirteenth century. In the armies of Baldwin of Hainaut at the end of the twelfth century, his landed knights were the central element, supported by sergeants who were sometimes mounted (and occasionally as well equipped as the knights) and sometimes not, and mere foot.[17] However, in 1184 the count became involved in the much greater conflict of Philip Augustus of France and Philip of Alsace, Count of Flanders, who invaded Hainaut in alliance with Godfrey of Louvain and the Archbishop of Cologne. Baldwin responded by strengthening and garrissoning his castles, and this required the efforts of his allies and even mercenaries, probably footmen, 2,300 of whom were placed in Binche. But he also had to hire 300 mercenary knights and some 3,000 sergeants, both horse and foot. Baldwin also enjoyed the support of about 300 knights from France and Lorraine, who were not paid but served for expenses: it may well be that some of these were ultimately well rewarded, for three French knights were subsequently taken into fief. These were professionals, young men who served "on spec", hoping for rewards.

Such professionals were a well attested phenomenon in twelfth-century Europe. Ordericus Vitalis referred to those drawn to the Norman wars under Robert Curthose by the hope of plunder and ransoms. The landless Bohemond was able to attract young men to his cause in South Italy because his military reputation offered the prospect of gain. In 1101, Henry I entered into an arrangement with the Count of Flanders, who promised to provide him with 1,000 mercenary knights, each with three horses, at need, and this arrangement was renewed during the reign of Henry II. After the conquest of Jerusalem, Western knights frequently went to the Holy Land for both adventure and employment. Gerard of Ridefort, later Master of the Temple, originally went to the Holy Land as a sword for hire and was employed by Raymond III of Tripoli. So commonplace were such paid men that under the terms of the Avranches agreement part of Henry II's penance for the death of Becket was to hire 200 knights to serve with the Templars. John's mercenaries were deeply unpopular and thirteenth-century England saw a decline in their employment, but this was unusual. Frederick II, the Italian cities, Charles of Anjou and the later Hohenstaufen, all employed paid cavalry to strengthen their armies. Robert of Flanders was a high-born ally in Charles's army of conquest, but he had a much more motley following.[18]

An enormous range of people could function as *milites*, even though they were not what the later twelfth century regarded as knights, lesser aristocrats sharing the lifestyle of their superiors. The distinction between such men and the noble knight serving by reason of his position in society and tenure of a great man is blurred in our eyes, although it probably was not to contemporaries, because by the early twelfth century kings and other major leaders paid knights for their military services. Endowed knights traditionally owed 40 days' service per year: they were not professional soldiers because they had other functions. Paid men, in our terms mercenaries, appeared very early. In Fulk Nerra's army, which defeated the Bretons at Conquereuil in 992, the *conducticiis* are contrasted with Fulk's own vassals. William the Conqueror's use of them before Hastings and during his wars in England is as well known, as are his sons' arrangements to recruit 1,000 from the Count of Flanders. Such people were not very clearly differentiated from knights, because they might themselves be vassals of a lord seeking employment, or close connections of knightly, and indeed aristocratic, families. Any commander would pay his own tenured knights to extend their service when he needed it.[19]

On the First Crusade there are references to people of considerable status being paid for specific tasks: at the siege of Antioch, Tancred was paid 400 silver marks to blockade the St George Gate, while the Count of Toulouse offered huge sums to draw all the other leaders into his service. The count's grants were, in effect, *fief-rentes*, a form of financial reward for service which was clearly regarded as totally honourable. This was the form of Henry I's treaty with Flanders, and in the twelfth century Henry II, Richard and John would all use it to enlist foreign allies. The Ottonians in the tenth century had used allocation of incomes rather than gifts of land to pay their armed retainers, while in the Latin Kingdom of Jerusalem the *fief en besant* was virtually the norm in a region with a buoyant money economy.[20]

In fact, the payment of knights tends to blur the relationship between the various groups who served in medieval armies as cavalrymen. The social exclusivity of the aristocracy from the late twelfth century lifted those who could afford to share their extravagant lifestyle and raised the status of the knight by confirming what it had always tended to be, a social rank. Below this rank were gentry, sometimes landholding, who shared the assumptions and manners of those above them but lacked the income or, in some cases, chose not to spend it in this way. This group of petty landowners, younger sons, young men with aspirations but few means, all of generally "gentle" origins, increasingly formed the recruiting base for cavalry. Because of their gentle status they were not usually referred to as mercenaries.

In the new socially stratified society sergeants were excluded – they might fight as cavalry and even be as well equipped, but they lacked the social connection. It was only the rich and well born, says Gislebert of Mons, who were allowed to hold sergeanties in heredity in Hainaut, and this may have been a highly significant distinction elsewhere. The term *miles* had always had the social implication of superiority and, as the twelfth century wore on, this was applied in an exclusive way, as it became an aristocratic rank. One consequence of this was the development of new names, most notably *squire*, to emphasize the gentle connections of those who fought on horseback but could not afford knighthood. Such men were the recruiting ground for the bulk of all retinues. Because contemporaries understood their social origins, there was little effort to describe them as mercenaries – that was a pejorative term, only rarely applied to these gentry who could aspire to upward movement with approval and who shared something of the lifestyle of the upper class and its aspirations, if not its wealth. Young men of great wealth seem to have created their own peripatetic establishments, often in opposition to their fathers, staffed by equally young social aspirants who were a vital component in the vogue for tournaments that swept Europe from the later twelfth century. Overall, anyone who aspired to be gentle or noble had to have a military capacity, even if they chose not to exercise it. Aristocratic society bred younger sons for whom it could not easily provide and also had a fringe of mediocres and aspirants – like the eighteenth-century gentry whom Jane Austen describes. These people, with all their refined distinctions, were also militarized, and some of them were specialists. This explains the ease with which even a relatively peaceful land such as England could raise large armies when required. These people were not wealthy but enjoyed a context of gentility, and this probably explains why wage rates for knights never seem to have been sufficient to cover the costs of military equipment, for they provided their own – and this was probably an important reason why kings were so anxious to maintain the system of tenurial military obligation.[21] By the end of the thirteenth century, armies seem to have found all the social distinctions distinctly unhelpful, especially as the increased availability of weapons made the military distinction between the gentle and others less relevant. The result was the emergence of the omnibus term "men-at-arms".

The elite of Europe were not simply the "officer class" of medieval society. In most areas they decided on war and peace, and in all they had to be consulted on such issues. They saw themselves as the only legitimate fighting force, and literate clerics justified their dominance in society in these terms. But in fact they were only the most effective element in contemporary armies, and in particular circumstances not even that. For war involved others – there were the sergeants who supplemented the cavalry and ended up amongst the amorphous group of men-at-arms. Then, of course, there were the infantry proper. Where did they come from?

# Chapter Six

## *Men of war: infantry*

Infantry were an element in all the wars of the period: in 984 their skills extricated Lothar and his cavalry from a difficult situation in Lorraine; their steadiness fought off Barbarossa's attacks on the *carroccio* to win the victory of Legnano on 29 May 1176, and they were vital to the victory of the Florentines at Certomondo on 11 June 1289. Of course, knights sometimes fought on foot while sergeants, a term normally associated with footsoldiers, sometimes fought on horseback. Broadly, the groups that we are considering here are those who normally fought on foot and were not in any sense gentle. Our sources in general pay much less attention to these people, dismissing them as mere *pedites*. The Bayeux Tapestry ignores all but the archers in its account of Hastings, probably because its public were the knights, upon whose doings the narrative sources also focus. Gislebert of Mons gives us much precise information about warfare in Flanders in the later twelfth century, including very believable figures for the numbers of cavalry involved in campaigns, but sometimes offers ridiculously high figures for the infantry.[1]

Gislebert makes it clear that the sergeants, whether mounted or not, formed a special group. Although sergeants on foot are sometimes lumped in with the rest of the infantry, just as those on horse are with other cavalry, they seem to be identical with the elite foot who figure in his narrative. These men were obligated to serve, even though they could not enjoy their status or tenement in heredity. The English evidence shows sergeancies as smallholdings. Some of those which were military in nature produced well armed men: a Suffolk sergeant was obliged to follow the king to the Welsh wars with bow and arrows, a sword and a studded leather or wool jacket. Such equipment would have raised him above the common ruck of infantry. But sergeanty in England covered "a hotch-potch of tenures that did not, for one reason

or another, conveniently fit into the general scheme of social grouping".
Crossbowmen, men with riding duties, occasionally knights and even King
John's Master Urricus, an engineer responsible for the royal machines, are
found in this category. The commander of William II's ship was a sergeant, as
was Thomas Buffin, who was to serve at his own expense for 40 days and for
the remainder at the king's. By the mid-thirteenth century in England, this
form of tenure had become obsolete and thoroughly demilitarized, although
this was not entirely typical across Europe.[2]

In the Norman kingdom of Sicily in the twelfth century, *servientes* were
non-knights obligated to serve in time of need, but by the time of Frederick
II a distinction between the fairly useless rustic sergeants and others was being
drawn. The Assizes of Capua of 1220 regulated their right to bear arms, and
this was later embodied in the *Liber Augustalis*. Sergeants certainly existed in
Germany and fought in its armies. Frederick Barbarossa was impressed by a
brave *strator* at the siege of Tortona, while after the siege of Cremona he
mourned the loss of active *servientes*. Nearly a century later, Count Frederick
of Zollern complained of the cruelties visited upon his sergeants and
*ministeriales* by the rebels against Frederick II. In Bruges, a list of municipal
troops of 1303 carefully distinguishes 183 sergeants from the 830 civic levies,
the mercenaries and others. They are frequently referred to in the armies of
the French monarchy. Under Philip Augustus, the *Prisia Servientum* suggests
that the monarchy could raise some 8,000, but only a limited number of these
were tenement-holders. The 300 provided by Tournai are described as well
armed infantry. The churches and cities of the Latin Kingdom of Jerusalem in
the late twelfth century were obliged to furnish the king with 5,000 *sergens* "in
time of great need".[3]

The smallholdings of sergeants must have originated in an age of limited
liquidity as a way of paying relatively humble servants. This must always have
caused difficulties, and it is evident that such tenements were relatively few.
In England they were clearly out of date by 1250, and while they continued
to exist elsewhere, their rank was increasingly just a synonym for infantry –
and, indeed, this seems to have been the case for a very long time. In the
twelfth century sergeants may sometimes have formed an elite amongst
infantry, but consistent practice is rare. What is certain is that most of those
who fought on foot in medieval armies were not serving because of this form
of tenure. Rather, they served from personal obligation as men of a king or
lord, or for pay, or through some combination of these factors.

It has long been assumed that there was, in most of Europe, an obligation
on all freemen to serve in arms, and that this formed the basis of large infantry
forces, at least in the earlier part of our period. In England the so-called *trinoda
necessitas* – the obligation of freemen to serve in the host (*fyrd*) and to do work

on bridges and roads – was believed to date back to the time of Offa and continued to be important into late Saxon times. But doubt has been cast upon the idea of a "nation in arms", and it has been suggested that England was always defended by the king's leading followers and their commended men, whose obligation was essentially personal and in part tenurial. The leaders of Anglo-Saxon society seem to have negotiated their military service to the king on an individual basis while acknowledging a general obligation to perform it as holders of land.[4]

If we turn to the continental evidence, we can see that the notion of an *arrière-ban* of all the freemen of a realm who the king could call out also often rests on very limited evidence, such as the reference to fines for failure to do military service in Poitou in the 1020s. In France, the first explicit summons was by Philip the Fair after the defeat of Courtrai in 1302, but the earlier evidence is exiguous. The Count of Flanders and the Duke of Normandy seem to have reserved a right to call out all men in times of foreign invasion, but the documentation emphasizes the fiscal and labour-service owed by humble men to their lords, while the counts of Anjou clearly relied on their vassals to bring entourages. The clear existence of some form of levy in Catalonia, albeit linked to landholding, was probably the consequence of living under constant threat of Saracen attack. The same fear of pagan neighbours probably underlay peasant obligation to military service in Saxony in the eleventh century. But whether such an obligation extended to anything beyond the local territorial defence to be expected on an exposed frontier is another matter. In Germany, thirteenth century law-codes assert *Folgepflicht* (a duty to follow) which bore upon the peoples of Saxony and Austria, but it is difficult to trace this back. Certain passages by Widukind, the Saxon chronicler, have been much discussed, but he never describes a peasant army. There were certainly peasants in the Saxon armies that rebelled against Henry IV, but according to the *Carmen* they were brought by the knights and nobles. Henry IV saw the treachery of some knights lead to the slaughter of his infantry at Bleichfeldt in 1086, but on what basis these men were raised is not known.[5] In fact, the evidence suggests that if there had ever been an ancient and universal obligation to bear arms, it was largely forgotten by the start of this period and was something that the rulers of the thirteenth and fourteenth centuries tried to invent for their own purposes.

They were able to do this because medieval society was an armed society. In his Assizes of Arms of 1181, Henry II laid down the weapons that all freemen, according to their status, were to possess. This was an attempt to ensure that the respectable elements in his lands could properly protect themselves and the public peace. The underlying assumption of the royal order was that most citizens were or could be armed. When rebellion threatened in 1193, or foreign invasion in 1205 and 1213, appeal could be made to these armed men for aid in defence of the realm in a situation in which it must have seemed common sense to respond. In 1230, the Assize was reformed to allow even some of the non-free to be armed; in 1242, the better-off were required to have horses, and archers were included. In 1253, the renewal was overtly concerned with law and order. In 1264, de Montfort raised troops against foreign invasion by selecting the best men each area could produce, and perhaps this involved calling out the levies created by the assizes. The legislation culminated in the Statute of Winchester, which systematized the holding of arms by virtually all men. In time of war, Edward I used Commissions of Array of king's men and local lords who selected soldiers from the local armed men to go and fight. The basis of selection is not known, but a mixture of coercion and cash probably explains the huge infantry forces which were raised at the end of the thirteenth century in England.[6]

It is very notable that in France the bulk of the sergeant-service was from the cities. The communal movement, there as elsewhere, was an armed movement in which resistance had played its part, and city-dwellers must have been keenly aware of the need to defend themselves against those from without the walls. In return for privileges and protection, the French monarchy in the twelfth and thirteenth centuries acquired vital sources of men and money for the conduct of war. In the Latin Kingdom of Jerusalem, 2,000 of the 5,025 sergeants came from the cities. In northern Italy, the communal movement was born in war against the German emperors. In Flanders, city militias are well attested to from the very beginning of our period, and by the thirteenth century it is clear that they were being summoned, as in Italy, according to the quarters in which they lived. It is not hard to see why cities produced good soldiers and sturdy foot. The Crusades are usually seen as an aristocratic preoccupation, but the cities of Europe and the Holy Land bred military confraternities of burgesses who were quite ready to fight, or at least to support warfare, in a very direct way. The city bred its own *esprit de corps* which could sustain men in the bloody business of war.[7]

There were plenty of armed men about in medieval society, and in the thirteenth century the powerful leaders of society tried to develop this situation to their advantage. "It is provided that if aliens come to our land, all should unanimously go to oppose them with force and arms without any interference or delay" – when he said this in 1213, John was not appealing to an unbroken tradition of militia service, but attempting to put a royal and centralist interpretation on a situation, and to good effect. But such an assertion of royal leadership, in circumstances when self-interest would predispose men to follow it, was quite different from a widespread obligation, either linked to land or not, which could be used to raise troops in any circumstances. Henry II in 1164 tried to get his barons to raise infantry in what may have been an effort to restore the old *fyrd* system of service by lordship, but it failed. Henry's response was to rely more and more on mercenaries to man his armies, and it can hardly be an accident that the later twelfth century was the golden age of mercenaries in France and England. The Capetians and Plantagenets needed larger armies than ever before but they had enough difficulties raising knights from their followers, let alone footsoldiers. By the thirteenth century, the city levies in France and the Assizes of Arms in England facilitated the raising of troops and money for war. But no ruler seems to have been able to raise troops for war simply by appealing to a tradition of universal obligation. There is a remarkable passage in the *Annals of St Bertin* under the year 859: "Some of the common people living between the Seine and the Loire formed a sworn association amongst themselves, and fought bravely against the Danes on the Seine. But because their association had been made without due consideration, they were easily slain by our more powerful people."[8] This "association", it must be noted, had to be made *ad hoc*: this was not the dying struggle of a militia system against a new seigniorial military system, but a specific reaction to particular circumstances which the wealthy bearers of arms saw as dangerous to their interests.

The development of sergeancies and the hiring of mercenaries, so evident from the late tenth century, are arguments against the idea of a universal obligation. It is not hard to account for the presence of sizeable numbers of infantry who took part in campaigns if we think of the reality of a medieval army. A knight needed servants and supporters. If he was well-to-do, an *armiger*, perhaps a man close to knighthood, was also desirable, but lesser men could only manage servants. Henry I's treaty of 1101 with Flanders specified that each knight must have three horses. Looking after horses was labour-intensive, and then food had to be cooked, tents erected and clothes stored. Undoubtedly, there was much doubling-up but, even so, if we allow for the demands of status, it is likely that there were two or three servants for every cavalryman. They could not have been allowed to twiddle their thumbs in the course of campaigns and must have formed part of the infantry of many armies, or at least an element that reinforced the sergeants and the more specialist troops, notably the archers and crossbowmen.

Archers were a formidable instrument of war. They helped to break down the shield-wall at Hastings, cut down French cavalry at Brémule in 1119 and Bourgthéroulde in 1124, and decimated the Galwegians at Northallerton in 1138. The Pisans contributed archers to the armies of Barbarossa in Italy, and Saracen archers fought at Benevento in 1266. Many, some mounted, accompanied Henry II to Ireland, while Roger of Wendover records the gathering of 1,000 against Prince Louis of France. When the killers of Charles the Good were besieged in Bruges castle in 1127, one Benkin the mercenary, said to be a very good bowman, was amongst the archers. At Barbarossa's siege of Crema and the Milanese attack on Lodi in 1159–60, the fighting was savage and bowmen supported the assault machines. The manuscript of Peter of Eboli's work, dating from the late twelfth century, shows numerous archers and crossbowmen at work, and they reappear in the mid-thirteenth-century Maciejowski Bible. Henry II's Assize of Arms for his continental lands required the poorest to produce either a quilted coat, steel cap and sword, or bows and arrows. Baldwin I (1100–18) of Jerusalem had a corps of bowmen under the knight Reinoldus, his *magister sagittariorum,* while on the Third Crusade Richard used large numbers of them. Archers were obviously a commonplace of medieval armies, to such an extent that one authority has suggested that in the Norman period "the normal infantry weapon was the bow".[9] Who were these bowmen?

Because of the statements of Gerald of Wales, it has been supposed that the Welsh were specialist archers. However, there is no evidence that the Welsh were hired as archery specialists, as Armenians were in the Middle East. The reputation of Welsh foot was formidable and once frightened Stephen into withdrawal, while they may have helped to defeat his cavalry at the Battle of Lincoln in 1141. Those hired by Henry II were used for ravaging and close-quarter fighting, and it may well be that they used bows, but this did not arouse special comment. In the armies of Edward I, many areas besides Wales provided archers. In the Middle East composite armies made up of people who adopted specialized military roles were common: in the West in the twelfth century, mercenaries came from particular areas, notably Flanders, Aragon and the Basque country, while later Genoa produced crossbowmen, but national specialities never developed in the same way. It seems likely that bowmen and infantry generally were raised from amongst the followings of lords who obeyed the ruler's summons to war. The sergeants who we hear about may well have been the leaders of such people and some of them were bowmen, but this was a skill diffused through the population: it is notable that many sculptural representations show them as hunters. In 1181, Henry II's Assize of Arms for England made no mention of bows, but in 1252 Henry III required the poorest men to have bows, and this was repeated in the legislation of his son, culminating in the Statute of Winchester. This English Assize, under which all Englishmen were obliged to keep weapons, produced a highly effective method of recruitment. This underlay the large infantry forces, including large contingents of archers, raised by Edward I. In 1295, Edward ordered the sheriffs of Hampshire, Dorset and Wiltshire, under Commission of Array, to collect 3,000 archers and crossbowmen. We do not know how these were selected from the armed freemen of the shires, but presumably a mixture of coercion and incentive was offered. The quality of those raised was not high.[10]

This was a general problem of all armies and a consequence of their *ad hoc* nature. The strength of an army is training and coherence, based on a uniform discipline: this was the burden of Vegetius, emphasized in his summary by Rabanus Maurus. The ethos of the upper class was highly individualistic, with a stress on personal qualities: in some sense, they were all present in any army as volunteers. At Dorylaeum on 1 July 1097, the massed knights of the crusader vanguard resisted a Turkish encirclement, but even so some broke away to demonstrate their personal valour, and examples of this kind of behaviour could be multiplied. In very unusual circumstances, armies developed coherence and discipline. William of Normandy's army spent much of the summer of 1066 exercising together at Dives, and this may in part account for the control that its commander was able to exert at Hastings, notably in the matter of the feigned retreat. However, his control was limited and groups within his forces were left with a great deal of latitude: when their infantry got into difficulties, the knights themselves decided to close with the enemy, fighting with swords. The growing cohesion of the First Crusade was a vital factor in its success.[11] Overall, any group of soldiers, cavalry or infantry, lacked cohesion and were likely to be of uneven quality. This is why commanders used mercenaries to such a considerable extent.

Mercenaries sometimes appear as the outcasts of twelfth-century society along with Jews and lepers. The Lateran Council of 1179 excommunicated them and their employers, explicitly associating them with heretics of southern France, an association later echoed by Walter Map and Innocent III. The decree promised to all who fought against them some of the privileges of the crusader to Jerusalem, laying the juridical foundation for the later Crusades against heretics.[12] But they were a fact of life. The Council of Anse in 990 mentioned them at about the same time as Richer of Rheims, at the very beginning of our period. They were much used by the Conqueror and his sons, formed an important part of the armies of Henry II, Frederick Barbarossa, Richard the Lionheart, Philip Augustus, John and the Latin Kingdom of Jerusalem, and served the Hohenstaufen and the Italian cities in the thirteenth century.[13] Our sources sometimes convey the impression of mercenaries as a people set apart by their brutality and barbarism, killers of the innocent and robbers of churches. They were often called by the names of the places they came from – Aragonese or Basques but most commonly Brabanters, a word which became a synonym for mercenary. The general terms Cotereaux or Routiers were applied to them, recalling their purpose as destroyers and pillagers and their wandering, rootless way of life.[14]

Churchmen excoriated mercenaries because churches were so often attacked. The protests of ecclesiastics, coming from a particularly disturbed area of central France, prompted the Lateran Council decree of 1179. Once this situation was brought to its notice, the papacy was anxious to play to the full its role in establishing social order: it is no coincidence that the same council passed decrees against tournaments and reaffirmed the Truce of God.[15] No-one can doubt that mercenaries were savage and destructive, but there was nothing peculiar to mercenaries about such behaviour. The *Chanson des Lorrains*, written between 1185 and 1213, describes an army setting out through enemy territory:

> The march begins. Out in front are the scouts and incendiaries. After them come the foragers whose job it is to collect the spoils and carry them in the great baggage train. Soon all is tumult . . . The incendiaries set the villages on fire and the foragers visit and sack them. The terrified inhabitants are either burned or led away with their hands tied behind their backs to be held for ransom. Everywhere bells ring the alarm; a surge of fear sweeps over the countryside. Wherever you look you can see helmets glinting in the sun, pennons waving in the breeze, the whole plain covered with horsemen. Money, cattle, mules and sheep are all seized. The smoke billows, flames crackle. Peasants and shepherds scatter in all directions.[16]

Mercenaries were often employed as ravagers, and the very word *raptores* is used as a synonym for them, but they were not alone in this. William Marshal was a great ravager, and delight in this savage business is often to be found in the *Chansons de Geste*, which were written for the consumption of the upper class. But although such gentry were also responsible and, as the ultimate commanders of ravaging armies, were at least as guilty as those they commanded, it was difficult for the Church to bring pressure to bear, and its efforts against the great were limited, to say the least. The mercenary was the surrogate for the wrath of the Church, which accepted the violence of the upper class in an effort to control it. Of course, the Church could justify its unequal treatment of the mercenary and his master by reference to intention. The famous penance imposed on the victorious Normans after the Conquest of England fell more heavily on those who served for gain than on those who served by way of duty to a lord, and this was echoed in canon law.[17] But in the end this was an evasion, because all conditions of men fought for gain. Churchmen were prisoners of one of the basic conditions of medieval society. The Church was staffed and run very largely by the upper class; it was part of that immense structure of power which sustained a very small proportion of the population in dominion over the rest. In a sense, ravaging was part of the taxation paid by the clerical aristocracy for the support of their lay colleagues, so there was a limit to criticism; after all, what the mercenary did, his master was usually responsible for.

Our view of mercenaries as deeply hated alien presences in Christian society is derived from particular incidents which have been given enormous prominence. There was alarm in the 1180s when large numbers of mercenaries paid off from the wars of Angevins and Capetians and the conflicts in Languedoc gathered in the Limousin and Auvergne and began to dominate the area. The Church encouraged confraternities of local people – peasants and gentry alike – to resist. A famous body of peasants, the "Capuchins", was led by the visionary carpenter, Durand, and they played a notable role in destroying the mercenary hordes. For relatively humble men in the form of mercenary bands to take power was entirely unacceptable – it is worth remembering that it was the raising of men of low status under King John that so aroused anger in England against mercenaries. Ultimately, the lords, with the support of the Church, employed the remaining mercenaries to destroy the peasant militias who had acquired a taste for freedom in arms. A century before, when Archbishop Aimo of Bourges had formed a peasant militia to enforce the Peace of God, that too had been destroyed.[18] In the early thirteenth century, Innocent III launched the Albigensian Crusade, denouncing the mercenaries in the pay of the heretics as subverters of the social order. The "Brabanters" were feared and hated, as were all soldiers, but this was given a different dimension when they went into business on their own account. In an armed society, that was a threat to the social order: it is very notable that the English barons complained bitterly about the mercenary leaders of King John, but it was those of low birth who were most hated and most harshly treated.[19]

Underlying feudal society and its celebration of noble chivalry was the blunt fact that armies needed large numbers of lesser men to perform necessary tasks, ranging from feeding horses to operating specialized siege machinery. Yet the arming of the "poor" was to be feared, and permitted only under controlled circumstances. The peasants who joined the peace militias of the early eleventh century ultimately inspired deep hatred, while the contempt of clerical writers for the masses of the "Peasants' Crusade", allegedly led by a goose and a goat, is well known. In the mid-twelfth century the movement of Eudes l'Etoile was savagely put down. On the Second Crusade, Odo of Deuil was shocked "For lords to die that their servants might live" when the humble escaped in the partial rout of Louis VII's army on Mount Cadmus. The peasant militias who helped to defeat the mercenaries of the Auvergne and the Limousin in the 1180s were crushed when the taste of armed freedom went to their heads. On the Third Crusade, the author of the *Old French*

*Continuation of William of Tyre* expresses satisfaction about the defeat of his own foot, who had become so proud that they had tried to do in war what their betters, the knights, had refused to contemplate – to seize Saladin's camp. In the thirteenth century the "Childrens' Crusade" of 1211–12 and the "Pastouraux" of 1251 were put down by main force. In Flanders the affair of the "Pseudo-Baldwin" in 1224–5 precipitated social conflict. In these cities, the militias were reorganized along occupational lines, so that they could the more easily be controlled by the urban patricians, who were increasingly in league with the rural aristocracy.[20]

As long as they did not threaten the accepted social order, mercenaries were such an accepted part of contemporary armies that they were often not clearly distinguished from others: some writers who described the Archbishop of Cologne's attack on Saxony in 1179 noted the presence of mercenaries, while others simply remarked on the number of foot, or even the total number of armed men. At the same time, there are casual references to them in the armies of Frederick I.[21] It is interesting that medieval writers adopted generic descriptions such as *Routiers* and regional designations such as Brabanter, rather than use blunter terms which intimately connected such people with money. They did so because so many others, often of gentle origin, were paid for fighting. John of Salisbury refers bluntly to "mercenary knights", but this is very rare. The plainer terms for mercenary were highly pejorative: *mercenarius* is the word for the self-serving hireling of John 10: 11–14.[22] Marianus Scotus did use the term in a neutral sense to describe the armed followers of an archbishop but, far more typically, Aimo of Fleury applied it to the inconstant Franks of an earlier generation, hiring themselves out to one side or another in royal feuds, while Robert Curthose rebelled against his father who, he claimed, treated him as a mere *mercenarius* by refusing to give him land to rule.[23] *Stipendiarius* carried with it the overtones of clerical income and it could imply one who held a fief; its frequent use as an adjective to describe knights suggests honourable connotations, and indeed Peter Cantor tells a very flattering story about story of a *miles senex et stipendiarius*. However, William of Tyre clearly intended an insult when he so described Reynald of Châtillon, as did Ordericus when he referred to Geoffrey of Anjou claiming Normandy as a *stipendiarius* of his wife. Robert of Torigni equated *stipeniarios et mercennarios* with the sole followers of Henry II in the Toulouse campaign.[24] The almost equally blunt *solidarius* seems to have developed in the later twelfth century. In 1168, Baldwin V of Hainaut sent a force to aid Henry of Namur against Godfrey of Louvain: it consisted of 700 knights, all of Hainaut, except for two mercenaries who were carefully distinguished as *duobus suldariis*. However, the term enjoyed little popularity until the thirteenth century, when it gave us the English word "soldier" and the French *soudoyer*.[25] This relatively mild and evasive language is simply a reflection of the fact that, in war, cash relationships were common and extended to the ranks of those considered honourable. Moreover, some mercenaries were mounted, and therefore doubly difficult to distinguish from their social betters. They were accepted to the extent that they could rise high if they were lucky. Mercadier lived to be the famous leader of Richard I's mercenaries and a baron of the Limousin, but we first hear of him as a leader among the notorious mercenary bands who were attacked by the "Capuchins", who they were later used to destroy. His association with Richard and his apparent conformity to aristocratic norms seems to have made him acceptable in a way which others were not.[26]

It is clear that the *Routiers* were peasants, the kind of people who were dragged into war by their lords anyway. What distinguished them was that they were willing to fight. Their regional designations have aroused much attention; our sources offer various lists, but always the most prominent are the Brabanters and other Flemings, closely followed by those from Gascony and Aragon. Overpopulation and the search for a living is a possible explanation, for Flemings were prominent in the colonization of eastern Germany. But what the areas mentioned all have in common is that they are zones of political turbulence, where an armed way of life was probably more than usually necessary. It is worth noting that, in the estimation of the twelfth century, the Count of Flanders could raise more knights than the king of France; this was the fruit of living in a disputed and fragmented border area. For the same reason, there were plenty of armed infantry – because war bred soldiers. Gislebert of Mons probably inflates the numbers of footmen in the armies of the various principalities of the Low Countries, but we can see these as indications of substantial numbers.[27]

Some confusion has been caused in thinking about mercenaries by an undue emphasis on their military qualities and organization. Despite assertions to the contrary, all the signs are that mercenaries throughout this period were recruited as individuals and were somewhat fallible as soldiers. In August 1173, a substantial number of Henry II's Brabançons were defeated at St Jaques-de-Beuvron by local peasants; in 1176, a peasant militia destroyed another group at St Mégrin, while in the following year those licensed by Richard of Aquitaine to ravage the Limousin were defeated by a local force. A few years later, as we have noted, large mercenary forces were defeated by peasant militias in the affair of the "Capuchins". Mercenary infantry of this type seem to have had their greatest successes when used with other forces and under proper leadership. For mercenaries were only retained for as long as they were needed, and this must have meant that, like all other forces, they lacked the cohesiveness which only corporate identity over a long period can bring. Everything points to mercenaries being raised as individuals or in small groups. Even in thirteenth-century Italy, where we hear an enormous amount about mercenaries, both infantry and cavalry, they continued to be recruited only to supplement the native forces of the cities and so retained their essentially casual nature. In England and elsewhere, the thirteenth century saw the raising of large infantry armies, but their quality was generally poor. The "Grand Catalan Company" is famous for its conquest of Frankish Greece after 1303, but it was formed in the long war of the Vespers, which came to an end with the Peace of Caltabellotta in 1302 – continuous existence gave it cohesion. It is interesting that the social inferiority of the company seems to have been the main reason why it was so universally hated.[28] In the fourteenth century, with the development and frequent use of Commissions of Array in England, forces which were in some real sense regular began to appear.

The ruling elite of the West controlled war. The ethos of decentralized political structures required them to be militarized as the guarantee of their social position. This is the obvious reason why all ruling castes must control the apparatus of war, but what is peculiar about the medieval situation is that the elite were not merely an officer caste. They claimed a monopoly of war, and this was accepted and legitimized by the Church. The system of landholding, by which men held of the great lords and castellans and in return were rendered military service, only worked very imperfectly as a military structure, and throughout this period household and paid knights remained common, while even those who did serve by reason of a tenurial connection came to be paid for their service. The real function of the tenurial system was political – to control the countryside. Its essential military function was to generate a sufficient supply of armed men who shared the honourable concerns of their social superiors. Social mobility meant that the ranks of the cavalry were filled by a wide variety of people who, by one means or another, could afford the right kind of equipment and find employment. From about the mid-twelfth century, the aristocracy increasingly closed ranks, but continued to employ cavalry from the ranks of the gentry below, who were associated with them. Cash was a vital element in the relationship between lord and armed follower, but it was modified by gentility and a common way of life, although the importance of the need for reward on top of it should never be overlooked. The growth of wealth and the development of states, opened to the elite and their followers new paths to fame and fortune; and, increasingly, those who adopted the military life were a specialized group, pre-eminently of the relatively young. But this was a group through which many passed to later eminence in civil life and, in any case, all who were of the elite had to remain militarized to a degree, because that was a mark of status.

This self-conscious military elite needed the services of others. Infantry could provide simple mass, which was at times useful, although they tended to play a more passive role in combat, where the initiative usually lay with the cavalry. Bowmen and crossbowmen added power to any army, while even in this age certain kinds of technicians were needed, to build and operate machines or dig mines. Such ranges and numbers of people could not be provided generally from the entourages and estates of even great lords and so had to be hired when needed. However, the episodic nature of war, and the obvious contempt of the ruling elite for all others, meant that such forces were rarely provided with the continuity that they needed to become coherent forces. Even in the thirteenth century, when royal and princely states waged war on a considerable scale, it was only rarely that units were kept together long enough to realize their military potential. This was largely the result of financial circumstance, but social exclusivity played its part: the Grand Catalan Company was universally hated when it destroyed the flower of the chivalry of Frankish Greece.

This period witnessed an aristocratic domination of war, but the official doctrine of a monopoly was a myth. War demands excellence, and this is rarely confined to a convenient social group. By the end of the thirteenth century in England, we find that catch-all term, "man-at-arms" emerging. The wide diffusion of good weapons and the growth of royal arsenals was expanding the range of those admitted to the military elite, but social exclusivity continued to influence armies throughout the Middle Ages.

# Chapter Seven

## *The nature of the castle*

Across Europe stand castles and the ruins of castles, enduring monuments to the place of war in medieval society and to the importance of the proprietorial imperative. Castles were many things at different times, but at heart they were the homes of the great and centres of their estate administration and government. The European elite had estates which, because they were acquired by death, inheritance, marriage, gift and conquest, were scattered. Rents were largely in kind and transport poor, so it was simpler for kings and lords to store renders in kind where they were collected, and to travel around eating them. In an age of insecurity, such residences needed to be fortified. It was these domestic needs that determined the location, and to a very large extent the form, of the castle: it was the stately home of its age.[1]

Kings always recognized the threat to their authority implicit in private fortifications. Charles the Bald prohibited them by the Edict of Pîtres. But in 868 Egfrid was killed by Count Gerald, when his "strongly fortified house" was besieged and burned despite the efforts of Charles the Bald. Such things happened when Carolingian government was a going concern; as the Carolingian line failed in the late ninth century the conflicts of competing "princes" made the fortified house even more of a necessity for those with something to lose and offered possibilities for the ambitious with something to gain. The castle was necessary because of the limited competence of medieval government. It was effective because of the technical limitations of the means of war, which meant that men had to come face-to-face before they could fight. The defender of a modest earth and timber ringwork enjoyed a considerable advantage, especially if it was a wet day and his attacker had to struggle up a slippery surface burdened by the weight of his equipment. Moreover, a fortification was a secure base for attack and a garrison, especially if mounted, could threaten the country round about. In fact, it is a mistake to see the castle as simply a defensive structure, because it could menace enemies as well as protect friends.[2]

Castles were built where proprietors had land. Modern visitors often wonder why a castle is built in a particular location which does not dominate routes, passes or river-crossings: the answer is that it was built where the owner had land important enough to defend in this elaborate way, and it was sometimes influenced by claims that he was pursuing against others, or enmities that he had incurred. Kerak and Showbak were called the "Lions of the Desert", but they were built in fertile enclaves which maintained them. Fulk of Anjou built Langeais to counter the raids of Gelduin of Saumur, but his great stone tower at Loudun enabled him to extort tribute from his neighbours. When Albert of Namur wished to challenge Godfrey's hold on Bouillon in 1082, he first built a castle on his own adjacent property at Mirwart. In England, the castles of Tonbridge in Kent and Clare in Suffolk formed centres for clutches of estates that belonged to the family of Clare. In France, the relationship between landholding and castles is very clear in the case of the counts of Champagne. At the start of the eleventh century, their holdings along the upper Seine were guarded by Montereau, Provins and Troyes, while those along the length of the Marne were protected by no less than six castles: Meaux, Château Thierry, Châtillon, Mareuil, Châtillon-sur-Marne and Vitry. Outlying holdings were guarded by their vassals at St Florentin and Vaucouleurs. Along the Aube, between these two valleys, lay a series of castles held by independent lords, amongst them Brienne, which was annexed only by negotiation in 1121. Since a castle could be a threat, this kind of interpenetration could lead to savage warfare, and it was to the end of averting raiding that the earls of Leicester and Chester demilitarized a whole section of Midland England during Stephen's reign. In 1176, Baldwin V of Hainaut and his brother-in-law Philip, Count of Flanders, tried to prevent friction by promising not to build castles in the lands of their common march.[3]

Everywhere, the stability of power depended on controlling castles. To remain dominant, a king or lord needed castles to protect his demesnes, to keep the loyalty of followers and to overawe enemies. Sometimes the need was passing: most of the castles built after the Norman conquest of England were allowed to decay. But castles often survived the demise of the initial impulse to build them: Beaujeu, built by Audouin, Bishop of Limoges (992–1012) with the support of the Duke of Aquitaine, against Jourdan of Chananais's efforts to encroach on the abbey of St-Junien, is a case in point. To remain strong, princes had to control castle-building: the counts of Champagne ensured that no vassal held more than two castles and the counts of Anjou controlled their castellans tightly. William Tallifer, Count of

Angoulême, viewed Aimeri of Rancogne's construction of the castle of Bouteville in 1024 as a breach of his oath of vassalage. Robert of Normandy and his brother William forbade castle-building in their joint effort to pacify Normandy in 1091. When, at Easter 1185, the Count of Vermandois declared that he held Bray of Philip Augustus of France rather than Philip of Flanders, it ended the truce between the two. The building of Dolforwyn castle by Llewellyn, Prince of Wales, contributed to the tensions that led to the Anglo-Welsh war of 1277. Failure to exercise control had disastrous consequences. In the early eleventh century, five great castellan families at Berzé, Beaujeu, Bâgé, Brancion, Uxelles and la Bussière rivalled the power of the counts of Mâcon. The multiplicity of such lordships and the common situation of multiple homage enabled castellans to bargain for independence, but the balance of advantage could be fine: the lords of Parthenay, first attested in 1012, established their position in the Gâtine of Poitou by playing off the counts of Anjou and Poitiers, but an open challenge to the latter led to their destruction, while their more politick neighbours at Lusignan went on to a great future.[4]

Even the strongest medieval sovereigns found it impossible to prevent castles emerging. Despite the prestige of Ottonian power, tenth-century Germany was turbulent and large numbers of earthwork fortifications appeared, many in the control of magnates. Modern writers have seized upon Ordericus Vitalis's comments about the absence of castles in Anglo-Saxon England as the reason for the speedy conquest of that land by William the Bastard. However, there were fortifications in Anglo-Saxon England, as the excavations at Goltho in Lincolnshire and Eynsford in Kent, amongst others, indicate. These earth enclosures around halls probably did not strike Ordericus, writing in the mid-twelfth century, as much resembling the castles of his age, but they were not so very different from the simple earth and ditch enclosures that the Normans built in the immediate aftermath of the Conquest and used long after, as the twelfth-century example at Deddington shows. Moreover, there is evidence that many *burhs* were fortified centres of lordships that functioned in much the same way as the later castles, and some may have been taken over unchanged in Norman times. All of this makes comprehensible Harold's promise in 1064 to garrison castles in England for William, amongst them perhaps the royal fort at Dover.[5]

Great crises such as succession conflicts weakened medieval authorities. The dukes of Normandy were powerful princes of France, but castles multiplied in the troubled minority of William the Bastard. In Anjou, the outbreak of a long succession struggle after 1060 enabled the count's castle-holders to annex public powers and found lordships; similar circumstances produced similar consequences in contemporary Champagne. The English succession struggle under Stephen led to the multiplication of castles, while that in Norman Italy after 1196 produced a rash of them, which was curbed only with difficulty by Frederick II. In France, the minority of St Louis produced large-scale warfare. In Germany, the Investiture Contest and subsequent dynastic conflicts fostered castle-building which is associated with the rise of great families such as the Hohenstaufen.[6]

In Italy, the tenth and eleventh centuries were the age of *Incastellamento*, a word that encompasses the planting of new villages, the fortification of new and old ones and their endowment with jurisdiction. However, it is significant that a word with such heavy military overtones is used, for in Italy the destruction of the native monarchy and the failure of the German monarchs to stabilize their control opened the way to political fragmentation and the multiplication of fortifications, especially in the later eleventh century when the Investiture Contest rented the land. These took various forms: villages might be surrounded by walls or dominated by the fortified *curtis* of a noble family. In Lombardy, the power of the Empire had prevented the rise of princely families, so the nobility were drawn into the politics of the fortified cities. The house of Tuscany were an exception but, significantly, their lordship, based on rural castles, lay on the fringe of the urbanized area of the Po plain. Fragmentation was even more marked in South Italy, where the Byzantine power jostled uneasily with the Lombard states such as Benevento and Capua, independent merchant-republics such as Gaeta and the influence of the papacy. Central Italy and the Roman principality after the mid-tenth century underwent the same process, with the creation of fortified hilltop villages, often embodying a *rocca castri*.[7]

History offered castle-builders many models, for fortifications are almost as old as man. Prehistoric fortifications, great "ring-works", studded the countryside. The inheritance of Rome to the medieval world was in stone and some of it survives to this day: the Porta Negra at Triers, the walls of Le Mans and Rome, the superb fortifications of Constantinople. Frontier defences such as Hadrian's Wall, permanent legionary camps such as Caerleon and way-forts provided further models of fortification for later ages. However, most Roman fortifications were ruinous, and stone was difficult and expensive to work, so earth and timber fortifications predominated. The Carolingians used them to stabilize their conquest of Saxony. The Vikings constructed them as bases for raiding. The Edict of Pîtres began the construction of earthwork forts along rivers to deny free movement to Danish raiders, and this may have influenced Alfred's decision to build a network of *burhs*, earth and wood fortifications, of which Cricklade and Wallingford are fine examples, which protected Wessex and its population. In the tenth century, royal burhs were a vital component in the re-conquest of England from the Danes and in the defence of Saxony against Hungarian attack.[8] But royal initiatives of this kind were becoming increasingly rare, as power slipped into the hands of lesser men.

Contemporaries used a vast variety of words to describe fortifications, so that it is often difficult to understand what kind of structure is referred to. In the tenth century most were of earth and wood, and they continued to be useful throughout the period: in the plain of the Po in the thirteenth century, earth and timber camps were a standard tactic of war. Earthwork remains are difficult to differentiate from the myriad mounds that dot the European countryside: one part of Normandy, $12 \times 20\,\mathrm{km}$, has yielded four stone castles and 28 earth mounds, not all of ascertainable date. But there was no simple transition from timber to stone. Forest was scarce in Spain and parts of Italy, where stone predominated.[9] In the Loire valley the counts of Anjou seem to have built in stone from a very early date, perhaps because of the availability of lime and stone. Langeais, built by Fulk Nerra in 993–4, is believed to be the earliest surviving stone tower, closely followed by Montbazon by 1006. Excavations at Doué-la-Fontaine reveal a process of adaptation: a splendid Carolingian stone hall was given a second storey in the mid-tenth century and strengthened in the eleventh with an earth motte heaped around the ground floor. At s'Gravensteen, the castle of the counts of Flanders at Ghent, the eleventh-century stone keep was built and later had earth piled around it to form a motte: there are indications that the timber buildings on the motte were contemporary with the stone structure. This all points to the difficulty of seeking simple models for the origins of castles and to the problems of definition. English and German fortifications may have been simpler than the stone castles of the counts of Anjou, but Goltho has many parallels in France.[10] The fact is that by about the eleventh century, fortifications were extremely variegated.

Our conception of a castle is dominated by existing ruins. But the reality was of much humbler structures which answered the need of proprietors for protection. Across this period almost any kind of fortification could, if well defended, become a major obstacle. In 1003, Robert II of France and his ally Richard II of Normandy were unable to capture the monastery of St Germain d'Auxerre, held against them by Landri of Nevers. In July 1128 William Clito, claimant to the county of Flanders, was repelled before a fortified house at Oostkamp, while in the thirteenth century Hen Domen was a wooden structure although in an exposed position on the Welsh March. In the early twelfth century, Ordericus distinguished between Robert of Bellême's "strong houses" and his castles. However, it would be impossible to define the point at which the one became the other. The Flemish example noted here suggests that all had military potential, and Stokesay and Acton Burnell in thirteenth-century England, or Tortoir and Les Bourines in France, are essentially similar. As late as the English Civil War, Basing House, a late medieval castle developed into a residence in Tudor times, withstood a long hard siege against a Parliamentary army in 1645.[11] What was actually built reflected the severity of conditions, the means of individual landowners and the pressures faced.

Of all these early castles, one type has been much discussed – the motte-and-bailey castle which modern English historians have been in danger of making into a norm, partly at least because it did not exist in England before 1066 and so has seemed to be startling evidence of the novelties supposedly imposed by the Norman Conquest. The motte is an artificial mound sur-rounded by a ditch, upon and around which defences were sited. Most commonly, a tower was set on it and a defended open area with buildings in it, the bailey, built to one side. Where the idea for this structure came from is uncertain, but the tradition of earthwork building is ancient. In the Rhineland, ring-works were sometimes raised because of the high water table. The *terpen* of the Netherlands were also built to raise houses above water level. The advantages of towers are obvious, and stabilizing them with heaped earth is a fairly natural process: out of this may have been born the motte-and-bailey. The great value of the motte-and-bailey was that it was a "go-anywhere" fortification. Lords located castles on their lands, but they did not always have some convenient eminence as a site. A motte could be raised in flat lands and it was effective. Moreover, it could be built with a minimum of expertise – the essential input was peasant labour, and proprietors disposed of that.

This structure exemplifies the social structure which created it. The bailey could serve as a protective enclosure for the people, livestock and goods of the area in time of war: this was the public function of the castle derived from the past. But in the end the really strong protection was afforded to the owner, the lord and his family and close dependants in the tower, which could usually be cut off from the rest. This was a compact fortification, economic of man-power for its defence, and capable of being built and supported by local ·resources. There are innumerable variations on this basic pattern: at Hedingham the huge motte was natural but improved by man, and the artificial plateau thus achieved was surrounded by a curtain wall around a central keep, while at Huntingdon there was only ever a modest mound with wooden fortifications and a ditch. This type of castle came to be built in virtually all the countries of the medieval West, except Spain, by the early twelfth century.[12] However, it was in no sense a norm, because proprietors wanted different things, and sites and the availability of materials varied.

In the Holy Land, plentiful supplies of worked stone from classical sites led to the rapid building of stone enclosures.

Even the simplest castle cost a great deal, and sheer expense limited the number of lords who could build them. In England only about 35 per cent of the 200 baronies had what we now recognize as castles as their heads in the twelfth century, although others probably possessed fortified houses, of which little trace is left. A large motte such as that at Clare probably took about 8,000 man-days, while even a modest one such as Huntingdon took 3,000. When castles had to be built quickly after the Norman Conquest, it was simple ring-works that went up, not time-consuming mottes, which came later. More-over, once built, a castle had to be manned and maintained, and this again tied it to the resources of its immediate locality; castleguard was a widespread obligation in medieval society. In 1199, a truce was agreed between Richard and Philip, under which the latter held a group of Norman castles while Richard held the lands. William Marshal regarded this as a triumph, for it imposed an enormous burden on the French, especially as the English harassed the garrisons. At Richmond in northern England, 186 knights owed castleguard to the lord and discharged this in a rota of six groups, each serving for two months. Here there was a specific castlery, an area dependent on Richmond castle, and such institutions were also found on the Welsh March; but in the main parts of England, arrangements such as the "Lowy" of Tonbridge had short histories as England gained in stability. Castleries are much more common in Europe in the eleventh and twelfth centuries. Such costs explain why only the greatest princes could own more than one or two castles.[13]

Even the greatest tried to build as few castles as possible, commensurate with their military needs and social status, and to economize as far as possible by simple constructions. Fulk Nerra of Anjou was a great builder of stone castles, but he certainly shared the costs of Château Gontier with the family to whom it was entrusted, and this may well have been his common practice. Hence most castles were, for long into the twelfth century, relatively simple structures, mainly of wood. They provided highly defensible homes for peripatetic noble households. Above all, they overawed the peasant who produced wealth, and made exploitation easier: "Castle walls helped to protect the ruling elements of medieval society against unrest at home as much as from threats from outside".[14]

Cost and landownership patterns determined much about the structure and nature of castles. Castles were not merely bunkers; they had to function as homes, and thus considerations of comfort and status loomed large. The fine ashlar finish of Hedingham, with its splendidly vaulted and arched Great Hall, was surely intended by the de Vere earls of Oxford in the 1140s as an assertion of their status and glory rather than as a mere functional military centre. Rochester is a mighty keep, but its upper stories are pierced with windows and it enjoyed elaborate kitchens. Now that they are ruins, or at best bare shells, it is easy to forget that the lofty halls and tower-rooms of Castle Rising or Pembroke, Angers, Münzenberg or Saone represented luxury in their age. Splendour and ostentation were part of the armoury of the owner. A lofty hall or great windows might actually weaken a castle as a military instrument, but they also showed the status and importance of the builder, making overt threat less necessary.

Castles were centres of estate management and, therefore, local government where lords or their deputies held court. In England, the Conqueror threw them up in great haste to control main centres of population, and accepted the need of his followers to do likewise in their lordships. In Flanders, Baldwin V (1035–67) established castles through which comital government was exercised, but this did not extend to the south and east of the county, where comital demesne was rare. Norman Sicily under Frederick II was divided into seven zones which, together, supported some 240 royal fortifications: a powerful expression in stone of the emperor's ideas of central government. As a result, castles had to have buildings to house all of the consequent comings and goings. Recent studies of the castles of the Holy Land emphasize their many functions, especially as centres of seigniorial administration. The presence of a sizeable community of consumers at a castle tended to attract merchants and, as a result, the castle-town "is almost the classic form of the medieval town in western and central Europe". The Flemish counts deliberately fostered commercial development around their castles. In the east Saône is an example of a castle-town that housed the Frankish population in this mountain lordship of the principality of Antioch.[15]

Much can be made of the wider functions of the castle, but at heart it had a military purpose – to defend the life and goods of its owner and to provide his troops with a base. The spread of castles intensified the basic character of war. The fact that a defender could take refuge in a castle decreased the attractions of battle and increased the need to ravage as an act of war. But castles were much more than merely defensive places of refuge. A garrison of mounted knights could harass enemies. In England, the castles of the Welsh Marches were a base for the conquest of Wales. William FitzOsbern, Earl of Hereford, built one of the earliest stone castles at Chepstow, at the southern reach of a line of fortifications which extended north to Wigmore. The outpost of Montgomery was established from the castles of Shrewsbury, Caus and Oswestry. In about 1106, Henry de Newburgh invaded Gower and founded Swansea castle and a network of others: Oystermouth, Oxwich, Penrice, Scurlage and Barham. Henry II built Orford as a check to Framlingham, which was held by the suspect Bigod family. Much has been made of Orford's luxurious aspects, but these simply served to reinforce the message of royal supremacy. Richard I built Château Gaillard as a base for the re-conquest of the Vexin, while Crac des Chevaliers, although it served as a bastion for the defence of the county of Tripoli, was also a means of extorting tribute from the emirs of Homs and Hama.[16]

In France, the number of castles seems to have been on the increase in the late eleventh and early twelfth centuries, although many had short active lives. A similar phenomenon can be observed in the Empire, where large numbers of castles were built between 1150 and 1300. This appears to be paradoxical, for this was a period during which the costs of building were rising, as stone replaced timber. However, we should remember that many were wooden and had short lives. Not all of this expenditure was simply military. Fashion and status were powerful influences. By the thirteenth century there was a cult of chivalry that may well have influenced aristocrats to build in a military style rather than with a military purpose. Frederick II's Castel del Monte was a sumptuously decorated hunting-lodge and palace, never intended for military purposes. Such structures became much more common in the later Middle Ages. In England, licences to crenellate were evidently in part a fashion and statement of status, but even those issued to clerics could have useful police and military functions.[17] But although fashion and comfort had their influence, most structures were built to be defended.

All castle-building was expensive, but stone was very costly, and in England this was an advantage to the king. Dover cost £7,000 to build between 1180 and 1190, but it represented an important investment for Henry II, who ruled a cross-channel empire. His tower-keep and curtain at Orford cost £1,400, spread over eight years, and a figure of about £1,000 seems to have been the minimum to build an up-to-date fortification, although some kind of stone castle could have been built for about £350. This was substantial expenditure, out of the range of most of his barons. As most of the castles of the Conquest ran down, the proportion held by the king increased. Between 1154 and 1214, the number of baronial castles in England fell from 225 to 179, while the number of royal castles rose from 49 to 93. This reflects the financial facts of life: in roughly the same period the average income of barons was £200 per annum and only seven seem to have had more than £400, while at least 20 had yearly incomes of less than £20. By contrast, normal royal income was never less than £10,000. Moreover, because of the relative peacefulness of England there was only a limited incentive to build them: a disproportionate number of English castles lay in the Marches of Wales and the North. The determination of the Angevin rulers to control castle-building there was a positive disincentive.[18]

But circumstances changed. The increasing wealth of Europe was not evenly distributed: the rich were getting richer. In England, honours became concentrated in the hands of a small number of greater barons, whose incomes were, therefore, very high. In the thirteenth century, Richard of Cornwall had £4,000 a year and Earl Ferrers £1,500–1,700, while it is no coincidence that the greatest castle of the age in the British Isles, Caerphilly, was built by Gilbert de Clare, whose annual income was about £3,700. The eminence of half a dozen noble houses in this period in England is very marked: by contrast, a knight might have only £30 per year and a squire less. At the same time, the counts of Champagne were able to extend their control by purchase and the bishops of western Germany pursued an active *Burgenpolitik,* purchasing castles from lesser nobles in difficulty. It is very notable that the kings of France were obliged to take a more permissive view of castle-holding and building than their Angevin counterparts: this was a simple recognition of the reality of their situation in a landscape dominated by castles. In Lombardy, the cities needed to control the area around, the *contado,* which provided food for their citizens. The countryside had been subject to the rise of private lordship and the fragmentation that accompanied it, but the most important castles were ruthlessly subjected to the collective lordship of the commune.[19] The nobility drawn into the cities interacted to form a new kind of political community, but the building of urban castles – of which there were 150 in Florence alone – reminds us of the strength of the proprietorial instinct and the value of castles to it. In central Italy, the papacy tried to impose its control over a multitude of communes and lordships, almost all fortified, by a mixture of force, diplomacy and bribery. Gregory IX in particular was responsible for the purchase or re-purchase of many castles.[20]

The new wealth of Europe favoured the dominant powers amongst the medieval elite – above all, kings – but no ruler could build equally strongly everywhere, and just as great lords had to make choices about which estates they defended, so did kings; but because in the thirteenth century their war was on a great scale, their choices took on a strategic character. In England, there is a contrast between the Marches of Wales and Scotland. By about 1100, Wales was surrounded by a ring of castles, some of the most formidable kind; this took much longer to develop in the north.[21] The reason for this seems to be in a sense economic. The Normans quickly perceived Wales as a suitable forum for their ambitions, so investment in castles was worthwhile and it was possible because the border zone was relatively rich. The Conqueror found in the north a huge area of uncertain loyalty, merging into clearly alien lands whose relative poverty made them unattractive. As a result, the royal and baronial presence in the north was for long confined to a few strongpoints which formed foci for the piecemeal development of the northern march.

The kingdoms of twelfth- and thirteenth-century Europe were, in principle, no different from other lordships. They were untidy agglomerations of rights and claims which interpenetrated and were interpenetrated by those of others. This is why the greatest concentration of castles in the Anglo-Norman world was where Normandy marched with the French kingdom in the Vexin. The Normans claimed that this bitterly contested area had been granted to Robert of Normandy in 1032 by Henry I, in return for his aid against his mother Constance's rebellion. The Vexin straddled the zones of influence, the *mouvances*, of two great feudal lords, the Duke of Normandy and the French king. Vassals of one held land of the other, and through it ran the trade route of the Seine valley. Many of the castles were baronial in origin, planted to safeguard particular interests, in a pattern that did not arise from the needs of overall defence. The Norman dukes had generally relied on their vassals for defence of the March, but the Conquest of England provided them with enormous resources and Henry I began systematic fortification, building new castles, notably at Châteauneuf on the Epte, Nonancourt and Verneuil on the Avre, and Vaudreuil on the Eure, as well as strengthening many others such as Gisors. Henry II developed these fortifications and established the rule that he could take over seigneural castles when public need pressed. He created a network of frontier castles supported by the hinterland of Normandy and paid for by the renders of the duchy and of England.

The bitter warfare which erupted at the end of the reign of Henry II and continued through those of his sons revolved around the possession of castles. The fortunes of war drove the frontier back and forth. In 1196 Richard I began Château Gaillard, which was completed by September 1198 at the astonishing cost of £11,500. The treaty of 1195 between Richard and Philip of France is really a catalogue of who holds what castle of whom. The dense network of castles in Normandy was unusual, but on the Loire Henry II developed fortresses to safeguard communications between Normandy and Aquitaine. The city of Tours was the key to the lower Loire, and the castles of Chinon, Loudun and Mirebeau were vitally important. Richard later built Saint-Rémy de la Haye.[22]

From the mid-twelfth century, castles were normally built of stone. Timber castles continued: Hen Domen near Montgomery existed by 1086 and became the stronghold of the de Boulers until they died out in 1207; in about 1215 it was abandoned in the tide of Welsh re-conquest, but it was soon reoccupied, but this time as a purely military outpost, down to the 1270s. Sometimes, as at Carisbrook, the form of the stone castle followed that of the wooden original, but commonly they were redesigned. There was a marked tendency for all structures to become more massive. In northern France and England, the primary element of a castle was often a single strong tower, but this was developed into massive structures such as those at Rochester, Loches, Norwich, Castle Rising or the Tower of London. Such great square or rectangular structures were often ringed by a curtain wall with a gate-tower, as at Hedingham or Goodrich. In these last two cases, we see the development of the notion of a multiple defence. The attacker must face a ditch, followed by a steep rise, then the outer curtain wall, strongly reinforced by the gate and projecting towers, then finally the *donjon* itself. Middleham is much the same. The shape of towers was experimented with: Henry II's Orford (1165–7) was circular with three great buttresses, and closely resembles Chilham (1170–4) and Conisborough with six (*c.* 1180), but John used an octagonal form at Tickhill and Odiham. However, Dover was built as a massive rectangular keep in the 1180s.[23]

Round keeps and towers were more common in France than in England: the earliest examples in both kingdoms are from the mid-twelfth century at Château-sur-Epte and New Buckenham. In the British Isles, round towers are common only in Wales and its Marches; Pembroke, rebuilt by William Marshal in *c.* 1200 being a notable example. However, most castle-building in the British Isles in the thirteenth century was in Wales. Philip Augustus's castles used round towers, notably at Gisors and Verneuil. The greatest example in France was at Coucy, where in about 1230 Enguerrand III built an irregular trapezium-shaped castle on a spur with four round towers at each corner, and in the middle of the approach side an enormous circular keep. R. A. Brown long ago attacked the idea that the circular tower was an innovation marking progress from relatively crude angular designs that ultimately owed their origins to wooden designs, but what were its origins and purpose?[24]

Ths most likely source of inspiration for round towers was Roman military architecture, of which round or D-shaped towers were certainly a feature, as witness the Porta Negra at Trier, the city walls of Rome and the bases of the towers at Le Mans. The Umayyads adopted them as at Anjar or Qasr al-Heir and their palaces in Jordan, while Armenian fortifications developed the rounded form very highly, as at Ilan. The crusaders took eastwards their preference for square keeps and towers: the very small round towers that flank the great square keep at Saône are rare exceptions. In general, the crusaders in the twelfth century built castles of fairly modest size: at al-Bara a simple stone keep about 10 m square and 12 m high was set on a low motte in a modest walled enclosure with small square towers at the corners, while at al-Burj al-Ahmar (the Red Tower) a solidly built tower 19.7 × 15.5 m, roughly 13 m high, was placed in an enclosure 60 m square, which probably had a fortified gateway and towers. The massive structure at Jebail (crusader Gibelet) represents a development of this basic plan; its strength indicated by the nineteenth-century British cannon-balls embedded in the west wall of the keep. The Islamic powers, who relied less on castles, tended to imitate the crusaders in the erection of large square constructions, although Saladin and his son built round towers on the citadel of Cairo. However, the massive oblong towers of Bosra and Damascus are much more typical of the later twelfth and early thirteenth centuries. The square towers of Muslim Subeibe, built in 1228–30, were supplemented only later, in 1260, with round ones.[25]

The round tower is reckoned to have had some advantages. It offered an excellent all-round view to the defenders, an important factor when it is remembered that a blind spot led to the fall of Château Gaillard in 1204. It is said that it may have been less easy to undermine: in 1215, the southeast corner of mighty Rochester was brought down by King John's miners and replaced, interestingly, with a cylindrical corner. The curving face presented a less solid target to heavy missiles. All of these were advantages, but perhaps most decisive of all was that the round tower could be made strong with smaller, more easily handled masonry, and this perhaps accounts for its lasting popularity. Moreover, it became popular at a time when many devices could be used to strengthen a castle in an integrated structure. However, there was a lot of experimentation. The main keep at Château Gaillard was beaked rather than round, while Frederick II's fortress at Castello del Lago, dating from the mid-twelfth century, has both square and round towers. Its greatest feature is a triangular tower set on a large gatehouse, closely resembling the contemporary one at Beaucaire.[26]

New features served to strengthen castles and particularly to increase their fire-power. Arrow-loops gave defenders better protection with a good arc of fire and could be sited to give overlapping fields of fire. Of course, counter-fire could clear the fighting-top of a wall or tower and even make life dangerous for marksmen behind arrow-loops, as witness the arrowheads lodged in the mortar cracks around them at Marqab. Projecting wooden hoardings could be used to drop missiles on attackers, and from the time of Château Gaillard stone machicolations were even more effective, particularly when the bases of walls and towers were splayed, enabling the defenders to drop rocks which ricocheted or smashed with a shrapnel effect. But there was no simple line of development and castles showed a bewildering variety of plans, mostly devised to suit the ground they were built on. This is no more than one would expect – after all, they represented the wishes and needs of diverse proprietors who were normally restrained only by cost and the limitations imposed by the site. In Lombardy, a castle with a keep was sufficiently rare to be a matter of remark for a writer of the early thirteenth century, and it may be significant that the word for it, *domigniono*, is of French derivation. The counts of Flanders rebuilt s'Gravensteen at Ghent very splendidly in 1180, but its plan is idiosyncratic and owes much to what was already there. Château Gaillard is carefully designed as a set of obstacles. The great beaked keep set in an inner bailey is in turn cut off from a well defended middle bailey by a moat. Set across the natural line of approach along the spur to these massive structures was a triangular outer bailey, isolated from the main centres of resistance by a deep moat. But this massive castle has no arrow-slits; here the defenders used stone machicolations set around the tops of the rounded towers and the keep.

In Germany, many castles consisted of a curtain wall with a strong gatehouse and towers, within which was set a *Palas*, a great hall and administrative centre somewhat in the style of royal palaces, together with a large tower or towers which might be square or round, called *Bergfriede*. Staufen, from which the royal family took their name, is a good example. In southern France, castles were somewhat less common than in the north, but often – as in the use of Puylaurens – were of rudimentary structure, deriving their strength from the crags on which they were set. Even in England, where castle-building was tightly controlled, there was no pattern. In early-thirteenth-century France, Philip II and his magnates created a considerable diversity of forms united by nothing except simplicity of plan and the round towers.[27] What is evident everywhere by the early thirteenth century is the tendency of fortifications to become ever more elaborate and massive.

The decisive development was integrated defence, in which advanced features were allied to a conscious overall design. That this was first made manifest in the Latin Kingdom of Jerusalem is hardly surprising, because the Franks of the East faced enemies on all sides. We have attached too much importance to castles in the military history of the Frankish states. Large numbers have survived because they were made of stone – but then Western aristocrats always built lots of castles. Some of those in the Holy Land are magnificent. For the twelfth century, Saône and Kerak, at the northern and southern ends of the crusader range respectively, and for the thirteenth Crac and Marqab, have attracted enormous attention, although they are quite atypical, for most of the castles were relatively humble – the Red Tower in the plain of Sharon is a good example – seigneural centres rather than military centres.[28]

The greatest surviving twelfth-century crusader castle is Saône (Qalaat Saladin) in the Jebel Ansariye. It guards a castle-town on the western edge of the ridge and its own towers are all distinguished by magnificent apartments. It is the model of a large-scale seigneury, whose business would have been the exploitation of the considerable wealth of this well watered mountain chain. It is one of a line of castles stretching north–south in the mountains (now Jebal Ansariyah) of the Antiochene principality of which the remainder are Bakas (Shugur Qadim) and Bourzey (Qalaat Burzey) to the north and Balatanos (Qalaat al-Mehelbeh), Bikisrail (Qalaat Ben Qahtan), Malaicas (Qalaat Maniqa) and Margat (Qalaat Marqab) to the south, but it seems unlikely that it was ever part of a chain of defence. All but Bikisrail (Qalaat Ben Qahtan) are on the site of earlier Byzantine or Arab fortifications, and it seems likely that they were simply seized as the Principality of Antioch established itself, as convenient strongpoints. They were able to develop because they tapped the considerable wealth of the Jebel Ansariye.[29]

It was once thought that castles formed a perimeter of defence for the crusader states, and especially the Kingdom of Jerusalem. Smail pointed out that castles could not stop an enemy, and showed that they reflected the proprietary pattern of the kingdom and the way in which it developed piecemeal, rather than anything else. Some castles were established for strategic reasons. Baldwin II built Shawbak to dominate the "pilgrims' road" to Mecca and Medina. In 1137, Fulk I began a strategy of building castles around Ascalon, which eventually included Ibelin, Blanchegarde, Beit Jibrin and Gaza, although he had to ask the Hospitallers to take over Beit Jibrin. Ascalon was isolated, but did not fall until 1153. Baldwin IV built Jacob's Ford to defend the frontier with Damascus in 1178 and asked the Templars to hold it. This frontier with Damascus was barely fortified. The key point was Banyas, which the crusaders held from 1129 to 1132 and then again from 1140 to 1164, but no effort was made to build a substitute after its fall, until Jacob's Ford in 1178, although this was a frequently used line of invasion.[30]

The crusaders did not lack a sense of strategy, but in their world, as in the West, the erection of a castle usually depended on giving somebody a vested interest in its construction. Political conditions never favoured that on the Damascus frontier, partly at least because royal policy was opposed to the creation of large lordships in this area. The condominium with Damascus endured until Nur-ed-Din became a major threat, and after that the kingdom was distracted by the Ascalon campaign and then the attack on Egypt, so that when Banyas fell the kingdom was faced by a dangerous open frontier. Elsewhere in the kingdom the crusaders built castles in virtually all of the strategic points, many of them brilliantly sited. The effect of the massive castle-building of the twelfth century was to create a network of fortifications, many of which were not particularly strong. They served the useful function of housing garrisons and providing refuge against raiding. Their worth was, however, limited. Most of the lordships of the Crusader Kingdom of Jerusalem were suffering severe impoverishment well before 1187, probably because of the increase in raiding and the commensurate increase in defence costs. The real defence of the kingdom was the Frankish field-army, which could deter sieges of the real underpinnings of the kingdom, the cities: it was a point well made in the debate before Hattin.[31]

The crusaders were very skilful at the exploitation of topography, and a number of their most famous castles are situated on ridges, with very limited approaches for an attacker. At Saône the obvious approach from the northeast is barred by a channel 27 m deep, cut through the natural rock, which served as the quarry for the stone of the castle, and dominated by the keep; elsewhere, curtain walls cling to the edges of the surrounding canyons. Bourzey crowns a massive crag overlooking the Orontes valley, where the crusaders strengthened an old Byzantine citadel by building an *enceinte* which clings to the very edges of the precipice around it.

Such strength is impressive, but topography does not always favour the castle-builder. At Belvoir, the Hospitallers took over an existing castle in a dominating position on the western edge of the Jordan valley, "set amidst the stars like an eagle's nest and abode of the moon". But the strength of its site is more apparent than real, for it actually stands on a flat plateau and is easily accessible on three sides. What the Hospitallers found there is uncertain, but recent excavation has revealed a structure that is the product of a single plan. The outer wall, 110 × 100 m, is massively built, with large square towers projecting from the corners and from the centres of each wall: the walls and towers have heavy splayed bases which project into and merge with the covering masonry of the 10 m deep and 20 m wide moat which surrounds the castle on three sides. Along the inner sides of the walls are strong stone vaults, which gave cover to the garrison. There is no keep: set 5 m within is a smaller twin of the outer castle, 50 × 50 m, from whose walls and towers supporting fire could be directed over the outer *enceinte*. Only on the cliffside overlooking the Jordan valley to the east is this impressive symmetry broken, for there stands a large tower enclosed within an outer wall down the slope. The masonry is massive, the rusticated blocks having coarse sharp-edged projecting fronts reminiscent of Hohenstaufen work called *Buckelquädar*. The gatehouse on the south side has an oblique approach that is well defended and features a tunnel entry. But all entrances are oblique, there are hidden sally ports and the arrow-slits give interlocking and mutually supporting arcs of fire. After Hattin, Belvoir was besieged for 18 months, and in the end the garrison was allowed to surrender, after which Saladin did some rebuilding.[32]

Belvoir is a concentric castle, conceived as a whole and built in a single campaign. It had a clear strategic purpose, to guard the fords of the Jordan at Jisr al-Majam'a and Sheik Hussein, although the Hospital used its acquisition as an opportunity to acquire and develop some 200 km² in the general area. In

1178, the King of Jerusalem built a rather similar fortress to command Jacob's Ford, a dangerous point of entry north of the Sea of Galilee over the Jordan. The structure is not unlike Belvoir, although in form it is a long, thin oblong enclosure, 130 × 35 m, crowning a hog's-back ridge that extends north–south above the Jordan. This area of the ridge was cut off from the rest by deep ditches and sculpted to form mutually supporting inner and outer tiers of defence, with massive rusticated blocks very like those used at Belvoir. It was probably intended that there should be barbicans north and south outside the ditch. The castle was entrusted to the Templars, but it was not complete and quickly fell to Saladin in August 1179. The square plan and massive splaying evident in these two castles reminds one of Caeserea, fortified by St Louis in the early 1250s. Templar Athlit has the same reliance on multiple lines of defence in an essentially squared structure, while the castle of the Ibelins at Beirut may have been similar.[33]

The greatest structures of the crusaders in the Holy Land – Belvoir, Crac, Marqab, Athlit and, by intention at least, Jacob's Ford – were all built by, or assumed their final form under, the Military Orders. These are marked by no obvious pattern; they represent skilful and carefully considered adaptations to well chosen sites. The central principle is of multiple and mutually supporting lines of defence, with carefully considered lines of fire from well protected points. They are marked by other common characteristics, most notably the enormous *casemes* for storage, which served as covered ways for the garrison. The huge volume of interior space with multiple uses is remarkable. The concentric castles of the crusader East, of which Belvoir is the earliest example, represent the application of careful thought to the problems of military architecture, but they were enormously costly and were not matched in the West until the thirteenth century.

Truly concentric castles, designed from scratch or radically rebuilt, were always rare and very much the preserve of truly mighty powers such as the Orders in the Holy Land and Edward I in North Wales. Rich nobles could still compete, as shown by Coucy and even more by Caerphilly, where Gilbert de Clare not only created a concentric castle which was the equal of those built later by Edward in the north, but set it amidst water defences that could deter miners and keep missile-throwers at a harmless distance. In the Holy Land, Ibelin Beirut was probably in much the same class. But even the greatest built only where there was need: the Orders to save the land, and Edward to secure a conquest which he seems to have long had in mind – the overwhelming power of his structures was intended to protect English colonists and act as a symbol of new authority. Not all of his castles are as ambitious as Beaumaris: Flint has a simple plan which, with its detached round keep, resembles Nesles-en-Tardenois. Strengthening of existing castles in a broadly concentric manner was more common – Edward I created the outer defences of the Tower of London while, at a more humble level, Goodrich was reinforced in the same general sense, as was Münzenberg, and Arques was given an outer wall.[34]

Frederick II was a great castle-builder, but his designs are eclectic. Lucera is skilfully adapted to its site and studded with pentagonal towers, but its main feature is a citadel which rather resembles *Mamluk* work: two round towers were added after 1270. At Enna in central Sicily, the castle's main strength is the site, although there is a double line of defence. But Frederick also developed a style that was to become highly popular in southern Europe and influential beyond. Castello del'Imperatore at Prato and Castello Ursino at Catania are large square single-block castles, the former with massive square towers and the latter with round ones, set around a central court. One might think of them as a reversion to earlier massive tower-keeps, such as Norwich or Loches, but these are on an even more huge scale, and the sophistication of their protective devices is remarkable.[35] These structures share one characteristic with Crac and Marqab, in that covered chambers line the walls, protecting the garrison.

By the mid-thirteenth century, the most advanced castles were massively fortified erections of brick or stone. They are consciously designed structures in a way in which castles had generally not been before. It is a mark of this that we begin to hear of specialized architects. Pierre Mainier rebuilt Chillon on an island in Lake Geneva to endow it with enormous strength, and Master James of St George, Edward I's Savoyard master architect who constructed the castles of North Wales, may well have built far beyond military necessity.[36] Almost all castles in the West continued to have open walkways and fighting-tops of towers protected only by merlons, with projecting wooden hoardings being used in times of war to widen fields of fire while protecting the garrison. But stone machicolations – and, more occasionally, box machicolations – gave much more protection. The greatest castles of the Holy Land embody huge vaults which served for storage, accommodation and stabling, but also as protected fighting areas where the defender was secure from missiles. Such structures are rarer in the West – below the walkway on the south wall of Caernarvon there are two covered fighting galleries that run the whole length of the wall, and similar structures can be found at Beaumaris. By the end of the thirteenth century, arrow-slits were carefully sited and directed so that tremendous firepower could be brought to bear, while approaches were made oblique. At Beaumaris, the gates of the inner *enceinte* are offset from those of the outer in such a way as to expose an attacker to murderous fire on his unprotected right side. Sites were exploited to the maximum: at Conway the inner bailey was almost unassailable except through the outer bailey to the east, but if an attacker could burst into that courtyard he would be subject to fire from the upper walkways and towers, which communicated with the inner bailey and could serve as an outwork of its defence.

No matter how strong, an isolated castle was vulnerable: even mighty Crac and Marqab fell quickly to a determined enemy. A network of castles supported by a field-army was a very different proposition, but only a few kings could afford such a combination. Edward I created a castle system in North Wales, but it was not often that such enormous expenditure could be justified. In creating these and other fortresses, Edward developed of a whole bureaucratic network which harnessed the resources of the kingdom to the needs of building and maintenance.[37] Thus the king as chief landlord was transformed into the king as sovereign. As for the other castles of England, they were chiefly centres of seigniorial administration which could serve as useful bargaining-counters in the dialogue of king and subject: it is worth remembering that Hedingham served the de Veres and their descendants down to the seventeenth century. Where the king's power failed, as in Germany, princes used castles in much the same way as kings. In areas of particular fragmentation, a pattern of fortified statelets arose in which virtually all substantial men needed defences to protect themselves from, or to prey upon, their neighbours. Thus arose a whole order of society, their bickering now frozen in the ruins of stone castles and towers.

# Chapter Eight

## Castles and war

At the start of this period, war was primarily a matter of plunder, destruction and skirmishing. The difficulties inherent in an attack on even minor fortifications simply intensified this. Ravaging undermined the economic base of the castle-owner and the morale of its garrison. The presence of a castle which could afford shelter to the defeated in battle added to the disincentives of risking men and political capital in the open field. This situation enabled substantial families who settled away from the centres of power of the great to maintain a degree of independence, by raising castles which increased their authority over the neighbouring countryside.

Sieges raised great difficulties even for the major rulers of the eleventh century. Brévol castle was the object of a bitter war in Normandy under Robert Curthose, which culminated in a set-piece siege, but its capture was a great effort involving the King of France and the Duke of Normandy. Philip I of France (1060–1108) confessed that the tower of Montlhéry had made him old before his time, while his son Louis VI cut his teeth in war against the castellan Bouchard of Montmorency. In Germany, Henry IV could not seize the fortresses of the powerful southern magnates and fought an unsuccessful war to gain control of the lands and castles of Mathilda of Tuscany. In England, the civil war under Stephen became a bitter stalemate in which castles formed the power-centres of the main parties. In 1142, Stephen's effort to push into Angevin territory by building a castle at Wilton was checked by Robert of Gloucester in a sharp battle, but shortly afterwards he seized the isolated Angevin outpost at Oxford. During this disorder, robber barons such as William de Launay, who built a castle at Ravenstone, emerged. It was only slowly and with great effort that King Stephen's superior resources began to tell, but even then a series of fortuitous deaths was almost as important in breaking the stalemate.[1]

This situation changed greatly in England and France during the period 1000–1300, because significant states developed. But even those states were limited in their articulation and highly dependent on the vagaries of the royal personality, so that it was impossible to assert an absolute monopoly of fortification for the public authority. As a result, castles remained as vital elements in the balance between kings and their great subjects, and although they were often elaborated in the directions of comfort and display, their military potential remained. Castellans could not afford to be too openly defiant of their masters, but they in turn could not afford to alienate large sections of their followers – and if they did, castles formed a core of resistance. Henry II was incontestably the greatest lord in his lands, and his resources enabled him to crush almost any combination which raised itself against him, but he was far from absolute and he faced constant revolt, especially in Aquitaine. Because of the confused and yet personal nature of allegiance, the conventions of the age made it difficult for him to execute rebels and so end plots. Only very powerful figures such as the vicecounts of Angoulême could really stand against him. In England, he established a massive dominance. However, when King John alienated many of his barons, the resultant war was marked by bitter sieges that required great military effort, the siege of Rochester being only the most famous of a long series. Castles formed a vital element in the balance between kings, princes and their more important subjects. That balance varied from time to time and place to place; and it is reflected in the differing policies of, for example, the Angevin kings who controlled castle-building closely and the Capetians, who were obliged to take a more relaxed attitude.[2]

In the first half of the twelfth century, the balance changed in favour of the monarchs and the very great princes in England, France and the Empire, because wealth increased and people looked to monarchy to provide order and stability. A series of strong personalities made their way into power and stamped the age as one of kingship. As a result, control became firmer. The military effect of this was to enhance the power of the king and to reduce that of the castellan, with only a handful of fortresses and no real field-army. Mighty royal castles such as Dover were strong in themselves, but they were also impressive as a reminder of the strength that lay behind them. The consolidation of Europe behind a few great rulers meant that individual castles were no longer what mattered; it was the existence of a network that could be supported in time of need which created a genuine fortress strategy.

On or about 1 November 1184, the county of Hainaut was invaded by the armies of Philip Count of Flanders (1168–91), of Philip of Heinsberg, Archbishop of Cologne (1167–91), and of Godfrey III, Duke of Brabant (1142–

90), who was accompanied by his son Henry (1190–1235). The campaign that followed is known to us in some detail, because it formed part of the narrative of a number of contemporary or near-contemporary sources, the most important of which is that of Gislebert of Mons, Chancellor of Baldwin V of Hainaut (1171–95). This war might almost have been conducted in order to illustrate the ideas of modern historians on medieval warfare: truces were more common and more sustained than military activity, it was without battles or major sieges, and in its military phase it was wholly inconclusive. It was a war apparently fought according to the dictate of Vegetius: "It is preferable to subdue an enemy by famine, raids and terror, than in battle where fortune tends to have more influence than bravery" and it was dominated by a castle strategy.[3]

The campaign involved much more than a policy of mere passive defence, and indeed shows us the castle in most of its major roles, although there were no real sieges. The Count of Flanders strengthened his castles on the southern march of Hainaut in order to prepare a base for his attack. This aggression, presumably combined with other factors, won over Jacques d'Avesnes, who was vassal both of himself and Baldwin V. From this base, Philip marched north to Baldwin's chief city of Mons with an army of 500 knights, 1,000 other cavalry equipped with hauberks and some 40,000 foot. *En route*, he devastated the land and seized some weaker castles; at Le Quesnoy the defenders burned the town lest he use it as a base for a siege of the castle. The Archbishop of Cologne with 1,300 knights and many sergeants on horseback and the Duke of Brabant with 400 knights and, so we are told, 60,000 other cavalry and foot, gathered their forces to the northeast and marched into Hainaut via Binches, where they took the Roman road to Mons, cutting a swath of destruction wherever they went. At Morlenwelz, Eustace de Roeux sallied out of his castle and inflicted heavy casualties upon them. By 10 November they had joined the Count of Flanders at Belmoncel near Mons.

The position of the Count of Hainaut seemed to be hopeless. His ally, the King of France, had for the moment abandoned him. Mons was not strongly fortified, although it had a garrison of 140 knights and crossbowmen. Baldwin could count on about 700 knightly vassals plus 300 mercenary knights and some 300, mostly French, volunteers; his 1,300 knights were badly outnumbered by the 2,200 of the allies, who also had many more mounted sergeants and footsoldiers. But because he was on the defensive he could count on his castles. In the words of Gislebert: "There is nothing very strange about the fact that the Count of Hainaut did not confront them in battle; he was totally preoccupied with securing his castles". Gislebert goes on to list all the castles of the count and his vassals which were strengthened and garrisoned. Only the weaker places fell to the enemy, and once that was clear all of these were totally abandoned. The Hainaulters concentrated their forces and resorted to a scorched earth strategy, adding their burning and destruction to that of their enemies, who were thus denied food.

This castle strategy was the rock of Baldwin's defence. He went to the garrisons and encouraged them: "Be brave, be assured, our enemies will go away one day and leave us our lands. After all, they cannot carry them off!" And it worked! For the devastation of the countryside deprived the allies of food and soon it came to Baldwin's ears that there was hunger in their camp. When the archbishop opened negotiations, Baldwin spun them out and soon the allied army had to retreat for lack of food. By 25 November, the allied forces had left Hainaut and the war degenerated into savage raiding which was brought to a halt 12 days before Christmas by a truce which was to last until Epiphany, 13 January 1185. Under the aegis of the King of France, this was extended until St John's day, 24 June 1185. By Christmas, the Count of Hainaut was paying off his mercenaries and sending his men home to their devastated lands. For the most part, hostilities were confined to luring vassals away from the Count of Flanders and his allies, until the truce was broken at Easter 1185, when the war was renewed.

This time, the Count of Flanders was on the defensive. He and his allies, the Brabanters, had to garrison their castles against the attacks of the Count of Hainaut, who was intent on revenge for the sufferings of his land. He had already destroyed 72 villages of the traitor Jacques d'Avesnes before the Christmas truce and subsequently he burned 110 more. In the face of such savagery, when the king of France challenged him before Amiens, with 2,000 knights and a huge mass of infantry, the Count of Flanders could mobilize only 400 knights and, perhaps, 40,000 other horse and foot. It was generally believed at the time that the Count of Flanders could call upon 1,000 vassal knights to the French king's 700, but on this occasion he had to leave garrisons against the ravaging of the Hainaulters – he was impoverished by the war of the previous year, while Philip of France was not. Although the two armies faced one another for three weeks, no battle resulted and in the end the Count of Flanders sued for a peace which greatly profited the French king and the Count of Hainaut.

At first sight, the story of this war appears to confirm the strength of castles and to represent a triumph for mere passive strength. But in reality there were other factors at work. No castle could hold out indefinitely against attack, but the Count of Flanders had to watch the King of France, who was dealing with the troublesome Stephen of Sancerre. Moreover, the situation of the Flemish and their allies was not easy, for they were caught in a ring of castles. These may have been built for a whole host of disparate reasons and they were never designed as a system, but all of them were loyal to Baldwin V. As a result, if the allies concentrated on one they could be harassed from another. The decisive factor in this phase of the story is that the army of Cologne and Brabant was starving in the face of a scorched earth policy. We may think it odd that Godfrey of Brabant should be in such straits only four days' march from his own land, and this brings us to the nub of the matter: the key factors in the war – as so often – were political, not military.

The allies had very different objectives. The Duke of Brabant was a cousin of Baldwin V, against whom he had pursued a long-running feud. The lands of these two potentates in southwest Hainaut were deeply interpenetrating, with consequential bickering. When Baldwin V began to fortify Lembecq in 1182–3, it was seen as an aggressive act. Moreover, there was another bone of contention. Baldwin V had persuaded Henry the Blind, Count of Namurs, to recognize him as his heir, in opposition to the claims of the house of Brabant. For them, this was an episode in a long-running family feud. Philip of Heinsberg, Archbishop of Cologne, was also a cousin of Baldwin V. He enjoyed a considerable patronage over the principalities of the Low Countries and Lorraine, and was undoubtedly concerned by the growth of Hainaut and the annexation of Namurs, especially as it lay across the important trade route between Cologne and Flanders.[4] For him, this was the moment to strike at a potential enemy.

The position of the Count of Flanders was rather different. Baldwin V had married the count's sister Margaret in 1169 and so was his brother-in-law, holding of him Bapaume as his wife's dowry. So good were their relations that as regent of Philip Augustus, Philip of Flanders had arranged the marriage of Baldwin's daughter Elizabeth to the young French king. But relations between Philip Augustus and his former regent cooled and each manipulated the problems of the other, culminating in a series of conflicts in the early 1180s, in which Baldwin V loyally took the part of Flanders. However, his enthusiasm dimmed as Philip Augustus threatened to renounce his daughter, and it was a pressure upon him that Philip of Flanders supported the Brabanters. This conflict was sharpened because Philip of Flanders' wife Isabel had died in 1182, and in 1184 he married Mathilda of Portugal, while keeping control of Isabel's vast dowry in Artois, which included Amiens, to which both Philip Augustus and Baldwin V had claims.[5]

For the Duke of Brabant, the attack was little more than the continuation of a series of raids, and he seems to have made preparations accordingly. Medieval armies could mount long-term expeditions for which they carried large food supplies, but this was not the purpose or spirit of this affair as far as the Brabanters were concerned. The Archbishop of Cologne seems to have been just as poorly prepared, but then essentially he was fishing in troubled waters. It was from the archbishop that feelers for a peace came, isolating Philip of Flanders and forcing a withdrawal.

What had the allies expected to happen? Probably they thought that their devastation would shake the loyalty of Baldwin's vassals. Jacques d'Avesnes was an important vassal of the counts of Flanders and Hainaut; early in the war he declared for the former against Baldwin V, and Rasse de Gavre followed suit. We may suspect that there were more, for our main source, Gislebert of Mons, is very devoted to Baldwin V and mentions Flemings who defected to him. But Baldwin V's castellans remained loyal, probably because he was determined and prepared to support them to the hilt. The Count of Hainaut held a large number of castles himself: he poured troops into these and assisted his chief vassals in the defence of their castles. In all, he hired 300 mercenary knights and 3,000 sergeants, and paid the expenses of another 300 who had volunteered for his service, plunging himself deeply into debt.[6]

The determination of Baldwin V and the support of his vassals had the effect of placing the allies in a ring of well held fortresses, and in these circumstances the differences between their objectives emerged. Philip of Cologne opened negotiations, and quite soon starvation in the Brabanter army forced the allies to retreat. Raiding and seducing vassals was the chief activity of the remainder of the war. It was primarily a political factor, the determination of Baldwin V despite a difficult situation, that governed the course of events, but one powerful influence must have been the threat of French intervention, which quickly became a reality in the following year. And this was a costly business. Gislebert notes the total cost of employing additional troops, but Baldwin also had to pay for fortifications. In addition, his lands were devastated, to such a degree that he was ultimately unwilling to desist from exacting revenge upon his enemies and had to be dissuaded by the King of France.[7]

So the outcome of this war was determined by a series of factors, primarily political, and the existence of castles was only one. There is no indication of their being particularly strong – in fact, Mons is explicitly noted as having weak walls, which the count later strengthened. Philip of Flanders was not lacking in the technology of siege, for he menaced Lewarde with balistas and mangonels, to no avail.[8] The outcome of this phase of the war was a result of political and personal factors, the threat of a French army and, ultimately, the resolution of Baldwin himself.

At about the same time, Henry II and his son Richard were reducing castles with relative ease. In 1152 and 1156, Henry II quickly seized Chinon, Loudun and Mirabeau when his brother Geoffrey rebelled, while his speedy capture of Thouars in 1158 was much remarked upon. In the course of squabbles with Louis VII, in 1166 Henry took Sées and Fougères, in 1167

Chaumont-en-Vexin, and in 1168 Lusignan and many fortresses in Brittany: this phase ended with the peace of Vendôme in 1170. As tension grew in 1173, Henry fortified his castles in England, and during the revolt there the royal castles of the Midlands provided important bases for quelling the East Anglian rebels. The great revolt turned on a series of sieges, most notably Louis VII's attack on Rouen, which was relieved by Henry. In the aftermath of the rebellion, Richard established a great reputation for himself, seizing castles and cities, notably in 1176 Châteauneuf and Angoulême and in 1178–9 Pons, Richemont, Gensac, Macillac, Gourville, Anvac and, most famously, Taillebourg. We simply do not know what these castles were like and how they compared with those of Hainaut, or indeed anywhere else. Verneuil, which defied Louis VII, is known to have been formidable, while the frequency with which the sources mention castles and defended towns being burned suggests many were of wood.[9]

In part, the explanation for these rapid successes was military organization. Henry and Richard used large numbers of mercenary troops, and the rapidity of their movements indicates that, on occasion at least, Plantagenet armies were well organized. The startling speed of the attack on Brittany in 1173 was followed by the successful siege of Dol, where it is probable that Henry employed prefabricated siege machinery brought along by his army. Henry, it has been said, "put up the cost of defiance" by using mercenaries, who could be resisted by elaborate castles of a kind that only he and a few other princes in his lands could afford. There is truth in this, but far more to the point in particular conflicts was his evident determination and, decisively, the fact that most of those whose castles opposed him were rebels who lacked a real field-army able to relieve them, and who were only too often let down by their ally, the King of France. Louis VII, for example, seems to have been quite happy to use the Breton rebels but unwilling to give real support. Quite simply, Henry II could raise relatively large armies able to isolate castles and small towns. An assault in force would nearly always succeed against any castle if the attacker was willing to sustain casualties: Bourzey, in the Latin Principality of Antioch, was not a particularly strong castle, but it occupied an immensely powerful position; Saladin simply overran it by sheer weight of numbers.[10] The individual castle was formidable against an enemy with limited wealth, but except for a few very strong places could no more than delay a monarch who could mobilize resources on Henry II's scale.

It was the combination of a network of castles and cities with a field-army which was the great strength of the Latin Kingdom of Jerusalem. Saladin invaded the Kingdom of Jerusalem in 1177 and Smail noted: "Saladin ignored all the strong places which lay in his path and swept on towards Ramla and

Jaffa; yet those strong places influenced the campaign in many ways. They did not halt the enemy at the frontier, nor prevent his temporary control of the open countryside. But intact they remained as the repositories of lordship." King Baldwin IV had retreated to Ascalon when he saw the size of the enemy army, but as it broke up to ravage he pounced and defeated it in detail at the battle of Mont Gisard.[11] In 1182, 1183 and 1187, when Saladin invaded Galilee, the crusader army concentrated at Saffuriyah where a small castle, no more than an enclosure and tower, stood at a vital road junction and guarded the springs. On each occasion, the army swelled as castle garrisons were stripped to feed it. Saladin's aim was always to provoke the crusaders into a battle against his superior forces by destroying the countryside. But an attack on a strongpoint was hazardous for him in the presence of a crusader army. Even if he took it, his army – like most – melted away at the end of the campaigning season, making it impossible to hold.

Until 1187, Saladin – like the Count of Flanders and his allies at much the same time – was caught in a web of castles and fortified cities. This did not take the form of a fortified perimeter of defence in either Hainaut or Jerusalem. The castles had been constructed where they mattered to individuals at different times. But, of course, most strategic points were covered, because it would normally profit somebody. The invader was ensnared in a *catenaccio* of castles which hardly barred his path but threatened him in minor ways, unbalancing his army before the threat of a field-force. In 1187, Saladin invaded the kingdom and laid siege to Tiberias. The king and barons of Jerusalem discussed how to respond to Saladin's attack: according to some of the sources, Raymond of Tripoli suggested that the army of Jerusalem should retire before Saladin to the vicinity of Acre "and be near our fortresses", where "if battle turns out badly for us we can withdraw to Acre and other cities that are nearby". Instead, King Guy of Jerusalem hazarded battle, with disastrous results.[12]

The great value of the castle was that it held down the land; without taking it there could be no secure mastery of the land that it dominated. No castle could hold out indefinitely, but its strength could pin down an attacker and make him vulnerable to the attentions of a friendly field-army. When the crusaders attacked Jerusalem in 1099, they were very conscious that their siege was a race against time, because the Egyptians were mobilizing to relieve it – this was why they risked an early assault, even though they had but one siege ladder. The civil war in England was sharpened by the invasion of Prince Louis of France in 1216. The castles of the royalist and rebel parties anchored the contending parties, and it was, significantly, a successful expedition by the barons to raise the siege of Mountsorrel that emboldened them to move on to attack Lincoln. But this was a siege too far, because the royal army under

William Marshal trapped them there. Prince Louis attempted to replace the army lost at Lincoln by forces from France, but this was frustrated by a royal victory at sea off Sandwich, which destroyed his fleet.[13] In the end, the lack of the field-army cost Louis his hopes of succession in England.

By the late twelfth century, it was only rarely that a single fortress could exert decisive influence. In the Holy Land, Crac des Chevaliers was a bastion of the failing Western power. This was a castle of extraordinary strength, but it could count on the resources of the whole Hospitaller Order and the support of the crusading movement. When that power ebbed, its great strength was no substitute and, like Marqab, which in some ways was even stronger, was eventually captured after a siege of only a month. But a fortress of such strength could impose a crippling cost on its attacker. In 1203, Philip of France concentrated his forces on Château Gaillard. It held for the astonishing period of six months against a major French army, but it was the miscarriage of John's attempt to relieve the siege and his subsequent inaction which led to its fall. After that terrible blow, the Norman defences fell like a pack of cards. Kenilworth was a strong castle, whose defences included large ponds, which prevented mining and kept throwing-machines at a distance. In 1266, Henry III besieged it from June to December. Its garrison had reason to hope for aid from abroad or from other centres of rebellion, and they may have thought a political settlement with the king possible. In the end, they surrendered on terms, but the siege had been cripplingly expensive, absorbing the income of ten English counties. In 1266, Charles of Anjou set out from France to claim the throne of the Sicilian–Norman kingdom, held by Manfred, who enjoyed enormous advantages. Charles faced a long and tiring march, and had to pass Manfred's allies in Lombardy and his fortresses in central–southern Italy. But Manfred offered little support to his allies, and his castle garrisons felt isolated and so fell easily. His failure to exploit webs of fortifications worked against Manfred, although in the end it was his decisions on the battlefield of Benevento which undid him. Edward I created a network of *bastides* and castles to anchor the defence of Gascony.[14]

The real strength of a castle was the garrison within it and their political connections beyond. However, if they were to play their part in war, castles needed to be fully prepared and garrisoned. Robert of Bellême surprised St Céneri in 1092, panicked its garrison and burned it to the ground. In 1098, he and William Rufus attempted to take Elias of Maine's Dangeul by surprise "out of season", when the garrison was dispersed. When they failed, Robert prepared his nine castles and other fortified places in Maine for a sharp war. As we have noted, Philip of Flanders prepared his castles on the March for his attack on Hainaut, while in 1282 the Welsh had great success in seizing unprepared castles from the English. It was essential that a proper garrison should be in place and supplies laid in; otherwise, a castle could neither serve as a base for aggressive operations nor be ready to withstand siege. Substantial parts of a castle's equipment were made of wood and tended to decay. This included the wooden hoardings, enclosures hanging out from the battlements that protected the garrison from enemy fire. Catapults were very important in the Middle East: at Marqab the great terraces so evident on the east wall were probably used for mounting large siege engines, but these would have been dismantled in times of peace and stored under cover.[15]

The castle may be thought of as having a defensive role but, as we have seen, its very construction threatened neighbours, and castles often served as bases for attack. In 1178, Baldwin IV of Jerusalem constructed the castle of Chastelleret at Jacob's Ford on the Jordan in upper Galilee. This castle would certainly have had a defensive role in protecting Galilee, but Imad ad-Din, Saladin's secretary, was convinced that its construction was part of a pattern of aggression by the crusaders. He may well have been right, especially in the light of the recent construction of nearby Belvoir. Saladin offered the Franks 60,000 dinars to dismantle it, raising the sum on refusal to 100,000. Ultimately, it took a ferocious campaign by Saladin to destroy a castle that was still incomplete when it fell in August 1179. Modern writers have perhaps been too influenced by Jaques de Vitry, who looked back on the building of these castles and, with the benefit of hindsight, saw their purpose as purely defensive, when in fact the fall of Chastelleret may itself mark the decisive turning point from offence to defence.[16]

The crusaders became established in the East by the conquest of important centres such as Antioch and Jerusalem, but they spread their control into the hinterland by building castles that subsequently served to defend them. Crac des Chevaliers flourished by threatening the nearby Islamic powers and extorting money from them. In southern Italy, Guiscard used the same technique to establish his supremacy. In England, the native population were overawed by a wave of Norman strongpoints. In Wales, Edward I secured a precarious conquest in a hostile land by establishing a network of castles that dominated the enemy heartland of Snowdonia. But although we speak of the Edwardian castles, it is essential to remember that Edward built fortified towns. He gave land within them to Englishmen and other foreigners, keeping out the Welsh and creating a new population that was secure in strong places and able to overawe the native people. Above all, he secured these places by sea-power – Caernarfon and Conway were important ports and the wealth that they generated made the countryside dependent. Even castles such as Rhuddlan and Harlech had ports, and from their trade towns arose. The scale and cost of Edward's building campaign in North Wales is often remarked upon, but it was less than the cost of war, and the security that it bred promised rich exploitation of his new lands – such were the rewards of a shrewd castle strategy. In Scotland, Edward I relied on hastily built timber castles and the rather limited native structures to secure his conquest, but they proved very vulnerable to surprise attack.[17]

In the decentralized world at the very start of this period, the castle protected the property of the powerful individual and overawed his neighbours. Its military power was vital in a violent world to protect and extend the rights of its proprietor and his friends. The castle literally shaped society around these wealth-centres of the powerful. War turned on the possession of such fortresses, and its most natural form in a primitive economy – devastation – was intensified by their existence. Where conflict and weak central power remained the norm, this situation continued, but where kings and princes grew in stature and wealth, and were able to assert the unique nature of their sovereignty, their possession of networks of castles enabled them to overawe and even absorb those of lesser men, particularly because they could sustain both castles and field-armies. However, the military potential of castles remained even in these circumstances. In an age when even in the most settled kingdoms all of those considered in any sense noble or gentle saw themselves as soldiers – even if they chose not to pursue a military career – there was nothing odd in the retention of a military potential in their houses, which acted as guarantees against the encroachments of kings and princes. But these leaders of society were able to develop castles in accordance with the possibilities opened up by the new wealth of the twelfth and thirteenth centuries, exploiting the defensive and aggressive potential of the castle to the full. For, right down to the end of the thirteenth century and far beyond, the massive strength of earth, timber and stone was a great asset of defence. Networks of castles, although rarely individual castles, remained repositories of lordship and even of sovereignty, because the technology available to attack them remained very limited. Castles continued to maintain the pattern of war in a primitive economy, a pattern of raiding and destruction that would continue throughout the Middle Ages and beyond.

# Chapter Nine

# *Fortifications and siege*

Castles were never the only fortifications in medieval Europe. By the end of the period there were cities everywhere, and most had stone fortifications. Large cities were more common in southern France, Spain, Italy and the Holy Land than in northern Europe. In Italy, Florence, Milan, Venice and Genoa, and in Spain Cordoba and Granada, all had populations of 50,000–100,000, but in northern Europe only Paris was of this magnitude, although Ghent and Bruges may have approached 50,000. Cities of 25,000–50,000 included Padua, Bologna, Verona, Pavia, Lucca, Rome, Naples and Palermo in Italy, Barcelona and Valencia in Spain, Toulouse in Provence and only Bordeaux, Lyons, Rouen, London and Cologne further north. In the 10,000–25,000 range, Italy had Cremona, Mantua, Modena, Parma, Pavia, Rimini, Forli, Faenza, Ravenna, Cesena, Orvieto, Perugia, Sienna, Pistoia and Pisa, and Spain had Zaragossa, while northern Europe could count Abbeville, Amiens, Arras, Lille, Ypres, Douai, Valenciennes, Mons, Louvain, Liège, Beauvais, Chartres, Troyes, Metz and Dijon. For the rest, the cities we hear of probably numbered between 2,000 and 10,000.[1]

Because many towns grew up around castles, the distinction between a small town and a castle was not at all clear-cut and, indeed, in the Holy Land and elsewhere we know of towns founded in castles, while Latin terminology often uses confusingly overlapping words which further obscures the distinction.[2] The basic strength of the fortified city, as of the castle, rested in its garrison and political connections, whether as part of a state, such as Ghent and Bruges within Flanders, or Paris within the Capetian monarchy, or as a city–state with alliances of its own. In this sense, the strategic problem for the attacker was the same – to isolate the target from a friendly field-army or the support of a network of castles. It was simply more difficult for a besieger to mount a successful assault on a city or to cut it off beyond all hope of relief, both because of its size and because of the problem of sustaining a large army over a period of time.

All besiegers faced certain common problems. Any city or castle could obviously be blockaded, and so would eventually fall from starvation if relief did not arrive. But the besieger himself was just as likely to suffer from supply problems as the besieged, and was more exposed to weather and disease. In 1184, hunger forced the retreat of an allied attack on the county of Hainaut, while in 1198 the Piacenzans could not assault Borgo San Donnino because of drought, followed by bad winter weather. The presence of a relief army imposed terrible risks on an attacker. At the siege of Acre, the crusaders dug earthworks that had to be manned when they attacked the city, lest they be taken in the rear by Saladin's army; Philip Augustus did the same against an English relief force at Château Gaillard. Richard I argued against an attack on Jerusalem in 1192 because Saladin's army could cut his communications with the coast. In 1199, the Piacenzans and Milanese were forced to withdraw from the siege of Castelnuovo Bocca d'Adda by the Cremonans, whose relief force established itself nearby in a fortified camp, and in 1237 the Milanese and their allies prevented Frederick II from besieging Brescia by establishing a similar camp 25 km to the south, on the Lusignolo.[3]

The problems of a major siege were aggravated by the loose and composite nature of medieval armies. Lack of discipline and a less than alert guard probably explains how Mathilda escaped from Oxford in 1142. At Ascalon in 1153, the Templars forced a breach in the walls, but refused to allow others to exploit it, with disastrous results. In 1238, Frederick II was anxious to follow up his great victory at Cortenova in the previous year, but he was unable to gather a sizeable army until July, and then it was with a very motley force that he attacked Brescia – Germans, Cremonans, Apulians, Saracens, Tuscans, English, French, Spanish, Provençals and even Greeks are mentioned, each with their own leaders. The siege seems to have been decided upon at a very late stage, for it was only after the arrival of the young King Henry in June that the army gathered. By that time, the four months' supply of rations that Frederick had commanded the Cremonans to take with them must have been running low. Although the only serious relief effort was an attack by the Piacenzans on Cremona, the siege, begun on 11 July, seems to have been conducted in a dilatory way which failed to prevent Brescian sallies, one of which, in August, captured Frederick's engineer, Calamandrinus, who was persuaded to work for the city. It was not until September that great siege towers were built and serious assaults made, but by then it was too late and inclement weather forced the imperial army to return to Cremona. In February 1248, Frederick II's army was encamped in his siege-city of Victoria outside Parma when the besieged noted his absence – he had gone hunting. A minor skirmish of a few knights on both sides led to a determined sally by the Parmans, which panicked the imperial army before Frederick could impose order – the result was a major defeat for the imperialists. Edward I's siege of Caerlaverock in 1300 began with futile assaults by notables intent on displaying their bravery; these were soon replaced by a systematic siege.[4]

The factor that distinguished siege warfare against important cities was their enormous potential for resistance. Street-fighting was just as costly in the Middle Ages as at Stalingrad. When the crusader army reached Toulouse in 1217, the city was virtually unfortified, but the crusaders were unable to enter because the citizens barricaded the streets and showered the attackers with missiles from the rooftops. At Mansourah, over 300 mounted knights were lost when they charged into the town and were overwhelmed by blocks of wood thrown down from the houses.[5]

When the First Crusade attacked Antioch in October 1097, their army of about 50,000 faced a garrison of no more than 5,000 Turks, who had limited support from the population, many of whom were Christians. But the walls were 10 km round and enclosed an area nearly 3 km long and 2 km wide. On the west they abutted the river Orontes, while to the east they rose abruptly up the mountainside to 500 m; the more vulnerable north side was reinforced by barbicans. This strong city wall dated from Justinian's time and it was defended by a hierarchy of great and lesser towers. The crusaders were not even able to blockade all of the main gates until April 1098, after seven months of siege. The risk that they ran was dispersal of forces, which might open them to defeat in detail by a determined sally, precisely the fate of Kerbogah's army on 28 June 1098, after his siege of the crusaders who had obtained entry to Antioch by betrayal. Similarly, in Italy, Barbarossa's first siege of Milan in 1158 was dogged by many sallies because his army was stretched out around the walls. By contrast with the garrison of Antioch, the Milanese enjoyed the support of the city population, whose limitations as soldiers counted for less behind city walls. Internal lines enabled defenders to launch effective sallies: it was probably for this reason that on the eve of the crusader attack in 1099, Jerusalem was reinforced with 400 horsemen. Medieval pictures almost always show knights in besieging armies; their mobility was necessary to defend against such sudden attacks. It is worth noting that the destruction of Frederick II's siege-city of Victoria began with a small cavalry skirmish.[6]

To attack a large city was an enormous undertaking, involving strong and able command, special equipment and personnel, persistence and, above all, organization to sustain forces. These qualities were not commonly combined in medieval armies, although they were demonstrated by the First Crusade at Antioch, to a remarkable degree. Baldwin I of Jerusalem maintained the siege of Tyre from November 1111 to April 1112 using earthwork fortifications to protect his army from relief forces, and constructing formidable siege-towers. In the end, he failed because the citizens put up a stubborn and intelligent defence, could count on supply by sea and knew that a relief army was imminent. In 1124, the same disciplined effort – this time supported by a Venetian fleet – was successful. The siege of Ascalon, from 1153 to 1154, was a triumph of organization and determination over adversity. The siege of Lisbon in 1147–8 enjoyed remarkable success, but there was tension between the Portugese, the Anglo-Normans, the Germans and the Flemings over booty. During the Third Crusade, the siege of Acre, sustained for two years from August 1189, was badly hampered by friction between various groups, notably those of Richard I and Philip Augustus.[7]

Frederick Barbarossa's enormous exertions against Milan illustrate the problems of siege very well. Barbarossa wanted to reassert imperial authority in the old Lombard Kingdom, but Milan was deeply opposed. After the failure of his early efforts to come to terms, Barbarossa besieged Milan with a great army in 1158, but he was never able to isolate the city, and many of his nobles tired of the bitter conflict, forcing him to come to terms at Roncaglia in September 1158. This settlement broke down, chiefly because Barbarossa needed the support of the imperialist cities; amongst them was Cremona, which wanted to weaken Milan by destroying Crema and the fortifications of Piacenza. The siege of Crema, from 2 July 1159 until 27 January 1160, was an immense effort by Barbarossa. Although relatively small, the city was well fortified and required an all-out effort, with the use of complex siege machinery. After its fall, Frederick's army melted away, leaving the initiative to Milan, which tried to seize imperial Lodi and to cut Frederick's communications by isolating Como: armed confrontations resulted, with a pitched battle at Carcano on 9 August 1160 in which Barbarossa was defeated. Only in May 1161 was Milan besieged, and by late August the bitter fighting prompted some of the German nobles to seek a settlement with Milan; Rainald of Dassel prevented this by ambushing their envoys. It was not until March 1162 that Milan capitulated. The attack on Milan strained even Barbarossa's resources. To sustain a war with so radical an objective – the destruction of an enemy city – was a major achievement in a world in which military activity was normally fitful. But a military solution in the Lombard plain was impossible, for the cities were too numerous and their political connections were too ramified, and Barbarossa failed to create a political solution after the fall of Milan. When Verona rebelled in 1164, much of eastern Lombardy followed – the emperor found himself with few Germans and "the Lombards were reluctant to come to his assistance".[8]

Toulouse, in southern France, was another great city which demonstrated its resilience in the face of a determined attack. It defied the army of the Albigensian Crusade in 1211: Simon de Montfort was unable to surround the city, whose walls were three miles round, and he could not depend on reinforcements. But, decisively, the crusaders were starving outside the city while Toulouse was able to buy food through its other gates, so after two weeks the siege was raised. The crusader army went on to attack Moissac, but even this small walled town defied them for a month, and in the end fell because of dissension between the garrison of knights and German mercenaries and the citizens.[9]

Through changing political conditions, the walls of Toulouse were almost destroyed in 1215–16, but in September 1217 Count Raymond of Toulouse regained the city and once again de Montfort and his crusading army laid siege in October 1217. The citizens were united in their defiance of the crusader army and they organized themselves efficiently – men, women and even children. They improvised fortifications with earthworks and timber, and, where these did not exist, poured down stones and other missiles from the roofs upon the attacking French, making the narrow streets impassable. The citadel, the Château de Narbonne, was held by the French, but it was completely cut off from the city. Once the fury of their first attacks was spent, the French settled down for a long siege. Focaud of Berzy advised Simon: "We must work out how to maintain a long siege so as to destroy the town. Every day we must make raids across the whole country so as to deprive them of corn, grain, of trees too and vines, of salt, timber and other provisions. In this way we shall force them to surrender." By January 1218, reinforcements from France were starting to arrive, and more poured in in May and June, but although savage assaults were mounted from both sides of the city, supported by elaborate siege equipment, it was never wholly closed off, and this enabled the citizens to receive reinforcements. When Simon de Montfort was killed by a stone from a mangonel on 26 June 1217, the siege was abandoned. The city was besieged for a third time in 1228, but ultimately it surrendered to the overwhelming power of the French monarchy.[10]

In fact, many sieges of cities were unsuccessful. Frederick II had huge resources, but at Brescia in 1238 his large army was poorly organized and unable to prevent effective sallies by the besieged. At Parma in 1247, his allies blocked the river to prevent food entering the city, which soon became desperate, but a sally caught his forces unprepared. In 1243, tiny Viterbo defected to his enemies at a time when he had dismissed his forces and defied the troops that he raised with Pisan loans. In 1241, the small city of Faenza eventually fell after a bitter six-month siege, which deflected his army from Bologna, its main goal.[11] By contrast, as we have seen, Henry II and his son Richard had been able to reduce castles with relative ease. The castle was

111

formidable against an enemy with limited wealth and where, as in thirteenth-century Germany, warfare was on a limited scale, but only an exceptionally strong castle could resist a monarch who could mobilize resources on Henry II's scale.

In Spain, the Christian kingdoms exploited the strength of cities to defend their frontiers. As the kingdoms advanced into Islamic territory, they planted cities to secure their new frontiers. Citizens were recruited by the offer of land, on generous terms. Fired by a mixture of religious zeal, well founded fear and anxiety to defend what they held, the settlers made good garrisons quite ready to sally out to attack Muslim ravagers and to offer determined resistance in the face of greater attacks. Even when Alfonso VIII was defeated at Alarcos in 1195, the Muslims were unable to make much progress in re-conquering the lands, because the cities stood against them, only three minor ones falling.[12]

Attacks on cities were relatively uncommon in northern Europe before the major growth of cities in the thirteenth century. London was besieged by Cnut in 1016, but it offered no resistance to Duke William in 1066 and stood no siege in the civil wars under Stephen, King John and Henry III, although it played a role in all three upheavals. In Germany, attacks on cities were very frequent, and were essentially "a by-product of the fractured political land-scape into which Germany and its sub-regions developed by the thirteenth century". The dissolution of the kingdom, especially after the death of Frederick II in 1250, produced a chaos of competing forces – many of them very small indeed – and free cities of one kind or another loomed large amongst them. These sieges almost always failed, in part because of the strength of town fortifications, but the major factor must surely have been the small size of the competing political units and their inability to sustain conflict over a long period of time.[13]

Siege was a test of political will and resources on both sides. The defenders needed to provide food and to maintain hope of ultimate success: the task was very much the same on the attackers' side, complicated by the need to provide shelter and an infrastructure of support. Strong fortifications were an impor-tant factor in this struggle of wills. The fortifications of cities were not, in principle, very different from those of castles. Milan's in 1158 incorporated a Roman arch which stood outside the main circuit, while Alessandria was a new city, whose fortifications at the time of Barbarossa's unsuccessful siege of 1174–5 were probably earth and timber. At the time of the First Crusade vulnerable sections of the defences of Antioch and Jerusalem were reinforced by double walls, and the twelfth-century sources indicate that most of the important cities of the Palestinian littoral enjoyed this form of protection: these were almost certainly the inheritance of the Roman past. The great walls of Constantinople were of course the example of systematic fortification. Such relatively sophisticated structures were rare in the West. Crema had a double wall at the time of its siege in 1159–60, while at Carcassonne in 1228–39 a strong concentric pattern was developed, and this was used in the new fortifications at Oxford shortly after. St Louis constructed Aigues Mortes as a modern fortification from which to launch his crusades. In the East, he re-created Caeserea with massive stone-lined ditches and a steeply raked talus on the wall side, on the model of Belvoir. Acre's walls were rebuilt on much the same pattern in the thirteenth century; the city fell to al-Ashraf after a siege of only six weeks, but its garrison was not numerous and the enemy was overwhelming. In North Wales, the walls of Conway and Caernarfon shared the modern sophistication of the castles that sheltered them. In these advanced fortifications, all of the devices found in the castle – machicolations, angled arrow-slits and sally-gates – were emulated. Such complex structures were probably as rare as concentric castles, although the strengthening of city defences with stone walls was a feature of the thirteenth century, and barbicans seem to have been a common addition at weak points. Determina-tion compensated for lack of walls at Toulouse in 1217, and at Alessandria from 27 October 1174 to 12 April 1175, when the threat posed by the army of the Lombard League persuaded Barbarossa to raise the siege.[14]

The defences of cities were often strengthened by the incorporation of a citadel. In Europe and the Middle East, castles often gave birth to towns, which nestled around them and were walled. At Ghent, the comital castle dominated the town. Montgomery was laid out as a town when the new castle was built there in the 1220s. Dryslwyn was a small castle-town of the later thirteenth century. But as cities grew, citadels became quite distinct entities within the defence. In Laon a "new tower", built by Heribert II in the 920s, held out after the city had fallen in 931 and 949, but fell to mining. During the siege of 985, the commercial quarter of Verdun seems to have served as an inner core for the defence. At Antioch, the citadel stood on the walls and at Jerusalem the famous Tower of David was on the west perimeter. In 1243, the citadel of Viterbo resisted when the city fell. An old Roman fort, the Château de Narbonne, was the citadel of Toulouse, but the demolitions of 1215–16 removed it from the circuit of the walls, and it served as headquarters of the Albigensian Crusade in the great siege of 1217–18. Thirteenth-century Acre was defended by double walls with a deep ditch between, and a similar arrangement cut off the suburb of Montmusard from the port proper, where the Templar castle served as a citadel. Citadels on the perimeter sometimes strengthened the defences of a city, although Antioch was an exception. The citadel there was so remote that during the crusader siege it had no influence whatsoever. When the crusaders seized the city, the citadel on its remote mountain-peak held out against them and admitted the forces of Kerbogah when he besieged them in Antioch shortly after their existence, like those of keeps in castles, must have given confidence to those of the defenders who might find an ultimate refuge in them. However, citadels often represented the menace of some outside ruling power and were intended to hold down the city rather than defend it, notably in early Norman England.[15]

In the end it was the garrison, not the walls, that mattered. Surprise was by far the best means of seizing a fortified place, and dissension within a city or garrison could be fatal. In 1236, an allied army of the eastern Lombard cities of Vicenza, Trevio, Padua and Mantua was being held off by Ezzelino of Romano when Frederick II suddenly marched from Cremona and seized Vicenza. This was possible because of the absence of many Vicenzan soldiers, and because Ezzelino had already enlisted sympathizers within the city. In the wake of this blow most of eastern Lombardy, notably Padua and Trevio, fell to the imperial cause. At Moissac in August 1212, as we have noted, the citizens lacked the will to fight off the crusader siege although the garrison was willing. Parma defected from the cause of Frederick II in 1247 when Parman exiles made a sally into the city and gained the upper hand.[16]

If surprise was impossible, a determined assault well pressed home was often enough, as at Tonbridge castle in 1088, which Wiliam Rufus's troops seized by storm on the second day of the siege. The army of the First Crusade tried to rush the formidable defences of Jerusalem equipped only with a single siege-ladder in June 1099. According to the *Gesta Stephani*, in 1144 Stephen captured Winchcombe by ordering his troops to rush at it under "a cloud of arrows". The castle was newly built on a high mound, which suggests that it was of wood, and it had only a small garrison. The assault failed, but the garrison quickly decided to surrender on terms. The fall of Winchcombe nicely illustrates the combination of psychological and physical factors which was called for in siege warfare. Stephen's assault was a clear show of determination and the garrison, feeling isolated and outnumbered, decided on the better part of valour. In 1144, Baldwin III was unable to take Li Vaux Moise but devastated the countryside, and so persuaded the inhabitants to turn against the Turkish garrison. Before he besieged Taillebourg, Richard's opening gambit was also destruction of the countryside, provoking the garrison to an ill-considered sally which enabled him to capture the place.[17]

Besiegers and besieged sometimes resorted to cruder methods to depress enemy morale. At Nicaea in 1097, and again at Antioch, the crusaders demoralized the garrisons by impaling the heads of their dead colleagues. Saladin did the same during his siege of Tiberias in 1187, while in 1153 the defenders of Ascalon hung the bodies of those killed in a failed assault over the battlements. During the siege of Milan, Adam de Palatio was hanged at the order of Frederick Barbarossa after a successful Milanese sally. When Barbarossa captured Corno Vecchio, all of the garrison had their right hands cut off. In 1224, Henry III swore that he would hang the garrison of Bedford if it failed to surrender, and duly did when the castle had to be stormed. Edward I reluctantly spared the gallant garrison of Stirling.[18] But if terror failed, specialized techniques and tactics were needed.

Castles were built to attack towns or other castles. William of Normandy used four against Domfront in 1052 and built one for his successful siege of Arques in 1053–4. The army of the First Crusade constructed three at Antioch. In 1102, Raymond of Toulouse began the famous Mont Pèlerin on a ridge dominating the city of Tripoli, which only fell long after his death in 1109; thereafter, the increasingly elaborate castle served as a formidable redoubt of defence for the city. At Tyre in 1111, Baldwin I built a fortified camp for his besieging force. At Alençon in 1118, the citizens admitted Fulk of Anjou into the town and he constructed what the sources refer to as a "park", an earthwork camp, as a base for his siege of the castle. Barbarossa built a camp for his siege of Manfred's castle near Castelleone in 1186, and the place surrendered on terms. In 1247, Frederick II created the grandiosely named "city" of Victoria, but his army was surprised by the besieged Parmans and destroyed. A camp provided shelter for the besiegers, protected them and their equipment from sallies, and provided a logistic base, as witness the huge booty of food seized by the Parmans at Victoria. At the same time, there was an obvious coercive purpose: Victoria was built only four bow shots away from Parma. However, fortified camps were not an invariable condition of success: the First Crusade built none during the siege of Jerusalem. By contrast, during the Third Crusade very elaborate fortifications ringed the crusader camp before Acre.[19] Sieges, especially of lesser castles, were often undertaken in a very casual way if no relief army was anticipated and the place was not strong, but bases were essential for operations against major fortifications.

There were a variety of stratagems for attacking fortifications. Wooden castles could be burned, although this was never as easy as we tend to think. An earthwork slope such as that of the motte made approach difficult – but not impossible, as the picture of Dinan in the Bayeux Tapestry shows. Setting fire against timber was by no means easy: Raymond of Aguilers spoke of mallets set with spikes being hurled at crusader machines during the final attack on Jerusalem in 1099, and another source tells us that a "newly invented" machine threw fire at the assault by the Count of Toulouse. The sources make fairly frequent reference to "Greek Fire" being used by the Muslims at the siege of Acre. The availability of naphtha and other oil derivatives in surface deposits probably explains why such fire-throwing was more common in the Middle East than in the West, where creating any form of "sticky fire" that could adhere to a wooden palisade and ignite it must have been difficult – and almost impossible in wet weather.[20]

A frequent stratagem was to undermine or batter down a wall with a ram or picks under the cover of showers of missiles. The approach of the attackers could be protected by mantlets, large panels of woven light wood. Armoured roofs or penthouses could be constructed, most simply of heavy logs leant against the defending wall, to shelter men working below. Alternatively, the roof could be mounted on wheels: such structures might be called "cats" or "sows". At Nicaea in 1097, most assaults were delivered by penthouses, some of which sheltered battering-rams. A battering-ram, used to break through the outer wall of Jerusalem in 1099, was then burned to make way for the siege-tower that was brought up behind it to dominate the main wall. Battering-rams suspended in siege-towers were used at Tyre in 1111–12, but the defenders used grappling irons and ropes to foil them. At Acre during the Third Crusade, a great ram protected by a penthouse was deployed, but the Muslim garrison managed to burn it. Edward I used a ram at Stirling in 1304. Penthouses could be employed to cover troops approaching a wall and to provide fire-cover: at the first siege of Toulouse in 1211 "cats" of boiled leather supported the attackers. An enormous wooden penthouse, massively armed, led the final abortive attack in 1217, in the course of which Simon de Montfort was killed.[21]

Deep mining was an alternative approach to undermining city or castle defences. Zengi seized Edessa in 1144 by undermining the walls using a system of natural tunnels. At Rochester in 1215, part of the curtain wall and then the southeast corner of the keep were undermined by a deep sap created by miners: in the case of the latter, the props in the sap were burned with the aid of the fat of 40 pigs. At Bedford, too, in 1224 the inner bailey and the keep were mined. In the Holy Land, both Crac des Chevaliers in 1271 and Marqab in 1285 fell to mining operations. But the success of deep mining depended on soil conditions: at Dover the soft rock made for easy progress and reduced the need for careful propping, but the miners with Edward I in Scotland in 1300 were of little use in the siege of marshy Caerlaverock. At Acre during the Third Crusade, countermining blocked French attempts to bring down the walls. At Bungay castle in Suffolk, a mine and a countermine, dating from 1174, are intact. At Alessandria, Barbarossa's "cat" covered the filling in of the ditch, supported a siege-tower and served to cover deep mining, but the defenders managed to collapse the tunnels. Even when mining was successful, the results were not always decisive; at Nicaea the breach was made late in the

day and filled in overnight, while at Dover and Acre defences were improvised after breaches were made. Mining was also relatively slow and demanded skilled labour, which might not be available.[22] Moreover,
fortifications could incorporate design features to prevent it. Heavy batters in
front of the wall could cause shallow mines to collapse before they reached
anything vital, while cisterns could be sited across likely lines of sap, offering
the possibility of flooding diggings. Overall, however, mining was the most
consistently successful tactic used against fortifications.

An alternative approach was to build huge wooden towers to overawe the
defences and enable others to attack them. The Vikings attacked Paris with
one in 885–6. At Verdun in 985, the siege-tower was dragged by ropes passed
around stakes close to the city wall, so that the oxen were moving away from
the enemy. In 1087, a Pisan and Genoese expedition employed similar towers
to capture Pantelleria. Such machines were not necessarily mobile. At the
siege of Pont Audemar in 1123, Henry I built a tower, but it was only used
to rain missiles into the castle, whose garrison had first to watch the burning
of the town around them and the devastation of the countryside. At Coria in
Spain in 1138, wooden towers acted as firing platforms, while at Bedford in
1224 the huge towers built for Henry III seem to have been used to mount
various kinds of stone-throwers which deluged the walls with missiles. At
Ma'arra on the First Crusade, the tower built by Raymond of St Gilles was
clearly mobile, but its purpose again was to act simply as a fire-base to cover
mining and assaults by ladder, which eventually carried the day. This was
probably the intended purpose of the towers in the siege of Jerusalem in July
1099, but that of Godfrey was fortuitously brought up close to the wall and
a bridge was improvised to make entry. Fully mobile siege-towers with
drawbridges to launch an assault became a feature of important sieges, notably
in the Holy Land where they were pre-eminent in the capture of the Muslim
cities of the coast. Barbarossa used them in Lombardy, and Edward I attacked
Bothwell castle in 1301 with a tower that had been transported in sections
and was covered in hides against fire. In the West, towers continued to be
important right down to the invention of cannons. At Lisbon, the Anglo-
Norman force brought up a tower some 28 m high and when this was
destroyed, they deployed another one, 25 m high, apparently built and commanded by a Pisan engineer; this proved to be the final straw for the garrison,
which surrendered.[23]

Such devices had very obvious limitations. The ground might be very
unfavourable, as at 'Arqa on the First Crusade, where the city walls crowned
a steep slope. In southern Italy, the relative isolation of inland places may have
made it difficult to get siege-machinery to them. Even where the ground was

117

generally suitable, it had to be smoothed and often ditches obstructed the route to the walls; at Jerusalem, the Count of Toulouse paid one penny for every three stones cast into the moat by the southern wall, while at Tortosa in 1148 a huge ditch 43 m wide and 32 m deep had to be filled. The clumsiness and weight of the towers meant that they needed to be built as close as possible to the point of attack. At Jerusalem in 1099, the defenders of the northern wall built up the walls, set up catapults and prepared beams and padding to repel the expected attack. The crusaders changed their assault point, and this was probably the decisive factor in the siege: near Zion Gate the Count of Toulouse had no room for manoeuvre and his tower was ultimately incapacitated by catapult attack and fire. A similar fate befell Bohemond's tower in the attack on Durazzo in 1108. Fire was the great enemy; the successful machine at Lisbon was covered with wet hides, with the animal tails hanging down for maximum flow, while at Jerusalem Godfrey's tower was soaked in vinegar against the defenders' "Greek Fire". During the siege of Tyre, the defenders built a war-crane on the city walls, which overtopped the crusader siege-towers and destroyed them by dropping incendiaries on to them.[24] Siege-towers were remarkable structures, but they were not a certain solution to the problem of attacking fortifications. Terrain was often a problem and countermeasures by the besieged could destroy them. Above all, they were costly and justified only for major objectives.

Artillery capable of battering fortifications and defenders into surrender, known in Roman times, continued to be used. At the siege of Paris in 885–6, *mangana*, *catapulta* and *balistae* are mentioned as hurling missiles. But these are only a few of the bewildering variety of words used by medieval writers to refer to siege engines. Unfortunately, their use is inconsistent and such descriptions as they give are confusing. Orderic tells us that at Brévol in 1092 a great machine was rolled up to the wall, which suggests a tower or penthouse, but adds that it hurled stones: it is possible that this was some kind of platform that accommodated a stone-thrower. Otto of Freising refers to a mangonel as a kind of *balista*, although this was a quite different kind of machine. The word *petraria*, rendered as *perrier* in French, is often, used but this merely means a stone-thrower. William of Tyre and Guillaume le Breton both clearly suggest that *perriers* were for heavy bombardment while *mangana* were lighter anti-personnel weapons, and the same notion about the latter is found in the *Chanson de la Croisade Albigeoise*.[25]

*Mangonella* would seem to be only a diminutive of *mangana*; in Roman times this referred to a weapon that depended for power on torsion. The *mangana* was a machine with a single arm, whose bottom end was embedded in a massive horizontal winding of sinew: the arm was bent back against the torsion of the winding and, when released, flew forward against a robust frame, hurling a stone out of a cup or sling on its end. The crash of impact between arm and bar probably explains the nickname *onager*, "the mule", for this machine. The missile was thus launched in an arc like the shell from a howitzer. The Roman *balista* was a crossbow-like weapon, but the "bow" consisted of two arms, each mounted in a vertically wound gathering of sinews, which provided the tension when the string was drawn to fire a bolt or ball: its trajectory would have been flat. The term *balista* in medieval sources generally refers to crossbows. Clearly related was the *arcu-balista* or later *springald*, a flat-trajectory weapon rather like a giant crossbow, which was widely used in sieges.[26]

The traction-trebuchet was the dominant form of artillery in our period. It was a device that originated in China and was transmitted to Europe by about the ninth century via the Arab world. It was essentially a beam pivoted between two high uprights: when the beam was pulled at one end by a team of men, the other flew up until a missile was released in an arcing trajectory either from a cup or, more effectively, from a sling. The pulling end of the beam was by far the shorter, in a ratio of perhaps 1:5, and the efficiency of the engine was enormously enhanced by the use of a sling on the throwing end. This kind of lever artillery varied in size, which partly accounts for the inconsistency of the language used to describe it; broadly, it would seem that *petraria* and *mangana* indicate sizeable examples and *mangonella* and *tormenta* lesser ones. There is no reason to believe that the principle of torsion was forgotten, but the impact of the throwing beam must have put enormous strain on the structure of the *onager*, which would have had to be very heavy to last any time, and of extraordinary size and weight to throw a large missile: lever-action machines were probably lighter and more durable. Moreover, the technology of lever-artillery could be easily assimilated by a society in which increasingly complex machinery, such as water mills with pivoting wheels and gears, was becoming common. At the siege of Jerusalem in 1099, both Albert of Aachen and Tudebode report that the crusaders used machines powerful enough to throw captured spies into the city; in the case cited by Tudebode, the machine had a sling, which, together with the presumed power, strongly suggests a traction-trebuchet and implies that they were not a novelty.[27]

None of these weapons could have had a decisive influence on siege-warfare. There is a good example of a traction-trebuchet at Caerphilly castle, which seems to approximate in size to those illustrated in the Maciejowski Bible and the work of Peter of Eboli: it throws a 15 kg ball about 120 m. It would have taken a long time to demolish stonework and was probably at its most effective against the fighting top of a wall or tower, the merlons, walkways, machicolations and hoardings that were so much more vulnerable.

This would have shortened its range to 50–60 m, although mounting it on a tower or a mound, as Edward I did at Edinburgh, would increase this. But machines were always very vulnerable to a sudden sally and had to be protected carefully: at the siege of Acre, Philip of France failed to do this and his artillery was burned. At the siege of Jacob's Ford, Saladin sent his men to find vine poles to set around his siege-engines.[28] Of course, the effectiveness of lever-artillery could be enhanced by continuous use and/or deployment of large numbers of machines. At Rouen in 1174, batteries of machines were kept going in eight-hour shifts. Uninterrupted action by massed forces of large machines would surely have smashed masonry in time, but the conditions in which large numbers of such machines could be gathered and operated were relatively rare, and before the end of the twelfth century there is little evidence of artillery smashing the main masses of castles and walled cities.

Moreover, defenders could make very good use of traction-trebuchets which, if they were mounted on towers, could certainly outrange attacking machines. In sieges in the Holy Land, siege-towers were the most important engines of assault. At Jerusalem in 1099, the defenders mustered 14 missile-throwers and concentrated nine of them against the tower of the Count of Toulouse, which was severely damaged. At Tyre in 1124, an Armenian artillery expert was brought in to direct counter-fire at the defenders' machines. At Milan in 1158, Barbarossa's troops seized the Roman arch and mounted a traction-trebuchet on it, but the defenders replied with two machines of their own, firing from the walls, and put this out of action.[29]

Accounts of late twelfth-century sieges do not suggest that siege-warfare had undergone any considerable change. On 26 July 1188, Saladin and his son al-Malik al Zahir besieged Saône. The Muslim army divided into two. Saladin attacked the east wall from across the great rock-cut ditch with four stone-throwers, causing damage at the northeast corner, where signs of repair are still evident. Al-Zahir's forces established themselves by the northern wall of the castle-town, where they set up two siege-engines, almost certainly at the spot where the walls follow the clifftop and leave a roughly triangular and relatively flat piece of land undefended. On 29 July, al-Zahir's forces made a breach and followed it up with a sudden assault, surprising the defenders and pouring into the town and the main fortress. The garrison fled to the great towers and negotiated terms of surrender.[30] The impact on the walls of the battering by a relatively small number of engines working over only two days is interesting, but it must be remembered that there was no counter-fire from within the castle. The main cause of the fall of Saône was simply that its garrison was hopelessly outnumbered, cut off from all hope of aid, and subjected to a two-pronged attack by Saladin's huge army, which divided their forces.

Again, at the siege of Acre we hear of severe damage being inflicted upon the walls of the city. Roger of Hovenden reports an unsuccessful attack made into a breach created by French engines, while Alberic Clement lost his life in another; although, interestingly, in this case only a part of the wall had fallen and the attackers had to carry in siege-ladders. Richard's men broke down a tower, but the rock-thrower seems to have supplemented mining, and this reminds us that, at the siege of Château Gaillard, Philip Augustus used a large traction-trebuchet to demolish the inner gate only after it had been undermined. The garrison of Acre were well supplied with engines of their own and destroyed the French traction-trebuchet, "Malvoisin". Their chief weapon against assault seems to have been "Greek Fire", brought to them by a Damascene coppersmith, which at least sometimes was projected by artillery. Descriptions of the damage inflicted suggest that it was largely on the walkways and that the walls were intact: a *petraria* built by the crusaders damaged part of a tower by shaking down two poles' length of its wall. This probably means a part of the walkway wall rather than the main structure. Moreover, Acre was besieged for a very long time and attacked by many methods – including mining, which may well have done much of the damage.[31]

In the very late twelfth and early thirteenth centuries, a new word comes to be used to describe hurling engines, variously spelt *trabuchetum*, *tribok* or *trabocco*. In about 1270, the French engineer, Villard de Honnecourt, drew a plan for a *trabucet*, and his description of the counterweight-trebuchet is supported by Egidio Colonna, writing in *c.* 1280, and Marino Sanudo, in about 1320. This kind of machine acted on the lever principle, but its load end was pulled down by a gang of men against a massive weight attached to its front end, normally using a winch for the purpose. The sling was then attached to the load end with a missile inserted, and when the rope securing it was released, the load end swung up, propelled by the massive weight at the front end. A radical improvement was the attachment of the weight in a pivoted basket. The range and power obviously depended on the size of the beam and the weights employed, but this kind of engine was capable of throwing substantial missiles. The front-end weight made for much greater accuracy than could be provided by a team of men, whose pull on the traction-trebuchet inevitably varied, thus altering the range. As in the traction-trebuchet, the principle was of a beam pivoted on a triangular frame. Comparison of two good modern replicas – one Danish and the other at Caerphilly castle – indicates the scale of the machine:

|                | Danish (m) | Caerphilly (m) |
|----------------|------------|----------------|
| Arm length     | 6.5        | 6.5            |
| Behind pivot   | 5.5        | 5.15           |
| Tower height   | 4.8        | 4.2            |
| Frame length   | 8.5        | 6              |
| Frame width    | 7          | 4.2            |

Massive beams of timber are used in both machines, and the Danish example has cast a 47 kg missile 100 m.[32] This would certainly be enough to inflict real damage on the main structure of a stone castle.

The earliest use of the term "trebuchet" is by Codagnellus, who says that a *trabuchis* was used at the siege of Castelnuovo Bocca d'Adda in 1199: this has been seized upon as evidence of the first appearance of the new counterweight-trebuchet in the west. However, on three of the occasions when he uses the word, Codagnellus seems to indicate a light weapon. The Genoese annals of the early thirteenth century mention trebuchets along with other weapons, sometimes specifically referring to them as quickly built. Rolandino of Padua mentions trebuchets and other machines mounted on a wooden belfry tower at the siege of Mussolente in 1249. This suggests that the term could be applied to a light weapon. But an illustration from the Genoese annals of 1227 offers very different evidence. It shows large traction-trebuchets with their firing beams in the characteristic semi-horizontal rest position; by contrast, two other machines at rest have their beams vertical, which is the characteristic position of the counterweight-trebuchets. The scale of the drawing makes it clear that these were very large, heavy machines.[33]

French evidence from the early thirteenth century indicates very clearly that the trebuchet was a large engine. The *Chanson de la Croisade Albigeoise* reports that Simon de Montfort used a *trabuquet* against Castelnaudary in September 1211: this was evidently a large and powerful machine, for with a single stone it demolished a tower, and with another a hall. Even allowing for poetic licence, this is suggestive. The Count of Toulouse attempted to retake the castle a little later, but was forced to abandon his camp and with it a trebuchet. Later in the *Chanson* there is a much clearer indication that the word *trabuquet* is being applied to a counterweight-trebuchet. As the defenders of Toulouse in 1217 prepared to meet the crusader attack, they "ran to the ropes and wound the trebuchets", while later we are told that, having set dressed stone in the slings of their *trabuquetz* "they released the ropes". These are very clear indications of what we are dealing with: the beam of a counterweight-trebuchet had to be "wound" or tensioned down and then "released": these actions are quite different from what was required of a traction-trebuchet. Moreover, the general descriptions offered in this poem suggest sizeable engines, for these weapons did great damage to the citadel of Toulouse held by the crusaders. At Toulouse in 1219, trebuchets were prepared for use against Louis VIII; they were differentiated from other stone-throwers by being put in the charge of men who were experienced in using them. The Tours chronicler reports that in 1226 the Avignonese used a similar array of machines, including trebuchets, against Louis. The first mention of a trebuchet in Germany, in 1212, says that it was then regarded as a new machine.[34]

English sources do not use the term "trebuchet" much in the thirteenth century. The Dunstable annalist says that Prince Louis of France brought a *tribuchetta* to the siege of Dover in 1217, but mentions only *petraria*, *maggunella* and *balisterii quam fundibularii* being used against Bedford in 1224, and Matthew Paris mentions the same range of machines. In 1224, Jordan the Carpenter made a trebuchet for Dover and in 1225 another for Windsor. At the siege of Kenilworth in 1266, Edward I deployed a number of *balistae*, some mounted on a tower, and 11 *petrarii*; the defenders replied with *mangonellae*. The huge machine built in August 1287 to attack Dryslwyn, and subsequently transported by between 40 and 60 oxen to batter Newcastle Emlyn into submission in January 1288, was probably a trebuchet, but the word is not used. The great engine which Edward I was so anxious to use against Stirling in 1304 is described by a chronicler as *immensis tormentis* and by neutral terms in the records, although it is almost certain, as Michael Prestwich comments, that a counterweight-trebuchet was actually used.[35]

The counterweight-trebuchet appears so suddenly that it was evidently an invention. Its creation must have been the outcome of careful thought and calculation, because performance depended on a number of variables, notably the shape of the hook that governed the release of the sling, the weight of the missile, the weight of the counterpoise, the ratio between the parts of the arm and the length of the sling. But formidable though it was, the counterweight-trebuchet did not radically alter the balance of advantage between attack and defence. Walls were built more strongly, and at Kenilworth, and later Caerphilly, the creation of large ponds around the main fortifications kept the weapon out of range. The construction and operation of the counterweight-trebuchet was the province of specialist engineers, who were not always available, and it was ponderous to transport. Its use was, therefore, limited, and traction-trebuchets remained popular because they were simpler and cheaper. The weapon had a limited range: trials on modern replicas suggest that it was of the order of 100–120 m, but at this distance projectiles would be striking the bases of walls rather than their weaker upper parts. Counterweight-trebuchets were deployed so close to their targets that the operators needed protection from the missiles of the defenders: the machine used against Dryslwyn and Newcastle Emlyn had a shelter to protect them. The dynamics of the traction-trebuchet are so complex that it must have been very difficult to change range. For example, a lighter missile will only go further if adjustments are made to the sling and the hook. The operator must have had to make very careful judgements balancing range against weight of missile, and taking into account local topography, weather and the strength of the target, in order to locate the machine; once *in situ* it was unlikely to be moved. Moreover, the quality of the missiles mattered. At Castelnaudary, stones that would not shatter had to be brought from "a long league away"; even so, one of them shattered, limiting damage. At Acre, Richard used very hard stones brought from the West, which were so unusual that they were specially shown to Saladin.[36]

Moreover, the counterweight-trebuchet could be as useful to the defender as to the attacker. We have noted that traction-trebuchets were deployed on towers that gave them enhanced range. Counterweight-trebuchets could be built within the walls. At Toulouse, Simon de Montfort's great "cat" was smashed by a stone from a counterweight-trebuchet, and he was killed by one thrown by a traction-trebuchet, allegedly worked by women. An illustration of the siege of Savona by the Genoese in 1227 shows a traction-trebuchet on the city wall being struck by a stone from a much larger machine fired by the attackers, and there is a similar picture in a manuscript of Peter of Eboli.[37]

In the Muslim East, enormous towers began to appear in the fortifications of the thirteenth century in order to carry counterweight-trebuchets: the most obvious example is the great square structure known as Baybars' Tower, which dominates the vulnerable southern wall of Crac des Chevaliers. The square towers at Bosra and the enormous round ones at Subeibe had the same function. This seems to reflect a much greater use of heavy missile-throwers in siege-warfare in the Middle East than in the West. Baybars even dragged such equipment up the terrible slopes of 'Akkar in 1271 after his success against Crac. At Acre in 1291, al-Ashraf deployed nearly 100 machines, including a great trebuchet called "The Victorious": this was siege-warfare on a scale unknown in the West.[38]

Western armies were occasional bodies, lacking a continuous existence which could nurture the special skills needed to build, operate and develop siege-equipment. Robert of Bellême and Gaston of Béarn were rare specialists at the turn of the eleventh and twelfth centuries. Even in the mid-twelfth century, Geoffrey of Anjou's engineering skills were evidently unusual. It is not strange that one of the penthouses built by the First Crusade to attack Nicaea in 1097 collapsed, while their mangonels were ineffective. In 1174, a Scottish traction-trebuchet was deployed against Wark castle, but its first missile fell on the team operating it. Many may have known in principle how to build machinery, but doing it was a different matter. However, military architecture was developing in the twelfth century and commanders needed weapons against it. It was a Genoese sailor, William Ricau, who built the siege machinery of the Provençals at Jerusalem in 1099. Guintelmus, a great engineer, was high in the councils of Milan during the conflict with Barbarossa. During the siege of Milan, Marchesius of Crema enjoyed rich rewards when he defected to Barbarossa. The rivalry of the Italian cities, their wealth and their commercial and maritime background, brought together all the skills needed for construction, but great kings were quick to follow suit. Henry II had engineers in his train, and specialized operators of siege-equipment.[39]

In the thirteenth century, engineers could enjoy great importance and their deeds are chronicled in the records of the period. Elias of Oxford served Richard I, while John bestowed a knight's fee upon Urricus. Masters Osbert and Bertram were prominent under Henry III. Edward I used a whole host of engineers and master-carpenters, supported by miners and others. Master Robert of Ulm supervised the mass of machinery deployed against Caerlaverock in 1300, and Master James of St George fulfilled the same role at Stirling in 1304. The engineer Jean de Mézos was raised to knighthood in 1254 by St Louis, while James I of Aragon employed the Italian engineer Nicoloso. Frederick II so valued his great Spanish engineer Calamandrinus that he kept him in shackles! By the end of the twelfth century, such people had become so important that the writer Guiot de Provins was dismayed at the prospect of their dominating war. There was little risk of this, because they were rewarded much more modestly than the traditional military caste: in war, status and conformity to the canons of chivalrous behaviour counted for more.[40] It is an interesting reflection on the importance of status in war that the siege of Lisbon, although it was a major victory over Islam and saw the employment of siege-equipment on a large scale, never seems to have enjoyed great renown in northern Europe, almost certainly because no notable person was present.

In fact, armies usually deployed every possible technique and instrument of war when they really wanted to capture a city or castle. No single method of attack was outstandingly effective, so they all had to be tried. No machine in this period actually altered the balance of advantage between attack and defence. The best way to seize a fortification was to isolate it with over-whelming numbers which, self-evidently, could prevent any relief. This required good leadership, skill, determination, organization and plentiful supplies – difficult enough to achieve when armies were transient.

It was pre-eminently kings who could achieve the conditions for success in siege-warfare. Strong centralized authority in England and France absorbed castles into the political system. They continued to have a military potential that could influence the political balance, and in times of weakness this could come to the fore. But their absorption into political systems reduced the need for sieges. In Germany after the death of Frederick II in 1250, political fragmentation mirrored that found in France at the beginning of our period, in a landscape dominated by castles; but large-scale siege employing complex machinery was rare, and the stalemate imposed by numerous cities and castles may even have increased the readiness to risk battle. In Italy, siege was more common because the area was dominated by great cities. The crusader settlements in the Holy Land after the Third Crusade were anchored by a few cities and great castles, and they were gradually reduced by a series of epic sieges, culminating in that of Acre in 1291, by an Islamic world with a highly developed siege technique. In all areas, fortifications continued to dominate the pattern of war.

Successful siege could achieve all that victory in battle offered and perhaps more, but at the price of much the same risks. Both kinds of action required enormous political and financial investment which could easily be lost. Duke William of Normandy's large force outside Gerberoi was taken by surprise by a sally and was scattered, as was Frederick II's camp before Parma in 1247. Relief forces could appear: William the Conqueror could not prevent a relief entering Arques in 1054; the First Crusade had to fight off enemy armies during the sieges of Nicaea and Antioch; Philip Augustus was forced to abandon the siege of Verneuil in 1194, when Richard suddenly cut his communications; and Charles of Anjou failed before Messina in 1282, because an Aragonese army came to its relief. Even when there were no such risks, the siege of a strong place was expensive: the siege of Bedford in 1224 was in part a political demonstration by the new king of his strength, but the employment of the latest in siege equipment and the concentration of large forces cost £1,311 18s. 2d. in wages alone, while the crushing of the Montforts in the siege of Kenilworth in 1266 required a huge effort and enormous expense.[41]

Sieges were simply a very specialized form of battle. They did what battle in other societies was designed to do – to destroy the basic strength of the enemy and acquire it for your own use. Strong central authorities absorbed cities and castles and used them where appropriate for large-scale confrontations of their own. But where an attack on a fortification was necessary, it remained as hazardous and difficult as ever, because no development or set of developments in the course of this period altered the balance between defence and attack. In 1310, Frederick of Austria gathered an army of Rhinelanders and Swabians, and allied with the Archbishop of Salzburg to ravage Bavaria and seize Wels, before besieging the castle of Schaerding. They had a large army, against which Otto of Hungary and Duke Stephen of Bavaria could muster only hastily raised forces, but lack of food, bad weather and loss of horses forced the abandonment of the siege – the failings of armies remained much as before.[42]

# Chapter Ten

# *Armies*

The face of war changed across the period 1000–1300. By the latter date, armies usually had more and better iron weapons. Many had siege-trains with specialized equipment and an apparatus of supply. But armies remained *ad hoc* bodies, whose structures were dominated by the gradations of landowning society and its preoccupations. It was always difficult to sustain them in the field and even the greatest of forces could melt away. There was a new professionalism, but it made little impact on command and its effect was limited by the inability of states to sustain armies in being.

Although there is some evidence that they tended to get larger by the end of the thirteenth century, armies varied in size considerably across the period. A great event such as the Conquest of England in 1066 could arouse even a small state to enormous efforts: in 1066, the Normans mobilized 14,000, amongst them 6,000–7,000 fighting men. Robert Guiscard gathered 15,000 for his attack on the Byzantine Empire in 1081–5. The sources often exaggerate numbers: Barbarossa's army at the siege of Milan in 1158 is said by both versions of the annals of Milan to have numbered 15,000 knights and an untold number of foot – Otto of Freising suggests 100,000 and the *Annales Sancti Disibodi* offers 50,000. The fact that on this occasion Frederick was forced to come to terms with Milan suggests something less than any of these figures: a reasonable guess would be about 15,000. Frederick probably raised an army of about the same size for the siege of Crema, for this was an enormous effort and we know that the emperor was supported by a number of German princes, including Henry the Lion, as well as his Italian allies. But after the fall of Crema this army went home, and at the battle of Carcano on 9 August 1160 Barbarossa could muster only some 400 cavalry and 2,500–3,000 foot. By May 1161, when Frederick moved to the siege of Milan, he had been reinforced, but still had only 2,100 German knights, with substantial numbers from his Italian allies and an unknown number of foot. The sources are somewhat clearer about the army that Frederick commanded at Legnano in 1176, which is reliably estimated at about 3,000–4,000 knights, supported by an unknown number of foot. Overall, the campaigns of Frederick Barbarossa suggest that in very favourable circumstances a major effort could raise 4,000–5,000 cavalry and about double that number of infantry, but that most of the time he had to rely on much smaller forces. Angevin armies were quite small – Henry II operated with about 600 mercenary foot plus cavalry, although armies 5,000 strong were raised in the years of rebellion, 1173–4. At Bouvines, there were less than 20,000 men in all.[1]

In 1277, Edward I could dispose of a maximum of 15,500 men in Wales, while for the war of 1282–3 around 20,000 were raised, and the rebellions of 1287 and 1294–5 required 11,000 and 31,000 respectively. It must be said that these are overall numbers: they were not raised at one time and were never deployed in one place. The Flemish campaign of 1297 raised 7,800, but 26,000 were recruited for the Falkirk campaign of 1298, although thereafter numbers fell off.[2] These figures contrast with the small size of the armies of Henry II, but Edward was certainly not alone in being able to raise large armies.

At Cortenova on 27 November 1237, Frederick II was said by Piero della Vigna to have led over 10,000 to victory, but they were only a part of the force with which he had attacked Mantua and Brescia that autumn, because he had sent others away to deceive his Milanese enemies into thinking that he was dispersing his army. Its precise number is difficult to arrive at, but a core of 2,000 German knights was augmented by the men of Trento and forces from Cremona, Parma, Modena and Reggio, together with a force of 500 knights under Ezzelino di Romano. Between 7,000 and 10,000 Saracen archers from Lucera also joined him, many of whom were mounted. If he had 3,000 cavalry plus about the same number of Saracen horsemen, we can guess at a total for his force of over 20,000, although since he had to garrison captured castles it is unlikely that so many were ever gathered together in one place. Against these were ranged the Milanese, who are alleged by imperialist propaganda to have suffered 10,000 casualties. The Piacenzan annals say that 800 Milanese knights and 3,000 foot were captured, together with rather more than 253 knights from amongst the allies. Since we know that this largely Milanese army had to use two roads to cross the Oglio, it does seem that a large army had been assembled, of about the same order as that of the emperor.[3]

In 1265, Charles of Anjou was designated King of Sicily by the pope, who preached a crusade to support his expedition. The result was a mixed force, including many notable French barons, and a mass of mercenaries who cannot easily be distinguished from crusaders. Contemporaries alleged that the whole army numbered 6,000 cavalry, 600 mounted bowmen and 20,000 foot, half of whom were crossbowmen. However, when it came to battle they had to struggle to defeat Manfred, whose cavalry did not exceed 4,000, so we might guess that we can reduce these numbers considerably. If we suppose that the accretion of allies and losses were somewhat in balance, this would seem to have been a very large and well equipped army of about 4,000 cavalry and 10,000–12,000 infantry.

Two years later, in the campaign that culminated at Tagliocozzo, Charles could raise only 4,000 knights against 5,000–6,000 under his enemy Conradin. In France, Philip III raised 8,000 men, including about 1,500 knights, for his crusade against Aragon in 1285, while Philip IV raised 1,600–1,700 cavalry and perhaps as many as 20,000 infantry against Flanders later in the century. Many of the foot may have been used for the low-grade tasks of occupation and spoiling. At Courtrai in 1302, 2,500 heavy French cavalry were supported by a substantial infantry force, perhaps 6,000 strong, with many crossbowmen.[4]

In Germany the greater princes, and certainly alliances between them, could also raise substantial armies. At Worringen on 5 June 1288, the Duke of Brabant and his allies pitted about 2,000 horse of varied quality together with 2,000–3,000 foot against a similar force led by the Archbishop of Cologne. But, according to the Osterhofen annal, in 1310 Frederick of Austria gathered what was simply recorded as a very large force, which was reinforced by the 15,000 horse and foot of Archbishop Conrad of Salzburg for the siege of Schaerding. They were opposed by 1,500 knights and 60,000 "rustics" under the command of Otto of Bavaria.[5] It should be noted that at Schaerding the attacking force melted away quickly for lack of food.

The fluctuations in the size of armies, even those gathered by the same leader, have fairly obvious explanations. Commanders tailored their effort to the demands of the situation that they faced. There was a limit to the pressure that they could exert on allies to produce troops. Above all, there were the political and social limitations imposed by the basis of recruitment. A king or great lord could levy as many troops as he could afford from his demesne, and these formed the core of his army. The more important of his vassals owed him service for their lands, but the basis of this was not always clear, and the German nobles resisted any fixing of quotas under Barbarossa. Even where service was admitted in principle, in practice norms were not fixed; and even when they were, as in England, there was a limit to what the king could demand – as King John discovered. The English monarchy was powerful, yet an English army was a snapshot of a king's political standing at the moment of its gathering. Barons saw their service as, in a sense, freely given in return for political influence. To accept money was to accept subordination, but to stand outside such a royal force would be to lose influence. Necessity pressed Roger Bigod to accept money for his service in Scotland in 1297–8, but in the following year he served at his own cost as a demonstration of his independence, for then he could leave as he wished. Many barons served Edward I on some occasions with more knights than they, in any sense, owed. In a strong monarchy this was the currency, or part of the currency, of political power. The system suited both parties in different ways. The king occasionally received more than he could ask for and the magnates felt that honour was satisfied and their influence acknowledged. It was an untidy situation, but it satisfied the social conservatism of the day, with its emphasis on tenurial relationships; formal contractual relationships for the provision of troops only began to appear in England and France at the very end of the period.[6]

In England and France, the wealth of the monarchy meant that their personal followings were enhanced by hiring troops for pay, and indeed kings increasingly paid most of those who served in their armies. In twelfth-century England, scutage became a form of tax, while in 1202–3 Philip Augustus was maintaining a standing force of 250 knights and about ten times that number of archers, crossbowmen and foot. Edward I tried to raise a wholly paid force for the Welsh war of 1282. This was possible because of the new efficiency of the administrative machines of England and France. Warfare was the motor of English administrative development under Henry I and Henry II. By the time of Edward I, the great offices of state had become established in London, but the king was surrounded by a complex administrative household, which undertook major functions in its own right. In France, one of our earliest detailed financial documents relates to military administration under Philip Augustus, while St Louis carried out a thorough-going reorganization of governmental structures. Philip IV, like his English contemporaries, was served by professional bureaucrats, amongst whom Nogaret and Flotte are only the most notorious. In northern Italy, the cities were developing professional administrations and systematic records. The frequent state of war there made the efficient raising of taxes for armies a necessity. The same impulse had much the same effects in the papal states, while Hohenstaufen and Angevin Sicily had long had an efficient administrative and taxation system. In Germany, Gislebert of Mons described the most notable of those who attended Barbarossa's great court at Mainz in 1184 in terms of the scale of their military followings. The governmental structure of the Empire itself was very limited by the thirteenth century, but the greater princes developed their administrations although there was enormous variation in size and efficiency. The eclipse of royal power in Germany after 1250 allowed some of these to develop and precipitated bitter rivalries and feuds. The great archbishopric of Cologne was virtually destroyed as a principality by the end of the thirteenth century, while by contrast the new dynasty of the Wittelsbachs emerged to dominate Bavaria. German history was dominated by "the political dynamics of diversity", but the greater German princes and towns were able to establish a highly profitable domination of communications and to secure and exploit their lands by castles administered by *ministeriales*.[7]

We should not exaggerate the effectiveness of this new machinery. No political power could yet make a budget and all were driven to desperate expedients to make ends meet. Edward I borrowed against his taxes on the wool trade, providing a liquidity which was very useful for paying armies, but the wars in Wales, Scotland and France in the 1290s ran him into debt. Philip IV needed to tread carefully to raise money after the defeat at Courtrai in 1302, negotiating carefully for taxes and fearful of rebellion. In both of these realms, the king had a permanent bodyguard and the nucleus of a military staff, but armies continued to be raised on an *ad hoc* basis, relied on voluntary support, and were paid off as quickly as may be. In Wales, Edward's great castle of Beaumaris remained unfinished, as a striking witness to his financial problems. Frederick II was caught out by the rebellion of Viterbo in 1243 because he had already paid off his troops. Charles of Anjou had an efficient military machine resting on the use of mercenaries, but heavy taxes drove Sicily into insurrection and ruined his vaunting ambition to dominate the Mediterranean.[8]

On the other hand, great strides were made in recruiting. In England, the *Statute of Winchester* of 1285 utilized the old obligation of freemen to bear arms, originally a product of the needs of public order, to create a new recruiting base. Under Edward I, influential men, supported by local officials, were appointed Commissioners of Array, to select troops from amongst the county levies.[9] This was the base from which Edward raised the huge infantry armies that he unleashed upon Wales and Scotland. Quite how the Commissioners operated we do not know, but presumably some men were ready to serve for money and others could be influenced in one way or another. In any case, the system was effective.

These mass infantry contingents were a European-wide phenomenon. By the mid-thirteenth century, the French monarchy had asserted a universal obligation to military service which would yield footsoldiers. Some of these were contributed by great lords and others by the urban communes. We hear of units of foot, the "constabularies" which contained between 50 and 150 men, being raised from the villages. The basis of selection is no more known than it is for England. However, it yielded similar results – very large masses of infantry. The Flemish cities produced large forces of such men, who defeated the chivalry of France at Courtrai in 1302 with a force of about 10,000. At Montaperti in 1260, the Florentine army defeated by Siena contained 14,000 infantry to 1,400 cavalry. In Germany, there were said to be 23,500 foot in the Hungarian army which fought at the Marchfield on 26 August 1278. These infantry masses were not an unmixed blessing. Peasant recruits to the Crusade against Aragon were said to have impeded the French army in 1285, while Edward I's forces deserted in huge numbers.[10] But these forces would not have been recruited had they been militarily useless.

The infantry were accompanied by increasingly effective and well equipped cavalry. The territorial obligation to military service remained important throughout our period, but increasingly it was for the creation of a pool of equipped, trained, mounted and, above all, willing cavalrymen, who were paid to serve. All from the upper ranks of society retained a military character and very large numbers must have served at some time in their lives: this is the pattern suggested by the French records. It was only a restricted group who chose the warrior's way of life. One such appealed for help in old age to the Capetian kings on the grounds that: "I have served you and your ancestors in the year when they went to Damietta, and to Sicily, and at the siege of Marseilles and that of Tunis". Such men had always existed, but the pattern of enhanced social choice which had developed by the later thirteenth century must have made them more specialized and probably more effective. Many nobles and gentry served on an occasional basis, however, and light forces were often included amongst them, so that the cavalry remained of very mixed quality. Edward I mobilized about 4,000 cavalry for the campaign of 1298, although these were probably never gathered together in one body, while in 1302 the French army at Courtrai had about 2,500 of the finest cavalry.[11]

Italy is sometimes seen as being rather different, because of its reliance on mercenaries. In northern Italy, the lack of a central authority resulted in a state of continuous war fanned by constant external interference – German, French and Aragonese – throughout the thirteenth century. The *contado* of most cities was relatively small, and so there was an enormous demand for mercenary troops, especially knights, drawn from the petty landholders of the Italian countryside or from German and other foreign adventurers who would strengthen their armies. In 1229–31, Siena recruited men from all over northern Italy, together with French and Germans, while Castilians and Germans fought in the Milan war of 1275–7. At the Battle of Campaldino in 1289, 500 of the Florentine contingent of 1,000 knights were mercenaries. The distinction between Italy and northern Europe was not, however, truly very great, because fighting for money was everywhere a norm. It was simply that the cities had to look far from their own territories for paid men and so the professionalization of war was simply more explicit than elsewhere, not least because the literate society of the cities and the state of continuous warfare produced standard contracts, *condotte*, with standard terms for service. It is interesting that the matters that they regulated – division of spoil, treatment of captured prisoners and compensation for loss of horses – were all precisely the kinds of matters that Edward I had to negotiate with his noble followers.[12]

What was novel about the armies of the Italian cities was the growing tendency to hire companies of mercenaries, using commanders as subcontractors. This was a great convenience for a city and saved enormous administrative effort. Militarily, it was a very significant step along the road to the great companies that would so influence war in the later Middle Ages, because regular existence under a single commander could make collections of soldiers into disciplined units. Perhaps the most spectacular example of one such was the Grand Catalan Company, which seized the Frankish duchy of Athens in 1311 and held it until 1388. Less notable, but no less important for the future, were the 60 men raised by the Earl of Cornwall for the Gascon war in 1294 for one year, for the sum of £1,000. But the companies raised in thirteenth-century Italy remained quite small; they seem to have had shifting populations and to have been much concerned with police functions within a city. William de la Torre was a Catalan commander who served 15 years in the armies of Siena, Florence and Bologna between 1277 and 1292, with companies that never amounted to more than 100. His employment was precarious in the extreme, and he never became one of the Captains of War being employed by cities in the late thirteenth century.[13]

These "Captains" of war – professionals set in charge of the whole military effort of a city – were an extremely important development in the cities of Italy. There were parallel developments, pointing the way to more regular organizations in northern Europe. Edward I was accompanied by a military household which acted as a nucleus and a command structure for the armies that he raised. When St Louis left the Holy Land, he continued to support a French regiment at Acre, commanded by Geoffrey of Sargines. Philip IV of France was served by Constables, Marshals and Masters of the Arbalesters, who were largely military specialists. Below them were regional captains such as Robert de Wavrin, Guichard de Marzi, Blayn Loup and Jean de Burlas, who were military governors in the disputed Aquitaine and could act as generals if required.[14] These men really were professionals of war.

Political and social conservatism were powerful in all armies. The great lords of a kingdom, the chief followers of a prince, had to be given honourable positions in war. It was to the "honourable" that the greatest rewards continued to go, and this was reinforced by the recruitment of cavalry from amongst their ranks. Men of rank, even if not fortune, needed to "look up" to those who led them into battle. The new needs of war introduced a group of highly skilled technicians – builders of castles and creators of siege-weapons – but they were never rewarded on anything like the scale of the "honour-able" soldier, as we have seen: hence that paradox, that armies, such as those of Edward I, which would spend much time in siege were dominated by men whose vocation was warfare in the open field. The armies of the French and English kings continued to be largely made up of magnate contingents, and this was reinforced as those who wished to please their prince would bring along volunteers in excess of their obligations. This social conservatism was less notable in Italy, although the new leaders who emerged, the "Captains", tended to be of gentle birth.

For the most part, the largely *ad hoc* armies of this period were rather like onions, in that there was always a core of loyal and fairly dependable troops around which the force was built. In England, the royal household troops were the core and usually formed a division in any army. On occasion, they could be expanded to count as many as 1,000 cavalry. The French too had a similar elite nucleus. James I of Aragon depended on his household men to form the centre of his army during the attack on Mallorca. Even forces that at first sight appear to be quite different took on this form. The conquest of the Baltic lands is associated with the monastic military orders of the Sword-Brothers and the Teutonic Order. But the Sword-Brothers formed an elite of heavy cavalry which spearheaded more occasional crusading armies. The Teutonic Order were much better organized. They had a grim and close discipline. They saw to the business of building blockhouses and establishing an infrastructure of conquest, but they too relied on other elements. They had their own knightly vassals and could call on military service from the towns that they founded. But it was the crusade, preached on an international scale, which drew in large armies around them, enabling them to take leaps forward – in the 1230s, Polish, Pomeranian and German forces played a crucial role.[15] But the heart of a medieval army was the commander's own troops and they were always its most crucial element.

Of course, the associated forces that supported commanders were them-selves organized. Some of Edward I's magnates seem to have had military households which they expanded in time of need, and this was true across Europe. But, like the royal household, these fluctuated in size and in person-nel. Warfare demanded that the retinues of nobles should be formed into larger units. In almost all descriptions of armies, we come across references to cavalry or infantry. The retinues of kings and nobles had to be incorporated within these great divisions. The foot and cavalry were divided into units, commonly called *acies*, a rather loose term which can be translated as battle-line or even squadron, "battle" in the old English sense of a unit or "*bataille*" in French: in Italy, *sclera*, related to the older word *scara*, is used, often in the form *schiera*. At Benevento in 1266, both the armies of Manfred and Charles of Anjou ordered themselves in three *acies*. Within these larger unities, knights seem to have been ordered in much smaller units of between 10 and 40, called *conroi*. In English armies of the late twelfth and thirteenth centuries, the knight–banneret seems to have been a minor commander with a force upwards of 13 knights, and was usually distinguished by carrying a square banner rather than a pennant. There were *milites bannerii* in the army with which Philip III attacked Foix in 1271.[16] But these were not standardized units like modern sections, platoons and companies, and "battles" varied enormously in size, being tactical units rather than organizational entities. Moreover, what little evidence we have shows that even within the smallest units there was little continuity of service in most cases. Moreover, considerations of rank disrupted these units as elements in a command structure.

It was only occasionally that medieval armies became highly cohesive and disciplined. This was nearly always the result of circumstance combined with good leadership. The army of William the Conqueror probably profited from its long sojourn at Dives, and the army of the First Crusade achieved a remarkable cohesion on its long march to Jerusalem. The protracted siege of Acre and the presence of Richard forged the army of the Third Crusade into a formidable fighting machine, despite quarrels amongst its leaders. Philip Augustus's army which he turned against Normandy in 1202–3 seems to have been unusually well ordered. In South Italy, Charles of Anjou was heavily dependent upon a nucleus of French settlers, and they seem to have formed a very professional army.[17] But there was no linear progression, no gradual and sustained improvement of armies, and in this respect those of the thirteenth were very little different from those of the twelfth century.

Maintaining armies also remained a difficult business. Edward I paid much attention to supply, but his armies in Wales and Scotland sometimes suffered from desperate shortages of food. Hardship was indeed a norm of war, and the rigours of the weather were especially severe in northern climes; the Crusades on Germany's northeastern frontier were generally limited to a few months because of the severity of the winter. Armies found it difficult to operate in any kind of extreme climate. In the summer of 1172, a huge Almohad army besieged Huete, whose defenders were almost driven to surrender by lack of water. They were heartened by a sudden storm, and the heat which had favoured the attackers now made it difficult for them to find food, so their great army broke up. In October 1199, the Milanese retired from the siege of a Cremonan fortified camp near Castelnuova Bocca d'Adda because of the autumn cold and rain. In 1216 in fighting near Pontenure, many horses died because of the heat, and the same happened in a battle between Verona and Ferrara in 1243. At Hattin, Saladin skilfully used the heat of the Palestinian July and the shortage of water to demoralize the Frankish army.[18]

Disease was a terrible scourge which could weaken armies. As late as the First World War, the ratio of battle to non-battle casualties was 1:1.3, while in the American Civil War twice as many died from disease as by violence. On the First Crusade, Anselm of Ribemont recorded the deaths of 13 of his acquaintances, seven by enemy action and six by disease: in the summer of 1098, as the crusader army rested at Antioch, plague struck. In 1167, Barbarossa's army at Rome was virtually destroyed by disease. The Christian army that won the great victory of Las Navas de Tolosa in 1212 broke up shortly after because of plague.[19]

Armies could do little to prevent or treat disease or to heal wounds. In his life of St Louis, Joinville gives us a horrific picture of the injuries suffered in battle at Mansourah: "Hugues d'Ecot received three wounds in the face from a lance, and so did Raoul de Wanou, while Frédéric de Loupey had a lance-thrust between his shoulders, which made so large a wound that the blood poured down his body as if from the bung-hole of a barrel. A blow from one of the enemy's swords landed in the middle of Erard de Siverey's face, cutting through his nose so that it was left dangling over his lips." The next day when the fighting was renewed, he and his knights could not wear armour because of the wounds that they had suffered. The wounded had to care for themselves or perish, in which case they would be lost to the army. During the battle of Santa Ponza in the Mallorcan campaign, James I angrily sent a knight back into battle because he had merely been wounded by a stone in the mouth. If men had more than superficial wounds their chances of survival in an age of very limited medicine were low, and even lesser injuries could be fatal: Richard I died of a crossbow wound in the shoulder. Efforts were made to care for the injured in Spain, and there is evidence that in the Holy Land the Order of the Hospital had a kind of field-ambulance service to care for the injured.[20] Wounds and disease were an attrition in all medieval armies which commanders were simply forced to accept.

The treatment of prisoners varied according to rank. The accounts of Tinchebrai barely mention the fate of the infantry, although many of them were cut down, while the massacre of the Frankish infantry after Hattin is mentioned only in passing by Western sources, which were far more interested in the noble and knightly. The sources for the wars in Lombardy mention the death of infantry in a casual and passing way. The slaughter of infantry was usual, simply because there was little alternative, especially if men were captured far from their homes. Armies found it difficult enough to care for their own, let alone prisoners. They were, after all, worthless in the literal sense of the word: in western Europe slavery was not an economic institution, so there was little profit in keeping them alive. In the Middle East and Spain, economic conditions were different and slavery was a viable alternative.[21]

But the well-to-do were another matter. Ransom was very profitable and all over the West the usual practice was to spare knights if possible in anticipation of a good ransom. It is a notable characteristic of the sources for the wars in Lombardy that defeated knights are noted to have been taken to prison in victorious cities, which suggests a kind of infrastructure of prisoner-exchange. So, for the most part, gentry could expect to survive. Even in the Crusader states, ransom was the common practice, and following Hattin, Saladin looked after his notable captives. Of course, captivity was not a pleasant experience. William of Bretueil was kept in a miserable cell through a freezing winter until he agreed generous terms with his captors; while, after Bouvines, Ranaud de Danmartin was laden with chains – but then he was a rebel. Joinville has left us an account of the terrors of the early stages of captivity, and of the terrible sufferings endured after Louis's surrender in the Nile Delta and the many resulting deaths. But the capture of an entire army thousands of miles from home was an unusual situation, and many of the captors were kind.[22] Ransom was so profitable that it could be regulated and controlled only by the strongest of commanders.

Armies changed across the period 1000–1300. By the end of the period they tended to be larger, better organized and better supplied. They contained more professional soldiers in that more and more of those who served in them were paid men who had chosen soldiering. But the persistent association of rank, political power and military authority meant that there could be no clear chain of command. Medieval armies were not monolithic. Their leading members, the knights and lords, equipped themselves and served, as they saw it, in a special position and of their free will. Armies remained *ad hoc* bodies. They had no infrastructure of training or uniformity of weapons. As a result, they depended on the personal valour of those who could afford to equip and train themselves. They belonged to a privileged caste whose habit was not to submerge themselves in the anonymity of mass, and while they clearly saw the need for a degree of cohesion and discipline, their whole social context generated a sense of individualism. The literature of the *Chansons de Geste*, which was written for them, represents war in highly individualistic terms, of man-to-man conflicts, and because much of war was small in scale, this corresponded to the experience of their audience. This whole ethos was bound up with the nobility's sense of social position and identity as a ruling elite. In these circumstances, armies changed only slowly.

# Chapter Eleven

# *Commanders*

If he wished to encourage and persuade his followers to risk their lives, the medieval commander had to embody the military values and so, perforce, he had to fight in the front rank. A man who has to persuade can hardly ask others to take risks which he himself refuses. This is how the Bayeux Tapestry portrays William the Conqueror at Hastings. When part of his army fled, he was on hand to rally the troops. When the Normans and North French were suddenly attacked by the Turks at Dorylaeum, Bohemond and Robert of Normandy were there to steady the panic. In an army of individuals and small groups, this was generalship of a very high order. Such exposure was absolutely vital. Suger is at pains to show Louis VI in the forefront of battle, while at Lincoln King Stephen displayed admirable valour, and at Bouvines both Philip Augustus and Otto IV were exposed to mortal danger. St Louis is shown in the thick of the fight by Joinville, while Charles of Anjou led the second battalion at Benevento. The appeal of brave leadership resting on shared values was very powerful, but of course it could have disastrous results, for these values were essentially individualistic. At Lincoln, Stephen gave battle because he scorned to fly, while Frederick Barbarossa seems to have been moved by similar motives to accept the challenge of the Milanese army at Legnano in 1176: both ignored advice to the contrary and neither seems to have been much reproached for this. By contrast, John's signal failure to lead his forces during the fighting in Normandy in 1203–4 earned him widespread opprobrium.[1]

But gallantry was not enough to command an army. The medieval commander needed to have sufficient troops of his own to form a central core for the army. Given the individual ethos of the European elite, such a dominance was what they repected – it represented a commitment of resources to parallel the commitment of the body in the front line. William the Conqueror recruited his own men for the Conquest of England, while Edward I's household troops usually made up a whole division of his army. While possession of such a force gave no certainty of victory, commanders who did not have one tended to come to grief: Otto IV at Bouvines and Conradin at Tagliacozzo are clear examples.[2]

A readiness to fight in the front line and a commitment of resources were not a guarantee of the ability to handle armies, and judge ground. That came with experience of the small-scale warfare which was the common experience of war. This kind of fighting must have made commanders were well aware of the need for intelligence about the enemy and his movements. Harold sent a spy to Normandy in the summer of 1066, and William had informants in England. Indeed, William was very careful to seek information about his enemies, and the Bayeux Tapestry shows his scouts watching the enemy army. As the crusaders approached Ascalon in 1099, they tortured prisoners to discover the dispositions of their enemies. The Angevins were no less aware of the need for good information. James I of Aragon used spies to gain entry into Almaçora, while as his army advanced towards Valencia he refused to allow an attack on an enemy force until he was sure that there were no obstacles such as watercourses that might bring a charge to grief.[3] But cunning and ruses are one thing – commanding a large force is quite another.

The performance of medieval commanders in major campaigns and battles has to be measured against the fact that such occasions were infrequent and might occur at any stage in their career. The generality of military experience, even for a king, was small-scale, and so there could be little training for these great occasions. Louis VI made prudent dispositions against an attempt by the Count of Champagne to raise his siege of Gournay in 1107, but at Brémule on 20 August 1119 rashness got the better of him, and he unleashed a poorly ordered charge against the well organized troops of Henry I, with disastrous results. Experience, force of personality and will were then, as now, vital elements in the make-up of a commander. Frederick Barbarossa, as a young man, was a virtually helpless witness of the destruction of the German army on the Second Crusade. Probably as a result, he controlled the German army on the Third Crusade very tightly indeed, but it fell apart when he died *en route*. Louis VII was very inexperienced in handling a large army and during the Second Crusade his vanguard simply marched away from the main body, exposing his forces to heavy losses. It was extraordinarily difficult to control the relatively incoherent forces of medieval armies. During the siege of Acre, for example, before the arrival of the kings of England and France, the footsoldiers forced the leaders to allow them to attack Saladin's camp, with disastrous consequences.[4]

It must have been extraordinarily difficult for kings and great nobles to live up to the expectations of their military followers. They had to be in charge, yet also be ready to consult – and all this under the pressure of nightmare events. In his account of the battle of Mansourah on 8 February 1250, Joinville paints a vivid picture of Louis IX as a commander under pressure. The premature charge of Robert of Artois and the Templars into Mansourah had greatly weakened his army, which was attacked by the Egyptians. In the wake of this emergency, Joinville reports blithely "In the meantime I and my knights had decided to go and attack some Turks who were loading baggage in their camp on our left": he had to be rescued from this diversion by the Count of Anjou. Louis was advised by Jean de Valery to move closer to the river, and agreed to this, but only after consulting his advisers, who were pulled out of the battle-line for this conference. Then the noble leaders of the next division begged him not to go, as they were under pressure, and the movement was halted, only to be resumed briefly until Jean de Valery returned. Shortly after, the king was persuaded to change direction towards Mansourah in the hope of rescuing Robert of Artois, and was nearly captured. Ultimately, he concentrated his forces by the river and was reinforced by crossbowmen, whose arrival frightened off the enemy.[5]

St Louis had never handled a large army in battle before, but the emphasis in this account on consultation was not simply a reflection of that inexperience. He may have been unusually punctilious, but any monarch or leader had to consult, because persuasion, not command, was the only way to get things done. In July 1187, Saladin besieged Tiberias. King Guy summoned the host of Jerusalem and a series of councils of war followed. As a king, he had a clear obligation to go to the aid of the Countess of Tripoli, who was shut up in the besieged city: aid to a vassal was a fundamental duty of any lord, even if it was contrary to good strategic sense. The debate on that July day in 1187 has attracted enormous attention because of the consequences of the decision to give battle at Hattin, but there was nothing unusual about the situation. As Charles of Anjou approached King Manfred's army outside Benevento, his advisers debated whether to attack immediately or rest. In the end, it was the determination of Giles le Brun, Constable of France and guardian of the young Count of Flanders, who tipped the balance, saying that he would fight instantly no matter what others felt; it was a display of mulish truculence to match anything in the debate before Hattin, but his side won the battle.[6]

It is hardly surprising that although rank continued to be all-important for the face of war, professionals began to take a more and more important role in the conduct of armies. Robert of Bellême is mentioned in 1091 as having a specialist knowledge of siege-machinery, which he later applied on the First Crusade. William of Ypres was a claimant to the county of Flanders, who became a trusted commander under Stephen in the English civil war. He fought at Lincoln, and then rallied the royal forces and led them to victory at the rout of Winchester, which rescued Stephen from captivity. He had worthy successors in Mercadier and Cadoc, who served Richard I and Philip Augustus, and the mercenary commanders of King John. But such men lived in the shadows of their masters. William Marshal was also a professional soldier, but he lived in nobody's shadow. He was a younger son of distinguished though not wealthy parents, and he was certainly well connected. He made his way as a soldier and a noted professional in the art of the tournament, displaying his undoubted skills before the magnates and kings of Europe. William was an experienced soldier, always careful to lead by example, sometimes to the point of folly – at the age of 50 he led the assault on the castle of Milli in person. It is significant that his biographer portrayed him as a model of chivalry, and that it is upon this aspect of his activities rather than his function as a general that modern comment has focused.[7] William Marshal exemplified the values of his class and age. By contrast, William of Ypres, although of high birth, was widely suspected of complicity in the murder of Charles the Good in 1127, while Mercadier and his like were people of obscure origins.

Because of the enormous demands on kings and great princes who were the ultimate leaders of war, specialized commanders did emerge. Philip Augustus created a whole corps of new men, amongst whom were distinguished soldiers such as Bathélemy de Roye and Henri Clément. At Bouvines, the effective military commander seems to have been a cleric, Guérin, the bishop-elect of Senlis, a Hospitaller knight who always wore his habit. In 1266, Charles of Anjou went ahead to Rome, leaving his army to follow him under the command of Peter and William of Beaumont, but they were assisted by notable soldiers, including Philip of Montfort, who would lead the attack at the battle of Benevento. The battle of Worringen on 5 June 1288 is recorded in great detail by Jan van Heelu's *Rijmkronijk*, which gives the leading role to the victorious Duke John of Brabant; Verbruggen, however, suggests that the real commander was the Count of Virneburg.[8]

As yet, such people played subordinate roles, and it was on the person of the king or great noble that the light played. There were many successful warriors, notably William the Conqueror, but the greatest commander within this period was undoubtedly Richard I. Richard took risks as a matter of policy and it was this which endeared him to his own generation. He too sought advice, but in the end he had the personality to impose himself on others and the skill to recognize military opportunities. At Gisors, he moved quickly to inflict a severe defeat upon Philip Augustus, although he later admitted that his counsellors had been against the risk. During the Third Crusade he managed to control a very disparate army and to adapt to conditions in the East. He also had a keen strategic grasp: he threw a network of alliances around Philip Augustus, while in the Holy Land he wanted, above all, to strike at Saladin's real heartland, Egypt.[9] But whereas we have only an external picture of Richard, one notable commander of the age, James I of Aragon (1213–76), has left us a personal memoir which is worth examining for the insight that it provides into the mind of a medieval commander.

James was only five in 1213 when he was captured after the Battle of Muret, in which his father was killed, and, throughout his long minority, relations with his important vassals were difficult; in Aragon, he had to face open noble defiance and in Barcelona he was not fully recognized until 1228.[10] He first came to prominence in the successful expedition to Mallorca of 1229. This was a Catalan project, and it was their church and nobility who took the initiative to create the army and fleet that sailed on 5 September 1229 – the Aragonese did not participate. James was not allowed to land until a bridgehead had been secured, and when he involved himself in a skirmish he was reproved by the nobles. On 12 September, the main Muslim force came to battle at Santa Ponza. James, in his memoirs, presents himself as being in charge. However, he admits that the nobles made their own decisions and that he could not control the Catalan infantry, who in the end joined them. However, the king acquitted himself well in what seems to have been a confused battle, apparently winning it with a charge uphill. This gallantry, and the death of the influential Moncada brothers, enabled James to take a more active role in the siege of Mallorca, when he stayed in the dangerous camp with his personal following, wielding a crossbow in the final assault. He makes much of the decision of many of the Muslims of the interior to submit to him personally; this probably simplified supply and thereby raised his prestige in the army. However, when the Mallorcans wanted to surrender on terms, the council of nobles rejected the idea against the king's wishes, because they wanted revenge for the loss of their compatriots. After the fall of the city on the night of 30–31 December, they imposed their own division of the spoils upon him.[11] James was not the prime mover in the Mallorcan campaign, and others dominated it, but he was an opportunist who skilfully exploited every chance that it provided to enhance his reputation.

The Mallorca campaign gave James great prestige, and by June 1233 he was in a position to support the Aragonese attack on the kingdom of Valencia. In 1234, the border between Christian and Muslim lay just north of Peñiscola, which at first resisted his attacks. The assault on Burriana was a vital phase of the campaign. James presents this as the opening of a grand strategy to seize

Valencia, but this was *post facto* rationalization. The initiative to attack Burriana came from the Aragonese nobles, and James was drawn into it because he feared that the greatest of them might establish themselves as independent powers. The garrison was determined and the city strong, forcing James to deploy a wide range of machinery. Mining was attempted and throwing-machines used, but the greatest effort was put into an elaborate siege-tower. A road of logs was laid for it and, under the cover of mantlets, iron rings were driven into the ground on the edge of the ditch in front of the city, so that it could be drawn up on ropes by men moving away from the enemy fire. The tower was intended to dominate the defences with firepower, but it was shattered by enemy throwing-machines. James's main problem was to hold together the barons of Aragon in the enterprise. A vital element in this was the provision of supplies, which he achieved by floating an enormous loan of 60,000 sols, guaranteed by the Orders of the Hospital and Temple. With this sum he was able to pay ships to bring food and subsidize the nobles. Ultimately they insisted, against his wishes, on allowing Burriana to surrender on terms.[12]

The surrender of Burriana was not immediately followed up, because James had preoccupations elsewhere, and it was the Aragonese nobles who pressed on to force the capitulation of Peñiscola and Morello. But James worked hard to interest the Catalans in the attack on Valencia, and a joint meeting of the Cortès of Aragon and Barcelona in October 1235 agreed to it.[13]

In 1236, the campaign entered its decisive phase when James attacked Puig de Cebolla, 3 km inland and only 17 km north of Valencia. Because of earlier defeats, Zayyan ben Mardanis, ruler of Valencia, had dismantled this hilltop fortress. James re-fortified the place, attracting further reinforcements to his 2,000 foot and 130 horse, and repulsed enemy attacks. Although James reports successful raiding, supplies ran low and he was forced go to Tortosa to borrow 60,000 sols; in his absence, his forces repulsed an attack from Valencia. James took an active part in raiding and supervised the transport of horses from Burriana for those who had lost them in the fighting. But the real crisis came when his commander at Puig died, because the Aragonese barons urged him to abandon the place. James refused and ostentatiously went to Puig with his wife and family, and took a public oath never to abandon it. This show of determination brought about the surrender of a number of local enemy forts, notably Paterna, which was less than 10 km northwest of Valencia, and an offer of tribute from Zayyan which emboldened James to lay siege to Valencia in April 1238.[14]

This was a major city with a strong garrison, although it was probably not as large as the 10,000 suggested by James. He had only 200 knights, 150 Almogavars and 1,000 foot. At the start of the siege, his Almogavars and camp followers, acting without orders, were ambushed in the suburb of Rucafa and had to be rescued. But the boldness of his action and the prospect of rich prizes soon brought reinforcements pouring in. James had encamped between Valencia and its port, and he persisted with this as his point of attack, despite being urged to move to the Boatella Gate by the Archbishop of Narbonne. He argued that there was no gate at this point from which the enemy could sally, that there were no towers and so the wall was vulnerable, and that they would in any case need to prevent the garrison communicating with the sea, a point emphasized when galleys from Tunis appeared but then sailed off, having been unable to land. James also sent a force to seize Silla to the south, isolating Valencia.[15]

The panoply of siege warfare was brought against the city, but the key factors that influenced the garrison were the lack of aid from Tunisia, which was much distracted by internal problems, and the lack of food, because the Christians had attacked early in the year before the harvest could be laid in. Even so, the city hung on until Zayyan came to terms for a surrender which spared the citizens' lives on 28 September. James accepted the surrender terms in secret and merely announced them to his barons as a way of underscoring his success.[16]

The *Chronicle* of James I is self-serving and often at pains to conceal the truth, but it reveals the problems and skills of a commander. First and foremost, he had to persuade, both in the conventional sense and by exposing his body to risk, by leading from the front. James's problems were particularly acute because of the independence of the barons and cities that was fostered by his long minority. Successful war was essential to the stability of his regime: his bravery and skill were a powerful incentive to follow him and they were reinforced by a flair for the dramatic, as in the oath of Puig. But the fruits of success were the most powerful incentive – James gave out far more land after the fall of Valencia than he had acquired. Like most kings he had wide interests, especially north of the Pyrenees, but internal pressures in Aragon and Barcelona drove him first towards Mallorca and then to Valencia. Once involved, he showed remarkable persistence and a clear awareness of the difficulties of the Almohad Empire in North Africa, then in a state of dissolution.[17]

James was far too preoccupied with his diverse interests to pursue consistent strategies. He claimed credit for devising a plan of attack on Valencia, but this was effectively dictated by the political and natural geography of Spain, and the gradual process of nibbling, fortress by fortress, by the episodic nature of medieval warfare. Much of the early fighting was entirely in the hands of Aragonese nobles. The Christian outpost of Teruel was 100 km from the coast, but it commands the upper valley of the Guadalaviar which flows down to Valencia and is close to the valley of the Mijares, at whose mouth stands Burriana; hence it served as a base for raids. Morella, which James was at pains to control once it fell, was the only Muslim fortress that could checkmate it. But James played a major role at Burriana and at a crucial stage seized the initiative at Puig, where he demonstrated great persistence. He was keenly aware of the importance of naval support and worked hard to persuade Barcelona to join the attack on Valencia. Once Valencia was besieged, he recognized that the key to sustaining the siege was supply, and Catalan ships guaranteed this to the extent that his army was lavishly supplied even with "apothecaries from Montpellier and Lerida". The failure of the Tunisian fleet to land at Valencia or to cause serious damage in his rear at Peñiscola was largely due to their fear of Catalan sea-power.[18]

In the field, James had a clear view of military realities. He made great efforts to control his troops properly: he was well aware that the loose order of his father's army at Muret had caused the disaster. Above all, he trusted his own household men and rewarded them, for they were the core of his army. He was careful about intelligence. Like all commanders, he was keen to keep order in his army and to establish the laws of the camp. The first such record of such a code that has survived to us is that of Frederick Barbarossa, drawn up in 1158, but such codes seem to have been an ancient institution, perhaps deriving from household laws. One of the most elaborate and stringent of such codes is that of the Templars. At Valencia, James's policy was skilfully adjusted to his means, and he caused the maximum disruption to the city at the minimum risk to himself. Only when his army had been swollen by news of his success did he allow forces to go south of the river to attack the Boatella Gate, where he was wounded in the fighting.[19]

James deserves his soubriquet, "the Conqueror". It was a very real tribute to him, because the nature of medieval armies meant that conquest in the military sense was peculiarly difficult. In his conquests there is a strong element of consent, albeit constrained. The Muslims of the Mallorcan countryside came to terms with him in return for recognition of their rights, and such agreements were frequent in the Valencia campaign. If we leave aside for the moment the Latin East and the German frontier, conquest in the simple military sense was difficult within the settled lands of western Europe. To take over an area with its own government, fortifications and military structure was likely, in the nature of things, to take a long time if there was real resistance, because sustaining armies was difficult. Alfonso VI (1065–1109) of León's ambassador was well aware of the problems of the Christian *Reconquista* when he collected tribute from the Granada: "Al-Andalus belonged first of all to the Christians until the time when they were conquered by the Arabs who drove them up to Galicia, the region of the country least favoured by nature. But now that it is possible, they want to recover all that was taken from them by force; and so that they may do so definitively, they have to weaken and exhaust you over a period of time. When you have no money or soldiers left, we shall take possession of the country without trouble."[20]

England is a rare example of quickly achieved conquest. William was skilful enough to take advantage of a whole range of random factors. Harold was distracted by enemies in the north, and it was with a weakened and reduced army that he confronted William at Hastings, in a battle which the Normans only narrowly won. Harold's death, and those of his brothers, left England with no obvious leader, so that the remnants of the royal council could accept William, who had a valid claim of sorts, with a good conscience. So many of the Anglo-Saxon elite had perished in the battles of 1066 that William's men were able to get a firm grasp on the southern part of the country. In this first phase, it should never be forgotten that William enjoyed easy communications with his Norman base. The North resisted, and in the end could only be conquered by the traditional method of destroying it totally. Such rule over ruins was hardly profitable: in this case, William was driven to it lest outside powers used the North as a base to attack him. But since conquest was intended to increase the wealth of the conqueror, there could be little point in such destruction. To eliminate the native population was to eliminate the source of wealth, so that most conquerors needed to come to terms, as William for the most part did, with the conquered. It was one of the major weaknesses of the Crusader states in the Middle East that their arrival terrified Muslims into flight, and that they were never able to attract a solid base of settlers. In Spain, every effort was usually made to come to terms with the mass of the population as noted, but the Christian kingdoms made strenuous efforts to resettle crucial border areas, granting land and privileges to cities whose inhabitants thus formed important bastions against reconquest.[21]

The closest parallel to William's achievement in England was the conquest of southern Italy and Sicily by Charles of Anjou. Charles was appointed king by the pope, in opposition to Frederick II's illegitimate son, Manfred of Hohenstaufen, who in 1265 seemed to be in a powerful position in Italy. Charles's expedition to Italy was backed as a crusade by the papacy, which also contributed enormous sums of money. But it was his boldness in striking into Italy that brought Charles victory at the battle of Benevento on 26 February 1266 and Sicily fell into his hands. The death of Manfred and the capture of his wife and children robbed resistance to Charles of any focus, and many Hohenstaufen adherents must have felt the need to keep their powder dry, pending the arrival of the legitimate claimant, Conradin: this situation too was paralleled in 1066. Moreover, like William, Charles was now at pains to gain assent to his conquest by recognizing the rights of all parties in the kingdom, and continued in this policy despite the pope's warning that he could not depend on the local nobility. He still had many of his French troops with him when Conradin challenged for the crown in 1268. On this occasion, Sicily, the Saracens of Lucera and some of the mainland nobles declared for the Hohenstaufen cause, and suffered accordingly after Charles's victory at Tagliacozzo on 23 August 1268. But Charles continued to distrust the native barons, especially in Sicily, where a revolt in 1282 was a reaction to alien rule which later was supported by the Aragonese. It is a mark of the problems of conquest that when revolt broke out on 30 March 1282 in Palermo, there were only 3,000 French, men, women and children to be massacred.[22]

The Norman conquest of England and the Angevin conquest of South Italy were remarkable achievements by well organized armies led by commanders who were able to exploit circumstances and were at pains to conciliate. By contrast, the Norman conquest of southern Italy began in 1017, or even as early as 999, and was not complete until 1091. It was a complex business, in which Normans frequently made arrangements with native Lombard lords, and married into their families. A recent scholar has questioned whether this should be called a conquest at all, but in fact conquest by persuasion was by no means uncommon, and it was always an element in the process. Geoffrey Martel of Anjou seized Tours by force, but he came to terms with the vanquished adherents of the house of Blois, while Geoffrey le Bel acquired Normandy by an adroit mixture of force and persuasion in support of his wife's claims, which was also the method used by his son, Henry II, to create what is now known as the "Angevin Empire". In 1203–4, Philip Augustus seized the Angevin lands in northern France from King John, largely because the elite of the Angevin lands, exhausted by war, were prepared to go with whoever won, provided that property rights were recognized.[23]

Barbarossa, by contrast, enjoyed the benefits of German military prestige, but was never able to create a consensus among the cities of the Lombard plain: military success tended to engender in Frederick further reliance on military success, which in the end was no substitute for adroit politics. The Albigensian Crusade, because its participants profoundly distrusted the nobles and people of southern France, found the gravest difficulties in conquering Provence and the Langue d'Oc, despite many military successes. At the end of the thirteenth century, as we have seen, Edward was able to conquer Wales only at enormous cost, while Scotland, which was larger and more distant, was beyond his means.[24]

The medieval commander was first and foremost a man of rank. This became more and more essential as society's divisions became more rigid. It was perfectly possible to rise as a soldier in all ages, but it became rarer to rise from very humble origins, as Guiscard did in South Italy in the eleventh century. The commander's essential skill was persuasion, for this was the only way to create an army and to hold it together. A vital part of his armoury of persuasion was personal bravery – it was imperative that he be seen to conform to this, the most prominent of the values shared by all soldiers. But affability and a willingness to consult counted for much, as did generosity in victory. Frederick II was in some ways a strikingly original and outstandingly exotic figure, but St Louis succeeded in war as in other fields by being the epitome of the commonplace values of his age. Competence in the handling of men and disposition of armies was a skill which could be bought – it was much respected, but soldiers knew that it could only occasionally coincide with rank. The commander had to impose himself upon the army even when relying on others for expertise, because he was the lynchpin of the force – his strengths made it work and, above all, prepared it for the supreme test – battle.

# Chapter Twelve

## *Campaign, battle and tactics*

Battle, it is often said, was relatively rare in medieval warfare. This statement requires some modification: we discount many incidents because by our standards they appear to be minor, and our sources tend to emphasize the great events. But this is war seen through a distorting mirror, and we need to be aware of this. The actual experience of battle, of close-quarter fighting in small units, must have been common amongst the arms-bearers of medieval society.

Every commander, every notable who aspired to influence in his theatre of power, had to contemplate battle. Without the will to battle, all other military activity was bluff, for in the end it was the ultimate hazard. And it seemed to offer the hope of decision, which was alluring. In 1044, Geoffrey Martel was besieging Tours when the Blésois advanced to relieve it. His Seneschal, Lisoius, advised him: "Leave the city which you are besieging. Summon your men from the fortifications, and you will be stronger to defend yourself. I shall hasten to you when you want to fight a battle. It is certainly better for us to fight together than to fight separately and get beaten. Battles are short but the victor's prize is enormous. Sieges waste time, and the town is rarely taken. Battles overcome nations and fortified towns, and an enemy beaten in battle vanishes like smoke. Once the battle is over, and the enemy beaten, there is a great domain waiting for you around Tours."[1]

This pursuit of decision explains why battle was so often contemplated and the merits of taking this course vigorously debated. Baldwin V of Hainaut considered and rejected it in 1184. Saladin's attack on Tiberias in 1187 precipitated a bitter debate, and both sides discussed the matter before Bouvines on 27 July 1214. In fact, commanders were well aware that battle was easy to lose and might sometimes have limited results, but it offered the exciting lure of decision, the opportunity to put one's case to the trial before God as in an ordeal. Writing of his victory over his brother at Brissac in 1167, Fulk le Réquin rejoiced that he overcame his brother "by God's grace".[2]

There were occasions when commanders sought battle, particularly in the context of conquest or civil war. In 1066, William the Conqueror deliberately refused to retreat into his fortifications, preferring to challenge Harold, while Charles of Anjou clearly pursued a battle-seeking strategy in southern Italy in 1266. This might also be the result of sheer opportunism, arising out of the general circumstances of war and raid. When Henry of France invaded Normandy in 1054, his ravagers were defeated in detail at Mortemer, and in 1057 his army was exposed to defeat at Varaville as it crossed a ford. Saladin was looking for battle in 1177, but his army was dispersed for ravaging when Baldwin IV attacked. It was in a similar context of raid and counter-raid that Henry II was able to inflict a severe defeat on Philip Augustus, while Richard almost captured him in an exciting encounter at Gisors.[3] But battle could easily occur without any specific decision in the context of the strategy of devastation. It was a situation in which small forces of attackers and defenders would inevitably clash, with consequences that might be difficult to control. The loose structure of medieval armies made this especially likely.

The bitter succession quarrels within the Empire after the death of Henry VI precipitated a long period of warfare in the Lombard plain between the Guelfs and the Ghibellines. Cities and alliances of cities and nobles fought in a pattern of raid and ravaging, punctuated by sieges of castles and other fortified places. Its object was to force rival cities into subordination: in 1212, Bobbio submitted to Piacenza after a severe raid. In 1213, the Cremonans established themselves in a camp in the marshy lands on the west bank of the Sério, close to Castelleone. There was nothing novel about this, for such field-fortifications were a familiar part of war in the Lombard plain, where they could be built to take advantage of the pattern of small rivers and drainage channels: in 1199, the Cremonans had checkmated a Milanese attack on Castelnuovo Bocca d'Adda with a similar camp. But in this case a major Cremonan force was ravaging the countryside very close to Crema, an important Milanese ally, and so a large army gathered from Milan, Novara, Piacenza, Lodi and Brescia. On 2 June 1213, the allies forced their way into the Cremonan camp and drove the defenders across the Sério; the allied army lost formation in pursuit and was defeated when the Cremonans rallied. Cremona captured the enemy *carroccio* in what is generally called the Battle of Castelleone.[4]

In June 1214, Milan and Piacenza struck into the lands of the Count of Sabaudia in the valley of the Trebbia, south of the Po. They were well equipped with siege-engines and were easily able to capture and burn small fortified towns, turning westwards in a great arc of destruction to capture Rovescala. But in the absence of their armies, Cremona counter-attacked dangerously close to Milan, and the Piacenzans and Milanese responded with raids close to Pavia. By the end of the month Thomas, Count of Sabaudia, made peace with Milan. In July, the Cremonans ravaged around Fiorenzuola, southeast of Piacenza, while the Milanese mounted a well prepared expedition with siege-engines, which captured Casale on the Po from the Marquis of Montferrat after an elaborate siege. In August, a Pavian raid against Borgonovo Val Tidone, southwest of Piacenza, developed into a series of heavy skirmishes, with losses on both sides. Pavia's allies, Cremona, Reggio, Modena and Parma, equipped with siege-engines, besieged the place, but they were distracted by Milanese and Piacenzan raiders. These raiders were not strong enough to hamper the subsequent withdrawal of the Gibellines from Borgonovo. In September, the Cremonan ambushed the Cremans close to their own city: they were only rescued by their Milanese allies. Thereafter, a cold winter ended the fighting. There had been no major encounter in 1214, but in 1216 Cremona, Parma, Modena and Mantua attacked to the southeast of Piacenza, and on 30 and 31 August were drawn into a savage skirmish in and around Pontenure, which the defenders had at first abandoned. This developed into a battle in which the Parman commander was captured. But the pressure upon Piacenza was telling, and in 1218 its Consuls attempted to come to terms with Parma and Cremona, but were defeated by the pro-Milanese party within the city. It was probably to boost the alliance that a major expedition of the Milanese and Piacenzans was mounted. At Gibello, near Fiorenzuola, its advance towards Parma was halted after a heavy and unsuccessful attack on a camp established by the Parmans and Cremonans. This was not a decisive defeat, for the army turned north and crossed the Ongino to seize Busseto to the north, and then turned east to ravage in the valley of the Stirone before dispersing. The attacking army had stayed in being throughout the month of June, with no notable success, and the war petered out in a truce arranged by the Church in January 1219, after which internal conflict began in Piacenza.[5]

This kind of campaign was common enough across the entire period. In the plain of the Po the wealth of the cities, the short distances between them, the flat terrain and the generally favourable climate all made the mounting of such expeditions, often on an elaborate scale, relatively easy. But in none of those described here does anyone seem to have sought a major battle. Ferocious encounters simply arose out of circumstance. At Pontenure, individual elements in the two armies drew their commanders into a sizeable conflict in and around the place. Here battle was a consequence of the loose structure of armies rather than any clear decision to fight. But it is important to recognize that such encounters, however accidental in themselves, took place as a result of a deliberate strategy. Armies and commanders set out for war with some idea of what they wanted to do and with a sense of how to achieve it.

Castles and fortified places were vital assets in the conduct of war, and very frequently battle arose out of sieges and relief attempts. In 1118, Henry I's garrison at Alençon was besieged by Fulk of Anjou. Henry approached with a relief army and engaged Fulk, but by chance another Angevin force had come up and took him by surprise – as a result, Alençon fell. In the summer of 1160, the Milanese recovered the initiative from Frederick Barbarossa, whose army had melted away after the capture of Crema. They sought to capitalize on this situation by seizing a number of settlements near Como, including the important castle of Carcano. Their purpose was to put pressure on imperialist Como, through which lay one of Frederick's routes back to Germany. Frederick moved his army quickly northwards from Cremona and cut the enemy army off from Milan. The Milanese army, faced with the alternative of starvation or battle, chose the latter and came to grips with Frederick, who was anxious for the opportunity to crush them: the Milanese won the subsequent Battle of Carcano. In 1167, the Romans attempted to prevent Reinald, Archbishop of Cologne, from occupying Tusculum, which would have served as a base for attack on Rome, but they seem to have been unaware that his small force was about to be reinforced by the army of Christian of Mainz, and were defeated, with terrible slaughter. Saladin's victory at Hattin was the result of a siege that was deliberately intended to provoke the Franks to battle. The siege of Acre was punctuated by a series of attempts by Saladin's field-army to drive off the attackers.[6]

A very notable battle that arose from the circumstances of raiding and siege was Frederick II's victory at Cortenova on 27 November 1237. In 1237, Frederick was delayed in Germany and did not arrive in Lombardy until 12 September, but he had evidently been making preparations because his army, including at least 7,000 Saracens from Lucera, was already gathering at Verona and would ultimately be about 20,000 strong. His star was in the ascendant: his ally Ezzelino di Romano who seized power in Verona in 1232 had, with imperial aid, fought off attacks by the Mantuans and the Brescians, while the support of Reggio, Modena and Parma gave him a strong position in eastern Lombardy. Frederick first turned against Mantua, a close ally of Milan. His was the classic strategy: he brought fire and sword to the countryside and picked off strong points, notably Góito, Marcaria (although the Mantuans retook it when they surprised its Cremonan garrison), Mosio and Redondesco. After a brief appearance before Mantua, he seized Vicenza. Gonzaga, due south of Mantua, did homage, and Ferrara and Saguinguera came to terms. Faced with isolation, the Mantuans had no alternative but to abandon their alliance with Milan and capitulate to Frederick.[7]

Then Frederick turned on Brescia, capturing Guidizzolo. On 21 October he captured Montichiari, despite a resolute defence, with the aid of machinery including a trebuchet. This was a victory noted in all the sources, because it was only some 17 km southeast of Brescia. From Montichiari, Frederick turned south and west, capturing more castles, including Pontevico where the road from Brescia to Cremona crosses the Oglio: this was presumably to secure his communications with friendly Cremona. But by this time Milan, alarmed at the possibility of losing yet another ally, had sent a major army at least 10,000 strong to aid the Brescians. The route of their outward journey is not known, but the quickest way lay across the Adda, whose bridgeheads were securely held by Milan, into territory disputed with Ghibelline Bergamo. We know that their return journey took them back through the county of Cortenova, so it seems likely that this is the course that they took, for Count Egidio was a former Vicar of Otto IV and had acted as Podestà of Guelf Brescia. His county virtually formed a corridor between the Sério and the crossings of the Oglio at Palazzolo and Pontoglio which he controlled, less than 20 km south of imperialist Bergamo. The Milanese were at Brescia by 2 November and there they stayed for seven days, until it became clear that the imperial forces were regrouping at Pontevico. They then marched south and made a fortified camp which the Piacenzan chronicler describes as being four miles from the emperor's camp on the other side of the River Lusignolo, at a place "inaccessible to horse and foot". The probability is that this was in the area of the modern Bassano Bresciano where the little River Lusignolo cuts the road from Brescia to Cremona, about 8 km north of Pontevico.[8]

Thus far, the campaign was taking a familiar form. A number of castles and cities had fallen and some allegiances had been changed, but the imperial army was now checkmated by the camp on the Lusignolo. The plain of the Po is flat, but here cut by numerous natural and artificial waterways, which made formidable even such a temporary camp. It is little wonder that the great imperial servant Piero della Vigna complained that the Milanese "hid amidst stagnant waters": Frederick could not assault the camp, but he did not dare move on towards Brescia leaving it in his rear, while even ravaging the lands of Brescia would have required care. The stand-off continued for 14 days until, on 22 November, the emperor built bridges over the Oglio and elements of his army began to cross, apparently on their way to winter quarters in Cremona. This was exactly what the Milanese had been hoping for. Campaigning was difficult in winter and all commanders were anxious to save expense by paying off their forces; this had obviously conditioned their entire strategy of deadlock. On 23 November, they began to leave their camp. By 25 November, the Guelf cavalry were crossing the Oglio at Palazzolo and Pontoglio, and by the evening of 26 November the *carroccio* was established by the strong castle of Cortenova, in friendly territory. This was a march of some 55 km, quite quick progress across the miry roads of winter, but clearly an army using two bridges had become disorganized and was intending to regroup in the shelter of Cortenova. Moreover, on the morning of 27 November the mounted vanguard at Cortenova were awaiting the arrival of the mass of their army, and its baggage and carts, which were still on the wrong side of the Oglio, while they themselves were encamped over a kilometre from other forces around the *carroccio*. In the meantime Frederick, leaving much of his army to continue towards Cremona, had taken 10,000 men and marched northwards some 32 km along the west bank of the Oglio, to arrive on 26 November at Soncino, only 20 km south of Cortenova. The next morning he set off northwards in haste.[9]

The outcome was a classic ambush. The first imperial forces fell upon the Milanese and Piacenzan cavalry, and as Frederick and more troops came up, drove them back on the *carroccio*. By this time, however, strong elements of the Guelf forces had arrived at Cortenova and they fought off the imperial attacks until night fell: this suggests that the leading elements of Frederick's army left Soncino early in the morning of 27 November, opened the fighting at Cortenova in the afternoon, and were only gradually reinforced as others came up. During the night, more imperial forces arrived, including troops from Bergamo, who seized Ghisalba and threatened the rear of the Milanese army. By the next morning, the Milanese army had dissolved and fled, with huge losses; the Piacenzan annalist speaks of 1,053 captured knights and 3,000 foot, but the Parman Chronicle mentions 6,000 – and in his letter to the Earl of Cornwall, Frederick boasted of nearly 10,000 slain or captured. The captives included the Count of Cortenova and his sons, and Pietro Tiepolo, commander of the Milanese army and son of the Doge of Venice. Victory enhanced the emperor's prestige and he made sure that all Europe knew about it. Imperial control of eastern Lombardy tightened, Lodi submitted to the emperor and all the Milanese outposts beyond the Adda surrendered to Frederick and his allies.[10]

This was one of those rare occasions when one side was able to impose battle upon another. In general, it needed both sides to resolve upon battle, because running away was fairly easy. Cortenova was a classic ambush, but beyond that we know nothing of the tactics or the way in which it was fought. This is not unusual, because it is only occasionally that we have close descriptions of battle. Most writers were clerics and this was hardly their natural environment. Moreover, even a participant was apt to see only part of an action, and by the time he wrote it down or passed it on to someone else to record, distortions would have set in. Letters proclaiming their victories by commanders, such as those of Saladin, Frederick II and Charles of Anjou, had a clear propaganda purpose. It is precisely because it attracted so much attention amongst contemporaries and near-contemporaries, and especially because of the Bayeux Tapestry, that Hastings has been so much written about.[11] Crusading warfare attracted much attention in the twelfth century and this influenced our view of medieval war, although it was hardly representative of Western warfare as a whole.

How were battles fought? How were armies controlled and commanded in this most stressful of situations? Commanders had at their disposal cavalry and infantry, which were nearly always organized separately. They were aware of the need for tactical control, and in the presence of the enemy they habitually drew up their armies in tactical groups, "battles" within which were incorporated the followers of the various lords who had brought forces. Amongst the cavalry there were probably smaller fighting units, *conroi*, but these were of varying sizes. Knights were very well protected formidable fighters, but their efficiency above the level of the small group would have depended on chance factors – such as how well secondary leaders knew one another. Perhaps the key factor was the overall commander and how well he set out to familiarize himself with the troops under him. The commander's banner was a vital rallying point and signal for the whole army, and we can suppose that the banners of the constituent forces acted similarly for every unit, while the sounding of trumpets, so commonly mentioned, may have been used to direct troops. Of course, the commander personally moved through his army, and could and often did rally his forces by his presence and his example, for this was possible in the small armies of the period. But we have no way of knowing if any effort was made to optimize the mix of cavalry and infantry or to establish a desired ratio of archers or crossbowmen to others. The general impression is that recruitment of foot was pretty haphazard and that finance was the chief limitation.

On most occasions, the infantry were ordered in separate units, although we know little of how they were organized. In the case of the Italian cities, the infantry seem to have fought in homogeneous groups raised from particular sections of the city. Each section seems to have provided a self-contained force within which the troops had specializations, ranging from the crossbowman and the heavily armed pikeman, down to the humble shield-bearer. This specialization was based on tactical requirements. In the Flemish cities, trade guilds became the primary recruiting base. There too, differentiation of function seems to have been marked. On the chest carved to celebrate the victory of the cities over the French at Courtrai in 1302, the infantry of the cities are shown in close-packed fighting order. From other sources, we know that the Flemish foot were divided into ten units, and it would seem that the archers and crossbowmen showered the approaching French cavalry with missiles, the pikemen broke the impetus of their charge and the *goedendag* men smashed at their horses, while lightly armed foot stabbed and jabbed where they could. In the eleventh century, the Spanish Muslim writer, Abu Bakr at-Turtusi, had advocated the drawing up of an army in a not dissimilar way:

> The tactics we use and which seem the most efficacious against our enemy are these. The infantry with their antelope [hide] shields, lances and iron-tipped javelins are placed, kneeling in ranks. Their lances rest obliquely on their shoulders, the shaft touching the ground behind them, the point directed towards the enemy. Each one kneels on his left knee with his shield in the air. Behind the infantry are the picked archers who, with their arrows, can pierce coats of mail. Behind the archers are the cavalry. When the Christians charge, the infantry remains in position, kneeling as before. As soon as the enemy comes into range, the archers let loose a hail of arrows while the infantry throw their javelins and receive the charge on the points of their lances. Then infantry and archers open their ranks to right and left and through the gaps they create, the cavalry rushes upon the enemy and inflicts upon him what Allah wills.

Infantry needed mass to give impact to its charge or to resist cavalry. At Worringen on 5 June 1288, the cry of the Brabanters, infantry and knights, was "Thick and tight! Thick and tight!".[12] Infantry, properly prepared and in solid formation, could hold off cavalry, break up their units and overwhelm them as individuals. But the quality of infantry was variable and until late in our period they were raised on an individual basis. The communal spirit of the cities of Flanders and Italy served to bind their forces together, substituting for the function of training in a modern army, but this emerged only slowly.

Before we can grasp how these rather inchoate bodies fought we have to come to terms with a myth that has dominated almost all modern consideration of medieval battle, the myth of the mounted knight and the idea that Western soldiers "were accustomed only to one development of tactics – the shock-tactics of heavily-armed cavalry". Oman, whose work was first published in 1898, is partly responsible for the view that by 1066 field-warfare was totally dominated by heavily armoured cavalrymen, lances couched under their arms, whose charge could sweep all before them. His treatment of the battles of Hastings and Dyrrachium (1081) was entitled "The Last Struggles of Infantry", and he went on, after an excursus on Byzantium, to a long treatment of the Crusades, which in his view pitted heavy Western cavalry against lightly armed Turkish horse. He was often more circumspect about the value of infantry, but in his analysis they came into their own only with the longbow in the fourteenth century. Hans Delbrück's work, published in 1923, gave enormous prominence to the role of knights, and saw their mounted style of war as dominant until disciplined infantry appeared in the fourteenth century. Verbruggen, writing in 1954, enormously deepened our knowledge of knightly fighting methods, but his very careful treatment of footsoldiers emphasized their contribution to warfare after 1300.[13] We were thus presented with an alluringly coherent view of medieval warfare: it was dominated by mounted knights whose tactics revolved around the charge with couched lance, relying on "shock", and its development followed a pattern essentially dictated by technical change, with the accoutrements of the knight, especially his stirrups, pushing mounted warfare into prominence, only for this to be superseded by the new technology of the longbow in the fourteenth century. In reality, there was never anything like this neat pattern of evolution and any examination shows a much more diverse experience of battle.

While it is obvious that a man on horseback has enormous advantages of mobility, weight and reach over a footman, all other things being equal, there are very obvious *a priori* reasons to question the notion of cavalry supremacy. Terrain and vegetation do not always favour cavalry, while much of war was concerned with sieges, in which their role is somewhat secondary. More simply, we have to note that, time after time, commanders took the trouble to provide themselves with large numbers of infantry and to employ them in carefully considered formations. The late-tenth-century chronicler Richer of Rheims was the son of a soldier and much interested in military matters. He described the battle of Montpensier of 892, where Odo is said to have confronted the Norse with an army divided into two parts: the infantry and archers in front of the cavalry. The Norse were subjected to a barrage of arrows, and then attacked by the infantry whose efforts were ultimately backed up by the cavalry. This is precisely the battle-order of the Normans at Hastings, where William employed large numbers of armoured foot.[14]

Rather different infantry tactics were used at Conquereuil in 992. Fulk Nerra had seized Nantes, whose citadel defied him, so he raised an army of vassals and mercenaries, but Conan of Brittany moved against him with a large force. At this point accounts differ: according to the Nantes chronicle, Fulk surprised the Bretons in their camp but was unable to break across its trenches and suffered heavy casualties, while Richer and Glaber say that the Bretons lured Fulk to a place where they secretly dug and covered over a deep trench, into which the subsequent Angevin cavalry charge fell. The use of such field-fortifications at Alençon and in Italy shows that this was certainly a viable tactic. At Tinchebrai in 1106, Duke Robert of Normandy's massed charge of infantry and cavalry was held by Henry I of England's infantry and dismounted knights, and then taken in the flank by Hélias of Le Mans and his cavalry. At Brémule in 1119, knights on foot stopped a mass cavalry charge in its tracks, while Bourgthéroulde in 1124 was won by archers. In 1139, a Scottish army invaded northern England and confronted an English force at Northallerton. All the Scots were on foot except for a small force led by King David's son, and the English dismounted their knights to stiffen the archers and foot of the local levies. When the Scots charged, led by wild but unarmoured Galwegians, archery caused heavy losses and their retreat sparked a general panic. David's son tried to rally the army by a cavalry charge: "But his mounted knights could by no means continue against knights in armour who fought on foot, close together in an immovable formation." Foot were very important in the wars of Barbarossa, were notable at Bouvines in 1214, and at Cortenova in 1237 held up Frederick II's army by rallying around their *carroccio*.[15]

The whole theory of shock tactics grossly overstates the value of the horseman as a "weapons-system". His true value was his mobility, and the fact that he was a trained, or at least semi-trained, warrior. By the age of 16, Godfrey de Bouillon was a soldier. Training for war began early amongst the military class, and it could be very brutal. One of the Giroie brothers was killed wrestling when he was thrown against the edge of a step, springing his ribs, while another was stuck with a carelessly thrown lance during practice. Knights fought by whatever means was available; William the Conqueror and Robert Curthose were excellent archers, while Godfrey de Bouillon wielded a crossbow at the siege of Jerusalem in 1099, a weapon that Richard I would use to great effect. Illustrations of knights mounted and using bows do exist, including one at Bouvines, while in 1150 Humphrey of Toron is recorded as pursuing Muslim mounted archers with his bow. The horse made knights mobile, enhancing their value as the best soldiers of the age.[16] This ability to move quickly was vital in wars which very largely consisted of raiding and small-scale encounters. In greater conflicts, the speed with which horsemen could strike meant that they held the initiative. However, it was not until the thirteenth century that the mass cavalry charge became the decisive element in battle.

Modern writers, obsessed with the shock role of the knight, have spent much energy on establishing when the use of the couched lance became common: this has been taken as the indicator of the use of shock tactics. It is very evident from the Bayeux Tapestry that knights sometimes couched their lances, but at other times stabbed, jabbed and even threw them, and no scholarly consensus has been reached on the vexed question of when couched lances became common, with dates as far apart as about 1000 and 1150 being suggested. In fact, the couched lance was a useful fighting technique, but not one necessarily connected with large-scale conflict or mass attack. Usamah, writing of his first scrap with the Franks in 1119, tells us that he thought he had run a Frank through when in fact he had done no more than pierce his armour with a thrust. From this, he drew the lesson "That he who is on the point of striking with his lance should hold his lance as tightly as possible with his hand and under his arm, close to his side, and should let his horse run and effect the required thrust; for if he should move his hand while holding the lance or stretch out his arm with the lance, then his thrust would have no effect whatsoever and would result in no harm". The frequency of representations of knights with couched lances is not so much evidence about shock tactics as of the common experience of individual combat while skirmishing, in which the technique recommended by Usamah was highly effective when possible. Moreover, it is not difficult to find quite late illustrations of knights using the lance with a stabbing movement – as in Matthew Paris.[17]

It is much easier to find occasions in the twelfth and early thirteenth centuries when footsoldiers played a vital role than it is to find instances of classic shock tactics by cavalry *en masse*. The main difficulty faced by a commander who wished to deliver a massed charge was organizational. Knights were most effective in close order, when they could throw their collective weight and fighting power against the enemy and support one another in any *mêlée* which might develop. Contemporaries were well aware of this. Both Suger of St Denis and Ordericus speak of the disordered way in which Louis VI's troops charged leading to their defeat at Brémule in 1119, while William of Tyre reports how Amalric's army, faced with superior numbers when trying to lift Saladin's siege of Darum in 1170, closed its ranks ever tighter.[18] Control of troops was the key to victory, and this almost always meant keeping together in tightly formed units. But such control must have been very difficult to achieve in armies made up of men who lived by an individualistic ethos and who were, by and large, unused to working in large groups. Even in the nineteenth century, cavalry were difficult to control. At Waterloo, both the British and French cavalry got out of hand, while the Charge of the Light Brigade is one of the most famous disasters in military history. British cavalry manuals of the modern period specified that cavalry should keep in tight order and only be allowed to move above a trot when they were within 40 yards of the enemy. This proved difficult enough to achieve with regular forces, and must have been remarkably problematic with the forces available to a medieval commander.

The nearest thing that we have to a cavalry manual is the *The Rule of the Templars*, which in its present form seems to date from the thirteenth century. It lays down painstakingly detailed instructions for the delivery of a charge, and this within the framework of monastic discipline. How could such coherence be achieved amongst laymen who might at best be used to working in small units? Moreover, what the *Rule* envisages is not simply a single all-out shock-effect cavalry charge. It insists firmly that the brothers should keep formation in units of ten, gathered close around a banner, and be obedient to the leaders of the Order – usually the Marshal. The squires with lances go ahead ready to hand them to the knights, but others hold spare mounts behind and they follow the main charge, with the fresh horses at the ready. Thus if the charge turns into a *mêlée*, the means exist to support the knights and enable them to charge again in their squadrons. The internal organization of the charge envisaged in the *Rule* would enable the cavalry to react to changing circumstances, or in a large-scale encounter to employ different tactics if they were appropriate. All-out charges were uncommon in the West – Muret in 1213 is a rare example. At Bouvines, the technique clearly envisaged in the *Templar Rule*, of small-scale repeated charges, was used to great effect, and this seems to be what happened at Hastings, where a series of charges were made.[19] The all-out single charge was a risky technique and probably very difficult to organize and time. It seems as if medieval cavalry were organized to facilitate a rather different tactic. This accounts for the relative rarity of the mass cavalry charge, at least before the thirteenth century, when the professionalization of the knights made it more practicable.

We know far too little of the internal tactical organization of infantry, although, as noted, density of formation was vital. Infantry's great strength was to defend, to give mass to an army and enable it to hold its ground, but they had to move with care, because in the open they were likely to lose formation and become vulnerable to cavalry attack. Medieval commanders usually placed their trust in combinations of cavalry and infantry. Of course, our sources are imperfect. There are battles of which we know very little, notably Nouy in 1044, Cassell in 1071 and Wilderen in 1129, but where we do have reasonable descriptions commanders seem generally, although not always, to have relied on a combination of arms, like William at Hastings. At Visé on 22 March 1106, for example, Henry IV's cavalry lured the cavalry of his rebellious son, Henry V, into an ambush which was sprung by a concealed force of infantry.[20]

In Spain, there were surprisingly few battles in the long period of the *Reconquista*, siege and raiding being much more common. In the open spaces of the Spanish plateau, mounted men had an obvious value, and this is reflected in the relative independence of the Spanish nobles. In 1085, Alphonso VI was at the height of his success after the seizure of Toledo, but the petty emirs of Spain had called in the fanatical Almoravids of North Africa. At the battle of Sagrajas (or Zalaca) on 23 October 1085, Alfonso VI could field only a very small army about 2,500 strong, including 1,500 cavalry, of whom perhaps 750 were knights in the full sense. The king fortified his camp, perhaps intending to use it as a refuge, and then led his cavalry in a charge against the huge Almoravid army, shattering the forces of the local Muslim rulers, but his impetus was halted by the large North African force, which surrounded him and destroyed his camp. 'Abd-Allah remembered in his memoirs that the defeat of the great cavalry charge of the Christians was the moment of victory. Clearly, this was an occasion when Alphonso was simply overconfident and – in spite of inadequate resources – engaged a vastly superior enemy.[21]

At Axspoele on 21 June 1128, Thierry of Alsace and William Clito, both claimants to the county of Flanders, met in battle. Thierry, with an army of about 300 knights and perhaps 1,500 infantry, had besieged a supporter of Clito at Axspoele. Clito arrived with an army of knights, estimated to be about 450 strong, and had a careful look to see "how much of it was a band of auxiliaries and how much a real army". Encouraged by the results of this reconnaissance, he resolved on battle and on the morning of 21 June took up position in three units, two in full view of the enemy on the brow of a hill overlooking the town and the third concealed behind the slope. Thierry's two units of knights attacked uphill, first with lances and then with swords, hacking their way through the enemy, who gave way, but this may have been deliberate feigned flight, for the hidden reserve of fresh knights then fell upon Thierry's disordered forces and swept down through the infantry, scattering and slaughtering almost at will. In his account, Galbert is not very explicit about the nature of the charge, except that lances were used at first, and then swords; but it seems likely that it was a mass charge by Thierry's men, lances couched, although probably at low speed because, as at Hastings, they were going uphill. The decisive thing was the control that William Clito exerted over his army, which enabled him to fall back and call up his reserve. It was, of course, a small force, but the skill with which it was manoeuvred was matched in the engagement at Gisors in 1188, when William Marshal pretended to disperse his knights and then reunited them to rout the French, or Richard's ambush in 1198, which defeated the French with heavy losses and made Philip Augustus "drink of the river" at the bridge of Gisors.[22] Axspoele was a triumph for cunning and control over a mass charge which relied on momentum and sheer weight of numbers.

In Anglo-Norman warfare of the late eleventh and early twelfth centuries, as we have noted, the mass cavalry charge was rare and commanders placed a heavy reliance on infantry. At Candlemas 1141, Stephen of England was besieging the castle of Lincoln when a strong relief army appeared, led by Robert of Gloucester and Ranulf of Chester. Accounts of the fighting are very confused, but the salient factor seems to have been that Stephen had few knights with him and was relying on his infantry, supported by some mounted troops and the militia of Lincoln, and that even these were outnumbered, or at least matched, by the rebels. As the relief force crossed the Withy, a debate erupted in the royal camp as many urged that the king should go and get new forces while Lincoln held out. The king, however, moved by pride (in the view of the chroniclers), marched down to the low ground to meet his enemies. In fact, he may have seen a good opportunity to eliminate the chief man amongst his enemies, and his yielding of the high ground may have been prudent, for he needed to be away from possible sallies by the Lincoln garrison. In the event, his small cavalry force scattered the enemy's Welsh infantry but, thus disordered, were overwhelmed. Stephen fought on with the foot and dismounted knights in the centre, but robbed of mobility he was defeated. Probably the decisive factor was that the king was outnumbered and should never have fought.[23]

At Carcano on 9 August 1160, Frederick I's German cavalry certainly destroyed most of the Milanese infantry, but the horse of his Italian allies was ambushed in fighting of which we know nothing. In 1176, Frederick was desperately short of men. Because of the weakness of his army he had been forced to withdraw from the siege of Alessandria in 1175, and to avoid battle with the relieving Milanese force, with which he concluded a truce. In response to his appeals for help, the Archbishop of Cologne and the other Rhineland bishops raised an army some 2000 strong, which crossed the Lukmanier Pass to Bellinzona, when their presence was reported to the Milanese: the make-up of this force is not known, but the Milan annalist carefully does not describe them all as knights. Frederick came with a small escort to Como, where he was joined by 500 troops and marched on to meet the new arrivals.[24]

The emperor then marched south towards Pavia, apparently in the expectation of meeting Pavian forces *en route,* but they seem not to have materialized. The movement to Pavia was a calculated risk, because it involved passing very close to Milan. Legnano, where he encountered the Milanese, is only about 30 km from Milan. In the meantime, the Milanese had assembled a very large force. As well as their own cavalry, there were 50 from Lodi, 300 from Vercelli and Novara, 200 from Piacenza, plus more from Brescia, Verona and the March, including infantry. Some footmen were left to defend Milan, but it seems likely that a force of about 3,000 knights was formed, backed up by very large numbers of infantry. This large force lay at Legnano on the night of 28 May while the Emperor was a little to the northwest at Cairate, near Busto Arsizio, with 1,000 German cavalry, the Comans, who may not have all been mounted, and whatever other forces had come across the Alps. The next morning the imperial army moved south and encountered a Milanese vanguard, which was brushed aside, and then crashed into the major allied cavalry force, which for the most part fled, apart from a few who joined the infantry around the *carroccio*. There then followed a long struggle – according to the historians of Cologne from the third to the ninth hour – but the Lombards resisted well, having resolved "to conquer or die". According to the *Chronica Regia Coloniensis*, the infantry had dug a trench: this may mean that they had fortified their camp in a style that we have noted was common in the Lombard plain, and would go far towards explaining their resistance. Two explanations are given for the breaking of the deadlock, and either or both could be true: (a) the scattered enemy cavalry returned and took the Germans in the flank; (b) Barbarossa, fighting in the midst of his army, fell off his horse and this caused a panic. The fact that in the subsequent rout the allies fell upon the German camp, killing many, suggests that some of the German and Coman army never engaged.[25] The battle nicely illustrates the contradictions of the commander's role between leading by example and exerting overall control. Frederick became absorbed in his role as leader in the thick of the fight, which must have taken the form of a series of attempts to force entry to a fortified camp, and lost track of events elsewhere. Confusion and the fog of war probably accounts for his failure, but it stemmed from his loss of control.

Across the twelfth and thirteenth centuries, war did not change radically. Its staple was destructive raiding punctuated with sieges and, more occasionally, by battle. The quality and mobility of the knights meant that they were the dominant element, although they needed infantry support and were vulnerable without it. In this style of warfare, confrontation between small groups was the norm, and the qualities of individual valour and initiative were decisive. Battle, when it came, might arise from a wide variety of circumstances and, indeed, it might be the result of accident. Once it was joined, the cavalry nearly always held the initiative, but they were not always the decisive arm. Mass cavalry charges were very rare events, and when they occurred they were not always successful. This was because mass cavalry formations were relatively rare and transient phenomena, so that the horsemen of an army lacked the coherence to execute such a difficult manoeuvre. In the close countryside of western Europe, infantry, although they too lacked training and coherence, could often find shelter and maintain a degree of solidarity that was sufficient to win the day. In fact, the decisive factor in the battles that have been analysed was the ability of the commander and the control that he exerted. This continued to be the case throughout the thirteenth century, although there are indications of a new coherence in both infantry and cavalry, but these appear unevenly and there is little sense of conscious development.

# Chapter Thirteen

# *Battle and the development of war*

In the early thirteenth century there were a number of battles, some of which had far-reaching consequences. In 1212, the Spanish Christians defeated the Almohads at the Battle of Las Navas de Tolosa, opening the way for Christian domination of the entire Iberian Peninsula. On 12 September 1213, Simon de Montfort won the Battle of Muret, which determined that the Languedoc would be attached to the French Crown rather than to that of Aragon–Catalonia. On 13 October of the same year, the Bishop of Liège was victorious over the Duke of Brabant at the Battle of Steppes. On 27 July 1214, Philip Augustus's victory at the Battle of Bouvines had enormous consequences: Flanders was firmly attached to the French Crown, King John's hopes of restoring the Angevin Empire were dashed, and the imperial pretensions of Otto IV destroyed to the advantage of Frederick II of Hohenstaufen. Bouvines set the pattern of European politics for centuries to come.[1] On 19 May 1217, the victory of the Regent of England, William Marshal, at the second Battle of Lincoln effectively ensured the succession of Henry III and ended the claim of Prince Louis of France to the English throne.

These battles were very diverse. Only one, Muret, was fought exclusively by cavalry. But at Muret and Bouvines cavalry played an important and disciplined role, and came to a prominence which it had not previously reached. Although cavalry charges were infrequent in the Welsh and Scottish wars of Edward I, the presence of cavalry exerted enormous influence on events. The importance of cavalry was a result of social and political factors as well as the development of tactical thought: in the end, it was the increased professionalism of the cavalry, already noted, which gave them their edge. This is not to say, however, that the armies of the thirteenth century were very much more cohesive than those of the twelfth, but only that elements of them were somewhat more so. Nor does it mean that infantry were in total eclipse. Rather, the development of war was uneven and it was hardly surprising that the arm of the proprietors, cavalry, became more effective. But in the uneven, unplanned development of war, armies remained the product of contingencies.

The victory of La Navas de Tolosa was the result of a carefully prepared campaign, intended to recover the initiative held by the Almohad Caliph Muhammad since the Christian defeat at Alarcos in 1185. A crusade was preached with considerable success, for despite the fighting between Léon and Portugal, whose rulers played no part, troops gathered from all over Spain. They included those of the religious orders, the King of Navarre – although he came late – and many French crusaders. So large was the army that, as it gathered outside Toledo, enormous sums of money had to be minted for its support and there were great difficulties over feeding it, as Alfonso VIII of Castille admitted in his letter proclaiming the victory.[2]

On 20 June the army, led by Alfonso VIII of Castile and Peter II of Aragon, left Toledo and seized Malagón and Calatrava. At this point, all but 130 French knights abandoned the crusade, although Sancho VII of Navarre then arrived with 200 knights. Encouraged by this desertion, the Muslim army left Jaén and moved to the foot of the Losa canyon. Topography now dictated events. The Islamic army effectively blocked this narrow pass and a vigorous debate ensued in the Christian camp, quite comparable to that before Hattin. However, a shepherd told them of a narrow defile by which they could descend, and this they followed, their vanguard debouching into the plain of the Mesa del Rey to the west of the Muslim advance guard. Both sides spent the whole of 15 July preparing. The Christians planned an attack, while the Almohads took up a defensive position on the slopes opposite them. The battle on 16 July was a confused affair, with the Christian army making a series of attacks with infantry and cavalry over the rocky slopes seamed with ravines, until a final cavalry charge broke the enemy.[3]

The next year saw Peter II, one of the victors of Las Navas de Tolosa, in battle against Simon de Montfort at Muret on 13 September. The battle arose as a consequence of Simon's ambition, supported by the Church, to forge a principality in southern France at the expense of the Count of Toulouse and other southern leaders who had been declared heretical. Peter, deeply opposed to such a creation, raised a great army and joined Raymond of Toulouse at Muret. The men of Toulouse besieged the city, while the Spanish army established a camp in the hills to the west of the River Saudrune, about 3 km away. The reasons for this dispersion of force are not in the least clear, but it was fatal. Simon de Montfort led his army into Muret in an effort to relieve the city, but his position seemed hopeless, because he only had about

800 knights against an estimated 1,400–1,500 in the allied force, which also had huge numbers of infantry.

The allied army then debated what to do. The Count of Toulouse wanted to continue the siege, for Muret was not a strong place. He seems to have assumed that this would force Simon's army into a sally, and suggested that the Spanish should fortify their camp so that they could shoot down Simon's desperate cavalry with crossbows, before emerging to crush a weakened enemy. But the Aragonese were offended by this proposal, perhaps overconfident after the victory of Las Navas de Tolosa, and they urged an immediate attack. This took the form of a mounted assault on Muret through the Toulouse Gate, which was left open, perhaps to facilitate negotiations that the clergy were conducting. It is possible that this was a ploy by Simon to draw in enemy forces but, if so, it was a great risk and the southerners all but seized the town before retiring to eat lunch. Simon de Montfort then led his forces out of the open gate to confront the southern army, which had taken up station about 2.5 km northwest of Muret between the Saudrune and the Pesquiès marsh, a position in which they should, given their numbers, have been invulnerable. They were drawn up in two lines, each of three divisions, and King Peter insisted on taking his place at the head of one of these, dressed only as a simple knight. They appear to have left all of their infantry in the camp, a kilometre to their rear, suggesting that they intended to fight a mounted battle on the open plain. Simon marched his men out of the city, divided them into three squadrons, and sent the first two hurtling into the mass of the enemy army, focusing their effort on King Peter. As they struck the southern army they became enveloped in it; Simon moved forward and to the right, crossed the marsh and took the enemy in the left flank, causing a panic which was intensified when Peter II was killed; "when the rest saw this they thought themselves lost and fled away".[4]

The sources are quite clear on the reasons for this disaster: the southern army was poorly organized, while Simon formed his squadrons in close order. James I had no doubt as to the causes of his father's defeat: "And thereon they [the French] came out to fight in a body. On my father's side the men did not know how to range for the battle, nor how to move together; every baron fought by himself and against the order of war. Thus through bad order, through our sins and through those from Muret fighting desperately since they found no mercy at my father's hands, the battle was lost." As Simon's army struck the Aragonese, the knights of Toulouse rushed up with no idea of what was going on and "paying heed to neither count nor king". It seems as if the forces between the marsh and the river had not expected an attack and had little time to prepare when it materialized.[5] It is not clear that anyone was in command of the allied army, which had dispersed its strength dangerously. A substantial force, including many cavalry, had tried to get into the Toulouse Gate and seems to have played no part in later events: a massive infantry force was left to do nothing, a kilometre behind the fighting. Once battle was joined, King Peter – imprudently positioned like Frederick I at Legnano – was unable to direct events. By contrast, Simon was very much in command and judged his moment to launch his reserve. His force was small, but it was the kernel of the crusader army and many of its members had been fighting together for a long time. It had the qualities of a highly cohesive force and fought as such against an uncertain and virtually leaderless enemy.

Steppes, on 13 October 1213, was an altogether smaller affair. The army of Hugh of Pierrepont, Bishop of Liège, was largely made up of foot spearheaded by a few knights: they were organized in two battles which formed the left and centre of the army. The right battle was made up of the cavalry, 300–400 strong, led by the Count of Loos and the Duke of Limburg, behind whom a few infantry had been drawn up, perhaps to prevent desertion; since some of Bishop Hugh's most important vassals had made peace with the enemy, it may well be that distrust was paramount. On the other side, Henry, Duke of Brabant, had set his foot in the centre, supported by strong wings of cavalry which certainly outnumbered the enemy's, although he probably had fewer foot. The Count of Loos led his battle against the Brabanter left, but was soon in grave difficulties. Henry of Brabant sent knights from his unengaged right wing to deliver the *coup de grâce,* but at this point Hugh launched his entire army and swept the enemy from the field. This was a victory for the army with fewer cavalry, produced by a grand (and probably rather confused) charge of all of the army of Liège. Cavalry were not the dominant element and the foot fought well – as they did at Cortenova in 1237, when the speed of the imperial knights brought them quickly to the ambush, where they were halted by Guelf foot and had to be supported by their own infantry.[6]

But of all the battles of the thirteenth century, the one about which we are best informed, and which was also the most important in its consequences, was Bouvines, fought on 27 July 1214. The fundamental issue was the strength and power of the French monarchy. King John was determined to regain the Angevin lands seized by Philip Augustus in 1204. He found potential allies in the princes of the lands between France and Germany, many of whom – notably Ferrand, Count of Flanders, Renaud of Danmartin, Count of Boulogne, and Henry I of Brabant, whose daughter married Otto IV in May – were deeply nervous at the prospect of French domination. John's diplomacy revived the strategy of Henry I, Henry II and Richard I, in seeking allies on the northern and eastern flanks of France. His intrigues were the more dangerous for Philip because of his family relationship with Otto IV, who claimed to be King of Germany and emperor. Philip decided to support the rival claimant to the Empire, Frederick II of Hohenstaufen, who enjoyed the support of Pope Innocent III. Papal diplomacy and French money created a Hohenstaufen party and plunged Germany into a civil war, which rapidly became deadlocked. Thus Otto was drawn into the web of John's plans for the recovery of the Angevin lands in France. Philip Augustus attempted to head off the coalition by invading England, but his fleet was destroyed at the sea-battle of Damme on 30 May 1213. At one stroke, England was freed from the fear of invasion, and Ferrand, Count of Flanders, was able to turn from the French king to an English alliance.[7]

John's strategy was essentially a repeat of Henry I's of 1124: Henry had called in his ally, the emperor Henry V, to invade France from the east while he fought on the Norman frontier. Through 1213 and well into 1214, John's allies skirmished against the French, while John prepared an expedition to Poitou. Although somewhat delayed by resistance amongst the English barons, on 15 Feburary 1214 John landed a substantial force at La Rochelle and struck northwards. William Longsword, Earl of Salisbury, was despatched to bring the coalition into action. John's attack was not a great success, but it tied down Prince Louis with 800 French knights and many more infantry, thus weakening the French king as his enemies assembled at Valenciennes on about 23 July. Philip marched north into Flanders with fire and sword, reaching Tournai on 26 July with an army of about 1,400 knights and 5,000–6,000 foot. On the very same day, his enemies encamped at Mortagne, some 12 km to the south. They had about the same number of knights and perhaps as many as 7,500 foot. But the most significant fact about the allied army was that its nominal commander, Otto IV, brought very few troops to the field. The army, therefore, had within it no dominant military figure and thus no central core. This was almost certainly a major factor in the events that followed.[8]

Philip decided to retreat due west from Tournai to Lille. The allies tried to ambush his army by travelling quickly across country in a northwesterly direction, to intercept his forces as they crossed the bridge over the River Marque at Bouvines. The decisive event was Philip's bold decision to move all of the cavalry of his rearguard southeastwards towards the allied army, as it debouched out of the forest in the vicinity of Cysoing. This prevented a pell-mell assault on his army, which was strung out on both sides of the bridge at Bouvines. Behind a huge cavalry screen, commanded by Guérin, whose front covered nearly a kilometre, the French army formed a battle-line that stretched about a kilometre northwards of Guérin's cavalry force. The allies deployed from column of march, and to screen the inevitable confusion they created a large cavalry force opposite Guérin. Under his able command, the

French knights fought with admirable discipline. They were ranged in contingents under their noble leaders, and Guérin launched each unit in turn, sapping the strength of the allied cavalry opposite. In the meantime, Otto led the rest of his army in a massive but disordered charge, resulting in the development of a gigantic *mêlée*, in which both Otto and Philip came close to being killed. However, when Guérin to the south managed to destroy the enemy cavalry formation, the rest of the allied army broke up.

Bouvines was a victory for cavalry. There can be no doubt that the knights were the decisive element, and that on the French side their discipline and order were remarkable. Guérin's tactics were not new; at Hastings, William's army fought in sections. But such tactics could only work under the kind of tight control and good leadership that we have noted at Muret and which certainly applied at Bouvines. It was enormously difficult to create those conditions in an age of *ad hoc* armies. The growth of military specialization in the European upper class and the improvement in armour for horse and man probably contributed considerably to French success, but good leadership was the decisive factor. Philip was firmly in charge and it was he who ordered the formation of Guérin's force, although he left him in charge of it once the battle had started. By contrast, Otto fought bravely, but he never seems to have been in control. On the allied side, the infantry were poorly handled – and some of the French infantry arrived late. The dogged resistance offered by Renaud of Boulogne's mercenaries reveals what infantry might have achieved with discipline and a good commander.

Although he was not present, King John of England was one of those defeated at Bouvines; as a consequence, many of his barons rebelled and accepted the claims of Prince Louis of France to the English throne. His was a perfectly serious bid, for England had been part of a French empire of one kind or another since 1066 and its upper class were, and would for long remain, French in outlook and culture. The rebels seized London on 17 May 1215, and by June 1216 Louis was firmly established there. The death of John in 1216 was not enough to end the rebellion, but Louis lacked decisive support from his father and the war was drifting towards a stalemate. In 1217, the rebellious barons seized Lincoln and were besieging its castle when a royal relief army led by William Marshal approached. The rebels refused his challenge to battle, leaving the royalists in something of a quandary. They tried unsuccessfully to get into the city through the castle, whose west gate stood on the circle of the city walls. However, Peter des Roches, who was in charge of the crossbowmen, found a secret gate and there followed a confused battle in the streets of the city in which the rebels were defeated.[9] The most interesting aspect of the Battle of Lincoln is the limited role of

William Marshal who, although he fought bravely in the *mêlée*, seems to have had little experience at commanding large bodies of troops. With the collapse of the rebellion, England enjoyed peace until the Battle of Lewes on 14 May 1264.

The context of the Battle of Lewes was the baronial reform movement led by Simon de Montfort, which sought to impose limitations on the personal rule of Henry III. The rebels seized London, but on 6 March 1264 Henry summoned his host to Oxford, where they dominated the Midlands. Simon de Montfort attacked Rochester, threatening communications with France. To safeguard the castle of Lewes, perhaps in preparation for an attack on London, the royal army marched there in early May 1264. Simon had numerous London levies of infantry, but only 300–500 cavalry, against 1,000 or more with the king. However, he had impressed upon them the worthiness of the reform cause so that, in the words of a contemporary, they had "the faith, will and courage to die for their country" and he was an experienced soldier who acted decisively. He moved swiftly southwards from London, and on the morning of 14 May took up a position on a spur of the Downs that rises 122 m to the northwest of the town of Lewes. In this favourable position he deployed his army, with the London levies forming his eastern or left flank and his cavalry squadrons to the right. The king, confident in the greater size of his army, clearly saw this as a favourable opportunity to destroy the opposition, and he drew up his army in three divisions, with his son Edward I commanding the bulk of the cavalry on his right flank opposite the Londoners, himself in the centre "battle" and Richard of Cornwall in command on the left. De Montfort's forces seem to have advanced down the slope until Edward and the bulk of the royal cavalry charged and scattered the Londoners. But the rest of Simon's army kept its nerve, while Edward – perhaps driven by contempt for the treachery of the Londoners, perhaps unable to control his men – engaged in a long and pointless pursuit which drew him entirely away from the battlefield, where the well organized forces of Simon first repulsed the attacks of royalists and then drove them back, capturing Richard in a windmill. However, because Simon had not captured Henry III or Edward, who remained at large at the head of a substantial cavalry force, the result of the battle was an inconclusive compromise, the "Mise of Lewes", and England remained in turmoil.[10]

In May 1265, Prince Edward began to reorganize the royalist party in a new political atmosphere, because many of the aristocracy had turned against Simon. The heart of Edward's army were the retinues of lords of the Welsh March, who had always viewed Simon with hostility. Simon marched west with an army much reduced by defections, but he underestimated the strength of the Marchers and the military skill of Edward who attempted to trap him, and he was forced to flee over the bleak Black Mountains to Hereford. His son Simon moved from Oxford to Kenilworth in his father's support, but a night march enabled Edward to surprise the young Simon's army there and seriously weakened his army. Edward returned to Worcester, and on 4 August 1265 trapped Simon de Montfort's army at Evesham. Simon's army took up position in a semicircle on a flat-topped high hill outside the city, but his Welsh troops were quickly scattered and this time there was no useless pursuit. Simon's cavalry charge against the royalists was overwhelmed by Edward's vastly superior army, which annihilated the enemy. Simon's body was grossly mutilated.[11]

The wars of Edward I in Wales and Scotland displayed a much more considered approach to warfare. Edward could rely on a competent and brave cavalry – much of it volunteer – and his enemies rightly feared it, for neither the Welsh nor the Scots could raise such a force. This is why battle proper was so rare in the long period of intensive warfare after 1277. But the Welsh and Scots had a strong sense of their own identity, comparable to that of the Italian cities, and they disliked foreign domination; this provided them with the spirit to counter the elitism of the English knights and their humbler followers. Edward clearly appreciated the risks in confronting such soldiers on their own ground, which is why he raised very large infantry forces of his own. Despite the construction of castles and the implanting of a loyal population in the fortified towns, the Welsh rebelled. Edward almost came to grief against the rising of Madog in 1294, because he ventured too far with only a part of his force and the Welsh captured his supplies, forcing him to take refuge in Conway, where he was short of food because adverse weather kept his ships away. On the night of 5 March, the Earl of Warwick made a forced march with about 200 cavalry and 2,000 infantry, surprising Madog at Maes Moydog. The Welsh force formed itself into a circle, bristling with spears to hold the cavalry off, but Warwick sent up archers who shot the enemy down until the cavalry could charge over them.[12] Maes Moydog was a nice demonstration of the advantages of having a strong cavalry force, and of their need for support from other troops.

The problem in Scotland was vastly greater. The Scots normally dared not stand and fight against Edward's huge armies, but the outbreak of rebellions in 1296–7 by Murray in the north and Wallace in the south terrorized Edward's supporters and undermined the whole basis of his rule in the northern part of the kingdom. Edward was distracted by continental wars and never seems to have been able to afford the great fortresses which anchored his rule in Wales. This was guerrilla warfare, waged by peasants and led by gentry, with the connivance of at least some of the magnates of Scotland. Moreover, the absence of the king's strong personality had an enormous impact on the conduct of the war, because his ruler in Scotland, John of Warenne, Earl of Surrey, was inactive and actually resided in England. When Warenne finally moved against the revolt, his failure produced a terrible crisis. His army concentrated at Stirling where, in effect, the bridge was the strap that held the north and south of Scotland together. To the north the rebels had prevailed, but if Warenne marched north he could undo all their work, so they concentrated their forces, largely native spearmen, to the north of the bridge. On 11 September 1297, Warenne prepared to force passage, but he seems to have stayed long in bed and as a result the English army deployed in a curiously dilatory way, some units marching across the bridge, then back again. Warenne finally arrived and sent infantry, archers and cavalry across the bridge; when the Scots judged that enough had passed for them to maul the English army, but not too many, they charged and slaughtered all who had crossed, including the Treasurer, Cressingham. Warenne's previous incredible passivity in watching his army march to slaughter now turned to panic – thus compounding the disaster, as he abandoned Scotland, leaving his garrisons open to attack and the north of England exposed to raids.[13]

But the limitations of the Scottish armies became obvious. Wallace had no great success in his attempts to seize the English-held castles, while he could do no permanent harm in northern England. In 1298, Edward gathered an army of 3,000 cavalry, 10,900 Welsh and 14,800 English foot and marched into Scotland. His army was soon starving because contrary winds kept his fleet away: there was massive desertion and the Welsh became so mutinous that there was a real danger of their joining the enemy. With the death of Murray in November 1297, Wallace became the leader of the Scottish resistance. Victory at Stirling Bridge had given him the confidence to confront Edward, particularly as he had a cavalry force provided by some of the Scottish magnates, and knew that Edward's army was in difficulties. He prepared to confront the English at Falkirk, north of Linlithgow. Wallace chose a position between dense woodland on his right and broken ground to his left, with a small loch before him which would make the approach to battle difficult for his enemy. He formed his spearmen into four great circular formations – schiltrons – girded with stakes roped together to check cavalry attack. Between the formations he set his archers, and behind he held the cavalry. The logic of this deployment was impeccable. Any frontal attack by infantry would be peppered with arrows before coming to grips with the schiltrons. Cavalry could scatter the archers, but they would then face a countercharge by the Scottish cavalry.

Edward's army marched in two groups, passing east and west of the loch to bring them up to the Scottish line. At this point, either through panic or treachery, the cavalry of the Scottish magnates fled. In fact, they were probably sensible to do so, because the English cavalry were so numerous that any countercharge that the Scots could mount would have been overwhelmed. In the event, the archers were soon driven from Wallace's line and the battle turned into a prolonged siege of the schiltrons. Their position was hopeless: English knights were in their rear and Edward used his archers to bombard the Scots preparatory to infantry and cavalry assaults. In the end, there was terrible slaughter, although Wallace escaped.[14]

There was nothing new about the tactics of the Scots. It was almost instinctive for infantry to gather in mass, and very effective, as the English had proved at Hastings: the schiltron is very like the formation that Richard I formed with spearmen when he was surprised by Saladin outside Jaffa, although he placed a crossbowman between each pair of spearmen.[15] Nor were Edward's methods of dealing with them novel. What was new was the spirit with which such footmen could fight and the way in which a well controlled army with a balance of infantry and cavalry could break them up. In the end, Falkirk was an empty victory. Edward did not have the means to occupy Scotland and he failed to achieve a political settlement with the Scottish magnates.

The lessons of his warfare were not passed on to the next generation, and Edward II suffered a catastrophic defeat at Bannockburn in 1314. Bruce created an army from a successful guerrilla campaign which had all but ejected the English from Scotland. Edward II attempted to reassert his rule by relieving Bruce's siege of Stirling with a large army. Perhaps 15,000 foot and more than 2,000 horse gathered at Berwick on 10 June 1314. As they approached Stirling, Bruce stood across their route with 7,000–10,000 foot and 500 light cavalry, experienced and battle-hardened troops who had fought together successfully over the previous years. The English seem not to have expected the Scots to stand and fight, and indeed the signs are that Bruce wanted to avoid a pitched battle. On 23 June, powerful cavalry forces of the English army suffered severe losses; that of Gloucester and Hereford charged under the impression the Scots were retreating, while that of Clifford and Beaumont may have been trying to bypass what they believed to be minor enemy forces. In both cases, unsupported cavalry was routed on broken ground by mobile formations of spearmen. These successes, and news of the low morale in the English camp, seem to have inspired Bruce to fight the next day. Edward was not a soldier and seems to have made no plan. On 24 June, Bruce's schiltrons took up position on a narrow plain and repulsed a series of frontal attacks, to win a great victory. Nothing could illustrate more clearly the importance of good leadership and tight control in war, for that is precisely what Bruce enjoyed and Edward II so signally lacked. Bruce's tactics repeated those of Wallace at Falkirk: Edward I found the means to prise open the schiltrons, while Edward II did not.[16]

The ascendancy of cavalry, which can be seen in English field-warfare in the thirteenth century, was never absolute. Almost everywhere, heavy cavalry dictated the terms of war, although not the outcome. They were most effective when supported by other arms. In the Baltic the heavy cavalry of the Sword-Brothers and their allies, supported by crossbowmen, were a powerful influence in driving forward the Christian conquests along the Baltic coast.[17] But amongst the most remarkable victories for cavalry in western Europe in the thirteenth century were those of Charles of Anjou.

The death of Frederick II in 1250 was hailed by the papacy as a divine delivery, but in the event it proved to be nothing of the sort, for Frederick had heirs. His son Conrad, already King of the Romans, was his heir in Sicily and was biding fair to make good his claim despite virulent papal opposition, when he died in 1254 leaving an infant son, Conradin. The vacuum of power in the south enabled Frederick's illegitimate son, Manfred, to gain the throne of Sicily, and by 1257 he was crowned and in full control of the old Norman Kingdom. But the determination of the papacy to oust any member of the "race of vipers" plunged Italy into a bitter conflict. The papacy, claiming overlordship of the Sicilian kingdom, was anxious to find a king to supplant Manfred, and alighted first upon Edmund of England; Henry III's efforts to tax England to support this adventure precipitated confrontation with his barons, forcing withdrawal of the offer in 1258. After many twists and turns of diplomacy, Urban IV recognized Charles, brother of St Louis, Count of Provence since 1246 and of Maine and Anjou since 1247. He had fought alongside St Louis on his Crusade, energetically repressed revolts by his own Provençal subjects and attempted to extend his power into Flanders. The papacy drove a hard bargain, but Charles seems from the first to have been sanguine about his prospects.[18]

To be granted the kingdom was one thing; to win it another. Manfred was in a very powerful position in both northern and central Italy as well as in Sicily, not least because of the victory of his Sienese allies at Montaperti on 4 September 1260. Manfred had sent Count Giordano as Imperial Vicar, together with substantial forces, to support Siena against Florence. The revival of the Ghibellines caused bitter conflict in Florence, many of whose Ghibellines sought refuge at Siena. Count Giordano had at his disposal a force of some 800 German and South Italian horse, and their aggressive attacks stirred Florence into inconclusive action in the early summer. It was an attack on the Florentine client-city of Montalcino which precipitated the battle.

The Florentines made a major military effort, raising 1,650 cavalry and some 13,000 foot from the city. Allies such as Bologna and Orvieto sent forces, and tributaries such as Lucca and San Gimignano made substantial contributions. Giovanni Villani suggests that the total force was 70,000, including 3,000 cavalry. This may be an exaggeration, but 20,000 is likely, outnumbering the Sienese whose city was smaller, although they were reinforced by 800 German cavalry.[19] This huge army, laden with supplies, went to Montalcino, marching directly past Siena on 3 September, probably hoping to intimidate the city – and not without reason, for there was treason in the air. The rise of Manfred had divided Italy, and there were Florentine Ghibelline exiles led by the Farrinata degli Uberti in Siena and Guelf exiles from Siena in the Florentine army.

According to Villani, the Florentine army had traitors in its ranks, amongst them one Razzart who, on the evening of 3 September, revealed to Siena serious divisions in the Florentine camp. Whatever the truth of this, the great army was poorly handled. From Siena it moved eastwards and settled 4–5 km east of the city, at the foot of the Monteropoli hills, which run north–south on the eastern side of the valley of the Arbia. This was an exposed position almost within sight of Siena, and on the evening of 3 September the Sienese, with the German cavalry and the Ghibelline exiles, encamped on the west side of the Arbia. In the morning the Imperial Vicar, Count Giordano, seems to have taken charge, forming his army into four divisions. Two divisions of cavalry under himself and Count Aldobrandino led the attack, supported by a third division of the infantrymen of Siena. But a fourth group of cavalry, under the command of Giordano's Seneschal, Count Arras, was sent on a long detour to approach the Florentine rear on their left.[20] The Florentines seem to have taken a very passive attitude, relying on their sheer numbers to absorb the shock of the Sienese and German charge; but as battle was joined, Count Arras's division fell upon the bulk of the Florentine cavalry on their left, who panicked and ran. Villani says that the treacherous Ghibellines in their own ranks started the panic, notably by striking down the Florentine standard-bearer. There was no pursuit, and virtually all of the cavalry escaped with their lives, but the Florentine footsoldiers were butchered on the bare slopes of the Monteropoli hills.[21] The surprise attack on the cavalry on the Florentine left seems to have destroyed the Florentine force. The comparison with Lewes is instructive: there, the dissolution of a whole wing of the rebel army was born stoically by the rest of a force, inspired by Simon de Montfort's leadership. But the Guelf army was an alliance of disparate forces, with poor leadership. It was formed at a time of deep intrigue and restless conflict in Italy. Struck a terrible blow by surprise, it simply fell apart.

That atmosphere of poisonous intrigue and distrust was turned against

Manfred in 1263–4. Charles's diplomacy, ably seconded by that of the papacy, which plunged itself into debt in support of its protégé, undermined the dominance that Manfred had built up in the Lombard plain. Supported by an enthusiastic and highly successful preaching of the crusade, Charles raised a great army in his Provençal lands for the invasion of Italy. At its core were highly experienced French knights. But before this army was ready, Pope Clement appealed for aid: Rome was isolated and Manfred had many friends within the city. Charles acted decisively: sailing from Marseilles, he slipped past the Sicilian squadrons in the Mediterranean and arrived at Rome with a small force on 20 May 1265. He quickly swung Rome and the Campagna to his side, and his small army was enough to dissuade Manfred from an attack on the city. In October, Charles's army left Provence under the command of Guy of Mello, Bishop of Auxerre, numbering in its ranks the counts of Flanders and Vendôme, Philip and Guy de Montfort and many other French and Provençal nobles. Manfred failed to support his allies in north and central Italy, and by 15 January this army was at Rome.[22]

As a would-be conqueror, Charles had no option but to pursue battle, and on 20 January he marched out of Rome and down the old Via Latina, crossing into the kingdom at Ceprano, where the bridge was intact and undefended. Manfred concentrated an army at least equal in size to that of Charles at Capua. He seems to have supposed that his garrisons would delay Charles while his nephew, Conrad of Antioch, gathered a large force in the Abruzzi. The problem was that the smaller garrisons, and even some of the larger ones such as Rocca d'Arce, capitulated quickly. Treachery may have played some part in these events, but Charles's army was large and well equipped – Saba Malaspina says that he used a trebuchet. Crucially, the great fortress of San Germano, above the Rapido on the slopes of the abbey of Monte Cassino, fell. Here the strong garrison, which included Saracens from Lucera, made a sally but were driven back by French forces, which then followed on into the castle itself. The collapse of this fortress opened the way for Charles to outflank his enemy at Capua by marching east towards Benevento. Manfred promptly occupied Benevento and awaited the arrival of the French army on 25 February. It is clear that he intended to give battle, for on that day his forces secured the bridge outside the city, across the swollen Calore. His motives have been much debated: Villani remarked that the French were hungry, and that if Manfred had waited he would have been joined by other forces from South Italy and the March. Manfred probably feared treachery if he waited, and perhaps he was heartened by the arrival of 800 well armed German cavalry. Many on the French side wanted to delay battle, for their army was tired, but Charles – as he proudly boasted in his own account – would have none of it, and delay might have enabled Conrad of Antioch to descend on his rear. On the morning of 26 February Charles's forces left their camp in nine divisions, which were then reorganized into five and marched to meet Manfred's troops on the west bank of the river, in the plain of S. Maria della Granella, with the bridge-gate of the city behind them.[23] This plain has a marked slope down towards the bridge-gate, which must have favoured Charles's army.

Andrew of Hungary's account incorporates a letter recounting the battle sent by a participant, Hugues de Baussy. According to him, Manfred's army numbered 5,000 cavalry and 10,000 Saracen foot armed with bows and crossbows. He reports that Charles arranged his force in four divisions against the enemy's three. The first division of the French army were the Provençals, amongst whom were the Montforts, and they engaged the division of Count Giordano who led the Germans and others. Charles commanded the second division which engaged that of Counts Bartholomeo and Galvano, who led Germans, Saracens and Apulians. Charles's army had a third division of Flemings and French, including the young Count of Flanders, and a fourth division was made up of Romans, Campagnans, Tuscans and Lombards, led by the Florentine exile Guido Guerra. They seem to have taken up a formation in depth; that is, each division was arrayed behind the other, with some footsoldiers ahead of all. The logic of this formation was that it enabled the commander to switch his mobile cavalry forces: a formation in line made this more difficult. Andrew's account focuses entirely on the cavalry. According to him, the Germans at first seemed to be successful moving up in tight order and cleaving into the French with their long swords, but the French closed with them and used their daggers, following the example of Charles, who cried out "Thrust with the point, stick them with it!". This can only remind us of the fate of Eustache of Malenghin at Bouvines: one French knight grasped him by the neck and tore off his helmet while another stuck him through the heart with a dagger. As the Germans began to give ground, Manfred called up his great division, but its members melted away, leaving him to fight on until he was killed.[24] This is a somewhat sketchy account. It is not clear how and when the Flemings engaged or what became of the Italian allies of the fourth division, and it describes the battle as a cavalry affair in which the infantry do not figure.

An essentially similar report – although filled out and with some variation – is given by Villani. According to him, the Angevin army was divided into three divisions, the first of which numbered 1,000 knights, including the Montforts. Charles commanded the second, which was made up of about 900 French, while Flemings and French, including the Count of Flanders, made up the third: there was also a fourth unit made up of Italian Guelfs, including

Florentines, and this had about 400 knights in it. Manfred's host was divided into three groups: a force of 1,200 German cavalry, a second group of Germans, Tuscans and Lombards numbering 1,000 cavalry, then the 1,400 horse in Manfred's own division, accompanied by the foot and the Saracen bowmen. Villani says that the Germans attacked and were successful, so that Charles had to move up his division, also drawing in the smaller force of the Italian Guelfs. It was when the French closed in with daggers and attacked the horses as well as the men that the tide turned and Manfred's division melted away rather than engage.[25]

The great puzzle is what the large forces of infantry did during this battle. Saba Malaspina says that the battle opened when the Saracen infantry rushed forward and did great damage to the French infantry, only to be routed by 1,000 French mounted sergeants who, in turn, were put to flight by the Germans under the command of Galvano and Bartholomeo. Charles then attacked and won a great victory. The Paduan annal suggests that the Saracen infantry were only deployed to one side of the battlefield, but concurs with this general account.[26] It is unlikely that this was their only part in the battle, for Andrew of Hungary's account makes it clear that they were present in large numbers. It seems likely that they formed an element in each division of the French army, for Malaspina says that Charles ordered his army so that there were two footmen with each cavalryman to kill horsemen whom he unhorsed. Manfred, however, seems to have concentrated the infantry in his division. Perhaps the lack of them hampered the Germans in their close-quarter fight with the French knights. The key factor, however, was the heavy cavalry. Andrew of Hungary gives a chilling picture of the German knights, moving slowly forward in tight formation like a juggernaut. The French army had many experienced warriors in its ranks and it was relatively homogeneous: the allied elements in it were small. It had been together for several months and had fought its way through hostile country. It seems to have been well disciplined and its knights, as at Bouvines, displayed a willingness to fight at very close quarters; it was this which broke up the initial German thrust. Manfred's force was very heterogeneous, and this lack of unity may have been a factor in the defeat. It was a battle which resulted in terrible casualties, especially on the losing side, for their forces, once broken, could not flee across the bridge. This was perhaps why Manfred's division broke so early – to get away while they had time. But there was probably another factor. Intrigue and divided loyalties were the norm by now in Italy, and many in Manfred's army must have remembered that there was another and more legitimate Hohenstaufen, Conradin, the grandson of Frederick II.

Charles of Anjou attempted to secure his conquest by a policy of magnanimity, pardoning even his most bitter enemies, and making it clear that he intended to rule in the tradition of his forebears. But his efficient government and insistent tax collectors stirred up discontent, while the adherents of the Hohenstaufen were soon flocking to Conradin in Germany. Charles tried to consolidate his position by destroying the Ghibellines in Tuscany and Lombardy, where a great parliament in March 1266 had signalled his triumph. Meanwhile, in October 1266 Conradin, although only 16 – and under the influence of the exiles – proclaimed his intention to seek the Crown of Sicily at Augsburg. In autumn 1267 he left Germany, while his agents stirred Sicily and the Muslims of Lucera into rebellion. But the decisive factor was Henry, Infant of Castille, an adventurer who had lent money to Charles and fought for him at Benevento. Charles was slow to repay and offered him few rewards. Henry put himself at the head of the anti-papal party in Rome, who made him Senator, and in October declared for Conradin. Charles seems at first to have wanted to meet Conradin in northern Italy, perhaps recalling the failure of Manfred to support his allies two years before. However, the revolt of Lucera threatened to spread disaffection all over the kingdom, and so in March 1268 Charles moved quickly south. Conradin had hitherto been confined to Verona and Pavia, but he was able to reach Pisa in April, and the revival of the Ghibelline cause after the retreat of Charles enabled him to advance to Rome, surprising and defeating an Angevin force near Arezzo on 25 June. On 24 July, he was received in Rome by Henry of Castille.[27]

Conradin was now somewhat in the position that Charles had been in two years earlier. The mountains of Italy present armies with sharply defined valley-routes, and Conradin, with his way south blocked by hostile fortresses, turned east on to the Via Valeria, aiming for Lucera via the Lancia lands. Charles quickly abandoned the siege of Lucera, reaching Scurcola, just to the west of Avezzano, on 9 August, from where he could command the narrow Mount Bove pass, at the foot of which is Tagliacozzo. Conradin marched to Carsoli and then left the Via Valeria, turning north to make his way over difficult and mountainous terrain to the upper reaches of the valley of the little River Salto at Borgocollefegato. This was a remarkable achievement, for it meant a journey of 50 km over very difficult country. His purpose may have been to bypass the narrow gorges towards Tagliacozzo, but it had a curious effect on Charles who, by his own account, moved his army some 25 km northeast, to Ovindoli: this may well have been because he feared that Conradin's march lay towards L'Aquila. He was soon disabused, and returned to Albe, on the high ground to the east, overlooking the mountain plain known as the Campi Palatini. Conradin's force now marched south down the narrow valley of the Salto, debouching into the Campi Palatini, where his vanguard skirmished with a substantial Angevin force before camping at Scurcola, on the west bank of the Salto. This skirmish may have been very important if Conradin had originally wanted to enter the plain by the east bank of the Salto. Scurcola lay to the west of the river, and Charles now moved his army down the Via Valeria to encamp by the east end of the bridge which carries it over the Salto, thus obliging his enemy to force a crossing. The two armies spent the night on opposite banks of the Salto before battle was joined on the morning of 23 August 1268.[28]

Conradin's forces seems to have numbered 5,000–6,000 and it would seem that there were only limited numbers of infantry amongst them, for they are not mentioned in the battle at all. The army was drawn up in three divisions, the first being that of Henry of Castille, which moved to the west end of the Salto bridge. Behind them was a corps of Italian troops and exiles from Sicily, stiffened with a few German knights, while a relatively small reserve of Germans remained under the command of Conradin and his cousin Frederick of Baden. Charles's army had about 4,000–5,000 cavalry and was also divided into three divisions. The first corps of Italians stood at the east end of the bridge and were supported by a second, commanded by Henry of Cousances, consisting of French and Provencal knights. A third group of 800–1000 hand-picked men remained under the command of Charles.[29]

Henry of Castille opened the battle by charging across the bridge, but at first made slow progress against the Angevins, until some of his troops found a shallow crossing of the Salto to the south and drove into the flank of the first two enemy divisions, breaking them totally. It is on the location of the third Angevin division and its action that interest has centred. The contemporary accounts suggest that Conradin crossed on to the battlefield east of the Salto, where most of his forces had scattered to pillage, only to be surprised and put to flight by a sudden onslaught of Charles's own division attacking from hiding. There was then a third phase of the battle, when Henry of Castille's force returned from pursuit and, after a grim fight, were defeated.

The French sources report that Charles was on heights some distance from the battlefield, and launched his attack when he saw his enemy scattered to loot, and it has been suggested that, on the advice of the crusader veteran, Alard of Saint-Valéry, who had joined his army, he had deliberately held this forces well back until the time was ripe, in order to spring a trap. However, this seems unlikely, for some time clearly lapsed between the defeat of his first two divisions and his reappearance, and a better moment to attack would have been when the allied army was turned away from him and engaged by the bridge. As it was, most of his first two divisions were wiped out. Moreover, the question arises as to where he could have hidden his third division and watched the battle from, for the bridge is somewhat isolated in the middle of a plain. The nearest high land is over a kilometre to the southeast, the Monte Felice, standing to the west of the road to Avezzano, towards which a spur reaches out to form a hidden valley, the Valle Vaccareccia. This was certainly a good hiding place, but it is so far from the scene of action that to have so used it would have been an impossible risk. However, it is on a natural line of flight from the battle, so if the Angevins had been shattered by the enemy charge, elements might well have fled in this direction, only to be rallied when they realized that there was no pursuit – this is probably what happened. From the high land, Charles could then direct his forces, about whom the enemy would have been in ignorance.[30]

But this was not the end of the affair. Henry of Castille had apparently pursued some of the enemy northwards, perhaps to the rising land near Magliano de Marsi: when he realized what had happened, his force – including formidable German cavalry – descended upon Charles's troops, who seem to have been outnumbered. Alard lured some of the enemy forces out of their strong formation by a feigned flight – an act which is probably responsible for the idea that he won the battle, and which may have owed much to his crusader experience – and hard fighting, in which Charles fought "like a lion", shattered Henry's troops.[31]

The Battle of Tagliacozzo demonstrates nicely the strengths and weaknesses of a thirteenth-century army. The cavalry were dominant in a campaign which was characterized by rapid movement, and the approach to battle saw both armies covering considerable distances across difficult country. Tactics on the battlefield were relatively simple and depended on disciplined mass charges, made possible because on both sides there were large numbers of hired professionals. However, Conradin's army was very diverse and lacked coherence, with contingents from many sources – Sicilians, South Italians, North and Central Italian Ghibellines and Germans. Furthermore, it lacked a clear and dominant commander: Henry of Castille was probably the moving spirit, but he commanded only a single division – Conradin was an inexperienced youth who seems to have been largely a bystander. Crucially, the bulk of these forces scattered to plunder as soon as they could – plunder was the wages of war, and this kind of diversion was always a risk in armies within which the individualist ethic still reigned. In 1099 before the battle of Ascalon, the Patriarch of Jerusalem had threatened excommunication against any who plundered without leave. Charles's army was also rather diverse, but its core were his hardened French and Provençal professionals, some of whom he had not been able to pay off for their efforts two years before. They rallied in defeat and saved the day. In tactical terms, the whole point of the story of Alard of Saint-Valéry is that close-ordered cavalry formations were very difficult to break up, and his feint served to loosen that of Henry's troops, who disregarded all warnings to remain in close formation. In the end, as so often in war, Tagliacozzo was a victory for control, command and cohesion, but these were qualities found only in parts of the two armies engaged.

The thirteenth century was truly the age of cavalry. This does not mean that they enjoyed an uncontested supremacy – far from it – but that it was clearly the actions of the cavalry, and the way in which they were handled, that dictated events. Paradoxically, as we have seen, infantry were now better armed than ever before. Moreover, in Italy, Wales and Scotland, and indeed elsewhere, infantry showed themselves to be formidable; Bannockburn in particular indicates the importance of terrain in any military equation. It was as if the victory of Bouvines had set a fashion in war and one which, because of the way in which it was portrayed, in terms of a courteous tournament, would have been doubly welcome to the armed elite of the West. Most of the great actions of the century happened to take place in country that was appropriate for this style of war and seemed, therefore, to confirm it. But it was only in quite exceptional circumstances that cavalry were totally dominant, and for the most part their commanders were well aware of the threat posed by disciplined infantry. At Worringen in 1288, two equally matched cavalry forces cancelled each other out, and the sudden appearance of an infantry force broke the deadlock. However, a more significant reminder of infantry power came at the start of the fourteenth century.

In 1302, the Flemish rebels attacked Philip IV of France's garrison at Courtrai with an army of 8,000–10,000 heavily armed foot from the rebellious cities. Robert of Artois marched to its relief with 2,500 of the finest French knights, supported by about 6,000 foot and crossbowmen. The Flemings under Guy of Namur took up a strong position just to the south of the town, with flanks resting on major waterways that flowed into the Lys behind them. In the marshy land across their front were a number of waterways enhanced by carefully dug trenches. Robert of Artois recognized that he faced a formidable task in assaulting such a position. There was a careful discussion of the possibility of drawing the Flemings from their position, and Robert obtained a map (which has survived) of the obstacles that his army faced. There was undoubtedly a battle-plan – there was no question of a pell-mell charge by the French cavalry. Robert of Artois's problem was how to bring his cavalry into action with the best chance of success across the unfavourable terrain. His foot were too lightly armed to risk close to the Flemings, so in the end, after an inconclusive exchange of archery, the French cavalry forded the great brook in front of the Flemish position to make an assault, but here it faced major problems. The Flemish line was quite close to the edge of the brook, which made it difficult for them to build up momentum for a charge after scrambling across; the difficulty was compounded by ditches and piled earth, all of it wet. In the resultant push at pike, the Flemish infantry held and began to drive their enemy back into the brooks. Robert of Artois led a final charge by his rearguard, but when he was killed the French army broke, with appalling slaughter in the brooks.[32]

The indispensable conditions of victory at Courtrai and Bannockburn were disciplined and spirited forces under prudent commanders. It is tempting to see these battles as turning points, when a new mode of war supplanted the chivalric warfare of the European upper classes. But in fact this would be a false perspective: it is worth remembering that victory at Bouvines was *also* the result of disciplined and spirited forces under prudent commanders. All medieval armies were the products of particular conditions, and their tactics were a result of the contingencies of the situation as understood by the commander. There was no doubt a predilection to rely on cavalry: the new spirit of aristocratic ostentation and exclusiveness, so characteristic of the thirteenth century, was only too ready to cling to this style of war as a norm. But in the day-to-day business of war, foot nearly always played a major role. Sometimes battle involved only knights, as at Göllheim in 1298. At Frechen in 1257, knights suppressed a rebellion by the city people after initial losses. At Hausbergen the knights of the bishop were intimidated by the mass of the rebellious Strasbourg foot. At Certomondo in 1289, the footsoldiers of the Italian cities of Florence and Arezzo carried the burden of a very bloody battle. We may also suspect our sources – the Marchfeld in 1278 is presented as a knightly battle, but we know that large infantry forces took part.[33]

Sometimes, a particular commander reflected very carefully on his task and came up with an army and tactics which were evidently appropriate – as Edward I did for his wars. But there was no means to refine and give continuity to such ideas – Edward II's disasters testify to that. War was part of the fabric of medieval society, but it was not institutionalized – as, for example, was education. Certain institutions served it – notably governmental administration – but war was the province of the proprietorial class, the leaders of society. In the thirteenth century, it was taking on a new professionalism. This showed itself first and most clearly amongst the cavalry, which generally held the initiative in field-warfare because of its mobility. But foot did not vanish, and commanders who had to use it could and did think up satisfactory ways of doings so. Because armies remained transient, there was no mechanism to bring ideas together in a systematic way. Each commander worked in his own way; each victory was *sui generis*; and even where there is evidence of clear thinking about combinations of forces, as in the case of Edward I, it was the product of his personality and died with him. Victory in battle depended, as victory always does, on the personality of the commander and his ability to adapt forces and employ them in particular circumstances – but it also depended on his having a large core of loyal troops around which his army could be built and manoeuvred. Unlike a modern general, the medieval commander had to do that without a staff, without a logistics service and, above all, without an institutional memory to serve him.

# Chapter Fourteen

# *Europe, ideology and the outsider*

The population of Catholic Europe came into contact with a number of peoples whom, for one reason or another, they saw as different – as outsiders. There was no settled term to describe such people, which is hardly surprising in view of the differences between them, but the word "barbarian" was occasionally used to describe them all. At one end of the scale of barbarians were the Celts of the British Isles. They were Christian, but the economies of Scotland, Ireland and Wales were far less advanced than that of England. In the European heartlands war was about possession of land and rule over its people, and as few wished to rule deserts, they did not try to remove or slaughter the population. In the Celtic fringe, economic conditions were much more severe, life was cheap and slavery remained highly profitable, to the scandal of chroniclers. At the same time, the reform of the Church in England after the Norman Conquest made educated Englishmen aware of the "primitivity", as they saw it, of Celtic religious practices. It is hardly surprising, therefore, that the chroniclers revile Celtic war practices. However, if we remember the horrors of war perpetrated by so-called civilized men – the harrying of the North of England by William the Conqueror and massacre of Vitry by Louis VII spring to mind – the excesses attributed to the Celts need to be noted with a pinch of salt. The peoples of the German frontier in northern and middle Europe were seen as primitive in much the same way, but here the differences were deepened, because they were not Christian. Moreover, it was far from unknown for the Germans to enslave those they conquered. And differences of religion did not prevent agreements between the Germans and their pagan enemies. Adolf of Holstein allied with the pagan leader Nyklot, and was notably hostile to the intervention of the Second Crusade in Baltic affairs, the more so in that it was led by his rival, Henry the Lion. Finally, Christian chroniclers did not wholly condemn the pagans, and sometimes praised their good qualities while criticizing Christian greed.[1]

The Muslims were another matter. Although the term "barbarian" was applied to them from time to time, the Church viewed them as heretics, although laymen seem to have regarded them as pagans.[2] In any case, there was an awareness of a formidable enemy with a rival civilization. In Spain, where Christian kingdoms coexisted with Islamic powers that ruled many Christians, religious hatred dominated relations, although this was tempered by political realities. After the collapse of united Muslim Spain in about the year 1000, the Christian kingdoms saw the opportunity to re-conquer the whole peninsula, but they knew that rivalries amongst themselves and the support that the Spanish Muslims could receive from elsewhere would make this a complex process. Their policy was to impose tribute whenever possible, making a war of conquest pay for itself. As a result, relations were complex, with Christian–Islamic alliances frequent, promoted by rivalries between the Christian kingdoms and by a common dislike amongst Muslims and Christians for the Muslims of North Africa, whose power stiffened the resistance of their co-religionists in Spain.[3]

In the Holy Land, Western Christians were only present out of deep ideological hatred of Islam. This was the spirit of the First Crusade – yet even then, in the full flush of animosity, alliances were made with the Islamic powers, especially Egypt, and even alliances against other Catholic Christians. Saladin later inspired admiration amongst his enemies for his martial prowess and humane attitudes. Frederick II pursued friendship with the Ayyubid ruler of Egypt to liberate Jerusalem by diplomacy. The Mongols at one and the same time raised hopes of an alliance against Islam for the recovery of the Holy Land and created such a terror that they were portrayed as eating human flesh.[4]

Relations between Europeans and outsiders were shot with ambivalence, but for most of this period were dominated by war. Some outsiders were divided, tempting the ambitious landowners of settled societies into expansion. At the same time, their savagery in war and their "backward" social structure justified such conquest. And it was made all the more tempting because western Europeans had a considerable confidence in their style of war. It has been suggested that the expansion of Europe owed much to castles, crossbows (or at least missile-throwers) and heavy cavalry.[5] Europeans enjoyed a degree of technological superiority over some of their neighbours. The relative prosperity of Europe enabled its leaders to afford good defensive armour and more sophisticated fortifications, but this certainly did not give them any advantage over Muslims or the Mongols.

The key to understanding the European expansion in this period is the social dynamic that underlay it. We have seen that social mobility existed, that military service could form an upward path for aspirants. They were attracted to the peripheries, where society was less rigid and prospects for elevation better. The lure of land and respectability, or the prestige of a share in high authority, were powerful incentives for the sons of Tancred d'Hauteville, who became the rulers of South Italy, and for thousands of other emigrants whose lives have passed into obscurity. But this did not motivate only those who aspired to nobility. Conquest offered considerable opportunities for established families to increase their influence and position. In 1066, William the Conqueror dispensed the fruits of success to his followers, and in 1282 Edward I granted to one of his commanders in the Welsh wars, Henry de Lucy, Earl of Lincoln, lands which he centred on the great castle of Denbigh. All over Europe, the proprietorial urge created a will to conquest – sometimes in the service of kings, sometimes not. Golden prizes were at stake and fuelled the dreams of thousands. A family such as the Montforts gained great influence in France, England and the Holy Land, while the Lusignans rose to be kings in Jerusalem, Cyprus and Armenia. This is the social dynamic of European expansion at the expense of the peoples of the periphery.[6]

When the Normans conquered England in 1066, they faced two peripheral areas, both Christian and each with a society radically different from their own. The Conqueror's priority was self-preservation, and in the North he established no more than a series of outposts holding the vast no-man's land which merged into the Scottish realm. Against Wales he established great earldoms at Chester, Shrewsbury and Hereford, to guard against princes who might well shelter Anglo-Saxon rebels, but the political fragmentation of Wales and the wealth of its vulnerable lowlands tempted the Anglo-Norman lords and their successors into a conquest which ebbed and flowed for two centuries – the proprietorial imperative of individual lords was the driving force of conquest.[7] The English Crown did not try to seize Wales until the end of the thirteenth century, but its will lay behind the establishment of a permanent frontier zone, the March of Wales, in which great lords and their vassals pressed on the process of conquest. This was very spasmodic – the greatest amongst the Lords of the March at all times had political preoccupations beyond it and for long periods of time left expansion to their followers. Occasions of weakness in England, such as the reign of Stephen, produced marked setbacks. At the best of times, the English monarchy took only a fitful interest. Henry II restored much that had been lost under Stephen, but by 1172 he was content to pursue a policy of stability in Wales. John checked the Welsh princes with a great expedition in 1211, but after this internal problems in England opened the way for the expansion of the Welsh principalities, especially Gwynedd, so that by the time of Edward I it was evident that advance could not be sustained by the Marchers alone.

Nonetheless, by 1200 Norman pressure had transformed Wales. From Pembroke to Shewsbury, the Marcher lords dominated, although in the north the advance was less successful. The Welsh resisted bitterly, although they were very divided. Geography was the main reason for the political fragmentation of Wales, but it also made the business of conquest difficult. The heavy Norman horsemen were at first a novel force in the military affairs of Wales, but it was their castles that secured the land. The Welsh were far from overawed by them and many were captured, notably Rhuddlan and Basingwerk in the north: for the Welsh, as their enemies freely admitted, were a warlike people, and the professional warriors who gathered around their princes in their *teulu* were formidable. The novelty of heavy cavalry was soon countered by ambush and raiding. In the period 1066–1296, Shropshire suffered 86 raids and 15 major Welsh incursions, often with savage destruction.[8] Guerrilla warfare came naturally to the hill people with their transhumance culture, and in broken land was very effective. The great highlands formed a natural place of retreat from English raids for a people who often lacked permanent infrastructures of wealth to destroy.

The Anglo-Norman assault produced more than merely a slow process of conquest. Welsh society was transformed, and that of the March modified, during the years of confrontation. In part, this was because Wales shared in the demographic growth of Europe. There was extensive colonization of land, with consequent growth in the wealth of Welsh leaders. The coastal areas assumed much greater importance than the hills. It has been said that the borders of wheatland marked the extent of Norman penetration, but in reality there were wheatlands beyond the area of conquest and these facilitated new growth in Welsh Wales. The development of lordships and the growth of towns in the March was not merely an economic phenomenon. The Marchers might occasionally enjoy friendly relations with the Welsh princes, but they were deeply aware of the racial divide. From its earliest times, the March was planted with English and Flemish settlers. Edward I continued this tradition, with English settlers in his great fortified centres, although he never neglected that other arm of conquest – coming to terms with friendly Welsh lords.[9]

The economic and military development of England and the March was matched and imitated in the Welsh lands. To exploit this wealth there was a new emphasis on princely power, especially with the emergence of the house of Gwynedd, whose ascendancy was well established by the mid-thirteenth century. This development was accompanied by a new military sophistication. Welsh lords imitated the weapons and fighting style of their neighbours, while Welsh castles appeared in the twelfth century and became quite numerous after 1180 – for the new wealth and more settled society generated the same imperatives as that of neighbouring England. However, even at the height of the power of the princes of Gwynedd, Wales remained a divided land. The efforts of Llewellyn ap Gruffudd (1246–82) to impose a unity threatened English hegemony and alienated many of the Welsh princes, and once Edward I was aroused to major effort, Welsh defeat was inevitable.

It was inevitable, but hard-fought, for the Welsh had learned much from their years of contact. Welsh armies inflicted a series of disasters on the Normans in 1094–8, prompting intervention by William Rufus. In 1136, the Welsh were victorious in Gower, and Owain and Cadwaladr of Gwynedd raised an army of 6,000 including 2,000 mailed horsemen, and defeated a substantial Marcher force in a pitched battle at Crug Mawr, near Cardigan. These were of course troubled years in England. But in 1157 Owain Gwynedd, in the words of Gerald of Wales, "badly mauled" Henry II at the battle of Coleshill. Henry was attempting to reassert Anglo-Norman power after the losses under Stephen when he encountered a strong Welsh force under Owain at Basingwerk. While his main army confronted them on the coast, Henry led an attempt to outflank them, but was ambushed in the woods, with heavy losses. The king's discomfiture did not prevent him forcing Owain to homage in a campaign in which he enjoyed the support of Owain's brother, Cadwaladr, and Madog of Powys, and in the following year Rhy ap Gruffudd of Deheubarth was forced to make restitution to the Marchers.[10] Owain was probably prepared to stand and fight on this occasion because he had profited from the growing wealth of Wales to build castles and develop his lands.

The first reference to a native-built stone castle in Wales is to Cardigan in 1171, which was rebuilt by Lord Rhys, but many others followed, including Dolwyddelan, Dolbadarn and Criccieth in Gwynedd, Dryslwyn and Dinefwr in Deheubarth and Dinas Brân in Powys. They were never as formidable as the greatest of the Anglo-Norman structures; the disparity in resources explains this and the lack of good building stone in Snowdonia contributed. However, Dryslwyn and Dinefwr, with their round towers, were quite up to date. Welsh castles tended to exploit strong sites, and some features of their construction – notably apsidal towers – remain to be investigated. In fact, the Welsh had never been overawed by castles. In 1095, Gruffudd ap Cynan destroyed castles in Anglesey and Gwynedd, and in 1182 the outer works of Abergavenny fell to a surprise attack.[11] Gerald of Wales describes a long and systematic siege of Pembroke in 1094, while at Rhuddlan in 1167 there was a sustained siege in which the Welsh may even have used a siege-tower – and the full panoply of poliorcetics is mentioned at the siege of Dinefwr in 1213.[12]

As the Welsh princes consolidated their lands in response to changing economic conditions, so they came more and more to resemble their Marcher neighbours, with whom they intermarried. This did not in itself end tension and hatred between the two groups – they were rival landowners between whom racial and cultural differences were strong. In 1214 Giles de Braose, Bishop of Hereford, excused himself from attending a church council because he was escorting a papal legate who had business amongst "the barbarous Welsh nations". It is a matter of record that his sister Mathilda was married to Gruffudd ap Rhys of Deheubarth. If this was ambivalence, there was also bitter hatred and atrocity. There is an inevitable bias in the English sources but, even so, the destruction of churches, the wanton killing of men with the taking of heads, and the enslavement of women and children, were seen as horrific and characteristic of this kind of frontier warfare. Decapitation seems to have had a cultural significance for the Celtic peoples, although it must be admitted that their enemies practised it, above all as a basis for reward.[13] But the rest of their behaviour is explicable in the terms of war. They could not hope to conquer, but only to raid – the emphasis was therefore upon removing all wealth and destroying what was irremovable as revenge. It was essentially the warfare of the weak against the strong: the conqueror does not in general wish to acquire a desert, but those who cannot conquer – who can do only limited harm – can at least do it intensely, and of course this generated retribution.

The skill of the Welsh in conducting raids into Marcher England was remarkable: they would slip in, make their first attacks deep in enemy territory where they were least expected and then burn their way out. The English also conducted raids, but the relative poverty of the Welsh made this less attractive. In a few places, the English developed light cavalry to counter the enemy. However, we should perhaps remember that atrocities occurred in all kinds of war and not simply on the frontier. They were a product of the undeveloped economy of the Welsh, in which slavery was still important, of the imbalance between the enemies in the March and of the stress generated by frequent war, not least amongst the different Welsh factions. The efforts of the princes of Gwynedd to extend their dominion over all the Welsh princes aroused enormous opposition, and even dissension within their own family.[14] Llewellyn was a great proprietor with high ambitions to dominate all who were Welsh, but this was not yet an age of nationalism and loyalties remained local; indeed, there were many Welsh in the armies of Edward I that destroyed him.

Wales was a hard land and Edward had to raise enormous forces. The Marcher lords assisted, but the war turned on three military commands at

Chester, Montgomery and Carmarthen. For his own advance along the North Wales coast, Edward ordered great clearances of forest and a fleet attacked Anglesey, seizing the grain supplies that were so vital to the mountain fastness of Snowdonia. The Treaty of Aberconwy of November 1277 saw an enormous advance in royal power in Wales and the humiliation of Llewellyn ap Gruffudd. But to conquer was not to hold, and Edward I was unable to come to terms with the Welsh particularism which had served him so well. His officials trampled upon its susceptibilities and the result was the rebellion of 1282, which had to be put down by more enormous forces, which finally destroyed the independence of Wales. But the cost was horrendous and the settlement had to be backed by an enormous building programme that almost bankrupted Edward.[15]

The determining factor in Anglo-Welsh relations was the will of the Crown. The creation of a March was a useful expedient for the Norman kings, but their will always underpinned it. The tide of conquest ebbed and flowed with "strong" and "weak" English kings. When Henry II decided to come to terms in 1172 he ushered in a long period of relative stability, while the fate of the Braose under John shows how aware the English kings were of the risks of a formidable military power emerging amongst the Marchers. When the royal will was turned against Wales, it was evident that the superior wealth of England provided larger and better-equipped armies with large cavalry forces, and it was only the land and weather that frustrated them. The Welsh reacted quickly to the Norman weapons of castle, cavalry and cross-bow, and by 1094 had established means of dealing with them; furthermore, they had their own tradition of archery. What is striking is the extent to which English progress depended upon command of the sea, and Gerald of Wales clearly recognized its importance. Many of the key centres of Marcher power – notably Kidwelly, Carmarthen and Pembroke – were on or accessible to the sea. According to Welsh tradition, Robert FitzHamon began the conquest of Glamorgan by a landing from the sea at Portkerry in 1093. Hugh of Shrewsbury was killed by Magnus Barefoot of Norway and his fleet off Anglesey. In 1114, Henry I supported his invasion with ships, while the Welsh paid for a Danish fleet to support their attack on Cardigan castle in 1135. Henry II used fleets to attack Anglesey and North Wales in 1157 and 1165, while shipborne forces from Ireland helped Henry III in the war that led up to the Treaty of Woodstock of 1247. Edward I used a fleet to great effect in his conquest of Wales, and the great castles that he built to enforce his conquest are by the sea and often have ports.[16]

Scotland was another peripheral area, but here conditions were very different. The North of England required a brutal military subjugation, and Norman rule there long consisted of little more than a series of embattled outposts beyond the Humber. Here, it was hardly possible to establish predator landlords with a vested interest in conquest. Any such development was effectively forestalled, because the kings of Scotland recognized the utility of reorganizing their kingdom and they invited in Norman barons, who were often established landowners in England – to the great chagrin of many of the native chieftains. Scotland was not as inviting a prospect as Wales for the Norman predators. But the issue between the kings of the two lands was the March, for both laid claim to Cumbria and Northumberland. It was to settle this point that in 1072 William the Conqueror led a great raid up the east coast, supported by a fleet, and received the homage of Malcolm Canmore at Abernethy. But this was inconclusive, and in 1080 Robert Curthose led another Norman attack and received another submission, but founded Newcastle – a significant advance of the Norman frontier, which Rufus extended yet further by the establishment of a castle at Carlisle in 1092. Normanization then proceeded apace in Scotland, and Henry I married a Scottish princess, bringing peace between the two lands.[17]

The Norman kings seem to have felt no urge to conquer Scotland, but only to safeguard their dominion over Northumberland and Cumberland, and essentially it was this quarrel, and not any great cultural or other gap, which stood between the two kingdoms. The main thrust of Scottish history down to the thirteenth century was the extension and intensification of royal power. David (1124–53) seized Northumberland despite his defeat at the battle of the Standard in 1138, but it was quickly recovered from his young son Malcolm (1153–65) by Henry II. William the Lion (1165–1214) tried to take advantage of turbulence in England in 1174 with a full-scale invasion which resulted only in his capture. In 1209, his sabre-rattling was checked by John at the Treaty of Norham. Alexander II (1214–49) allied with the rebellious barons in 1216, invading England both then and again in 1217, when the defeat of the French brought peace. In 1244, he settled outstanding problems with Henry III, inaugurating half a century of harmony.[18] In the end, it was the very closeness of the two realms – cemented by family relationships between their ruling houses and the closely related families that they ruled over, who had lands under both – that led to Edward I's intervention in the succession crisis and his effort to conquer Scotland.

In many ways, relations between England and Scotland resemble those between England and France, where the consolidation of French government brought it into conflict with the English kings as rulers of Gascony, and this indeed is precisely what was happening. What gave Anglo-Scottish warfare its particular character were the allegations by English writers of atrocities by elements of the Scottish army. This body was made up of two kinds of troops. On the one hand were the Anglo-Norman lords and their followers, who owed service in respect of their landholding, and on the other the "common army" of the realm mustered compulsorily at need. It was this latter force that was accused of atrocities described as bestial during the invasion of 1138 and on later occasions. There is evidence that the Scottish kings condoned such behaviour even if their "feudal" forces did not participate. It has been argued that this constituted the special characteristic of war in the North.[19] The trouble is that, as with Wales, our evidence is rather one-sided. However, the uniformity of the charges suggests that war on the northern frontier, as often on the Welsh March, had a special horror. The Scottish king was only partially in control of his army in 1138: at the battle of the Standard, the Galwegians insisted on advancing first against the king's wishes. He may have mobilized his army to conquer territory, but many of his people had come to plunder – of which slavery, rapine and murder were natural by-products. It may well be that such savagery was unusual in Anglo-Norman warfare, but it was paralleled in Italy and elsewhere.

For the most part, the thirteenth century saw peace between England and Scotland. When war came again, it was the result of Edward's intervention in the succession dispute in Scotland. Edward adjudicated in favour of John Balliol, whom he then proceeded to treat as just another English vassal. When Balliol rebelled in 1296, Edward crushed him and took his great army as far north as Elgin. Then, as on so many subsequent occasions, he was supported by a powerful fleet. Edward's broad strategy seems to have been to bring the great nobility of Scotland, who were so intimately connected with the English court, to terms, but their feuds and factions, which had favoured his incursion into the northern kingdom, now made it difficult for him to build a party; those minded to resist could always find shelter in the inaccessible north of the country. Moreover, Edward's overbearing ways alienated wider Scottish opinion, which exploded in the rebellion of William Wallace and his defeat of the English army at Stirling Bridge in 1297. But Wallace was crushed at Falkirk on 22 July 1298 and by 1304 most of the nobility of Scotland had made submission to Edward. Edward made a moderate settlement by the Ordinance of September 1305, but his earlier arrogance, and the horrors of a war that had been increasingly brutal after 1297, increased distrust; after his death, the weakness of Edward II opened the way for further resistance.

In Scotland, Edward faced a strong unit with its own sense of political community, which was in many ways comparable to, if poorer than, his own. He never enjoyed the consistent support of a group amongst the English nobility with a vested interest in conquest, as he had in his attack on Wales. The Marchers lent their military aid to that effort, and through their connections created a mood favourable towards the enterprise. The Scottish war, by contrast, cost money and helped few. Edward I's death in 1307 was a body-blow to his policy of assimilation.[20]

More truly and radically different was the Baltic frontier of northeastern Europe. In a great band of land, stretching from the foot of the Jutland Peninsula around the eastern shore of the Baltic to what we now call Finland and 200–300 km deep into the hinterland, lived a huge array of pagan peoples. From Jutland to the Vistula were the Western Slavs, under the names of Wagrians, Abotrites, Polabians, Liutizians, Rugians and Pomeranians. Each people had a prince, but the countryside was dominated by magnates, with military followers ruling from earth and timber forts; near the mouths of the great rivers draining into the Baltic were urban communities who made a living from the needs of Baltic trade and so possessed fleets. East of the Vistula were the Prussians, Lithuanians, Latvians and Curonians. They too were led by a military aristocracy who built forts and dominated trade, giving them a close interest in sea-going. To the north lay Estonia and the Finnish peoples, who had close contacts with the great trading focus of Novgorod, the northern outpost of Russian Orthodoxy. All of these peoples were linked by a vigorous trade in the goods of the north – furs, slaves and amber – which the Scandinavians and Germans were anxious to share in, by constant war and piracy. Centralized kingship was growing only slowly amongst them, but for the most part they were obdurately pagan, their leaders seeing in the activities of Christian missionaries only foreign elites threatening their own domination. There was some christianization, notably amongst the West Slavs. They had paid tribute to the Ottonians and their church before 983, and early in the twelfth century the Pomeranians became Christian, as for a short time did the Abotrites under their Prince Henry, but they soon reverted to paganism under Nyklot.[21]

A number of Christian powers were interested in this complex of peoples. The Scandinavians, whose old power had waned, and Denmark in particular, were subject to raiding, and their Baltic trade to piracy. Before the great revolt of 983, the German monarchs had imposed tribute and service upon the West Slavs but left their society and religion alone; this policy had been followed by the Saxon lords in their tentative attempts at re-conquest. In the twelfth century the proprietorial imperative drove Saxon landowners on the Elbe frontier, notably Adolf of Holstein, to extend their lands. The chroniclers of the new phase of expansion from the mid-twelfth century strongly disapproved of the old methods of tribute-domination; Helmold was critical of the way in which the Saxons in the eleventh century had made peace with idolaters for money, and Henry of Livonia criticized thirteenth-century Russians for adopting the same attitudes to the pagan tribes. Territorial lordship, buttressed by religious conformity, was the main form of social organization in Europe, but the Saxon princes were chary of offending their Slav subjects; Adolf of Holstein founded Segeberg and imported settlers from Flanders to strengthen his hold on Wagria.[22] However, he was reluctant to impose Christianity and prepared to accommodate to the political realities of the world into which he was venturing, making a treaty with Nyklot, prince of the Abotrites.

But a new spirit was at work in the West. In 1147, the Second Crusade was proclaimed: the expansionist nobles of the German frontier were not anxious to rush off to the Middle East, not least because they were mainly Welf in sympathy and were unwilling to follow a Hohenstaufen crusade; they probably pleaded their preoccupations with nearby pagans as an excuse. As a result, they were encouraged to fulfil their vows by crusading against them. The purpose of this new Crusade was forced conversion: St Bernard made it very clear that if the pagans adopted Christianity they were to retain their traditional organization, but if not, their nations were to be destroyed – although he did not condone actual massacre. The Saxon princes were not happy with this new spirit. Adolf was unwilling to abandon his alliance with Nyklot, and Helmold suggested that Henry the Lion of Saxony was at pains not to damage lands which he hoped to rule. It was a sign of the times that the ordinary soldiers criticized their leaders for temporizing. When Süssel, a fortified Frisian settlement, was besieged by the Slavs, its people were on the verge of coming to terms; the local priest charged into the enemy army, seeking his own martyrdom as a means of preventing an agreement.[23]

By and large, the great Saxon nobility and their dynastic ambitions were the driving force of this phase of the conquest which, by the end of the twelfth century, had annexed most of the West Slav lands to Germany, with a coastal share to Denmark. Adolf of Holstein re-forged his alliance with Nyklot, not least as a counter to Henry the Lion, and only reluctantly did he begin to impose Christianity on his Slav subjects. The Danes under Waldemar I (1157–82) were anxious to end raiding by the pagans of the Baltic coast and co-operated in conquest with Henry the Lion; neither, however, was much interested in the advance of Christendom. Henry, indeed, indulged in a bitter feud with the Church over control in his newly conquered land. Ultimately, both recognized the advantages of the new crusading culture in enlisting support and pacifying newly conquered lands.[24]

In this first impulse of conquest on the eastern frontier, proprietorial ambitions and ideology tended to be in opposition, but matters worked differently in Livonia. There, the precursors of German conquest were the German merchants, striving for a share of the Baltic trade with Russia and the north. But the archbishopric of Bremen was also strongly interested in saving the souls of the many pagan peoples, while the papacy was uncomfortably aware of the possibility of Orthodox penetration into the Baltic from Russia. The decisive factor in establishing the Baltic mission in Livonia was the appointment of the Archbishop of Bremen's nephew, Albert of Buxhoevden (1199–1229), as its bishop. He was extremely well connected and encouraged members of his family to join the conquest, notably his brother, John of Appeldorn. Albert co-operated closely with the papacy; as a result, he was able to raise Crusades from Germany year in year out. He was also able to establish a permanent warrior group with a vested interest in conquest – the Sword-Brothers. These were modelled on the better-known Templar, Hospitaller and Teutonic Orders of fighting monks, but they were never as coherent or disciplined. They seem to have formed around Albert's relatives and friends. In effect, they made up for the absence of a native or neighbouring Christian aristocracy with a vested interest in conquest: in 1204, Bishop Albert agreed a partition that gave them a third of Livonia. They were a turbulent lot and gave Albert trouble, but he was their founder and the formidable administration that he built he seems to have kept them in order. After his death they became the dominant force in Livonia, alienating the papacy and the Danes, so that when their order was almost annihilated by the Lithuanians in 1236, the papacy called in the Teutonic Order.[25]

In Prussia the missionary-bishop, Christian of Prussia (1215–45) founded a new religious order, the Knights of Dobrzyn, but they too were replaced by the Teutonic Order. In both areas, these various orders acted as a kind of regular military core who could hold the Christian pale, around whom armies of crusaders, mostly from Germany, could be built from time to time. Indeed, after a series of defeats in the 1260s, the Teutonic Order in Prussia was saved by crusaders from Germany. The Teutonic Order was a landed institution with great ambitions, who insisted on autonomy for their conquests. In Prussia, they created a monastic state. They thus fulfilled the role of predator aristocracy, comparable to the Marchers of Wales. At the same time "the dominant motive of the Teutonic Knights, and of all crusaders, was the desire for atonement through self-sacrifice" and thus they could exploit the idealism of the European upper class. Their prestige created for them resources all over Christendom, so that their commitments in any one theatre, such as Prussia, could be financed and supported from elsewhere.[26] In short, the Teutonic Order represented, along with the Church in general, the bishops, the Danes and various other interested parties, an implacable will endowed with the means to conquest.

The Christian conquest was a remarkable achievement, for war in the Baltic world faced special obstacles. The miserable wetness of the spring and autumn greatly hampered movement, which meant that fighting was effectively confined to summer, either in May–June before the harvest, or August–

September after it. In winter, communications were better, because rivers, lakes, marshes and even the sea froze over, but it was then impossible to feed large armies for any period of time, so that this was a season of raiding. Even in the summer there were formidable problems. Beyond a narrow coastal strip, the great forest was all but impenetrable except by the river valleys, and this meant that expeditions tended to rely on sea transport. It was these general conditions which dictated the limited ends of the military interventions of the princes of Novgorod – to impose a peace and extract tribute was what was most easily possible in these conditions – and doubtless this had weighed with the Ottonians too. In these circumstances, how was it that relatively small numbers of Germans – the Sword-Brothers never numbered more than 120 – were able to impose themselves?[27]

Fundamental to this victory was the will of the Church, which inspired men such as Bishop Albert to go out and conquer. The secular conquerors whom we see at work in the twelfth century might in time have driven the frontier forwards, but like the Marchers of Wales they lacked a common will and had many distractions. There were adventurers all over Europe ready to look abroad for advancement, but without the appeal of the crusade few would have ventured to the harsh and dangerous north: only very slowly did individual knights appear, ready to take up lordships in the new land. They could certainly never have formed themselves into corporate bodies – the religious orders – without that appeal. Moreover, the crusade enlisted behind the conquest enormous numbers of part-time fighters, whose wealth and energy was given to a cause which only the Church thrust before them. Here, then, were the roots of victory.

This iron will to expand was enhanced by technological advantage. One of the earliest missionaries to Livonia, Bishop Meinhard, tried to persuade the Livonians to convert by sending for stonemasons from Gothland to build a castle at Uexküll, which would be invulnerable to Lithuanian attack: the Livonians accepted the fort but lapsed into their old pagan ways. The trilogy of castles, cavalry and crossbowmen had great effect, although this must not be exaggerated. The north was peculiarly unsuited to the classic tactics of heavy cavalry, as the enemy quickly learned. The Sword-Brothers were destroyed on marshy ground, and in Prussia the Teutonic knights suffered many severe reverses. But the Germans enjoyed a mobility which matched that of their enemies on their light ponies. Their strong armour was a huge advantage, both physical and psychological. It is difficult to believe that without this Conrad of Meiendorf and the German followers of Bishop Albert would have charged the huge mass of the Lithuanian raiders in 1205, shaming their Semgall allies into joining them. So prized was armour that it was used for diplomatic gifts – such as that made to Vladimir of Pskov in 1207. Crossbows are frequently mentioned and clearly gave the Germans a great advantage over the pagans. They were especially useful in defending Christian forts and attacking those of the enemy: when the Russians approached Uexküll in 1206, they knew there were Germans in the castle, because some of their men were wounded by crossbows. By the 1220s some of this technology was rubbing off on the pagan tribes, who consciously imitated it.[28] But without the industrial base which generated such weapons and techniques there were grave limits to what they could achieve, and they never seem to have changed their fighting methods in any significant way.

The castle was the key to conquest. The pagans had their own earth and timber castles, and the Germans built many similar structures, but they were gradually reinforced or replaced by stone. In this way, lines of fortresses were established down the key river valleys. In the conquest of Livonia, Bishop Albert took an important decision when he moved the centre of all his operations to Riga, close to the mouth of the Dvina, which was strongly fortified. Castles were the keys to the land, and time and time again resisted pagan assault. In 1211, a large Estonian army supported by a fleet attacked Caupo's great fort on the Aa, which was partly held by Christian Livonians; they were able to hold out until a relief force from Riga arrived.[29] But not only were the forts of the Christians stronger – they had also developed the art of siege warfare much more highly.

As early as 1147, Henry the Lion was deploying siege-machinery against Nyklot's fortresses of Dimin and Dubin: the Russians tried to imitate a catapult in 1206 when they besieged Holm, but it misfired and wounded some of their own men. It was not merely siege-machines that enabled the Germans to seize enemy forts: they were better organized and more persistent. In 1211, the Germans and their allies attacked Fellin: they ravaged the land around, killing its inhabitants, and then used archery to clear the enemy from the outer ring of defences, while the moat was filled and a wooden siege-tower was moved up to dominate the ramparts. When an attempt to fire this was fought off, the besiegers brought a stone-thrower into action: "Since the Estonians had never seen such things, they had not strengthened their houses against such missiles". The Germans then mounted the outer defences; when they failed to penetrate the inner citadel, they set it alight, so forcing a surrender. In the next year the Germans attacked rebel Livonians in Dobrel's fort; when one siege-tower was blown over by the wind, another was built and the besiegers "were digging day and night at the ramparts . . . until the rampart was cut in two". By such means, the crusaders established a network of castles, usually of very simple construction, which anchored their conquest and created a framework within which immigrant vassals of the dominant powers, the Teutonic Knights and the bishops, could flourish. The castles were financed by the wealth of the Order, by donations from the Church in the West and, increasingly, as peace established itself, by taxes on the con-quered population.[30]

The decisive technical factor which sustained the German conquest was not military at all, but a by-product of the economic expansion of Europe, the merchant cog or round-ship. These were large, solidly built craft up to 30 m long and 9.5 m wide – by the end of the thirteenth century, deadweights of 200 tons were possible. They were popular with merchants in the Baltic and elsewhere because they could carry an immense load, up to about 250 tons, with a crew of only about 18–20, and so they were available to the German crusaders. By contrast, their pagan enemies did not have the means to build such expensive vessels. The cog could carry 500 people – very useful for bringing in and supplying crusaders and their settlements. As fighting ships, they were helped by a high freeboard, which meant that they towered over anything else that could float, like a castle at sea: indeed, one was turned into a floating fort to guard the mouth of the Dvina against enemy attack. The cog was never fast or manoeuvrable, but it was very seaworthy, especially after the introduction of the stern-post rudder, and it could be towed up rivers. Henry the Lion came to recognize the need for sea-power, as we have noted, but the increase in Baltic shipping brought a decisive advantage to the Germans. In 1215, two cogs were enough to scatter the Estonian fleet in the mouth of the Dvina, and a little later that year nine cogs bearing pilgrims returning to Germany were trapped by bad weather in Oesel, where large numbers of Estonian ships tried in vain to destroy them.[31]

The Germans owed something of their success to the political circum-stances of the northern world. Their chief rivals in the northern and eastern Baltic were the Russian principalities. These, however, were disunited and Orthodoxy lacked the institutional power to bind them together. They clung to the old model of tribute-hegemony and made little effort to expand in a territorial sense. Moreover, they were soon diverted by a new force – the Mongols. In 1237, the Great Khan Ogedei (1229–41) sent his armies, perhaps 150,000 strong, into Russia and the West. Although bad weather prevented them from taking Novgorod, Kiev fell in 1240 and Mongol supremacy was quickly established. In 1241, the Mongols moved west in two great arms of attack. The southern arm destroyed the Hungary of Bela IV at Mohi on 11 April, while the northern arm defeated the Poles at Leignitz on 9 April. The Poles had allied with the Teutonic Order against the Lithuanians and others, which is why the Order sent troops, but they were overwhelmed.

The Mongols had built a magnificent military machine. Their style of warfare was a reflection of their nomadic way of life. They were horse-archers, riding hardy ponies which were so small that each man needed a string of remounts – up to 20 is mentioned – to maintain mobility. Under Chingis Khan, a centralized government was imposed on the tribes and an army created. The Khan was guarded by the *Keshik*, a personal guard of about 10,000 men. The major unit of the army was the *tumen* of about 10,000, divided into *mingan* of 1,000, *jegun* of 100 and *arban* of ten. They were supported by specialist troops and later by infantry drawn from the conquered peoples. The whole army was subject to a severe discipline, but its great strength was coherence. Man for man, the Mongols were poorer and less well armed than most of their enemies, but huge numbers could be gathered – the thrust west involved 150,000 men. Each unit was co-ordinated by a system of signals, and selected archers could change the direction of fire by using whistling arrows. The basic tactic was to envelop an enemy, pour in arrows, probably from about 50 m, and charge home only when opposing formations broke up. In time, the Mongols acquired more armour, but it was their highly disciplined and organized light cavalry, with their strings of remounts, which won their battles. Of course, their tactics were akin to those of the Turks, to whom they were related, but it was their discipline allied to overwhelming numbers that made them successful. The Mongols did not stay in Europe: in 1241, Ogedei died and the Mongol armies withdrew as a succession struggle loomed. That they never returned, however, is probably due to the lack of grazing for their horses – Mongol armies depended on finding grazing, and this was much more difficult in the confines of the West. But they remained in Russia, whose principalities were from now on deeply preoccupied by the politics of the "Golden Horde".[32]

The Germans enjoyed some support from other Christian peoples around the Baltic. The Germans regarded Danish expansion into Estonia with suspicion, but it diverted their enemies. In Prussia, the Teutonic Order enjoyed considerable Polish support in its early years. But more important than these were the divisions amongst the Baltic peoples themselves. Defections to Christianity amongst the West Slavs have already been noted. The pagan Semgalls were as often allies as enemies of the Livonian crusade, partly because of their hatred for the Lithuanians. The Selones accepted Christianity for a time, although they later returned to their alliance with the Lithuanians. The Teutonic Knights profited from the failure of the Prussian tribes to combine against them. The alliances between these pagan peoples and the crusaders were very unstable, but in this they resembled the alliances that the pagans made amongst themselves. The newcomers had the enormous advantage of identifying themselves as a single force opposed to all paganism, while each pagan tribe sought to preserve its independence against all-comers. There were efforts to combine, but the pattern of war bred by conditions in the north made them short-lived. The last pagan state of the north was to be Lithuania, whose royal house emulated their Christian enemies and built a great state which would defy conquest far beyond the period covered here.[33]

What distinguished war in the north from that elsewhere was the scale and horror of atrocity. The war of the north was harsh and brutal – tribes raided incessantly, slaughtering men and enslaving women and children, burning crops and houses. Slavery was a profitable business and powerfully increased the incentive for such attacks. In essence, these were the tactics of waste, universal in war, applied by peoples who did not seek territorial aggrandizement. This was how war in the north was conducted amongst the native peoples of the area, as Henry of Livonia shows. This style of war was not alien to the Germans, who had indulged in it under Henry the Lion, even to the taking of slaves. But in the thirteenth-century Crusades, the Germans quickly adopted it and waged it with every conceivable horror.[34] This savagery was amplified by the racial arrogance of the Germans and their religious fanaticism, which sanctioned slaughter in the name of God. Inevitably, the pagans committed horrific atrocities against Christian priests who fell into their hands.[35] The warfare along the Baltic was about as near to total war as medieval men could get – a war of atrocity and counter-atrocity in which no quarter was given. Its brutalities must be seen in the context of harsh tribal competition for limited resources in an inclement climate. However, clearly, war against "the other" took on a quite different and extreme form compared to that fought within western Europe, where it only rarely reached this level of bitterness. Much modern reaction to the horrors of the Baltic conquest springs from the fact that they were committed in the name of God – on behalf of a notion of meritorious war which we call a crusade, which was first invented for use against quite different enemies.

# Chapter Fifteen

# *Crusading and warfare in the Middle East*

Conquest in the Middle Ages was always difficult. Even the greatest kings found collecting resources complicated and persuading followers problematic, which is why it was usual to try to come to terms with the existing population. Distance, geography and weather made the process complex and liable to miscarry. Yet in 1095 a pope, Urban II (1088–99), proposed a military expedition to seize the city of Jerusalem, some 4,000 km distant from Clermont where he was preaching, in a land strange to most of his listeners, with a climate they would find harsh, occupied by people of an alien religion who would brook no compromise. There was no great leader with a retinue of predatory followers to take command, and he offered no pay to those who went. What was proposed appears as ideological warfare in the purest sense: that men should leave their riches, their wives and their lands to free Jerusalem from the infidel, thus gaining an indulgence – release from the burden of sin – and, if death should overcome them, immediate entry into the kingdom of heaven.

It is strange is that such an idealistic appeal should be directed to a class whose primary preoccupation was landholding by one who was, after all, drawn from their ranks. What is even stranger is that it succeeded, for the First Crusade brought together an army of over 60,000, including in its ranks 6,000–7,000 cavalry drawn from the ranks of the leaders of society.[1] But this is not such a great paradox. Men and women did not make their decisions, even about peace and war, solely on the basis of proprietorial considerations – it was simply that in any serious matter these played a major, and often *the* major, role. It would be an impossibly narrow view of human motivation to believe that it was always entirely material. Moreover, and this is critical to our understanding, the Crusade was presented in a way which had a powerful appeal to the proprietorial instinct.

There is little doubt that religious sentiment had increased enormously from about the year 1000. Lay patronage of churches, the cult of saints and pilgrimage, especially to Jerusalem, are all evidence of a new religious spirit. Men and women were painfully aware of their own sinfulness and its terrible consequences, and deeply anxious to escape from them. Urban offered to the leading groups in European society an opportunity to purge their sins by a meritorious act of war. Although he played on older ideas, the novelty of the synthesis was striking and must have seemed like a window of opportunity, a moment in which to escape from the burden of sin that weighed men down hitherto beyond all hope of escape.[2]

But Urban's language, if we can trust our sources, cast this in a particular way: "May you be especially moved by the Holy Sepulchre of Our Lord and Saviour which is in the hands of unclean races". The crusaders were called to liberate God's land, Jerusalem, from the infidel, upon whom they should wreak God's vengeance. Almost a century after Urban's appeal at Clermont, an unknown French poet lamented the fall of the kingdom: "As I love God, we have delayed too long to travel in His service and seize that land from which the Turks have ejected and exiled us". During the Third Crusade, Richard I wrote to Saladin summarizing, in remarkably material terms, what lay between them: "The points at issue are Jerusalem, the Cross and the Land". Innocent III compared the crusader's duty to that of a vassal obliged to come to the aid of a dispossessed lord. One of those who took the cross in 1095 was Hélias of Maine, who subsequently found his lands threatened. He excused himself in terms of defence of property, whose sanctity he virtually equates with the liberation of Jerusalem: "I wished to fight the pagans in the Lord's name, but now I see that I must wage a war nearer to home against enemies of Christ". He seems to have been little blamed for his failure to fulfil his vows.[3]

The Crusade, therefore, was presented in terms comprehensible to the military leaders of Western society with their proprietorial instincts. Urban was at pains to stress that only those who went to Jerusalem "from pure devotion, not for reputation or monetary gain" could gain the spiritual reward, but this was not a bar to plunder, loot and land. Urban knew perfectly well that an army could only exist by ravaging and that territorial gain would be the inevitable result of the crusade; he would not have dreamt of prohibiting this. If spiritual concepts were expressed in rather crude material terms, material gain could also be seen as a witness to spiritual success. Urban's own language, if we can trust Robert the Monk, in fact tended to incite the desire for gain. It was, therefore, a heady cocktail which Urban offered and which he publicized with enormous care. It had an enormous appeal which would endure across the centuries: pious nobles, adventurous young knights, the desperate poor, even the urban patriciate – all saw something in it for them. This was the propellant, the underlying driving force, of a great movement which was to make itself felt in every corner of Europe in the centuries to come. The power of its appeal explains why crusader armies could stay in the field so much longer than was normally the case. Each individual provided his own finance, commensurate with his status and the task in hand. For a knight, this meant raising at least one year's income: for the feudal summons he was only obliged to support himself for 40 days. Crusades mobilized resources on a scale only exceptionally available to Western commanders.[4]

The First Crusade, and indeed some subsequent crusades, had allies. Urban arranged for the Western armies to gather at Constantinople, which most of them reached in the spring of 1097. Some crusaders, but probably not the leaders, may have expected Alexius to lead them, but in the event they had to settle for imperial support and aid. This was vitally important. The imperial forces took over captured territory, relieving the crusaders of the need to detach garrisons, provided guides and diplomatic help in dealing with groups such as the Armenians, and, above all, provided absolutely irreplaceable logistic support during the long siege of Antioch. The importance of Byzantine help was self-evident to the crusaders, who were bitterly disappointed by what they saw as the failure of Alexius to come to their aid when Kerbogah attacked them in Antioch. But despite the quarrel which ensued when Bohemond took over Antioch, relations between Byzantium and the West remained reasonable. There was some tendency to blame the Byzantines for the failure of the Second Crusade, but this was fairly limited, and, very soon after, the crusader states began a phase of close alliance with Byzantium.[5] It was events at the time of the Third Crusade which created a gulf between Byzantium and the West. The fall of Jerusalem after Hattin in 1187 shocked the West, and the first major army to set out was the huge force of Frederick I Barbarossa. But because of the political turbulence in Constantinople the Byzantines had allied with Saladin and did everything they could to frustrate Frederick – to no avail. This was a bitter business and helped to create the climate of opinion in which the Fourth Crusade could capture Constantinople. Thereafter, although the prospect of a Byzantine alliance and a resolution of the schism of the churches continued to haunt the Western Church, nothing concrete ever came of it.[6] The failure of Byzantium and the West to forge a common understanding had important military consequences. It prevented the Byzantines from re-conquering Asia Minor, so there was no land-bridge for mass pilgrimage which could have provided manpower for the crusaders in the East. Moreover, without a land-bridge the Crusader states had to rely entirely on sea-communications.

The Crusades were dependent from the first on sea-power. Urban II personally appealed to the Genoese, who provided a fleet for the First Crusade. This, together with Italian, English and, above all, Byzantine shipping, was indispensable to the success of the crusade.[7] Once that was achieved, fleets were vital for communications with the West. The Second Crusade was crippled because its fleet had become absorbed into the siege of Lisbon. The army of Barbarossa on the Third Crusade was the last to try to force its way through by land: the armies of Richard of England and Philip of France came by sea, as did every crusade to the East thereafter. It was the absence of a fleet that delivered the leaders of the Fourth Crusade into the hands of Venice. The voyage of the Rhenish and Frisian fleets on the Fifth Crusade was a remarkable undertaking. Frederick II raised his own fleet for the East, as Charles of Anjou did later. St Louis made an enormous naval effort, absorbing local shipbuilding capacity to the extent that one of his companions, the Count of St Pol, had to have his ship built in Scotland. After the Third Crusade, the only route to the Holy Land was by sea, and even horses needed special transports.[8]

Sailors and the material that they brought played a major part in the sieges of the First Crusade, and it was with their aid that the cities of the Palestinian littoral – without which the crusader bridgeheads established in 1099 would never have been viable – were captured. It was the fortuitous arrival of a pilgrim fleet which saved Baldwin I of Jerusalem after his defeat at Ramla in 1102, while the fleet of William of Sicily saved Tripoli after Hattin in 1187. The twice-yearly pilgrim fleets from the West were the lifeline of the kingdom. They brought with them pilgrims who could be conscripted in moments of emergency. They carried the trade in luxury goods which was vital to the incomes of the kings. One important consequence of dependence upon sea-power was that the Italian city–states that controlled it acquired special privileges. They had their own quarters in the cities and lived by their own laws. When the monarchy weakened in the thirteenth century, they plunged the kingdom into their own quarrels, of which the most disastrous was the War of St Sabbas. But they were always essential to the survival of the Latins in the East. This maritime supremacy was rarely challenged by the Muslims. The Islamic world lacked wood to sustain shipping. Only Egypt had a fleet, but its ships were smaller and they suffered from problems of water supply. This was one area where the crusaders enjoyed a clear technical superiority.[9]

After the triumph of the First Crusade in 1099, the crusade became an established institution of the medieval West. The papacy directed crusaders to many different places at different times. Here we are concerned with what was always its most characteristic purpose, the maintenance of Latin domination over the Holy Land. To achieve this end, the crusade was an imperfect instrument. Crusading came in fits and starts, often with long intervals in between. The absence of a major effort after the failure of the Second Crusade undoubtedly helped the Islamic powers in their assault on the crusader principalities. All who took the cross did so as individuals, and, theoretically were equals. In fact, the social structure of Europe persisted in the crusader armies, but this left the problem of command.

The First Crusade was led by a committee of princes, and it was only in extreme circumstances that the leaders agreed to the appointment of a single commander – and then only for a limited period. Serious strains arose after the fall of Antioch in 1098, to such an extent that the siege of Jerusalem was undertaken by what were virtually two armies. The crusade of 1101 involved huge numbers of troops, but they fought in separate contingents which were defeated by small numbers of Turks in Asia Minor. A similar fate overtook the Second Crusade, because Louis VII of France and Conrad III of Germany failed to work together. The quarrels of Richard and Philip Augustus delayed their departure for the Third Crusade and once there they failed to co-operate. After Philip had departed, Richard was a brilliant commander, but there were considerable tensions between the English, French and Germans, and prevalent attitudes in the army forced him to pursue the attack on Jerusalem when he might well have preferred to attack Egypt. In the end, he withdrew from Jerusalem because of the dangers of a siege in the face of a hostile army and the sheer difficulties of holding it once the crusade had departed. For this decision he was much reviled, but he had taken the best advice and he was almost certainly right.

On the Fourth Crusade the nobles elected Boniface of Montferrat as their leader, but he had to work with others, most notably Baldwin of Flanders and the Venetians who controlled the fleet: as a result, the crusade was directed largely by incident and circumstance rather than decision. On the Fifth Crusade, the comings and goings of leaders and contingents were such that leadership was vested in Pelagius, the papal legate. On the First Crusade, Adhémar had been legate and he had exercised great influence even over military decisions, but he was unusual in that he had military experience. Pelagius rose to his position of command by default, and made a series of poor decisions which contributed to the failure of the expedition. Frederick II had only a small army, and was spurned by the forces of Jerusalem because he was excommunicate. But he liberated Jerusalem by skilful diplomacy, showing what limited force shrewdly applied could do. The Crusade of Theobald of Champagne and Richard of Cornwall has been called "a burlesque of the crusades": the two main leaders never met, Theobald's army was bitterly divided and disobedient and the barons of Jerusalem were fractious. The result was a series of bizarre decisions, yet also an astonishing success, for as a result of diplomatic circumstances the kingdom lost in 1187 was restored, albeit briefly. St Louis was incontrovertibly the sole commander of his army, but his forces were barely adequate for the conquest of Egypt and his errors as a commander brought defeat; in particular, he failed to make an early decision to withdraw after Mansourah, a failure to contrast with Richard's withdrawal from Jerusalem.[10]

Uncertain and often divided leadership was inevitably accompanied by uncertain purpose. Much of the success of the First Crusade was due to the limited but specific objective – Jerusalem. When its leaders were at their most ignorant and hesitant, their army was large enough to overcome by sheer weight of numbers the Sultanate of Nicaea. Very quickly, they took the measure of their enemies and maximized their strength by an adroit diplomacy, winning allies and buying off enemies by pacts of friendship which they were perfectly prepared to break. This diplomatic aspect to their crusade was vital, for although the Middle East was fragmented, many of its component parts were more than a match in military terms for the invaders. What the Muslim powers did not understand was that the invaders posed a threat to their very existence. Once that was understood, the scale and quality of their resistance to new crusades was enormously enhanced.

The Second Crusade simply had no clear purpose: the occasion of its calling was the fall of Edessa to Zengi, but this had not in itself stirred the West; it was only the incredible activity of St Bernard that created what became a general onslaught upon the non-Catholics who confronted Europe. This vast concept never generated any central control and Louis VII, the only leader to arrive in Jerusalem with an army, had little idea what to do with it. Richard of England, as we have noted, had a crusading strategy – to seize Egypt, the real heart of Saladin's power – but the religious goal of the expedition (and probably the personal animosity which Richard so obviously generated) proved too strong. But the problems of the Third Crusade were pondered. The union of Syria and Egypt under Saladin had caused the fall of the Latin Kingdom, but the quarrels of his descendants, the Ayyubids, created opportunities which could be exploited. The leaders of the Fourth Crusade made a secret decision to attack Egypt. This was actually carried out by the Fifth Crusade, probably acting in accord with the decisions of the Fourth Lateran Council, although it was their decision to attack Damietta rather than Alexandria. Once the city had fallen, the crusade was for long paralysed by failures of command, and it was probably popular demand for action that led to its ultimate failure near Mansourah.[11]

The problems of command and strategy on crusade reflected in a more acute form the general problems of command in medieval armies. Even the most capable commander had to impose himself and persuade, developing methods of uniting his forces. But on crusade, far from home and in grave peril before determined enemies, such weaknesses were more dangerous. And crusader armies shared many of the other flaws of the generality of Western forces. Those who summoned medieval armies could never be quite certain who would turn up or how suitable they would be for the task in hand, and this was particularly the case for crusades. The extent of support for the First Crusade astonished contemporaries, and the Second Crusade may well have exceeded it, but only a third of the expected 33,500 men arrived at Venice for the Fourth Crusade. Even on the First Crusade, some forces arrived a month after hostilities at Nicaea had begun. On the Second, the French and Germans operated to their own timetables, while the English fleet became involved in a full-scale action in Portugal, and something of the sort happened to the northern contingents of the Fifth Crusade. On the Third, conditions in the West meant that the Anglo-French expedition did not arrive until four years after the defeat at Hattin. The Fifth Crusade suffered from an endless turnover of leaders and forces – Andrew of Hungary left in January 1218 before the attack on Egypt had even begun. Desertion had always been a problem for crusades – during the First there was bitterness against apostates who had not fulfilled their vows, while Philip Augustus left the Third Crusade, and on the Fourth there were sizeable numbers who either did not arrive at Venice or left the army at Zara. And the crusade had an international appeal which all too often enlisted mutually hostile peoples. On the First Crusade there was considerable tension between the Provençals and others. The French and the Germans quarrelled bitterly on the Second Crusade, while there was an enormous amount of bickering on the Third between nationalities. The diversity, the random appeal of the crusade and the different kinds of contingents raised, the lack of any central command – all of this meant that crusader armies were even more *ad hoc* than most medieval armies. There were some notable exceptions. The army of the First Crusade became hardened by three years of fighting together, and by its later stages the army performed with exceptional skill and coherence. Barbarossa recruited a huge and tightly organized army which fought its way across the Byzantine Empire and the Sultanate of Iconium – but its unity lay in the dominant personality of Frederick himself and after his death it broke up, much to the relief of the Muslims. Richard I had a fine army drawn from his own lands, but he experienced grave tensions with other contingents. St Louis had a magnificent army, although its total of 15,000 was barely adequate for the job in hand.[12]

These problems came to be understood very clearly. Richard I took in hand the organization of his Crusade, which was virtually an official Angevin expedition. The crusade was probably never preached in England because

Richard preferred to raise effective troops by other means, notably from amongst his mercenaries. Philip Augustus's state machinery had rather more difficulty in launching his crusade, but by the time of St Louis it was highly effective in raising, supplying and organizing troops. The Saladin Tithe was inspired by the shock of the destruction of the Latin Kingdom in 1187, but it laid the foundations for regularizing the key area of finances. Innocent III tried to create a sound basis in his plans for the Fifth Crusade and at the Lateran Council. After the defeat of St Louis, a new strategy of substituting for the *passagium generale* a number of *passagium particulare* was discussed. This involved sending specific bodies of troops, even mercenaries, for particular functions; the regiment maintained by St Louis in the East after his departure is an obvious example. Ultimately, organizing and sustaining the crusading movement proved to be beyond the means of the papacy. This is why kings became so prominent in the movement, but their willingness to support it proved limited.[13]

Crusades raised diverse and loosely organized armies which enjoyed no clear technical or tactical advantage over their enemies. Although the environment into which they were moving was unfamiliar, it was inevitable – and indeed desirable – that crusading armies would stick to tried and trusted methods of fighting. The timespan of individual Crusades was far too short to make any serious alteration. But the basic condition which had favoured the success of the First Crusade was the fact that their enemies were not united, although it cannot be said too often that many of the Muslim powers which it encountered had very formidable armies. After its success, Muslim resistance stiffened. An alliance of Islamic powers crushed the crusade of 1101. Thereafter, dynamic leaders emerged: Zengi (ob. 1146) at Mosul and Aleppo, Nur ad-Din (ob. 1174), who added Damascus, and Saladin (ob. 1193), who unified Syria and Egypt. These new rulers had great power, and enjoyed the enormous advantage of fighting on their own ground with established methods.

Warfare in the Middle East was heavily conditioned by geographical and climatic factors. In general, the countryside was much emptier than in the West, and there were large tracts of desert and semi-desert. This placed a heavy emphasis on mounted warfare, because large distances had to be covered between the main population centres. In the open lands of North Syria east of the Orontes, on the Golan, the Galilee and in the desert between Gaza and Egypt, infantry were at a huge disadvantage. Water was vital in an arid land and any army without it would perish.

Islamic armies, like those of the West, were largely *ad hoc* bodies. The rulers of the area kept small standing forces and formed armies round these nuclei at need. At the heart of the Islamic system was the Diwan, the ministry responsible for troops and their finance. In Fatamid Egypt this supported arsenals, barracks and a paid army based on 4,000–5,000 cavalry and the African heavy infantry. This could be augmented by forces drawn from peoples with specialized styles of war; particularly Berber, Bedouin and North African light cavalry. In the Seljuk lands the nucleus could be augmented by heavy cavalry as well as light horse and archers from Iran, archers from Armenia and Syria, and infantry from the Daylami of the Caspian. But the core of the Seljuk armies were *Māmluks*, slave soldiers, Turkish horsemen whose speciality was mounted archery. Increasingly, these forces were supported on *Iqta*, grants of land and authority made to Emirs and other princes. Such grants were in the gift of the ruler and were controlled by the Diwan. The troops that they provided were the most effective element in the Islamic armies, although they continued to be augmented by other forces and by volunteers, men doing military service as a religious duty. Saladin destroyed the influence of the Africans in the Egyptian army when he came to power in Egypt, and favoured Kurds and Turks in positions of authority, retaining only a personal guard of about 1,000. He raised the rest of his army at need from the provinces of his empire. This created similar problems to those noted in Western armies. In the twelfth century, it took at least two months for Fatimid Egypt to raise an army and get it to Palestine. In the conference before Hattin, according to Ibn al-Athir, Raymond of Tripoli urged King Guy to avoid battle and proclaimed his indifference to the fate of Tiberias because "if he [Saladin] chooses to stay there he will be unable to keep his army together, for they will not put up for long with being kept away from their homes and families". Saladin later had great problems keeping his army together over a long period of time against the Third Crusade.[14]

The make-up of Islamic armies was very different from those of the West. Horsemen of all kinds were predominant and infantry played a limited role. There were always heavily equipped, mailed horsemen in Islamic armies: *Agulani* whose horses were protected with "iron plates" were noted on the First Crusade, while similar troops were the core of the Fatimid army. There was in fact a tendency for Islamic armies to use more and more heavy cavalry, and the Middle Eastern *ghulām* of the twelfth century was not so very different from a Western knight. But the really obvious difference was that Islamic armies used clouds of light cavalry and horse-archers.[15] The consequence of this different make-up was different tactics.

There was much reliance on ambush, partly because this was an obvious tactic for light cavalry. But the really great contrast between East and West was in the approach to battle. Everywhere, close-quarter confrontation was decisive, and the Western tradition was to bring that about as quickly as possible. In the East, light cavalry could outflank and unhinge formations by rapid movement: Raymond of Aguilers vigorously testifies to the concern of the Franks on the First Crusade to guard their flanks. But even more significant was the tactical use of large bodies of horse-archers who fired from the saddle. Their bows had a range of 50–80 m, which enabled them to kill horses and men at a distance. Archers alone could only decide a battle if the enemy's nerve broke, but they could demoralize and unpick enemy formations, opening gaps into which the light and heavy cavalry could pour. The clouds of Turkish horse-archers had an enormous psychological effect on the knights of the First Crusade, who had no means of reply to this kind of bombardment. The natural response to this kind of attack was an intensification of the Western tradition of close order. Knights in tight formation could protect one another from bombardment and threaten a charge, which could scatter the lightly armed archers, who had to come quite close to fire effectively. The First Crusade employed this tactic in their first major battle at Dorylaeum. The formations of the crusade of 1101 a showed grim determination in the face of such attack, but in the end they were defeated. On the Second Crusade, Conrad's Germans were scattered by these tactics, which also prised open the rather loose formation of the French army at Mount Cadmus. Louis VII reacted by putting his army in the charge of the military religious orders, whose veterans improved their formation.[16]

The presence of veterans of the Frankish East on the Third and Fifth Crusades was of great importance, but their advice was not always heeded. When the Crusade of Theobald of Champagne marched south in November 1239 to Ascalon, Peter of Dreux led a very successful raid, and in emulation of this many of the Western knights, and Walter of Brienne, Count of Jaffa, decided to raid the vicinity of Gaza. The protests of the masters of the religious orders were ignored and the whole enterprise suffered a disastrous defeat when they were ambushed by the Egyptians at the Battle of Gaza, on the site of the present village of Bayt Hānūn, just 10 km northeast of Gaza city. On the Crusade of St Louis, Robert of Artois charged into Mansourah, despite the reservations of the Templars.[17]

It was hardly strange that the people who came to the East on Crusade stuck to tried and tested methods, and often failed to understand the problems that they faced. But what of the warfare of the eastern Franks? Fundamental to our understanding of the Latin states of the East is that they all shared a common problem – a shortage of manpower. This considerably influenced their ability to sustain warfare and conditioned their response to it. It is very difficult to arrive at figures for the total population of either the Crusader states as a whole or the Latin Kingdom. The army that fought at Hattin contained about 1,200 knights, of whom the Orders probably produced about 600; so the remainder, 600–700, must have come from the nobility. This suggests that the upper classes, knights and nobles, numbered no more than 3,000 in the kingdom, and perhaps about the same in the other principalities. It is known that some 5,000 sergeants normally owed service to the king, but that on this occasion there were over 15,000. A total Frankish population for the kingdom of 120,000 or 140,000 has been therefore surmised. Archaeological investigation has recently uncovered a surprising number of Frankish villages, raising the possibility of a larger Frankish population. They ruled over a native population of about 500,000, of whom 75–80 per cent must have been Islamic. The initial intolerance of the crusaders had driven out many Muslims and so there was always much empty land within the kingdom. Increased tolerance of a Muslim population, as in Spain, inevitably produced grave consequences for internal security.[18]

The building of castles has often been linked to the small size of the Frankish population. At best, this is a simplification. The leading nobility established castles to guard their proprietorial rights. The hostility of much of the native population was certainly a serious consideration, but they would have built them anyway, because building castles is what proprietors did to guarantee their power. In the twelfth century, castles contributed to the security of the kingdom, but it was chiefly underpinned by the cities and the existence of a powerful field-army. In the thirteenth century, cities remained the essential base of the kingdom, although some castles – notably Athlit, Crac and Marqab – were very important.[19]

There was little unity between the principalities of the Latin East. In part, this was because of rivalries between princes. However, it was also the case that each state had very different possibilities for expansion and was therefore forced to consider different strategies. Even before the city of Antioch was besieged in 1097, the crusaders had seized Ruj, part of the lower valley of the Orontes, and with it the vital crossing of the Orontes at Jisr as-Sugar. Because of this, the Franks of Antioch were able to overrun the Jabal Ansariyah. Before them the land fell away into the Orontes valley, whose eastern bank was capped by the limestone scar of the Belus Massif. Beyond that lay a rich plain, in the north of which was Aleppo, only 100 km from Antioch along a good Byzantine road, which went via Artah and a gap in the Belus Massif past Sarmada and al-Atharib. It was a tempting prospect, but Norman Antioch was always distracted by threats from the Byzantines and later the Armenian kingdom of Cilicia. In 1104, Antioch and Edessa were defeated at Harran, but what had been lost was quickly recovered. Roger of Antioch's (1111–19) victory at Danith in 1115 opened the way for a great expansion which, by 1119, was threatening an encirclement of Aleppo, but Roger was defeated and killed at the "Field of Blood". Again, the Franks soon recovered their losses. But civil strife in Antioch from the 1130s, and the dominance of Byzantine power from the mid-century, halted the expansion of Antioch.

The kingdom of Jerusalem had different choices. The leaders of the First Crusade seriously considered attacking Damascus on their way to Jerusalem. They also debated the idea of an attack on Egypt as an alternative to the siege of Jerusalem. These two possible axes of attack would set the strategic dilemma for the kingdom. Both were tempting. Damascus was easily accessible from Galilee across the bare landscape of the Hauran, which posed no significant barrier, although it is fairly arid. Egypt was also close and any attack on it could be supported by a fleet. The major barrier to any southern strategy, however, was the fact that Ascalon remained in Egyptian hands until 1153.

Under the first two Baldwins, the implications of this difference of orientation between the kingdom and the northern states were masked, because both had ruled in Edessa and were deeply interested in the affairs of the north. Moreover, while paying much attention to the north, the kings of Jerusalem were at the same time able to mount attacks on Damascus, notably under Baldwin II in 1126 and 1129, when a crusade came from the west to his assistance, but suffered defeat at Marj as-Suffur. Egypt mounted several major attacks on Jerusalem in its early years, including that which defeated Baldwin I at Ramla in 1102. In 1118, Baldwin II attacked Egypt and it was perhaps the fear thus aroused and the opportunity arising from Baldwin's death in that year that led Damascus and Egypt to ally in a great attack, but it was beaten off and thereafter the threat from Egypt subsided. In the 1120s, Baldwin II founded the lordship of Oultrejourdain to the east of the Dead Sea, and it has been suggested that Jerusalem was consciously seeking to establish a desert frontier from the Red Sea to Damascus. Whether there ever was such a doctrine is debatable, not least because expansion was very dependent on circumstance and on personality. In any case, the rise of the North Syrian power of Zengi and his ambitions against Damascus ultimately led to an alliance between Damascus and the kingdom which would endure until the Second Crusade.[20]

The decision by the Second Crusade to attack Damascus has attracted considerable criticism from modern historians, who have seen it as an act of folly to have attacked the only ally that Jerusalem had in the Islamic world. But after the death of Zengi in 1146, Damascus had allied with his successor, Nur ad-Din, and in 1147 there was open hostility between Damascus and Jerusalem when Baldwin III led an expedition which narrowly failed to seize Bosra in the Hauran. When the crusaders and the magnates of Jerusalem met in the kingdom at Easter 1148, they seem to have given up hope of helping Edessa, whose fall in 1144 had provoked the Second Crusade, and discussed two projects – an attack on either Damascus or Ascalon; the final decision was in favour of the former. In fact, in general terms it was not a bad decision, for even a neutral Damascus was a barrier to expansion. However, the attack was a total failure. This has often been ascribed to tensions between the Franks of the East, who were later accused of being bribed by the Damascenes, and the crusaders, but careful examination of the sources suggests that the crusader force was not strong enough to overcome Damascus, which was supported by a considerable Muslim relief force.[21]

Neither this defeat nor that of the army of Antioch at Inab in June 1149 ended Jerusalem's interest in Syria. Baldwin III began the siege of Egyptian Ascalon, which lasted from January to 22 August 1153. Partly because of this effort, the kingdom was unable to prevent Nur ad-Din from taking over Damascus on the death of Unur in 1154. Shortly after, Baldwin III tried to undermine Nur ad-Din's power by mounting a joint expedition with Antioch against Shaizar. There was every possibility that this great fortress would surrender, but Raynald of Châtillon, an adventurer from the West who had acquired Antioch by marriage to its heiress, refused to accept Philip of Flanders as its ruler, perhaps because he would have been the man of Jerusalem in an area he saw as his own: the siege was abandoned. However, Baldwin defeated Nur ad-Din before Banyas and in the Battle of al-Batihah in 1158, and pursued a policy of friendship towards Byzantium, presumably with the intention of checking him. But a joint expedition with the Byzantines in 1159 ended inconclusively. In 1160, Raynald was captured and Baldwin III died in 1163.[22]

The union of Syria under a single ruler was a threat to both Antioch and Jerusalem, which Baldwin III had done his best to counter, but his successor, Amalric I (1161–74), turned to that other axis of Frankish expansion, Egypt, where the Fatimid regime was being increasingly undermined by factional strife. The contending forces in the civil conflict there were prepared to ask outsiders, including the Franks, for help. Amalric mounted a series of expeditions which culminated in the brief installation of a Frankish garrison at Cairo in 1167. But Nur ad-Din's forces, under his general Shirkuh, eventually took control in 1169, and when he died in that year Saladin took over. The cost to Jerusalem had been enormous, and the whole strategy was abandoned when Amalric died in 1174 and was succeeded by Baldwin IV, the Leper King.[23]

The union of Syria and Egypt under Saladin resulted, as we have seen, in the fall of the kingdom and, in the thirteenth century, in a new focus for Crusades from the West. Divisions in the Ayyubid family, which separated Syria and Egypt, meant that the old strategic dichotomy of Jerusalem continued. Frederick II exploited this to regain Jerusalem, but St Louis failed to do so. The Fifth Crusade was somewhat distracted by the possibility of attacking Damascus, while that of Theobald of Champagne, under the influence of the barons of Jerusalem, actually attacked both Damascus and Egypt. The bitter civil war in Jerusalem precipitated by Frederick II ended in the triumph of the Templars, at whose bidding the kingdom sided with Damascus against Egypt in the campaign which ended in disaster at Harbiyah in 1244. Even thereafter, the old dilemma re-emerged in a different form when the Mongols erupted into Syria, taking Damascus in 1260. They enjoyed the support of Bohemond VI of Antioch, but the barons of Jerusalem were appalled by the prospect of an alliance with such a terrible people, even if their general was a Christian – in any case, he was not a Catholic. In the event, the Egyptians defeated the Mongols at Ain Jalut, while the Franks stood by, helpless to influence the fate of the Middle East. It would not be long before Mamluk Egypt destroyed them.[24]

Strategic dilemmas are not easily resolved, but the kings of Jerusalem in the twelfth century made every effort to come to terms with theirs. This was complicated by their uncertain relations with Antioch, Edessa and Tripoli, and the need to gain the support of their own vassals. In the thirteenth century the central fact was that Jerusalem was without an effective king. In these circumstances, differences amongst the real powers of the kingdom inevitably emerged. The Temple leaned to friendship with Damascus, the Hospital to an Egyptian strategy and the barons were drawn into one party or another. In 1244, these two parts of the Ayyubid Empire were in bitter confrontation and the kingdom decided to back Syria at the behest of the Temple. It was a perfectly reasonable decision: the terrible defeat of Harbiyah (La Forbie) which followed was the result of tactical errors, not strategic misconception.

It is conventional to divide the history of the Latin states into two periods, a first when they were aggressive and a second when they were defensive. The dividing point is usually seen as the Second Crusade. This is partly based on the gloomy view taken by William of Tyre about events in the second half of the twelfth century and partly on Usamah's well known comments on the caution of the Franks in war. But the Franks were often impetuous in war, as Usamah himself shows, while William of Tyre was anxious to paint a picture of a kingdom in difficulty, anxious for overseas help.[25] In reality, the Franks were almost always aggressive.

This is very well illustrated by the defeat of Roger of Antioch on the "Field of Blood" on 28 June 1119. Roger was threatening Aleppo: by 1119 Frankish power extended to Buza'ah to the east and 'Azaz to the north, while the fortified settlements of al-Atharib and Sarmada were little more than 30km to the west. It was to rescue Aleppo that Il-Ghazi of Mardin raised a great army and laid siege to al-Atharib on 27 June. When Roger heard about Il-Ghazi's army, he asked Baldwin II for help and mobilized his own army at Artha. He was advised by his Patriarch to await the army of Jerusalem, but Roger had enlisted his nobility in the process of conquest by giving them lands. Robert son of Fulk, also called the Leprous, lord of Saône, held Sarmada, and Renaud Mazoir of Marqab had extensive lands that were now exposed to attack. These lords persuaded Roger to move forward to rescue al-Atharib. Roger's army of 700 cavalry and 3,000 infantry moved through the pass at what is now the Turkish/Syrian border post of Bab al-Hawa into a bowl-like plain, surrounded on all sides by hills, whose eastern exit is through the modern village of Tell Aquibrin. Il-Ghazi heard of this, infiltrated his troops on to the hills around the bowl and brought his main army up to the attack. This probably need not have been the end for Roger, because the plain is well watered and on its eastern side the village of Sarmada was fortified. We know that Antioch was not bereft of troops, despite the scale of the army that Roger had raised, and Baldwin II was on the way. Roger chose to attack the enemy although he was outnumbered and surprised. He sent a rearguard to prevent his force from being attacked from behind, threw his infantry forward to bombard Il-Ghazi's army and charged with his cavalry in a V-formation with its open end forward, so that his five squadrons struck the enemy in echelon. He appears to have attacked northwards, because a wind from the north blew dust into his men's faces, which suggests that the final confrontation took place near to Tell Aquibrin, which provided a convenient route into the plain from al-Atharib for Il-Ghazi's army. Roger's Turcopoles were thrown back, throwing his whole force into confusion, and a massacre of the Franks ensued in which Roger was killed.[26] Even so, Antioch recovered most of the lands lost in the wake of this defeat.

This aggressiveness continued. Despite defeats and internal problems, Raymond of Antioch challenged Nur ad-Din in 1149, although he was defeated. Baldwin III of Jerusalem pursued high ambitions and even after the accession of Baldwin IV, the Leper King, the Franks were ready to challenge their enemies, victoriously at Mont Gisard, but with less success later. At the Springs of Cresson on 1 May 1187, a small force of perhaps 140 Templar and Hospitaller knights attacked 7,000 of their enemies and was annihilated. It was rashness on the part of the lords of Jerusalem which lost the Battle of Harbiyah in 1244, after which the Franks ceased to be an independent force in the Middle East.[27]

It is not difficult to account for this pugnaciousness. The Franks were small in numbers and they needed to maintain a reputation for ferocity and success. Saladin had united Egypt and Syria in an empire with huge resources. In the early 1180s, he ravaged the kingdom savagely. The crusader leadership, notably in 1183 under Guy of Lusignan as Regent, responded with

Fabian tactics – staying close to Saladin's army and checkmating it. This was not the earlier tradition when, even under Baldwin IV, confrontation had been the rule, and Guy was bitterly criticized. Fabian tactics had a high price in destruction of the land, but an even higher price in the erosion of the Frankish reputation for ferocity and success in war. By 1187, when Saladin came again, many Franks must have felt the need to reassert themselves. Their heavy equipment made them masters of close-quarter warfare, which was the essence of battle tactics at this time, and they seem to have come to a good understanding of the limitations of the Turkish horse-archers. The consequence was that their tactics relied heavily on close formation. Clearly, they were somewhat at a disadvantage when it came to manoeuvre in the open lands of the Middle East. When faced with the necessity of making a long journey in the presence of the enemy, the crusaders formed themselves into a tight-packed column for a fighting march through the enemy forces. It is not the least tribute to Richard I's military genius that he was able to establish and hold precisely this formation in the march from Acre to Arsuf, which led to the victory at Arsuf in 1191. On this occasion, Richard ordered his cavalry in three divisions and threw around them a cordon of footsoldiers and crossbowmen, who held off the enemy. As infantry tired, so they retreated to the seaward side of the march, where the fleet shadowed their progress.[28] Conventional Frankish tactics, emphasizing mass and close order, with co-operation between infantry and cavalry, were brought to new heights in the Holy Land. This was possible because this was a heavily militarized society, whose members must have served together time after time. These methods served the crusaders well and so they were not radically altered.

Much ink has been spilt on one other component in the Frankish armies – the *Turcopoles* – because they do seem to represent an adaptation of Frankish methods to Syrian conditions. They formed a substantial unit in the army of Roger of Antioch which was defeated at the "Field of Blood", were "innumerable" amongst the Franks at Hattin and even accompanied Louis IX in 1252. In the early twelfth century, Albert of Aachen and Raymond of Aguilers both described Byzantine Turcopoles as the children of mixed Turkish–Christian marriages. As a result, some historians see this as a name given to any kind of native soldiery enlisted under the crusaders, while others think that it refers to light cavalrymen. It is fairly certain that they were light cavalry employed to raid, harass and ambush enemy forces. In major battles, they seem to have been amalgamated with the traditional Frankish heavy cavalry. Usamah unequivocally calls them the "archers of the Franks", and other evidence bears out the suggestion that at least some of them were mounted archers. The balance of the evidence by the end of the twelfth century suggests that they were light cavalry and often mounted archers, sometimes of native and sometimes of Frankish origin, used in special roles, as scouts, messengers and above all raiders who harassed the enemy. However, they were not numerous enough in pitched battle to face the light cavalry and mounted archers of the Turks, and so were used simply as a supplement to the heavy cavalry. This probably explains why the *Templar Rule* distinguishes between them and mounted sergeants, while associating the two in time of war.[29] Conditions in the Middle East favoured the use of light cavalry, and the Frankish Turcopoles were a useful adjunct to the Frankish army.

There is no doubt at all that contemporaries were impressed by the power of the Frankish cavalry. At Marj as-Suffar on 25 January 1126, the forces of Damascus had pushed the Franks into retreat, but they turned on their enemies and defeated them with their "famous onset". In the fighting around Damascus on the Second Crusade, we find the Frankish cavalry "delaying to make their famous onslaught until the opportunity should be offered" and seeking a "clear field for their own charge", while in 1149 at Inab the Franks "made their famous charge". Their horses were much admired – to Ibn al-Qalanisi, they were "magnificent" even in death. The importance of cavalry arose from the general conditions of fighting in open empty land characteristic of much of the Middle East. This tactic of the massed charge was a necessary riposte to the greater range of tactical expedients open to the Muslims. Tight formation could hold off envelopment, but eventually mounted bowmen could take a toll of even the most closely knit formation. The Franks, therefore, needed infantry; bowmen to hold the enemy at a distance and spearmen to protect the archers, because their relatively low rate of fire would expose them to being ridden down. This involved a high degree of discipline by all, and in particular the knights had to time their charge to the point where the enemy offered a good target, a formation whose defeat would be decisive. At the same time, they had to be able to mount small-scale attacks to counter enemy movements, all without upsetting their basic formation. It was a fundamental condition of this kind of war that Frankish armies had to hold together even when surrounded.

This fast-moving warfare was very different from European warfare and represented an impressive development of Western tactics. It depended on discipline and co-ordination within the Frankish field-army of a very notable kind. The formidable nature of the Frankish army can be judged by the respect conceded by their opponents. In the great campaigns of 1182 and 1183 Saladin, although enjoying superiority of numbers, was very wary about risking battle: the Franks for their part were prepared to checkmate him by shadowing his army, although many disliked this and reviled Guy for it. But the fact was that for the Franks a stalemate campaign was a success: it was Saladin, not they, who needed to conquer.[30] However, by the mid–1180s the charms of these Fabian tactics must have been wearing thin, as the cumulative effect of enemy raiding and major expeditions imposed enormous costs on a nobility that was already in difficulties. In addition, the accession of Guy had divided the kingdom: he had many enemies prepared to criticize whatever course of action he took. The Battle of Hattin was an occasion when all of the military and political factors went wrong and destroyed the Latin Kingdom.

The cause of the war that broke out in 1187 was a raid during a period of truce by Raynald of Châtillon, now lord of Kerak, on a Muslim caravan for which he refused, despite the urgings of King Guy, to pay compensation. But Saladin was already well prepared and his call to *jihad* was quickly issued. The scale of the threat that he posed was clearly understood, for Raymond of Tripoli renounced his understanding with Saladin after Cresson and became reconciled, at least outwardly, to his bitter enemy King Guy and his support-ers, although acute tensions remained. The Franks now made a full muster of all the forces available to the kingdom, about 1,200 knights and 15,000–18,000 foot and Turcopoles. The figure for cavalry seems reasonable – an amalgam of the forces of the barons and those of the Orders plus mercenaries and pilgrims. But the figure for infantry represents an enormous scale of mobilization. We know that the kingdom could provide 5,000 sergeants, but we can only guess that Guy had called up virtually every able-bodied man, and possibly recruited natives and mercenaries. It was remarkable that a kingdom of this size could produce an army larger than that of Philip Augustus in 1214. It points to the military nature of the Frankish settlement, where every man must have been a soldier. Of course, all Western societies were militarized, but the degree varied according to their situation, and the exposure of the Holy Land to attack meant that it was perhaps the most militarized of all, with every fit man being prepared to serve. Against them, Saladin had mustered 12,000 first-rate cavalry, supported by others and foot, making a total of perhaps 30,000.[31] The crude overall figures indicate a huge numerical advantage to Saladin, but in reality it was far greater, for even if there were as many Turcopoles as heavy cavalry in the Frankish army, he still had four times their numbers of front-line cavalry, and cavalry was the decisive arm. In this light, Frankish losses at the Springs of Cresson seem enormous.

Guy's army gathered in late June at Saffuriyah, where a castle with ample springs, set in the ruins of an ancient town, offered a good base. Saladin crossed the Jordan just south of the Sea of Galilee on 27 June and then moved up to Kafr Sabt, halfway between Tiberias and Saffuriyah, where he estab-lished his main base. After a reconnaissance failed to provoke the Franks to leave Saffuriyah, he attacked Tiberias on 2 July, capturing the town and besieging the wife of Raymond III of Tripoli in the citadel.[32] King Guy called a council of war and on 3 July marched out against Saladin. Historians have devoted enormous attention to this council in order to discover why Guy sallied out from his safe base. Most of our accounts have something to say on this, but Muslim ones are inevitably speculative, while Christian writers were concerned to affix blame on the basis of party allegiances. For example, in both *De Expugnatione* and the *Continuation of William of Tyre*, Raymond of Tripoli is portrayed as urging the army to leave his countess to her fate, but other sources suggest that he begged Guy to go to her aid. There is no doubt that the arguments rehearsed in our sources were the kind deployed, but they are probably somewhat simplified and their attribution is highly suspect. In favour of the Fabian tactics so far pursued, it was argued that even if Tiberias fell it would gain Saladin no permanent lodgement, because in time his army would break up: this is a somewhat doubtful argument, because since the Franks had lost the castle at Jacob's Ford much of Galilee had been devastated and Baisan abandoned, so the fall of Tiberias might well make a permanent lodgement possible. It was certainly true that if Saladin wanted a battle it would be better for the Franks to let his army march around until it could be attacked at a point of their choice, but the price of that in devastation might be very high. Certainly it would be hazardous to attack him before Tiberias, because it was 26 km away, with little water along the road. But Guy had to be concerned that a vassal had begged for aid and that an opportunity existed to smash the menace of Saladin once and for all. Moreover, Guy's Fabian tactics against Saladin's attacks in 1182 and 1183 had earned him great hostility, so he may have felt the need for a victory. This may have struck a sympathetic note with the barons of Jerusalem, exasperated by Saladin's harassment and perhaps eager for a settling of scores.[33]

The intensity of interest in this debate has somewhat masked the question of just what Guy intended to do when he left Saffuriyah on the morning of 3 July. It is not enough to assume that he was simply incompetent. Guy had shown himself to be a sensible leader in 1183, as his Muslim enemies testified, and he would do so again at the siege of Acre, when he achieved wonders in a difficult situation. Smail has suggested that Guy's intention was a fighting march to relieve Tiberias, but it has been pointed out that Tiberias was about 26 km away, and that the longest march ever covered in the face of serious opposition was rather less than half this.[34] Of course, in a general way Guy must have intended to relieve Tiberias, but how? We shall probably never know, but a fighting march seems unlikely, for Saladin was known to be determined, and if such a strategy worked it could lead to the army being isolated in largely destroyed Tiberias. On the other hand, a fighting march could lead, in favourable circumstances, to a deployment and full-scale battle. It must be the case that Guy had resolved to give battle and to destroy Saladin, not merely to try to reach Tiberias. That could only be done by an advance, and so the army set out in order of march with the cavalry in three blocks, Raymond of Tripoli in the first, Guy in the second and Balian of Ibelin and the Templars in the third, with infantry arrayed before and around them.

It has been suggested that Guy's real intention was to reach the water at Turan, some 12 km to the northeast on the northern edge of the rich valley (Sahel al-Battof) which carries the Acre–Tibèrias road. Turan was a strong position comparable to Saffuriyah but closer to the enemy. The idea, it has been suggested, was to draw Saladin's army into the valley where, if he was minded to give battle, the crusaders would be able to pin his army against the north–south ridge where it mounts to the higher ground to the east near Maskana. If this failed, the crusaders could then retreat to Turan, repeating the manoeuvre at will and checking Saladin. This might have been the case, or Guy could have intended to fight his way to Saladin's camp at Kafr Sabt: the sources suggest that the movement northeastwards to Hattin was a change of course from the road leading in that direction.[35]

We will probably never know for certain, but battle must have been Guy's intention and the reason why he was never able to deploy his forces in a satisfactory way was quite simple – he was outnumbered. In his own letter, Saladin said that the departure from Turan was a disaster for the Franks. The sources make clear that the crusader army was by then surrounded, with the main enemy attacks coming in from the rear, where the Templars held the line. This in itself would not have been fatal, but as they struggled the 4–5 km up the slope to the vicinity of Maskana, it became clear that Saladin had enough men to harass them to the point at which they could not deploy for battle, while keeping his main force to the south, comfortably out of range of a sudden charge. Approaching Maskana, the Frankish army was only about halfway to Tiberias: it faced a choice of routes – to press on to Saladin's camp or to turn northwards to seek the springs of Hattin. These were only 5 km distant, but then that was pretty well the distance that they had managed since Turan in the course of a whole afternoon and the move downhill disrupted their formation, with infantry falling behind. In the event, the army encamped for the night at Maskana, surrounded by the enemy on a bare dry broken plain. The primary reason for this halt seems to have been that the rearguard, under massive attack, could not keep up and, in addition, there was disorder in the vanguard. The sources blame either Count Raymond or King Guy for the delay, which in retrospect was seen as the crisis of the battle, but there was probably little choice because of the exhaustion and disorder of the army.

Moreover, there was some water at Maskana, while Saladin's forces already held Hattin.

The crusaders spent a bad night, surrounded, tired and thirsty on the the dry plain. On the morning of 4 July, the Muslims were found to have backed off from the Frankish army and did not resume their attacks until the heat of the day and lack of water were starting to enervate their enemies. Quite possibly, they also feared that a sudden break-out might pierce their ranks. What happened on that day is not at all clear. We do not know what the crusader army was trying to do: Prawer suggests that it was attempting to force the springs of Hattin, but Kedar thinks that they were trying to reach the lake. They were caught on a mountain plain, with the higher land to north, south and east held by the enemy, who blocked the way ahead. We know of a number of episodes – the Muslims lit fires to increase the misery of the crusaders, the Templars tried to break out, Raymond of Tripoli broke through towards Tiberias, the demoralized infantry deserted and fled to the old volcano of the Horns of Hattin, Guy ordered tents to be pitched to create a fighting camp – but making a coherent picture of them is impossible. Crucially, the army was desperately short of water and their ranks had become disorganized. The whole disaster seems to have ended with desperate cavalry charges from the Horns of Hattin, but the day was lost and with it the only army of the Latin Kingdom, whose main outposts fell very quickly.[36]

We should note that Guy's army held together very well under adverse circumstances, apparently until quite late in the day, for when they reached the Horns of Hattin they still had their tents with them. It seems that the army, desperate for water, simply broke up as the enemy attacks went on and every effort at a break-out failed. There was hard fighting – at one point, a crusader charge almost broke through to Saladin, while the Muslims opened their ranks for Raymond's division to escape, perhaps rather than face its impact. King Guy has been much blamed for the disaster at Hattin. But we do not know what he intended to do in leaving Saffuriyah, because the Western sources were either ignorant or more concerned with the laying of blame. In the end, he was responding to that most powerful of imperatives – proprietorial need. A vassal had appealed to him: he faced the prospect of devastation to his lands coming on top of earlier devastation. His vassals followed him – given the record of some for insubordination, they would not have done that if he had not been in some way responding to their needs and with a rational plan. He disciplined and controlled his army well, or it would not have remained intact for so long. His tactics of marching with cavalry and infantry in co-ordinated formations were sensible. But in two respects he seems to have ignored the canons of fighting in the Middle East. He seems not to have made provision for water, nor to have recognized the strength of

Saladin's army. He must have known that he would be outnumbered, but he would hardly have left Saffuriyah if he had known to what extent. In the Sahel al-Battof he was faced with a fast-moving swirl of horsemen, as he must have expected, but superior numbers counted, and whatever his intentions were, he was trapped as they raced around the army, unable to do anything except march further into the trap set for him. Saladin had an army so superior in numbers that throughout 3 July he harassed the crusaders to the point at which they could not deploy, while still holding his main force of cavalry out of range of their charge. He could still have lost: a well directed and timed charge by the body of the Western knights could have destroyed enough of his army to force a retreat, and could even have killed him. But he was circumspect – harassing the crusaders throughout 3 July so that they could not deploy, and then holding off on the morning of 4 July.

The fundamental weakness of the crusader kingdom was revealed by the aftermath of the battle – there was nobody left to defend Jerusalem and the cities, and they fell quickly to Saladin. The ruling class had been wiped out: it is worth recalling that it took three great battles in 1066 to reduce the thegnly class of England to anything like this situation. They were, of course, an elite fighting an elite, but Saladin's recruiting base was much the greater. In the thirteenth century, Syria could probably support 30,000 horsemen and Egypt a further 24,000. The loss of knights at Hattin removed the kingdom's main defence, and the slaughter of infantry must have annihilated most of the rest of the male population. In the event, enough remained to hold Tyre as a base for the Third Crusade's efforts to restore the kingdom.

The dominions of conquest which western Europeans created on the periphery all suffered from a shortage of dependable people – it was inherent in conquest. They all sought to recruit from the heartlands – in the case of the Latin Kingdom, very vigorously. We find Flemish settlers in Wales, on the Baltic and in the Holy Land. But the problem for the kingdom was that it was distant, and because there was no land-bridge, could only be reached after a long and expensive journey. The Holy Land was an arena of conquest that attracted mercenaries and adventurers such as Gerard of Ridefort, the Lusignans and the Montforts, and we can assume that there were many others who enjoyed less sparkling careers. But there were other fields where glory and land could be won, and the Holy Land was distant and difficult. We know that, on the eve of Hattin, Guy was enlisting mercenaries on a large scale, using money donated by Henry II, and undoubtedly such people had always been a feature of life in the East. But they were not enough to compensate for a major disaster in the face of a determined enemy: the crusader states were never able to attract enough people to form anything like the border cities of the Spanish *reconquista*, which were such a bulwark of defence. But then in

Spain the enemy too was something of a colonialist, based on North Africa and facing many distractions. Moreover, the aristocracy of Jerusalem did not have access in the twelfth century to the wealth of the kingdom. This was generated by international trade and their only path to this was royal favour, for the king and the Italian cities controlled the trade.[37]

To a certain extent, the military religious orders compensated for this situation. Their ethos was war against the infidel, but they had an obvious vested interest in conquering and defending land. Their assets in the West gave them a resource base that could compensate for losses. Every contemporary testifies to their military effectiveness and they have been called "the regular army of the Latin Kingdom". It is true to say that they provided a regular force, but they were too few to be decisive. They were a vital supplement to the forces of the King of Jerusalem. Moreover, the Orders were autonomous and were not always obedient to the king. Also, the two major Orders did not always agree: thus the Hospital strongly backed the Egyptian campaigns of Amalric, but the Temple did not. This kind of disagreement became endemic in the thirteenth century when there was no effective king.[38]

The consequence of this manpower shortage for the crusader kingdom was that everything depended on good leadership and sound tactics. In essence, although infantry could provide mass and solidity, and a vital defence for the cavalry as they prepared themselves, everything depended on launching a well timed cavalry charge against a critical mass of the enemy. This tactic was possible because the nobility of the kingdom were small and coherent – they knew one another and very regularly fought together. They must have had some of the characteristics of a regular cavalry force. The situation of the crusader states was not unlike that of the German settlements in the Baltic: they needed time to develop behind a military screen. At Hattin, that screen failed and the vulnerability of what lay behind was exposed. In the thirteenth century, the cities of the Holy Land became very prosperous, but there was no development of the hinterland and the kingdom remained vulnerable, the more so in that it lacked an effective king. For a while it could still muster considerable military force, but there was no uncontested leader. Moreover, the army would lacked a core under the close control of the ruler. At Harbiyah, a committee tried to run the battle, with disastrous results.

In 1291, Mamluk Egypt extinguished the last remnant of the Latin Kingdom of Jerusalem with the capture of Acre, and soon after that the final shreds of crusader power vanished. After the defeat of St Louis, a Mamluk clique seized power at Cairo. *Māmluks*, military slaves, have a long history in Islam. Under the Sultan Baybars (ob. 1260) and his successors, Egypt brought military slavery to a new development. Segregation, discipline and intensive training created a highly disciplined elite. The troops were provided with sizeable fodder-fed horses and robust armour, and trained in the best techniques of mounted bowmanship and close-quarter fighting. They were supported with a good logistics service and backed by well trained infantry and volunteers. In short, they were a regular army with a recognized command structure, a system of training and even a genuinely military literature of their own. This was a highly successful response to the Mongol threat. This force was able to seize the strongest castles of the crusaders, who were never again to challenge it in the open field.[39] The emergence of an efficient military regime in Egypt doomed a weakened and permanently divided kingdom.

It is remarkable that any Crusade ever succeeded, given the problems of organization and logistics which they faced. Such success as they enjoyed – the First Crusade apart – is largely a tribute to the power of the Italian cities and their fleets. The settlements that they made in the East were alien to the world that they found themselves in. That could have been overcome, but they were never allowed time to establish themselves. There was nothing inevitable about the destruction of 1187, for Saladin's unity in the Islamic world was fragile, but so brittle were they that a single major defeat was enough to sweep almost all away. Thereafter, the kingdom was massively dependent on outside powers – and especially on the West, whose preoccupations meant that help on a sufficient scale was never forthcoming. However, it must be said that despite all the difficulties the Fifth Crusade and that of St Louis came near to success.

"Crusade" is often used as a synonym for savage, even total, war, and in the Baltic and southern France there can be no doubt that it was just that – massacre and murder were its hallmarks. It is widely believed that the Crusades in the Middle East were the same. In fact, although this was a struggle between religions, to a degree at least some of the conventions of war were observed by both sides. The Crusades began with a massacre, of the so-called People's Crusade in western Asia Minor in October 1096, and ended with another at Acre, when it fell in 1291 to the Sultan of Cairo, al-Ashraf. After Ma'arra was stormed in December 1098, the population were either killed or enslaved, and there were incidences of cannibalism. The massacre of the inhabitants of Jerusalem after its capture in 1099 has made a great impression. But it is important to recognize that any town anywhere which held out until stormed was at the mercy of the enemy, not least because it was impossible to control an army with its blood-lust up. Moreover, in the case of Ma'arra, the cannibalism occurred well after the seizure of the city, and was a result of starvation in the crusader host, which was occupying a zone that they had long pillaged, while later generations of Muslim writers exaggerated the sack of Jerusalem to foster the spirit of *jihad*. It should be remembered that, on the First Crusade, Roger of Barneville made a great reputation by arranging ransoms for captured crusaders during the siege of Antioch, and that the crusaders made a series of treaties with Muslim powers.[40]

In siege-warfare there were often massacres in the early stages of the crusader settlement; as at Tortosa in 1102, where the population were slain or sold into slavery, while that of Acre were treated cruelly. There was a terrible massacre when Tripoli fell in 1109, but Arsuf surrendered on terms in 1101. In 1109, Jabala accepted terms, as did Sidon in the following year and Tyre in 1124. Conversely, Nur ad-Din accepted the surrender of Banyas in 1164, while Saladin was very careful to offer good terms after Hattin to any place which wished to surrender. In the thirteenth century, when the Mamluks were somewhat more savage, Marqab in 1285 and Crac in 1271 surrendered on terms, while at Arsuf in 1265 and Safad in 1266 Baybars tricked the garrisons into captivity, and in the latter case, massacre. Kalavun's army stormed Tripoli in 1289 and carried out a general massacre, including cutting off the arms of an English Franciscan.[41] In general the normal "rules of engagement" for sieges were accepted on both sides – basically, he who holds out dies – but there were substantial exceptions.

Capture in battle or skirmish was also subject to much the same rules as in the West, at least as far as the "gentry" was concerned. This was a world in which Western military adventurers could serve in Muslim forces, while the greed for money was an obvious motive for sparing the life of a noble prisoner. Broadly, therefore, the kinds of rules that we have noted in the West applied here too, notwithstanding the rival clash of Crusade and *jihad*. There were some terrible exceptions: after the "Field of Blood" in 1119, the Frankish prisoners were subjected to terrible tortures and killed in Aleppo. But this was rare: in the mid-twelfth century, Usamah acted as a go-between for the exchange of captives and ransoms. A number of well known and high-ranking Franks were held prisoner against ransom, of whom the best known was Baldwin II, who was imprisoned twice, in 1104–8 and 1123–4. After Hattin, Saladin spared all of the knightly and noble prisoners for ransom, with the special exception of Raynald of Chatillon. So firmly was the habit of ransom ingrained, however, that he had to pay their Muslim captors to give up the Templar and Hospitaller prisoners for execution. Members of the military orders could expect rougher treatment than lay notables because of their vocation, but even they were often ransomed. The end of the Fifth Crusade was marked by an exchange of prisoners, but the scale of the surrender of St Louis's forces created enormous problems and there was great suffering, although Joinville had kind things to say about his captors. The financial gain from ransom was in general sufficient to preserve the life of a captive of rank – others were simply slaughtered or enslaved. However, ransom was always something of a lottery and many were never released, perhaps less because of religious hatred than because of the accidents of distance and the ravages of disease. The military orders did help in negotiating ransom and release, to the benefit of both Christians and Muslims, but their primary concern seems to have been profit for themselves, and the elaborate infrastructure for releasing captives found in Spain never came into existence in the Latin East, although the Trinitarians had outposts there. Pierre de Queivilliers, a knight from Picardy, was held captive at Saône, possibly in the prison, which is a dank hole in the wall of the great castle ditch, but died in 1227 while the Hospitallers were negotiating for his release on behalf of his family. His must have been the story of many others.[42]

Crusading was a pretty horrible experience. Distance, hunger, disease and brutal fighting made it a terrible undertaking. To live in the Holy Land was to be constantly at war. Usamah's *Memoirs* show that between the great expeditions skirmishing was commonplace, and that when major fighting was taking place in one theatre small groups of men were fighting and dying in obscure places. To go on crusade was to suffer a specially intensive kind of war experience, and to live in the Latin states was to undertake war as a way of life.

# Chapter Sixteen

# *Perspectives*

Medieval warfare in the period 1000–1300 was influenced more than anything else by the nature of the people waging war, by the climate and geographical circumstances in which they fought, and by the available technology, which itself was also in part governed by political and social factors. War was the instrument of landed proprietors because land was the primary source of wealth, and power over men and women sprang from ownership of it. Kings and emperors claimed a special authority but generally lacked the means to make it real: they too were primarily influential as owners of land. It was the needs of a landowning elite which gave rise to the characteristic institutions of medieval warfare, the castle and the knight. These were guarantees of their social domination over the masses who worked the land, title deeds to impress rivals and bargaining-counters in the business of power-broking. Since states were rudimentary, and in major areas never really developed, the ability – or at least the potential – to wage war was a vital factor in political life. Castles and armed followings were the currency of political influence and those without them served, at best, as followers.

The noble's armed retinue were the guarantee of his social position and political influence. They were so fundamental to his being that when armies gathered, considerations of rank, based on differences in landholding, dictated command structures. Armies were collections of personal retinues centred on the following of the commander. The sheer cost of war meant that nobody could afford to maintain regular standing forces, and it is doubtful whether political circumstance would have permitted it if it had been possible. Richard I seems to have wanted a regular army of 300 knights supported by taxation, but this sank without trace. Any such development would have struck at the influence of the great. It was not that the leaders of society necessarily wished to be soldiers themselves, but they knew that so much influence

– and even moral justification – was caught up in their military function that it could not be abandoned. The machinery of the state developed to the point where, by the end of the thirteenth century, some armies in some areas were better administered and organized than ever before, but it barely affected the way in which they worked, and so did not challenge the dominance of the elite in war. Moreover, in much of Europe state-building remained rudimentary.

The style of war reflected the nature of landholding and its central importance. Raiding and devastation were the primary activities and mounted men who could be easily mobilized were necessary, both to wage it and to guard against it. This kind of war generated individual confrontations, placing emphasis on the personal qualities of a soldier rather than his position within a disciplined hierarchy. But in the countryside of western Europe, with its hedges, coppices and woods, the mounted man was vulnerable to ambush, especially to archery, for the ground gave cover to infantry. The knight could not, therefore, fight alone and needed infantrymen to support him. When retinues gathered in larger armies, this style of war was simply reproduced on a large scale. An army was never a monolith in these circumstances, it was simply a loosely organized collection of retinues. Discipline and order, which were essential if men were to support one another in large formations, were very difficult to achieve. Command required persuasion – both to create and then to manoeuvre armies – and the demonstration of personal valour was a vital element in this.

Mobility was always important and the cavalry always held the initiative, but their potential in battle was not always realized because of the problems of organization and discipline. However, although mobile, they were hardly fast-moving, especially when coming into action. This and the simple polarity of Western armies between heavy cavalry and armed foot, meant that speed and manoeuvre on the battlefield were not common: muddy fields rather than open plains were the normal theatre of war in Europe. This accounts for the Western emphasis on close-quarter fighting. It is hardly surprising, therefore, that when they spent money on war the European elite spent as much as possible on themselves, on their protection and on their weapons of offence. Hence so much of weapons development went on what they used – at the expense of other kinds of development.

This style of warfare was adaptable, precisely because it was so centred on close-quarter fighting, which was everywhere the ultimate skill in war. Everywhere they fought, Europeans adapted their characteristic methods and weapons of war. The Normans in Wales, and the Germans in the Baltic, thought about how best to fight in new circumstances. In the Middle East the style underwent a fairly radical adaptation to the circumstances of a very different environment, in which the crusaders enjoyed no technical advantages. Even so, the European style of war remained part of the identity of the Franks in the East, and was adapted rather than transformed.

Change was very evident in the society of this period. Economic growth and the revival of learning, which we call the "Twelfth Century Renaissance" for short, gave rise to new elites. Merchant patricians emerged in the growing cities. The schools and universities created their own leadership and produced educated administrators who developed systematic administration in royal government. But this penetrated little into the world of war, for here the nobility were the dominant force, and there could be no academy of war – no career structure of merit – which might challenge their position. This explains the conservatism of armies and the erratic nature of change in Western warfare. It also explains why it was in architecture and poliorcetic that technical change made most impact on war. Engineers and architects were the product of the vast building programmes of the twelfth century that generated a new technology, of which war leaders were largely ignorant. Hence experts, clearly and consciously defined as such, had to be employed.

Change also affected the kind of men who fought. The diversity of twelfth- and thirteenth-century society and its many economic opportunities meant that the children of the nobility and their followers had a greater choice of career. Increasingly, it was paid specialists who formed the cavalry. Mercenaries could provide a greater expertise amongst the infantry. This professionalism could in theory have challenged the noble stranglehold on command war, but it never did. The cavalry might be more professional, but they were predominantly drawn from the same milieu as the leaders of society to whom they were deferential. They had no standing armies in which to make their careers – only passing service in retinues gathered by the great. Mercenaries were vital to war, but they were never part of its direction. When they tried to assert themselves, mercenaries, just like free peasant soldiers, were crushed. Even mercenary leaders were kept in check and were rejected as soon as their job was done. King John paid a high price for promoting them. The contrast between attitudes to John's mercenary captains and "the best knight in the world", William Marshal, is highly instructive, for the Marshal was "one of us" in a way that, for example, Fawkes de Bréauté never could be.

The social exclusivity of the aristocracy dominated war. Because of it there were no forums to develop the theory of war, the improvement of weapons or even the systematic use of cavalry and infantry. There is no doubt that because of their social origins commanders favoured cavalry warfare, but infantry could not be totally ignored. Too often, climate and topography made the effective use of cavalry very difficult. By the late thirteenth century, the English monarchy faced military challenges that required it to think carefully about their role. At the same time, the rise of cities created efficient and motivated infantry forces which, as at Courtrai, thrust themselves firmly upon the attention of all. This was hardly welcome, and the savage treatment of defeated foot was a long-standing tradition of medieval warfare.

War between elites, however, was marked by a degree of moderation and even mercy. Even in the Middle East, where a European Catholic elite confronted an Islamic nobility, a degree of contact and mutual appreciation was possible. Usamah enjoyed the company of some Franks and frequently negotiated ransoms for prisoners taken in the fighting against them. The rivalry of the Angevin and Capetian monarchies did not prevent their knights from showing courtesy and respect to one another. Mercy to a captured opponent was profitable because he could ransom himself, and ransom payments were amongst the most important of the profits of war. Of course, this did not extend to the infantry, who were too poor to redeem themselves and too expensive to keep in prison. Civilian populations were normally treated with casual brutality, but massacre was avoided simply because war tended to be about possession of land and they were indispensable to make it produce wealth. Slavery was not economically viable in the West. In the Holy Land, however, it was profitable, and there civilian populations were treated much more harshly by Catholics and Muslims alike.

Economic expansion and rising standards of luxury impelled ambitious young men out to the fringes of Europe to make and enhance fortunes or to support and satisfy family pride. Military service always provided opportunities for social advancement, so the lure of land and status on the frontier could facilitate the recruitment of retinues. But acquisitiveness was not all, and never was. War could be fought for a wide variety of motives, although its implications for proprietary right were always considered. Even ideological warfare, the crusade, was powerfully influenced by it, for the crusade was presented as the recovery of God's land and His city. But the need to calm religious anxiety was great – Christianity pervaded the life of the upper classes. It was the Church that acted as the agent of colonization in remote and difficult places, drawing in the European elite to the war in the Baltic, although it is interesting that, here and in other places, the Church created fighting monastic orders – religious lordships with a powerful interest in landed expansion – to serve as the cutting edge of Christian penetration and conquest. Such ideological war, especially when informed by feelings of racial superiority, produced something like total war, in which whole populations could suffer terribly. Crusade and conquest in the European experience were justified by religious exclusiveness, and produced a savagery that was otherwise reserved for heretics and those who were perceived of as disturbing the social order.

War, therefore, was primarily a product of social and political forces interacting with the technology of the age. Technical innovation was not the expertise of the European elite, and technological limitations meant that there were sharp limits to tactical ideas. War changed, but slowly and erratically, because the forces for change were beating upon powerful elites who regarded control of warfare as the vital factor in maintaining their social position. This is why they clung so tenaciously to their style of war, even in strange and distant places. This is why it is so difficult to make sense of military development in the medieval West. There was no linear development but, rather, a series of impulses produced changes that were not always sustained, and in the end much depended on powerful personalities. The course of change in military affairs was the product of the shifting forces of experience and conservatism. Hence every military experience is unique – and the only apparent pattern is diversity.

The only rival system of war that struck the West in this period was that of the Mongols. Western Europe really had no real response to offer to this systematized tribal warfare which, to a remarkable degree, adapted the natural instincts of a steppe people and made of them a highly disciplined mass army. That this threat was lifted owed nothing to the martial prowess of the West and everything to political developments in the Far East. Egypt faced the same threat, but much more consistently, and as a consequence developed the regular *Mamluk* army which, for a time, became the most advanced military organization of its age. There was no comparable impulse to change in the West, where the pattern of military development remained painfully slow.[1]

# Appendix I

# The Battle of Bouvines, 27 July 1214

*See plans of the battle which appear on pp. xiv–xv of this book.*

By 23 July 1214, Otto and his allies were gathering their army at Valenciennes. Philip marched north into Flanders with fire and sword, reaching Tournai on 26 July with an army of about 1,400 knights and 5,000–6,000 foot. On the very same day his enemies encamped at Mortagne, some 12 km to the south. They had about the same number of knights and perhaps as many as 7,500 foot. When the French and allied armies became aware of how close they were to one another, the leaders were forced to make decisions.[1]

We do not know their precise intentions at this stage. However, the coalition needed to break Philip's power and prestige quickly, and so were probably seeking battle. On the night of 26 July, when Philip learned of the presence of the allies at Mortagne, he called a council of war. He considered an attack, but was advised that the ground near Mortagne was not suitable, and in any case he was reluctant to fight on the next day, which was a Sunday. It was decided to withdraw to Lille, 30 km away, and so find another route by which to invade Hainaut. This account by Guillaume le Breton, the story of a precipitate retreat in the Anonymous of Béthune, and the subsequent behaviour of the king, all suggest that he really wanted to checkmate the allies rather than challenge them in the open field, in the hope that their army would fall apart. There was every prospect of this: Henry of Brabant had married his daughter to Otto in May 1214, but he had recently been in the pay of Philip, whose daughter Marie he had married in April 1213. His sons were held hostage by Ferrand of Flanders. On the other hand, Philip was suspicious of the Count of St Pol, who quipped bitterly as he led his forces into battle that he would "be a good traitor today".[2] The whole coalition was cemented by King John's largesse, which in the end had limits, and this may well have been what Philip was counting on.

On the morning of 27 July 1214, Philip's army broke camp and marched in good order for Lille, at a speed which impressed contemporaries. It was possible because there were sufficient carts for the arms of the infantry. Medieval armies rarely moved at very high speed and often were forced to crawl along. However, the Roman road west from Tournai crosses flat lands and it was a fine day – optimum conditions for rapid movement. There was every prospect that they would reach Lille, a 40 km march, before nightfall. The assumed average rate of march would be a very brisk 7 km per hour. The major obstacle was the bridge at Bouvines, 16 km west of Tournai, where the road crosses the little River Marque in its marshy valley, and this would inevitably form a bottleneck. If we assume that the French king's early start was at about 6 am, we have to allow time for the army to begin its march. Moreover, its column would have been about 5 km long. The Anonymous of Béthune says that Philip was eating at a time when the lead elements of his army, including all the infantry, had crossed the Marque and reached 2–3 km beyond. Since the river crossing, like leaving the camp, would have taken time, it seems reasonable to believe that by this time it was midday. Much of the French army in its column of march would have been strung out east of the bridge for about 2–3 km.[3] It was in this embarrassing position that Philip learned that the enemy was closing upon him.

The allies must also have been aware of the presence of the French army on the 26 Augustus road, because the next morning they were informed of its departure and summoned a council of war to decide what to do. Roger of Wendover says that all were unanimous in wanting a battle, but there was sharp disagreement over when it should take place. Otto, supported by Renaud of Boulogne, was reluctant to fight: after all, it was a Sunday, when blood should not be spilt. Hugh of Boves had a high military reputation and he angrily accused Renaud of treachery, urging that it was their duty to their paymaster, the English king, to seize the opportunity presented to them. Underlying this dispute would have been the certain knowledge of Philip's predicament as he crossed the Marque and the opportunity that it presented. Conditioning the whole debate was the lack of an overall commander, for whereas the French leaders advised their king, in the coalition Otto was clearly only one amongst equals, and the English interest, represented by the Earl of Salisbury, must have been for a swift conclusion.[4] The allies resolved on a pursuit, and for very good reason. They knew that the French would be strung out along the Tournai–Bouvines–Lille road and that crossing the Marque would take time. They set out to march north some 6 km and turned northwest on to another Roman road that joined the Tournai–Lille road just east of the bridge at Bouvines, with the clear intention of catching the French in disarray as their army crossed the bridge. This plan very nearly succeeded.

King Philip was ignorant of his enemies' movements, and seems to have taken no steps to discover them, but that morning the Viscount of Melun and Guérin, bishop-elect of Senlis and an important military adviser, had set off southwards from Tournai. They observed the movement of the allied army and Guérin returned to report to the king, while the Viscount and his forces seem to have occupied the northwesterly road to Bouvines in an effort to harass the enemy advance. When the situation was reported to Philip, he held a short council of war and decided to press on towards Lille; it may then have seemed that the allies simply intended to occupy Tournai. But if the French had made impressive speed, that of the allies was even more remarkable. They had presumably set off somewhat later than the French and they had to cover a rather longer distance, about 20 km: it has been suggested that the column must have been about 7 km long. Philip first realized that the enemy was close in the early afternoon. He had eaten, and was resting close to the bridge at Bouvines, which "the greater part of the host had already crossed", when messengers arrived. They explained that the rearguard of the army, under the Duke of Burgundy, were in the presence of the enemy, who were brushing aside the Viscount of Melun's small force, which was in full retreat.[5] This calls for some explanation. The only force covering Otto's advance was that of the Viscount of Melun. The road along which the allies were marching passed through wooded country which opened up near the abbey of Cysoing, about 3 km southeast of Bouvines. Since the enemy were not actually upon the rearguard, which would have been the rearguard of the main army on the Bouvines–Tournai road, this suggests that they were within 2 km of the bridge; and since the French army would have been strung out along at least 5 km of road, this bears out Guillaume le Breton's statement that most of the army had passed the bridge.

Philip was now in the greatest peril. If he continued the retreat he would at the very least lose substantial sections of his finest cavalry, which formed his rearguard, and a vigorous pursuit inspired by such a success might then overtake his main force on the road to Lille. At the urging of Guérin he decided to fight, and ordered the bridge to be enlarged to speed the return of the elements that had already crossed. But, most importantly, he gathered about him a sizeable force of cavalry and led it towards the enemy. The speed of his response seems to have taken the allies by surprise and it is possible, therefore, that he had already deployed some of his forces south of the road to protect the crossing of the bridge.

Both armies were in a state of disarray. The French needed to get their infantry from across the river, and in the meantime their great anxiety must have been to prevent a sudden rush by the enemy from the direction of Cysoing, against the bridge. If the allies could rush upon the French army as it tried to deploy, all would be lost. This was the reason for Philip's bold move towards the enemy, who were disconcerted by it. The Duke of Burgundy's rearguard was then enormously reinforced until it grew to 600–700 knights, and it was placed under the command of Guérin: this formed the right (southern) flank of the French army. This formidable force was assembled very quickly in order to deter the allies from a sudden thrust out from their defile by threatening their left flank. According to the Anonymous of Béthune, "As the hosts came close enough to see each other clearly, they stopped for a long time and put their affairs in order".[6] It requires little imagination to see why. The allies had to deploy from column of march, while the French needed to get their infantry back across the Marque. Philip's boldness in creating a massive mounted rearguard had wrested the initiative from the allies – they had been deprived of the fruits of surprise and now had to deploy in unfavourable circumstances.

The allies were debouching into the southeast corner of an open plain, bounded to the north by the Marais de Willems, to the south by the Marais de Louvil and to the west by the marshy valley of the River Marque. The problem for the allies was to unscramble their army and arrange it in such a way as to make an attack possible. In order to confront the French, whose main force was feverishly deploying to the north, they had to swing north-wards off the road in the general vicinity of Cysoing, a complicated, untidy and time-consuming business, made highly dangerous by the presence of Guérin's huge and mobile force on the French right. To mask the deploy-ment, the allies created a similar force on their own left, of something like 600 knights from Flanders, Hainaut and elsewhere.

The French for their part were in a quandary. There was an obvious temptation to use Guérin's huge force to attack the milling forces deploying before them, but the rest of the French army was still forming up behind and to the north of Guérin's cavalry; if his cavalry became drawn into a *mêlée* they could be separated from the main force and defeated in detail. On the other hand, the French did not want to do nothing, because that would leave the allies entirely free to do as they liked. Guérin's solution was to extend his front to about 1,000 m, placing his right wing firmly on the Marais de Louvil, and to begin the battle by sending a contingent of mounted sergeants forward to harass the Flemings. This was the opening of the battle, and it must have occurred towards mid-afternoon, for Guillaume the Breton, who was with Philip, states that the Sun was a factor in the battle, shining on the shoulders of the French and into the eyes of the west-facing allies.

The Flemish knights scorned the sergeants, and repulsed them, but Guérin followed this up with a series of limited charges by various contingents from within his division. Because Guillaume le Breton's narrative focuses on the leaders of these contingents, it has been seen as romantic, a reworking of the battle as tournament, and indeed the Anonymous of Béthune speaks of the fighting in terms of a tournament. And what was actually happening probably was rather like a tournament, as each group accompanied its leader in a charge against the enemy in close order. The parallel with the large-scale tournaments that often involved hundreds – reported, for example, by Gislebert of Mons – is very striking. The difference was that each group was acting in a disciplined way in the context of a much larger unit. Guérin knew that the knights had come to the army in contingents under the command of their great lords: the relative coherence of such units made them formidable in the attack, but he controlled the sequence and the target of each assault. In this way, he subjected the enemy to attrition without ever overcommitting his forces. It was a skilful adaptation to the needs of the situation. After the repulse of the sergeants, a large force of perhaps 180 Champenois knights charged but were forced back by the Flemings. Attacks followed by the Count of St Pol, the Count of Beaumont, Matthew of Montmorency and Duke Odo of Burgundy, who was unhorsed and rescued by his knights closing around him. The Viscount of Melun succeeded in penetrating the enemy line and charging back through it – a sign that the Flemish were weakening. This process must have been incredibly tiring and the Count of St Pol is portrayed as being exhausted.

But why is it that the charges were so one-sided? There was certainly bravery on both sides, but the allies seem to have been disordered from the first. In the words of the Anonymous of Béthune: "The king [Philip] put his echelons in formation and they rode forward. You could see among them noblemen, much rich armor and many noble banners. The same was true for the opposite side, but I must tell you that they did not ride as well and in as orderly a manner as the French, and they became aware of it."[7] As Verbruggen rightly remarks, this disorder stemmed from the march and the conditions of the deployment, and also, perhaps, from overeagerness for action. In addition, no single leader seems to have been in charge of this huge mass of cavalry, and their entire stance seems to have been passive. The French fought as a whole, and the allies as individual contingents. Guérin sacrificed the sergeants to open more disorder and then used his sections of heavy cavalry to batter at the gaps which were appearing. In this area of the field, the most resistance was put up by Ferrand of Flanders and his immediate followers, so we should perhaps see Guérin picking off the other sections which were more loosely controlled. The capture of Ferrand, who never seems to have established proper control over his huge division, resulted in its total dissolution, but it must be said that, long before this, he succeeded in doing what was required – embroiling the French cavalry so that they could not interfere with the main attack.

The regrouping of the French army had taken a good deal of time, and the remainder of the allied army had turned across the rear of the large cavalry block and formed up around the banner of Otto IV, which was mounted on a great carriage. This force was free to advance because the French cavalry were locked into their own battle. It was the purely cavalry fight which caught the eye of those who recorded the battle; Guillaume le Breton describes it as a self-contained action whose events preceded this charge, but the cavalry battle must still have been in progress; otherwise, Otto would never have dared to launch his great charge at the heart of the French army to the north. The main French force was gathered about King Philip on a front of about 1,000 m, with its left flank resting on the Marais de Willems, near the village of Gruson. The speed of Otto's movement meant that he attacked just as the last of the French infantry – in fact, the communal infantry of Corbie, Amiens, Arras, Beauvais and Compiègne – came into line. They rushed past the king's forces, but were driven back on them and scattered by some of the allied cavalry, which seem to have been leading the general charge. But the signs are that this charge was not well co-ordinated, because German foot crashed into the royal division and threw the king off his horse, only to be defeated by the knights of the king's immediate entourage, all of whom went on to attack Otto and his entourage, who seem to have been elsewhere in the fight. Guillaume le Breton describes this fight vividly while failing to give us any overall picture of what was happening, but the isolation of the German foot suggests an ill-co-ordinated attack, albeit one which almost succeeded. Moreover, the Anonymous of Béthune says that, in this phase, "both sides charged each other" and this would certainly have made for a chaotic situation.

There were thus two battles within the battle, a cavalry battle to the south and a general *mêlée* to the north. The relationship between events on these parts of the battlefield is difficult to establish, because the detailed account of Guillaume le Breton treats them separately, but the Anonymous of Béthune suggests that it was after the general *mêlée* had developed that events in the cavalry battle took a decisive turn: the Count of St Pol charged through the coalition cavalry, completing its attrition and causing the Duke of Brabant, who had as yet played no part, to flee: "he took flight and initiated the defeat". Shortly after, Count Ferrand was captured. The collapse of their left wing had its effect on the struggle to the north and is probably what underlay the retreat of Otto, during which he was nearly overwhelmed by determined

French attacks. The men of Bruges were on the left wing of the general attack and they retreated when they saw the collapse of their cavalry.[8] But many on the allied side continued to fight on, and there was yet another distinct phase of fighting. Renaud of Boulogne had an infantry force about 700 strong. He formed them into a double-ranked circle, bristling with long lances and double-edged axes. His knights made constant sallies and then sought refuge in the circle. In the end, they were overwhelmed by Thomas of St-Valéry with 50 knights and 2,000 foot. Quite where this action took place is not at all clear.[9]

Bouvines could easily have been a successful ambush on the retreating French. That it was *not* was due to the vigilance of the Hospitaller Guérin and Philip's boldness in creating a powerful and entirely cavalry wing which masked his deployment. This rearguard became the right wing of a French battle-line which extended northwards across the plain in front of Bouvines. The controlled battle that Guérin fought shows what a knightly army could do, although undoubtedly he was well served by subordinate commanders. The tactics of well disciplined small-group attacks reflect closely those anticipated in *The Rule of the Templars*. Guérin was greatly helped by the fact that his troops were all French, and that Philip's bold sally gave him time to organize his troops. His main enemy, Ferrand of Flanders, had to deal with a motley collection who he had first to extract from the ruck of a deploying army. To the north, Philip seems to have marshalled his forces into a defensive line, although it was incomplete when Otto launched his attack. Why, then, did it survive? It was extended over a kilometre, so it must have been fairly thin. It is possible that part of it was anchored by a baggage-park, as suggested by Roger of Wendover. But more crucial was the apparent disorder of the allied attack. In his *Philippidos*, Guillaume le Breton says that the enemy leaders had sworn to kill Philip and had aimed their assault at him, but the separation of forces suggested by Guillaume le Breton's account, and Roger of Wendover's explicit statement that the allied units became widely separated, both point to a degree of confusion from which the French were able to profit, in order to launch a vigorous counter-attack that nearly killed Otto. Otto's violent assault failed to produce a decisive result, and was itself cruelly exposed by the final collapse of Ferrand of Flander's division and his own surrender – and when that became known, the allied army fell apart.[10]

# List of Abbreviations

| | |
|---|---|
| AA | Albert of Aachen. *Historia Hierosolymitana*, RHC Oc. 4. |
| *Battle* | *Anglo-Norman Studies, Proceedings of the Battle Conference.* |
| BT | Wilson, D. M. (ed.). *The Bayeux Tapestry* (London: Thames and Hudson, 1985). |
| Contamine, *War* | Contamine, P. *War in the Middle Ages*, tr. M. Jones (Oxford: Blackwell, 1987). |
| Gabrieli, *Arab historians of the Crusades* | Gabrieli, F. *Arab historians of the Crusades* (New York: Dorset Press, 1989). |
| GF | Anonymous. *Gesta Francorum et aliorum Hierosolimitanorum*, R. Hill (ed.) (London: Nelson, 1962). |
| Gislebert | Gislebert of Mons. *La chronique de Gislebert de Mons*, L. Vanderkindere (ed.) (Brussels: Kiessling, 1904). |
| Glaber | Rodolfus Glaber. *Histories*. In *Rodulfus Glaber opera*, J. France (ed.) (Oxford: Clarendon Press, 1989). |
| Guillaume le Breton, *Gesta* | *Gesta Philippi Augusti*. In *Oeuvres de Rigord et de Guillaume le Breton, historiens de Philippe-Auguste*, H. F. Delaborde (ed.) [2 vols] (Paris: Librairie Renouard, 1882–5), vol. I, pp. 168–333. |
| *Philippidos* | *Philippidos Libri XII*. In *Oeuvres de Rigord et de Guillaume le Breton, historiens de Philippe-Auguste*, H. F. Delaborde (ed.) [2 vols] (Paris: Librairie Renouard, 1882–5), vol. II. |
| Halphen, *Chroniques* | Halphen, L. & R. Poupardin (eds). *Chroniques des Comtes d'Anjou et des Seigneurs d'Amboise* (Paris: A. & J. Picard, 1913). |
| Howlett, *Chronicles* | Howlett, R. (ed.). *Chronicles of the reigns of Stephen, Henry II and Richard I*, [4 vols] (London: RS, 1884). |
| Maciejowski | *Old Testament Miniatures*, S. C. Cockerell (ed.) (New York: George Braziller, 1969). |
| Mansi, *Concilia* | *Sacrorum Conciliorum Nova et Amplissima Collectio*, [31 vols] (Venice, 1759–98). |
| MGH | *Monumenta Germaniae Historica.* |
| SS | *Scriptores*, G. H. Pertz et al. (eds), [32 vols] (Hannover, Weimar, Berlin, Stuttgart & Cologne, 1826–1934). |
| Nicolle, *Arms and armour* | Nicolle, D. C. *Arms and armour of the crusading era 1050–1350*, [2 vols] (New York: Kraus International, 1988). |

| | |
|---|---|
| OV | Ordericus Vitalis. *Historia aecclesiastica*, M. Chibnall (ed.), [6 vols] (Oxford: Clarendon Press, 1969–79). |
| PL | *Patrologiae cursus completus. Series Latina*, J.-P. Migne (ed.), [221 vols] (Paris, 1841–64). |
| RA | *Le "Liber" de Raymond d'Aguilers*, J. H. & L. L. Hill (eds) (Paris: P. Geuthner, 1969). |
| RHC | *Recueil des historiens des croisades*, Académie des Inscriptions et Belles-Lettres (ed.), [16 vols] (Paris, 1841–1906). |
| Arm. | *Documents arméniens*, [2 vols] (1896–1906). |
| Lois | *Recueil des ouvrages de jurisprudence composé pendant le XIIIs siècle dans les royaumes de Jérusalem et de Chypre*, [2 vols] (1841–3). |
| Oc. | *Historiens occidentaux*, [5 vols] (1844–95). |
| Or. | *Historiens orientaux*, [5 vols] (1872–1906). |
| RHGF | Bouquet, M. *Recueil des historiens de France et des Gaules*, [24 vols] (Paris, 1738–1904). |
| Rigord, *Gesta* | *Oeuvres de Rigord et de Guillaume le Breton, historiens de Philippe-Auguste*, H. F. Delaborde (ed.), [2 vols] (Paris: Librarie Renouard, 1882–5), vol. 1, pp. 1–167. |
| RIS | *Rerum italicarum scriptores*, L. A. Muratori (ed.), [25 vols in 28] (Milan, 1723–51). New series in progress 1900–. |
| RS | Rolls Series: Chronicles and Memorials of Great Britain and Ireland during the Middle Ages, published under the direction of the Master of the Rolls, [99 vols in 251] (London, 1858–96). |
| Runciman, *Crusades* | Runciman, S. *A history of the Crusades* [3 vols] (Cambridge: Cambridge University Press, 1951). |
| Setton, *Crusades* | Setton, K. M. (ed.). *A history of the Crusades*, [6 vols](Philadelphia & Madison: University of Pennsylvania Press & University of Wisconsin Press, 1955–86). |
| Stubbs, *Chronicles* | *Chronicles and memorials of the reign of Richard I*, W. Stubbs (ed.), [2 vols] (London: RS, 1864). |
| Usamah | *An Arab–Syrian gentleman and warrior in the period of the Crusades. The memoirs of Usamah ibn-Munqidh*, P. K. Hitti (ed.) (Princeton: Princeton University Press, 1987). |
| Verbruggen, *Art of warfare* | Verbruggen, J. F. *The art of warfare in western Europe during the Middle Ages* (Amsterdam and New York: Boydell & Brewer, 1997). |
| WT | William of Tyre. *Chronicon*, R. B. C. Huygens (ed.), [2 vols], Corpus Christianorum, continuatio mediaevalis, 63–63A (Turnhout: Brepols, 1986). |

# Notes

## Chapter One

1. The author would like to acknowledge his debt to the rather different but highly stimulating discussion of the importance of property by J. C. Holt, "Politics and property in early medieval England", *Past and Present* **57**, 1972, pp. 3–52; **65**, 1974, pp. 130–2; reprinted in *Landlords, peasants and politics in medieval England*, T. H. Ashton (ed.) (Cambridge: Cambridge University Press, 1987), pp. 65–114 and J. C. Holt, *Colonial England* (London: Hambledon, 1997), pp. 113–60.
2. OV, vol. 4, p. 272, and see J. France, *Victory in the East: a military history of the First Crusade* (Cambridge: Cambridge University Press, 1994), pp. 41–2.
3. J. F. Fino, *Forteresses de la France médiévale* (Paris: A. & J. Picard, 1967), p. 111. On Caerphilly, see C. N. Johns, *Caerphilly Castle, Mid-Glamorgan* (Ministry of Works: Cardiff, 1978). At the siege of Nicaea during the First Crusade, Henry of Esch seems to have passed for an expert, but the armoured roof he built collapsed, killing those manning it: France, *Victory in the East*, p. 163.
4. S. Reynolds, *Fiefs and vassals* (Oxford: Oxford University Press, 1994), pp. 48–74; E. Lewis, *Medieval political ideas*, [2 vols] (London: Routledge & Kegan Paul, 1954), vol. 1, pp. 88–139; R. van Caenegem, "Government, law and society", in *Cambridge history of medieval political thought*, J. H. Burns (ed.) (Cambridge: Cambridge University Press, 1988), pp. 174–211.
5. J. Flori, *L'idéologie du glaive: préhistoire de la chevalerie* (Geneva: Droz, 1983), p. 168.
6. Rodolfus Glaber, *Histories*, in *Rodulfus Glaber opera*, J. France (ed.) (Oxford: Clarendon Press, 1989), pp. 104–5 n6, 268 n1; Gislebert, p. 181.
7. E. John, "English feudalism and the structure of Anglo-Saxon society", in *Orbis Britanniae and other studies* (Leicester: Leicester University Press, 1966), pp. 128–53; R. P. Abels, *Lordship and military obligation in Anglo-Saxon England* (London: British Museum Publications, 1988).
8. T. Reuter, "Plunder and tribute in the Carolingian empire", *Transactions of the Royal Historical Society* **35**, 1985, pp. 75–94; J. Gillingham, *Richard the Lionheart* (London: Weidenfeld and Nicholson, 1978), pp. 9–23, has quite rightly argued that what was at issue was rebellion rather than merely buried treasure, but it is interesting that the story that it was treasure which was at stake could be believed.

9. On the nature of monarchy in the early Middle Ages, see J. M. Wallace-Hadrill, *Early Germanic kingship in England and on the continent* (Oxford: Blackwell, 1971); P. H. Sawyer & I. Wood, *Early medieval kingship* (Leeds: University of Leeds Press, 1977). For a general survey, see H. A. Myers & H. Wolfram (eds), *Medieval kingship* (Chicago: Nelson-Hall, 1981); Lewis, *Medieval political ideas*, especially vol. 1, pp. 241–8.

10. B. Arnold, *German knighthood 1050–1300* (Oxford: Oxford University Press, 1985), pp. 14–16; T. Reuter, *Germany in the early Middle Ages, 800–1056* (London: Longman, 1991), p. 214; Otto of Friesing and Rahewin, *The deeds of Frederick Barbarossa*, C. C. Mierow & R. Emery (eds) (Columbia: Columbia University Press, 1953), pp. 124, 150.

11. Fulk Réquin, *Fragmentum Historiae Andegavensis, auctore Fulcone Réquin*, in Halphen, *Chroniques*, p. 237, and for the precise date see L. Halphen, *Le comté d'Anjou au XI siècle* (Slatkine: Geneva, 1906), p. 147 *n*4; C. Verlinden, *Robert I le Frison, comte de Flandre* (Antwerp/Paris/'S Gravenhage: De Sikkel, E. Champion, M. Nijhoff, 1935); H. W. C. Davies, "The battle of Tinchebrai", *English Historical Review* **24**, 1909, pp. 728–32; **25**, 1910, pp. 295–6; K. R. Potter (ed.), *Gesta Stephani* (Oxford: Clarendon Press, 1976), p. 173; F. R. Vegetius, *Epitome of military science*, N. P. Milner (ed.) (Liverpool: Liverpool University Press, 1993), p. 108; Glaber, pp. 56–61; on Tagliacozzo, see below, pp. 181–4.

12. D. Whitelock (ed.), *The Anglo-Saxon Chronicle* (London: Eyre and Spottiswoode, 1961), p. 159; Suger of St Denis, *Vita Ludovici Grossi Regis*, H. Waquet (ed.) (Paris: H. Champion, 1929), pp. 36–9.

13. As an indication of the scale of the problem of feeding horses, in August–September 1914 von Kluck's army marching on the German right wing had 84,000 horses, each needing 24 lb of grain and hay each day – a total requirement of 2 million pounds weight of fodder per day. This was not forthcoming, and even though there was plenty of grass in summer, his horses were in terrible condition within a month of campaigning and the whole efficiency of the army was declining: J. Terraine, *The white heat: the new warfare 1914–18* (London: Sidgwick and Jackson, 1982), p. 97; Vegetius, p. 111; G. Fournier, *Le château dans la France médiévale: essai de sociologie monumentale* (Paris: A. & J. Picard, 1978), pp. 158–60; D. F. Renn, *Norman castles in Britain* (London: Baker, 1968), p. 14, Map D.

14. OV, vol. 2, pp. 231–3; Henry of Huntingdon, *Historia Anglorum* D. Greenway (ed.) (Oxford: Clarendon Press, 1996), pp. 143–5; A. L. Poole, *From Domesday Book to Magna Carta 1087–1216* (Oxford: Oxford University Press, 1955), pp. 146–7. On the limitations on war, see M. Strickland, *War and chivalry: the conduct and perception of war in England and Normandy 1066–1217* (Cambridge: Cambridge University Press, 1996), pp. 132–203 who, however, does not place my emphasis on proprietorial right and its consequences as the governing factor; W. S. Jesse, "Urban violence and the *coup d'etat* of Fulk le Réchin in Angers, 1067", *The Haskins Society Journal* **7**, 1995, pp. 75–82 discusses a rare occasion when there were political executions.

15. B. W. Scholz (ed.), *Carolingian chronicles: the Royal Frankish Annals and Nithard's Histories* (Michigan: University of Michigan Press, 1972), pp. 64–5; on outsiders, see W. R. Jones, "The image of the barbarian in medieval Europe", *Comparative Studies in Society and History* **13**, 1971, pp. 376–407. For a view of warfare on the peripheries of Europe as "beyond chivalry", see Strickland, *War and chivalry*, pp. 291–329, 337–8, and the rather similar comments of J. Gillingham, "Conquering barbarians: war and chivalry in twelfth-century Britain", *The Haskins Society Journal* **4**, 1992, pp. 67–84. See also my discussion below, pp. 187–203.

16. Vegetius, p. 108; J. France, "La guerre dans la France féodale à la fin du ix et au x siècles", *Revue Belge d'Histoire Militaire* **23**, 1979, pp. 177–98; J. Gillingham, "William the Bastard

at war", in *Studies in medieval history presented to R. Allen-Brown*, C. C. Harper-Bill, J. Holdsworth, J. Nelson (eds) (Woodbridge: Boydell & Brewer, 1989), pp. 141–58, "Introduction of knight service into England", *Battle* **4**, 1981, pp. 53–64; S. Morillo, *Warfare under the Anglo-Norman kings, 1066–1135* (Woodbridge: Boydell & Brewer, 1994).

17. OV, vol. 3, pp. 294–5; Glaber, pp. 158–63; M. Bur, *La formation du Comté de Champagne v. 950–v. 1150* (Nancy: Université de Nancy II, 1977), pp. 106, 126–8, 169–70, 173; W. M. Hackett (ed.), *Girart de Roussillon, Chanson de Geste*, [3 vols] (Paris: A. & J. Picard, 1953–5), vol. 2, pp. 280–1, 6,200–9: I owe this reference to Strickland, *War and chivalry*, p. 159; D. Crouch, *William Marshal. Court, career and chivalry in the Angevin empire* (London: Longman, 1990), pp. 30–2, based upon P. Meyer (ed.), *Histoire de Guillaume le Maréchal*, [3 vols] (Paris: Société de l'Histoire de France, 1891–1901), vol. 1, pp. 30–41, 805–1106.

18. B. S. Bachrach, "Fortifications and military tactics: Fulk Nerra's strongholds *ca.* 1000", *Technology and Culture* **20**, 1979, pp. 531–49, "The Angevin strategy of castle building in the reign of Fulk Nerra, 987–1040", *American Historical Review* **88**, 1983, pp. 533–60, "The cost of castle building: the case of the tower at Langeais, 992–94", in K. Reyerson and F. Powe (eds), *The medieval castle: romance and reality* (Dubuque: Kendall-Hunt, 1984), pp. 47–62; F. Chalandon, *Histoire de la domination normande en Italie et Sicile*, [2 vols] (Burt Franklin: New York, 1969), vol. 1, pp. 258–84; B. Z. Kedar, "The battle of Hattin revisited", in *The Horns of Hattin*, B. Z. Kedar (ed.), (London: Variorum, 1992), pp. 190–207; H. Delbrück, *Medieval warfare* tr. W. J. Renfroe (Lincoln: University of Nebraska, 1982), p. 417.

19. J. Gillingham, "William the Bastard at war", pp. 151–3, "War and chivalry in the history of William the Marshal", in J. Gillingham, *Richard Coeur de Lion: kingship, chivalry and war in the twelfth century* (London: Hambledon, 1994), pp. 321–2; R. C. Smail, *Crusading warfare 1097–1193* (Cambridge: Cambridge University Press, 1995), p. 185; Delbruck, History of the art of war, vol. 3, *Medieval warfare*, tr. W. J. Renfroe (Lincoln: University of Nebraska, 1982), pp. 334–6. For my comments, see below, p. 153; J. Bradbury, "Battles in England and Normandy 1066–1154", *Battle* **6**, 1983, pp. 1–12.

20. Salimbene de Adam, *Chronicon*, G. Scalia (ed.) [2 vols] (Bari: G. Laterza, 1966), vol. 1, pp. 292–3; Otto of Friesing, pp. 283–306; O. Holder-Egger (ed.), *Gesta Federici Imperatoris in Lombardia: Annales Mediolanenses Maiores* (Hannover: MGH, 1892), pp. 37–40, 48–54; F. Barlow, *The feudal kingdom of England* (London: Longman, 1961), p. 373.

## Chapter Two

1. British Library Ms. Royal 2.A.XII, London; Nicolle, *Arms and armour*, vol. 1, pp. 344, 398; vol. 2, nos 870–870AP, 957A, 772F, 898, 899, 900a., b., 944, 1047a–i. The Artillery Museum at St Petersburg has a very early complete set of cavalry equipment – mail hauberk and helmet, together with sword, spear and stirrups, spurs, etc. The helmet is conical, of one-piece design, but lacks the pointed top, which seems to have corroded away so evenly that it was possible this cone was made separately and attached later. There is no published description of his set of armour; D. C. Nicolle, "Impact of the European couched lance on Muslim military tradition", *Journal of the Arms and Armour Society* **10**, 1980, pp. 6–40; V. Norman, *Arms and armour* (London: Weidenfeld and Nicholson, 1964), Pl. 5, p. 10.

2. Compare Plate 1 of this book, showing the simple pointed cap of the Normans as worn in the Bayeux Tapestry, with the great helm of the mid-thirteenth century knight in Plate 3; Nicolle, *Arms and armour*, vol. 1, pp. 344, 398; vol. 2, nos 870–870AP, 957A, 772F, 898, 899, 900a, b, 944, 1047a–i. The Artillery Museum at St Petersburg has a very early complete set of cavalry equipment – mail hauberk and helmet together with sword, spear and stirrups, spurs, etc. The helmet is conical, of one-piece design, but lacks the pointed top, which seems to have corroded away so evenly that it was possible this cone was made separately and attached later. There is no published description of his set of armour; D. C. Nicolle, "Impact of the European couched lance on Muslim military tradition", *Journal of the Arms and Armour Society*, **10**, 1980, pp. 6–40; V. Norman, *Arms and armour* (London: Weidenfeld & Nicholson, 1964), Pl. 5, p. 10.

3. C. Blair, *European armour c. 1066–c. 1700*, (London, B. T. Batsfield, 1958), Pl. 3, clearly shows the mask on flat-topped helmets, as does Norman, *Arms and armour*, Pl. 7 p. 12; C. Gaier, "Le problème de l'origine de l'industrie armurière liégeoise au moyen âge", *Chronique Archéologique du Pays de Liège*, 1962, p. 26; Norman's Pl. 9 shows the two statues of knights on the west front of Wells cathedral, datable to *c.* 1230–40, one with a great helm and the other with an arming cap over a mail coif. Nicolle, *Arms and armour*, vol. 2, nos 1161A and B.

4. Blair, *European armour*, p. 52; Nicolle, *Arms and armour*, vol. 2, nos 964–66, 970, 773a & b. According to Gaier, the bascinet appeared only in the fourteenth century in the Liège area: C. Gaier, "L'évolution et l'usage de l'armement personnel au pays de Liège du XII au XIV siècle", *Zeitschrift der Gesellschaft für historische Waffen- und Kostümkunde* **4**, 1962, p. 75.

5. Blair, *European armour*, Pl. 5 & 6, pp. 22, 42, 47; helmets worn under the coif; Nicolle, *Arms and armour*, vol. 2, nos 953, 955, 656AA, 772K and T 956, 1161a & b, 1424a, 1476: K. Devries, *Medieval military technology* (Ontario: Broadview Press, 1992), p. 73, sees the kettle-hat as an infantry protection. A very notable example of a knight wearing a kettle-hat is Godfrey de Bouillon in the thirteenth century; Ms. Boulogne-sur-Mer Bib. Mun. 142, *Histoire d'Outremer*, for which see J. Folda, *Crusader manuscript illumination at St Jean d'Acre* (Princeton: Princeton University Press, 1976), Pl. 119; Gaier, "Notes sur les origines du heaume chevaleresque", pp. 105–6, remarks on the complex evolution of the helm.

6. See Plate 1 of this book where the mail hauberk being carried, illustrates the split at the groin and its short sleeves, while BT Pl. 58, 59, 68 illustrate long arm protection, and Pl. 58, 68 the *chausses*; Blair comments that representations of the aketon being worn under mail are rare before the mid-twelfth century and points out that in the mid-thirteenth century Maciejowski Bible, soldiers caught by surprise putting on hauberks appear to be wearing no more than shirts, *European armour* p. 33, but for a possible earlier example see Nicolle, *Arms and armour* vol. 1, p. 280; vol. 2, no. 678 and for the ventail 934a.

7. Leiden University Library, Ms. BPL 20, f. 60, Geoffrey of Monmouth, *History of the kings of Britain*, used as Pl. 24 in R. H. C. Davis, *The medieval warhorse* (London: Thames and Hudson, 1989), p. 56. Nicolle, *Arms and armour*, vol. 1, pp. 303, 351; vol. 2, nos 751, 895a–c. For examples of flowing drapery under the hauberk, see Duby, *L'Europe au Moyen Age*, Pl. 32, the fighting knights on Angoulême cathedral, and (Pl. 34) the Vannes coffer (both early to mid-twelfth century) where long drapery hanging from under the hauberk is especially notable, as it is in the contemporary F. Wormald (ed.), *The Winchester Psalter* (London: Harvey, Miller & Medcalf, 1993), fol. 14, Pl. 17, and the figure of the knight from St Zeno Maggiore at Verona dated *c.* 1139 and illustrated by Norman, *Arms and*

*armour*, Pl. 4, p. 10; on iron gauntlets, see M. Prestwich, *Armies and warfare in the Middle Ages: the English experience* (Yale: Yale University Press, 1996), pp. 21–2 and Gaier "Le problème de l'origine de l'industrie armurière liégeoise", p. 26; Prestwich, *Armies and warfare*, p. 21, suggests that these *chausses* and the integral shoes of the Westminster Psalter crusader are plate, but if that were the case they would have to be articulated. My own guess is that they are leather studded with mail rings.

8. Nicolle, *Arms and armour*, vol. 1, p. 311; vol. 2, nos 772a.–m., 949, 955a–j, 771, 934c, 937. Blair, *European armour*, pp. 28–9, 34–5, 38–9, Pl. 1, 42–3; Norman, *Arms and armour*, p. 16; Prestwich, *Armies and warfare in the Middle Ages*, pp. 21–2.

9. *The song of Roland* tr. D. L. Sayers (London: Penguin, 1957), p. 90, v. 79, v. 99, p. 101; Guillaume le Breton, *Philippidos*, vol. iii, pp. 83–85, ll. 485–534; Prestwich, *Armies and warfare*, pp. 21–2; Gerald of Wales, *Expugnatio Hibernica*, A. B. Scott & F. X. Martin (eds) (Dublin: Royal Irish Academy, 1978), pp. 76–7. The point about the "thrice-woven mail" in Guillaume le Breton has been missed because of the odd Latin, *thoraca trilicem*, but the substantive here is of Greek origin and the adjective agrees. Guillaume was a learned man, educated at the University of Paris, on which see H. F. Delaborde (ed.) *Oeuvres de Rigord et de Guillaume le Breton, historiens de Philippe-Auguste* [2 vols] (Paris: Librairie Renouard, 1882–5), vol. 1, pp. lxxvii–lxxxii. E. M. Burgess, "Further research into the construction of mail garments", *Antiquaries Journal* **33**, 1953, p. 197 and Pl. 23b shows a modern example of six-in-one mail. The idea of inserting two rings for every one used in ordinary mail was suggested by C. Ffoulkes, *The craft of the armourer* (London: Constable, 1988), p. 45, but without any evidence that it was ever used in the Middle Ages: I owe this last reference to Matthias Pfaffenbichler of the Kunsthistorischer Museum in Vienna; B. Thordeman, *Armour from the battle of Wisby 1361*, [2 vols] (Stockholm: Antikvitets Akademien, 1939–40), vol. 1, pp. 285–8; for a discussion of the figure of St Maurice in Magdeburg Cathedral, dated *c.* 1250, see Blair, *European armour*, p. 40.

10. D. C. Nicolle, "Arms and armour illustrated in the art of the Latin East", in Kedar, *Horns of Hattin*, pp. 333–5 and *n*18; S. Duparc-Quioc (ed.), *La Chanson d'Antioche*, [2 vols] (Paris: P. Geuthner, 1977–8), l. 8133, portrays Engelrand of St Pol in the battle against Kerbogah in June 1098, equipped in a splendid "hauberc jaseran"; Smail, *Crusading warfare*, pp. 110–12; France, *Victory in the East*, pp. 200–6, 358–60; J. France, "Technology and the success of the First Crusade", in *War and society in the eastern Mediterranean, 7th–15th centuries*, Y. Lev (ed.) (Leiden: Brill, 1997), pp. 163–76; see below, p. 213.

11. William of Malmesbury, *Gesta regum Anglorum*, T. D. Hardy (ed.), [2 vols] (London: English Historical Society, 1840), vol. 2, p. 479; OV, vol. 6, pp. 238–9; Usamah, pp. 80, 88, 90; Meyer, *Histoire de Guillaume le Maréchal*, vol. 1, ll. 1701; for the comments of medieval writers on the protective worth of mail, see OV, vol. 6, pp. 350–1; Guillaume le Breton, *Gesta*, vol. 1, p. 282, *Philippidos*, vol. 2, p. 323: I. Pierce, "Arms, armour and warfare in the eleventh century", *Battle* **10**, 1987, p. 240.

12. Thordemann, *Armour from the Battle of Wisby*, vol. 1, pp. 149–209, 165–6, 180–3; Usamah, p. 86.

13. BT Pl. 62 shows Norman cavalry with their shields slightly trailing, attacking the solid line of overlapped Saxon shields; see Pl. 67 for the shield slung on the neck and Pl. 66 for unarmoured men with shields. For rounded convex shields, see Pls 64, 71, 72(2), and for the squarish one, Pl. 70; the Angoulême carving is illustrated in Duby, *L'Europe au Moyen Age*, (Paris: Arts et Métiers Graphiques, 1979), Pl. 32.

14. Nicolle, *Arms and armour*, vol. 2, for the flat-topped long kite, 924a, and its later persistence, 757; for small shields, 908a & b, 912a, 913; for wide shields, 759a.–j. There is a good discussion of the shield with useful illustrations in Gaier, "L'évolution et l'usage de l'armement personnel", pp. 67–70.

15. *Henry II, Rotuli de Dominabus et pueris et puellis de comitatibus, an. 1185*, Pipe Roll, vol. 35, p. 59; BT Pls 10, 19, 51, 67: Nicolle, *Arms and armour*, vol. 1, pp. 344–5; vol. 2, nos 870E, J, Q.

16. Nicolle, *Arms and armour*, vol. 1, pp. 308–9; vol. 2, nos 763 a & b, 768. Nicolle does not have a picture of the Christian knight in Rheims cathedral.

17. Nicolle, *Arms and armour*, vol. 1, pp. 263–4, vol. 2, nos 656a–ag; vol. 1, p. 242, vol. 2, nos 607a.–u.; see also the comments of E. Lourie, "A society organised for war – medieval Spain", *Past and Present* **36**, 1966, pp. 54–76; A. B. de Hoffner, *Arms and armour in Spain: a short survey* (Madrid, 1982).

18. Nicolle, *Arms and armour*, vol. 1, pp. 72–4, 525–6, 562–3; vol. 2, nos 154–74, 1382–431.

19. BT Pl. 66 is a good example of the contrasting types; Nicolle, *Arms and armour* vol. 1, p. 366, vol. 2, nos 955E, 956; vol. 1, p. 311, vol. 2, no. 772D; very finely illustrated in the *Life of St Edmund*, written at Bury St Edmunds *c.* 1135. The original is Pierpoint Morgan Ms. 136, fol. 7v and is used in Davis, *The medieval warhorse*, Pl. 7. On this style of warfare, see below, pp. 157–61.

20. See the complex typology in R. E. Oakeshott, *The sword in the age of chivalry* (London: Lutterworth Press, 1964), p. 24. There are variations in length of blade and handle, and later examples tend to have curved quillons and a heavy round pommel which acted as a counterweight. However, it needs to be stressed that these weapons are highly individual in detail but, broadly, are intended for slashing rather than pointing. The Conyers Falchion in Durham Cathedral Treasury is a ceremonial example, beautifully decorated. More utilitarian weapons in various forms are shown in the Maciejowski Bible: Nicolle, *Arms and armour*, vol. 1, pp. 310–11, 356, 497, vol. 2, nos 772AD, AM, 916, 1374; Galbert of Bruges, *The murder of Charles the Good*, J. B. Ross (ed.) (Toronto: Toronto University Press, 1993), p. 174, and see below, pp. 32–3.

21. BT Pls 54, 57, 61 (thrown), 68; Nicolle, *Arms and armour*, vol. 1, pp. 41, 114, 147, 173, 270, 292, 310–12, 353, vol. 2, nos 667, 772AE, Y, AB, AN, 903. Devries, *Infantry warfare in the early fourteenth century* (Woodbridge: Boghill & Brewer, 1996), pp. 12–13, citing J. F. Verbruggen, "De Godendag", *Militaria Belgica* **1**, 1977, pp. 65–70, "Het epos der Vlamme gemmentenaren. De Slag der Gulden Sporen 11 juli 1302", *Revue Belge d'Histoire Militaire* **22**, 1977, pp. 285–312. In modern Dutch, the form would be "Goedendag"; BT, esp. 65, 72; William of Poitiers, *Gesta Guillelmi ducis Normannorum et regis Anglorum*, R. Foreville (ed.) (Paris: Les Belles Lettres, 1952), pp. 186–9; Nicolle, *Arms and armour*, vol. 1, pp. 377, 392–3, vol. 2, 772k, AI, AO, 956; OV, vol. 6, p. 542; Wace, *Roman de Rou et des Ducs de Normandie*, H. Andresen (ed.), [2 vols] (Bonn, 1877–9), vol. 2, pp. 372–3, and see M. Bennett, "Wace and warfare", *Battle* **11**, 1988, pp. 37–58; Otto of Freising, *Deeds of Frederick Barbarossa*, p. 304.

22. R. H. C. Davis, "Warhorses of the Normans", *Battle* **10**, 1987, pp. 67–82; France, *Victory in the East*, p. 73; GF, p. 49; on early Turkish and Islamic horse armour, sometimes lamellar, Nicolle, *Arms and armour*, vol. 1, pp. 4, 18, 24, 108, 127, 157, 196, 237; for felt and padded armour, pp. 108, 110, 153; for Byzantine, p. 51; for Egyptian, p. 214; Gislebert, p. 197; Roger of Hovenden, *Chronica Magistri Rogeris de Hovenden*, W. Stubbs (ed.), [4 vols] (London: RS, 1871), vol. 4, pp. 58–9; Gaier, "L'évolution et l'usage de

l'armement personnel", p. 80; BL, Lansdowne 782, fol. 27, used as illustration by Davis, *Medieval warhorse*, p. 59, Pl. 25; for mail armour, Nicolle, *Arms and armour*, vol. 1, pp. 248, 264, 356, 365, 368, vol. 2, nos 656, 953, 956, 959; Gaier, "Le problème de l'origine de l'industrie armurière liégeoise", p. 26.

23. I. Pierce, "Arms, armour and warfare in the eleventh century", *Battle*, **10**, 1987, pp. 237–57, "The knight, his arms and armour in the eleventh and twelfth centuries", in *Ideals and practice of medieval knighthood*, C. Harper-Bill & R. Harvey (eds) (Woodbridge: Boydell & Brewer, 1986), pp. 157–64; Devries, *Medieval military technology* (Ontario: Broadview Press, 1992), p. 84; France, *Victory in the East*, pp. 37–9; Davis, *The medieval warhorse*, pp. 21–2, ignores the weight of the Bayeux Tapestry knights' shield and weapons, and appears to ignore these same factors for the late medieval knight in the complete steel; J. Larner, *Italy in the age of Dante and Petrarch 1216–1380* (London: Longman, 1980), p. 216; J. H. Pryor, "Transportation of horses by sea during the era of the Crusades, eighth century to AD 1285", *Mariner's Mirror* **68**, 1982, pp. 9–27, 103–18; A. Hyland, *The medieval warhorse from Byzantium to the Crusades* (Stroud: Sutton, 1994), pp. 144–6, with a picture (p. 58). I would like to thank Mr G. Dennis and the Museum of London for an early sight of their preliminary findings on the London horse-burials, and thank them for the discussions that we have had.

24. Gislebert, pp. 171, 182–3, 197; for sergeants in the crusader states, see C. Marshall, *Warfare in the Latin East* (Cambridge: Cambridge University Press, 1992), pp. 49–50, 87, 158; Philip Augustus had 257 knights and 267 mounted sergeants in 1202–3, as indicated by Verbruggen, *Art of warfare*, p. 142.

25. R. Barber, *The reign of chivalry* (Newton Abbot: David & Charles, 1980), p. 129, showing the illustration from Bib. nat. lat. 10525; Henry of Huntingdon, *Historia Anglorum*, D. Greenway (ed.) (Oxford: Clarendon, 1996), pp. 454–5, 472–3; OV, vol. 6, pp. 350–1; Nicolle, *Arms and armour*, vol. 2, 772F, 955E, and see his comments in vol. 1, p. 310.

26. It is possible that the six archers in the main panel wear quilted protection. However, if we compare the two right-hand archers in BT 60 with the obviously humble woodcutters of 35, it is difficult to see any difference. The figure at 60 upper left may be wearing padding, but this is very uncertain. Nicolle, *Arms and armour*, vol. 1, p. 343, suggests a difference between the professional archers of 60 and the marginal figures in 69. These last, like many of the marginal figures, are much less elaborately portrayed, and in general their garments seem to be just like those of humbler people in the main panel; William of Poitiers, *Gesta Guillelmi ducis Normannorum et regis Angloram*, R. Foreville (ed.) (Paris: Les Belles Lettres, 1952), p. 184; France, "La guerre dans la France féodale", pp. 194–8; William of Malmesbury, *Gesta Regum*, **2**, p. 335; OV, vol. 2, p. 357; bows were always "long" – the short bow is a product of historical imagination, on which see J. C. Holt, *Robin Hood* (London: Thames and Hudson, 1982), p. 79; J. Bradbury, *The medieval archer* (Woodbridge: Boydell & Brewer, 1985), pp. 71–5; R. Hardy, *Longbow. A social and military history* (Cambridge: P. Stephen, 1976), pp. 53–4, 202–3, 208; Gerald of Wales, *The Journey through Wales and the description of Wales*, L. Thorpe (ed.) (Harmondsworth: Penguin, 1978), pp. 49–50; for an illustration of the composite bow in the West, see Pl. 2, an early-thirteenth-century copy of Peter of Eboli; Nicolle, *Arms and armour*, vol. 2, no. 657 and elsewhere, notes Spanish examples. On the Turkish bow and its limitations, see C. R. Bowlus, "Tactical and strategic weaknesses of horse archers on the eve of the First Crusade", in *Autour de la Première Croisade*, M. Balard (ed.) (Paris: Publications de la Sorbonne, 1996), pp. 159–66; France, *Victory in the East*, pp. 147–8; there is an illustration of a composite bow in the early twelfth century "Bible of Stephen Harding", illustrated in J. Bradbury,

*Stephen and Mathilda: the Civil War of 1139–53* (Stroud: Sutton, 1996), p. 67. AA, pp. 380–2, says that in the Lake Battle the Turks were hindered because their bows would not fire in the wet weather.

27. On the early use of the crossbow, see France, "La guerre dans la France féodale", pp. 187, 197, "The military history of the Carolingian period", *Revue Belge d'Histoire Militaire* **26**(2), 1985, p. 99; Bradbury, *The medieval archer*, pp. 45, 76–7, 146–7; Contamine, *War*, pp. 71–2. There is a good survey of the history of the weapon in C. Gaier, "Quand l'arbalète était une nouveauté. Réflexions sur son rôle militaire du Xe au XIIIe, siècle", in *Armes et combats dans l'univers médiévale* (Brussels: De Boek-Wesmael, 1995), pp. 159–82, with comments on range, etc. (p. 176); V. Foley, G. Palmer, W. Soedel, "The crossbow", *Scientific American*, 1985, pp. 104–10; Devries, *Medieval military technology*, pp. 40–2. For a goatsfoot trigger in a Spanish Ms. dated 1086, see Nicolle, *Arms and armour*, vol. 2, nos 768, 669b, and for a possible composite bow, vol. 1, p. 282, vol. 2, nos 654 F and G.

28. F. M. Powicke, *The loss of Normandy 1189–1204* (Manchester: Manchester University Press, 1913), p. 333–6. See also H. Round, *The King's sergeants and offices of state* (London: Woburn, 1971), p. 16. The subject of castles and siege-equipment is dealt with below (Chapter 9); Nicolle, 2. No. 945 English late twelfth century, nos 695a–c Spanish, later thirteenth century, nos 330H, 807, 833E, 808, 835 Outremer, late thirteenth century, in 2. contrast 772U with 772K; Verbruggen, *Art of warfare*, p. 142; Marshall, *Warfare in the Latin East*, p. 50; Beha ed-Din, *Anecdotes et beaux traits de la vie du Sultan Youssof (Saladin)* RHC Or 3. p. 251; see Plate 2 of this volume, an illustration of Henry VI at the siege of Naples, which shows a very clear contrast between bowmen and crossbowmen; Barber, *Reign of chivalry*, p.13.

29. The peasants in the "Dream of Henry I" are wielding tools, on which see below, p. 32 *n*5: there is a sling in the early-twelfth-century "Bible of Stephen Harding", illustrated in Bradbury, *Stephen and Mathilda*, p. 67. Staff-slings are also known, as in Matthew Paris's drawing of the siege of Damietta, illustrated in S. Lewis, *The art of Matthew Paris in the Chronica Majora* (Cambridge: Scolar Press, 1987), p. 273. J. Kiff, "Images of war", *Battle* **7**, 1984, pp. 177–94, discusses representations of cavalry in Anglo-Saxon art and stresses the influence of the Utrecht Psalter, while noting that the kite-shaped shields may be contemporary (pp. 185–6). M. Strickland, "Military technology and conquest: the anomaly of Anglo-Saxon England", *Battle* **19**, 1996, pp. 360, 382, thinks that the Anglo-Saxons concluded that infantry fighting was perfectly adequate and that we have exaggerated the advantages of cavalry. For the Norman heavy foot, BT Pl. 65 shows a Norman footman behind a horse, striking an enemy with an axe, and Pl. 70 a similar figure, curiously with two swords, killing an unprotected Saxon footman. The Norman spies on foot in Pl. 56 are presumably dismounted knights; C. W. Hollister, *The military organisation of Norman England* (Oxford: Clarendon Press, 1965), pp. 219–60, summarizes what we know of the *fyrd* and suggests that some of those who served were substantial men, comparable to later sergeants. On Tinchebrai, see H. W. C. Davis, "The battle of Tinchebrai", *English Historical Review* **24**, 1909, pp. 728–32, **25**, 1910, pp. 295–6; Roger of Hovenden *Chronica Magistri Rogeris de Hovenden*, W. Stubbs (ed.) 4 vols (London: RS, 1871), vol. 2, p. 345; William of Newburgh, *Historia Rerum Anglicarum*, in Howlett *Chronicles*, vol. 2, pp. 194–6; OV, vol. 6, p. 543; on the Italian wars, see below, pp. 163–4; on Outremer, see Smail, *Crusading warfare*, pp. 88–137; Marshall, *Warfare in the Latin East*, pp. 47–92.

30. *Itinerarium regis Richardi*, in *Chronicles and memorials of the reign of Richard I* W. Stubbs (ed.), [2 vols] (London: RS, 1864), vol. 1, p. 99; Nicolle, *Arms and armour*, vol. 2, nos 718A & B, 719A & B, 720B & C, 1296A–C, 772AQ, 772AR, 772K, 772AI, 772AM.

31  Guillaume le Breton, *Gesta*, vol. 1, pp. 282–3; on Courtrai, see below, pp. 184–5; Nicolle, *Arms and armour*, vol. 2, nos 7720A & F, 772C, T & X, 772AF & AM, 772J & Z, 772K, T, AI, AO, 772AI & AN.

32. J. Boussard, "Les mercenaires au xii^e siècle. Henri II Plantagenet et les origines de l'armée de métier", *Bibliothèque de l'Ecole des Chartes* **106**, 1945–6, pp. 189–224; Powicke, *Loss of Normandy*, pp. 333–6; for Richard's use of Saracens, see his article in *The Scottish History Review*, 1910, p. 104; Nicolle, *Arms and armour*, vol. 2, no. 955B from Canterbury Apocalypse, Douce 180 has a lion on his shield, but 951B, Oscott Psalter BL add. Ms. 50.000 954 and 954 Pierpoint Morgan Ms. 302 may represent footsoldiers.

33. Note the contrast between the figures of peasant and noble rebellion in the famous illustration of the "Dream of Henry I" in Corpus Christi Oxford Ms. 157 of the *Chronicle* of John of Worcester, in which the former bear scythe, pitchfork and spade, while the latter appear as fully equipped knights: C. N. L. Brooke, "The structure of medieval society", in *The flowering of the Middle Ages*, J. Evans (ed.) (London: Thames & Hudson, 1966), p. 15, Pl. 7.

## Chapter Three

1. For a detailed survey, see R. Sprandel, *Das Eisengewerbe in Mittelalter* (Stuttgart: Anton Hiersemann, 1968), pp. 93–220; Gaier, "Le problème de l'origine de l'industrie armurière liégeois", p. 45; R. J. Forbes, "Metallurgy", in *History of technology 2: the medieval civilizations and the Middle Ages 700BC–AD1500*, C. Singer, E. J. Holmyard, A. R. Hill & T. I. Williams (eds) (Oxford: Clarendon Press, 1956), pp. 68–9; A. M. Bautier, "Les plus anciennes mentions de moulins hydrauliques industriels et de moulins à vent", *Bulletin Philologique et Historique du Comité des Travaux Historiques et Scientifiques* (1960), pp. 567–626; on Cistercian involvement in iron making, see Sprandel, *Eisengewerbe*, pp. 359–62 and J.-F. Finó, "Notes sur la production de fer et la fabrication des armes en France au moyen âge", *Gladius* **3**, 1964, pp. 47–66; R. H. Bautier, "Notes sur le commerce du fer en Europe occidentale du XIII au XVI siècle", *Revue d'Histoire de la Sidérugie* **1**, 1960, pp. 7–35, **4**, 1963, pp. 35–61; C. Gaier, *L'industrie et le commerce des armes dans les anciennes principautés belges du XIII à la fin du XV siècle* (Paris: Les Belles Lettres, 1973), pp. 194–9.

2. For Flanders, see Gaier, *Industrie et le commerce des armes*, pp. 115–60, 191–4, "Le problème de l'origine de l'industrie armurière liégeoise", p. 48; for Italy, see E. Motta, "Armaiuoli milanesi nel periodo visconteo-sforzesco", *Archivio Storico Lombardo* **41**, 1914, pp. 179–80; for France Finó, "Notes sur la production de fer at la fabrication des armes en France au moyen âge", pp. 47–66; on Germany, B. Kuske, *Köln, der Rhein und das Reich* (Köln: Bohlau, 1956): for England, Ffoulkes, *Craft of the armourer* (London: Constable, 1988); Poole, *Domesday Book to Magna Carta*, pp. 81–2; M. L. Bazeley, "The Forest of Dean in its relations with the crown during the twelfth and thirteenth centuries", *Transactions of the Bristol and Gloucester Archaeological Society* **33**, 1910, pp. 3–19.

3. Forbes, "Metallurgy", pp. 56–7, 63, 69–71; more "Damascus" blades were probably forged in Toledo than in Damascus, on which see A. Bruhn de Hoffmeyer, "An introduction to the history of the European sword", *Gladius* **1**, 1961, pp. 30–75; J. Wadsworth & O. Sherby, "On the Bulat–Damascus steel revisited", *Progress in Materials* **25**, 1980, pp. 35–68;

H. Maryon, "Pattern welding and Damascening of sword-blades", *Conservation* **5**, 1960, pp. 25–37; Gaier, *Industrie et le commerce des armes*, pp. 161–3; on the forging of steel sword blades, see Finó, "Notes sur la fabrication du fer et la fabrication des armes en France au moyen-âge", p. 61; Barber, *Reign of chivalry*, p. 13. The importance which has been attached to the work of the German Benedictine monk Theophilus, whose *De diversis artibus*, C. R. Dodwell (ed.) (London: Nelson, 1961), was produced between 1110 and 1140, is a revelation of the limitations of our knowledge of medieval technology. On him, see L. White, "Theophilus redivivus", *Technology and Culture* **5**, 1964, pp. 224–33.

4. *The Romance of Alexander*, Bodleian Ms. 264, has some fine illustrations of medieval armourers at work. There is a facsimile edition by M. R. James (Oxford, 1913), fol. 165.

5. The reference to the dream illustration is in Chapter 2, *n*33 above; Maciejwoski Pl. 2r; Contamine, *War*, pp. 58, 95–97 and *n*72, 73; J. Farmer, "Prices and wages", in *The agrarian history of England and Wales*, vol. 2, J. Thirsk (ed.) (Cambridge: Cambridge University Press, 1988), p. 747.

6. A. Boretius (ed.), *Capitularia regum Francorum*, [2 vols] (Hannover: MGH, 1883–97), vol. 1, pp. 123, 136–8, 167, 171; Roger of Hovenden, *Chronicon*, vol. 2, p. 253; D. C. Douglas (ed.), *English historical documents*, [12 vols] (London: Eyre & Spottiswoode, 1953), vol. 2, pp. 416; vol. 3, p. 462. The English Assize prescribes swords for no class of person and never mentions bows. This may be because it was issued with law and order rather than defence in mind.

7. Gaier, *Industrie et commerce des armes*, pp. 67–8, "Le problème de l'origine de l'industrie armurière liègeoise", pp. 39, 31; D. Waley, "The army of the Florentine Republic from the twelfth to the fourteenth century", in *Florentine studies*, N. Rubinstein (ed.) (London: Faber & Faber, 1968), pp. 75–6, "Papal armies in the thirteenth century", *English Historical Review* **72**, 1957, pp. 1–30; Y. Renouard, *Les villes d'Italie du X au début du XIV siècle*, [2 vols] (Paris: Société d'Édition d'Enseignement Supérieur, 1969), vol. 2, p. 290; Larner, *Italy in the age of Dante and Petrarch, 1216–1380*, pp. 215–23.

8. The classic formulation of the "Three Orders" was by Adalbero of Laon and Gerard of Cambrai and is analyzed by G. Duby, *The Three Orders: feudal society imagined*, tr. A. Goldhammer (Chicago: Chicago University Press, 1978), esp. pp. 21–55; John of Salisbury, *The Policraticus*, C. J. Nederman (ed.) (Cambridge: Cambridge University Press, 1990), pp. 66–8, 125–6; on the monetary explosion and the subsequent social diversity and fluidity, A. Murray, *Reason and society in the Middle Ages* (Oxford: Clarendon Press, 1978), pp. 50–8, 81–109.

9. OV, vol. 6, pp. 350–1; Guillaume le Breton, *Gesta*, vol. 1, p. 282, *Philippidos*, vol. 2, p. 323; Roger of Wendover, *Flores Historiarum*, H. J. Hewlett (ed.) [3 vols] (London: RS, 1886–9), vol. 2, p. 281; Strickland, "Military technology and conquest", pp. 355–6; J. Gillingham, "The unromantic death of Richard I", in *Richard Coeur de Lion: kingship, chivalry and war in the twelfth century* (London: Hambledon, 1994), pp. 155–80; see below, pp. 121–5.

10. Gillingham, "William the Bastard at war", p. 157; F. J. Schmale & I. Schmale-Otto (eds), *Frutolfs und Ekkehards Chroniken und die Anonyme Kaiserchronik* (Darmstadt: Wissenschaft Buchgesellschaft, 1972), pp. 90–1; D. S. Evans (ed.), *A medieval Prince of Wales: the life of Gruffudd ap Cynan* (Llanerch: Llanerch Enterprises, 1990), p. 75; P. Latimer, "Henry II's campaign against the Welsh in 1165", *Welsh History Review* **14**, 1988–9, pp. 523–52; Lyons & Jackson, *Saladin*, p. 345, detail the attacks on Richard's supply-lines; Joinville, *Life of St Louis*, pp. 197, 240; J. R. Strayer, "Crusade against Aragon", in *Medieval statecraft and the perspectives of history* (Princeton: Princeton University Press), pp. 112, 109.

11. RA, p. 157.

12. Terraine, *White heat*, p. 97; A. C. Leighton, *Transport and communication in early medieval Europe AD 500–1100* (Newton Abbot: David and Charles, 1972), pp. 102–24; L. T. White, *Medieval technology and social change* (Oxford: Oxford University Press, 1962), pp. 62–7; AA, p. 277; Odo of Deuil, *De profectione Ludovici in Orientem*, V. G. Berry (ed.) (New York: Columbia University Press, 1948), pp. 104–5; on Roman roads in Asia Minor, see D. H. French, "A road problem: Roman or Byzantine", *Istanbuler Mitteilungen* **43**, 1993, pp. 445–54, and D. F. Graf, "Camels, roads and wheels in late Antiquity", in *Donum Amicitiae*, E. Dabrowa (ed.) (Krakow: Jagiellonian University Press, 1997), pp. 44–5.

13. See Plate 4 for an example of a four-wheeled cart drawn by two horses, and for other examples see Maciejowski, Pl. 5v, 9r, 12r, 27v; Leighton, *Transport and communication*, pp. 112–24; White, *Medieval technology*, pp. 62–7; on Bouvines, see below pp. 170–71, 235–41, on fighting in the plain of the Po see pp. 151–3 and on Hattin pp. 221–5; D. W. Lomax, *The reconquest of Spain* (London: Longman, 1978), pp. 94–6; Smail, *Crusading Warfare*, p. 204; J. France, *Victory in the East*, p. 94; Davies, *Age of conquest*, pp. 24–55; N. Brooks, "Medieval bridges: a window into changing concepts of state power", *The Haskins Society Journal* **7**, 1995, pp. 11–29; Christiansen, *The Northern Crusades*, pp. 13–16, 160–66.

14. R. R. Davies, *The age of conquest: Wales 1063–1415* (Oxford: Oxford University Press, 1987), pp. 52–3; Prestwich, *Armies and warfare*, p. 133; on Edward I and Scotland and Wales, see below, pp. 192–3, 195–6; France, *Victory in the East*, pp. 211–12; on British naval history in the Middle Ages and the use of fleets, N. A. M. Rodger, *The safeguard of the sea: a naval history of Britain vol. 1 660–1649* (London: HarperCollins, 1997), pp. 31–50.

15. B. S. Bachrach, "Some observations on the military administration of the Norman Conquest", *Battle* **8**, 1985, pp. 1–26; on Tagliacozzo, see below, pp. 181–4; J. W. Nesbitt, "Rate of march of crusading armies in Europe: a study in computation", *Traditio* **19**, 1963, pp. 167–82; E. N. Johnson, "The crusade of Frederick Barbarossa and Henry VI", in Setton, *Crusades*, vol. 2, pp. 92–4; France, *Victory in the East*, pp. 122–42; Prestwich, *Armies and warfare*, p. 246, in a chapter (pp. 245–62) that discusses logistics.

16. Oakeshott, *The sword in the age of chivalry*, pp. 32–4; Maciejowski Pl. 3v, 12r, 40 r.; see Chapter 2, *n*29; Nicolle, *Arms and armour*, vol. 2, nos 772K, T, AJ, AM.

## Chapter Four

1. J. Gillingham, "The unromantic death of Richard I", in *Richard Coeur de Lion: kingship, chivalry and war in the twelfth century* (London: Hambledon, 1994), pp. 155–80.

2. J. D. Tooke, *The just war in Aquinas and Grotius* (London: S.P.C.K., 1965), p. 11; F. H. Russell, *The just war in the Middle Ages* (Cambridge: Cambridge University Press, 1975), pp. 21–2, and on the Church's role according to Gratian and distinction from crusade, pp. 68–85; J. Brundage, *Medieval canon law and the crusader* (Wisconsin: University of Wisconsin Press, 1969); K. F. Werner, "Kingdom and principality in twelfth-century France", in *The medieval nobility*, T. Reuter (ed.) (Amsterdam: North Holland, 1978), pp. 243–4; F. Barlow, *The feudal kingdom of England*, pp. 52–62; G. Barraclough, *The origins of modern Germany* (Oxford: Blackwell, 1957), pp. 234–7.

3. Reuter, *Germany in the Middle Ages*, pp. 139–41, "*Filii matris nostrae pugnant adversum nos*. Bonds and tensions between prelates and their *milites* in the German High Middle Ages", in *Chiesa e mondo feudale nei secoli x–xii* (Milan: Università Cattolica del sacro Cuore, 1995), pp. 247–76, "*Episcopi cum sua militia*: the prelate as warrior in the early Staufer era", in *Warriors and churchmen in the High Middle Ages: essays presented to K. Leyser*, T. Reuter (ed.) (London: Hambledon, 1992), pp. 79–94; on Italy, see below, pp. 50–1; *L'Estoire de Eracles empereur*, RHC Oc. 2, p. 34, translated in J. Richard, *The Latin Kingdom of Jerusalem*, tr. J. Shirley, [2 vols] (Amsterdam: North Holland, 1979), vol. 1, p. 96; on England, see above, pp. 4, 10.

4. *Triumphus Sancti Lamberti*, MGH SS 20, pp. 497–511; Reuter, "The prelate as warrior", pp. 86 *n*27, 92 *n*65; O. Guillot, *Le comté d'Anjou et son entourage au XI$^e$ siècle*, [2 vols] (Paris: A. & J. Picard, 1972), vol. 2, p. 25, no. 8, for 989, pp. 119, no. 162, for 1056; William of Poitiers, *Gesta Guillelmi*, p. 67; France, *Victory in the East*, p. 53.

5. The origin of the principalities is a controversial subject. The fundamental work of J. Dhondt, *Etude sur la naissance des principautés territoriales en France (IX–X siècles)* (Bruges: De Tempel, 1948), supported recently by J. F. Werner, "Kingdom and principality in twelfth century France", argued that royal favour to important servants who took over old Carolingian *regna* was the basis of princely power; but others, including J. Dunbabin, *France in the making, 843–1180* (Oxford: Oxford University Press, 1985), have seen usurpation and conquest as having played a major role. On Burgundy, see J. Richard, *Les ducs de Bourgogne et la formation du duché du XI au XIV siècles* (Paris: Les Belles Lettres, 1954) and Dunbabin, *France in the making*, pp. 63–6; J. Gillingham, *The Kingdom of Germany in the High Middle Ages*, Historical Association Pamphlet G. 77, Historical Association, 1971; Reuter, *Germany in the Early Middle Ages*, pp. 148–220; Verlinden, *Robert I Le Frison*, pp. 46–70; Dunbabin, *France in the making*, pp. 184–90.

6. Dunbabin, *France in the making*, pp. 162–9, 173–9, 188–90, 204–5, 295–9; Fulk gave his own account in his *Fragmentum Historiae Andegavensis*, in Halphen, *Chroniques*, p. 234; J. Boussard, "L'éviction des tenants de Thibault de Blois par Geoffroi Martel en 1044", *Le Moyen Age* **69**, 1963, pp. 145–7; J. F. Lemarignier, *Recherches sur l'homage en marche et les frontières féodales* (Lille: Bibliothèque Universitaire, 1945); R. Fawtier, *The Capetian kings of France: monarchy and nation 987–1328*, tr. L. Butler (London: Macmillan, 1960), pp. 20–2; G. Duby, *La Société aux XIe et XIIe siècles dans la région mâconnaise* (Paris: S.E.V.P.E.N., 1971), pp. 155–71; on Otto-William, see also Glaber, pp. 104–5 *n*6 and J. France, "Rodulfus Glaber and French politics in the early eleventh century", *Francia* **16**, 1989, pp. 101–12; Gislebert, pp. 11–13; D. Bates, *Normandy before 1066* (London: Longman, 1982), p. 73.

7. See above, pp. 4–6, for this confusion of sovereignty and property.

8. Guillot, *Le comte d'Anjou et son entourage*, vol. 1, pp. 3–9, 131–8; Halphen, *Comté d'Anjou*, pp. 1–2, 14.

9. Bachrach, "The Angevin strategy of castle-building in the reign of Fulk Nerra", pp. 533–60; Bachrach, "Fortifications and military tactics: Fulk Nerra's strongholds circa 1000", pp. 531–49; B. S. Bachrach, "A study in feudal politics: relations between Fulk Nerra and William the Great 995–1030", *Viator* **7**, 1976, pp. 114–15; Halphen, *Comté d'Anjou*, pp. 39–41; Guillot, *Comte d'Anjou et son entourage*, vol. 1, pp. 21–38, 43–55, vol. 2, p. 26; R. W. Southern, *The making of the Middle Ages* (London: Hutchinson, 1953), pp. 83–8, which is now superseded by Bachrach, "Angevin strategy'. For the importance of castles in a particular episode, see J. Martindale, "Conventum inter Guilelmum Aquitanorum comes et Hugonem Chiliarchum", *English Historical Review* **84**, 1969, pp. 528–48.

10. Glaber, pp. 56–61; Halphen, *Comté d'Anjou*, pp. 33–45; Bachrach, "Angevin strategy"; Halphen, pp. 33–4, refers to Thietmar of Merseburg's knowledge of the battle; on Nouy, see Glaber, pp. 242–5.

11. Halphen, *Comté d'Anjou*, pp. 49–50: Guillot, *Comte d'Anjou et son entourage*, vol. 1, pp. 327–33; Boussard, "L'eviction des tenants de Thibault de Blois par Geoffroi Martel", pp. 191–203; W. Ziezulewicz, "An argument for historical continuity", *Medieval Prosopography* **8**, 1987, pp. 93–110; Barlow, *Feudal kingdom of England*, pp. 88–95. On Frederick I and II, see below, pp. 50–2, 108–10, 114, 128–9; C. W. David, *Robert Curthose, Duke of Normandy* (Cambridge, Mass.: Harvard University Press, 1920), pp. 46–51, 53–69; F. Barlow, *William Rufus* (London, Methuen, 1983), pp. 70–98, 273–96; J. Gillingham, "The Fall of the Angevin Empire", in *Richard Coeur de Lion: kingship, chivalry and war in the twelfth century* (London: Hambledon, 1994), pp. 193–200; Powicke, *Loss of Normandy*, pp. 280–307.

12. Suger, pp. 20–5; OV, vol. 6, p. 159, vol. 4, pp. 287–96; France, *Victory in the East*, pp. 41–3; F. M. Stenton, *The first century of English feudalism 1066–1166* (Oxford: Clarendon Press, 1961), pp. 252–4; J. Richard, *St Louis* (Paris: A. Fayard, 1983), pp. 46–7, 65–6; B. Arnold, *Princes and territories in medieval Germany* (Cambridge: Cambridge University Press, 1991), pp. 273–4; D. Crouch, *The Beaumont twins: the roots and branches of power in the twelfth century* (Cambridge: Cambridge University Press, 1986), p. 54.

13. M. Pacaut, *Louis VII et son royaume* (Paris: S.E.V.P.E.N., 1964), pp. 188–94; Richard, *St Louis*, pp. 46–7; J. H. Round, *Geoffrey de Mandeville* (London: Longman, 1892), pp. 207–21; Potter, *Gesta Stephani*, pp. 108–10; T. C. van Cleve, *The Emperor Frederick II of Hohenstaufen, Immutator Mundi* (Oxford: Clarendon Press, 1972), esp. pp. 396–400.

14. Bur, *La formation du comté de Champagne*, p. 403; I have drawn this account from J. Gillingham, *The Angevin Empire* (New York: Holmes & Meier, 1984), pp. 11–24, 34–5.

15. W. L. Warren, *Henry II* (London: Eyre Methuen, 1973), pp. 65, 72; Gillingham, *Angevin Empire*, p. 26.

16. William of Newburgh Historia rerum Anglicarum, in Howlelt, *Chronicles*, vol. l, p. 17, vol. 2, p. 491; Gervase of Canterbury, *Historical works of Gervase of Canterbury*, W. Stubbs (ed.), [2 vols] (London: RS, 1879–80), vol. 1, p. 167; Ralph of Diceto, *De Regibus Anglorum in Opera Historica*, W. Stubbs (ed.), [2 vols] (London: RS, 1876), vol. 1, p. 303; Robert of Torigni, *Chronica*, in Howlett, *Chronicles*, vol. 4, p. 202; Roger of Hovenden, vol. 1, p. 217. See the comments of K. Norgate, *England under the Angevin kings*, [2 vols] (London: Eyre Methuen, 1887), vol. 1, pp. 461–3, and Warren, *Henry II*, pp. 82–91, 117, 144–6; Robert of Torigni, pp. 229–31; . Boussard, "Les mercenaires au XII siècle", pp. 201–3.

17. Warren, *Henry II*, pp. 122–3; William of Newburgh, vol. 1, p. 181, tr. Warren, p. 125; J. Boussard, "Les mercenaires au XII siècle", pp. 211–13.

18. Bradbury, "Battles in England and Normandy", pp. 1–12; Boussard, "Les mercenaires au XII siècle", p. 11: see for Breton victory, p. 207, Fornham, p. 208, and Alnwick, p. 209.

19. This is a brief survey of a complex period. For an elucidation of developments in Italy, see D. Waley, *The Italian city–republics* (London: Longman, 1969), pp. 56–109; G. Tabacco, *The struggle for power in medieval Italy* (Cambridge: Cambridge University Press, 1989), pp. 182–36. On the general policy of Barbarossa, P. Munz, *Frederick Barbarossa: a study in medieval politics* (London: Eyre & Spottiswoode, 1969), pp. 44–145, and for Italy pp. 148–86; M. Pacaut, *Frederick Barbarossa* (London: Collins, 1970), pp. 41–56, and for Italy pp. 57–92; Otto of Freising and Rahewin, *The deeds of Frederick Barbarossa*, C. C. Mierowa and R. Emery (eds) (Columbia: Columbia University Press, 1953), pp. 125–8.

20. Munz, *Frederick Barbarossa*, pp. 162–77; Pacaut, *Frederick Barbarossa*, pp. 84–8; *Annales Mediolanses*, MGH SS 18, p. 367; Otto & Acerbus Morena, *Historia*, F. Güterbock (ed.) (Berlin: MGH, 1930), p. 66; *Annales Coloniensis*, MGH SS 17, p. 770; *Annales Egmundani*, MGH SS 18, p. 461.

21. On this subject in general, see J. R. Strayer, *On the medieval origins of the modern state* (Princeton: Princeton University Press, 1970), and on Frederick's ideas, van Cleve, *Frederick II*, pp. 237–80, and see also pp. 179–93, 391–424, 498–512; H. Mitteis, *The state in the Middle Ages*, tr. H. F. Orton (Amsterdam: North Holland, 1975), pp. 339–44; Otto of Freising, pp. 125–9; Munz, *Frederick Barbarossa*, pp. 167–9; K. Hampe, *Germany under the Salian and Hohenstaufen emperors*, tr. R. Bennett (Oxford: Blackwell, 1973), pp. 284–6.

## Chapter Five

1. Justinian, *Leges Selectae*, PL 72, col. 1106.

2. J. Flori, "Sémantique et société médiévale: le verbe adouber et son évolution au XII siècle", *Annales ESC* **31**, 1976, pp. 915–40; John of Salisbury, *Policraticus*, pp. 104–17; J.-P. Poly & E. Bournazel, *The feudal transformation 900–1200* (New York: Holmes & Meier, 1991), pp. 87–119, esp. pp. 87–118; Arnold, *German knighthood*, pp. 112, 69–75.

3. Galbert of Bruges, *The murder of Charles the Good*, J. B. Ross (ed.) (Toronto: Toronto University Press, 1993), pp. 96–118, shows that the effort of the count to treat the Erembald clan as servile precipitated his murder in 1127; Gislebert, pp. 209–15, reports the affair of Robert of Beaurain, who was finally forced to admit his servile origins under threat of judicial duel in 1188; Richer of Rheims, *Histoire de France 888–995*, R. Latouche (ed.) 2 vols (Paris: Les Belles Lettres, 1937), vol. 2, pp. 160–3; Bur, *Comté de Champagne*, pp. 427–42, 459–60; William of Jumièges, *Gesta Normannorum Ducum*, J. Marx (ed.) (Rouen: Société de l'Histoire de Normandie, 1914), pp. 106–8; D. W. Lomax, *The reconquest of Spain* (London: Longman, 1978), pp. 99–100; E. Lourie "A society organised for war – medieval Spain", *Past and present* vol. 36 (1966), pp. 54–76, pp. 55–6; J. P. Poly & E. Bournazel, *The feudal transformation 900–1200* (New York: Holmes & Meier, 1991), p. 101; Reynolds, *Fiefs and vassals*, p. 101; S. Harvey, "The knight and the knight's fee in medieval England", *Past and Present* **49**, 1970, 3–43; A. L. Poole, *The obligations of society in the eleventh and twelfth centuries* (Oxford: Clarendon Press, 1946), p. 57. There are some interesting points about the diversity of knights in B. S. Bachrach, "The *milites* and the millennium", *The Haskins Society Journal* **6**, 1994, p. 92.

4. J. F. Lemarignier, *Le Gouvernement royal aux premiers temps capétiens (987–1108)* (Paris: J. Picard, 1956), pp. 67–140; Murray, *Reason and society*, pp. 81–109; Glaber, pp. 32–5; S. Reynolds *Fiefs and vassals* (Oxford: Oxford University Press, 1994), pp. 40–1; F. Vercauteren, "A kindred in northern France in the eleventh and twelfth centuries", in *The medieval nobility*, T. Reuter (ed.) (Amsterdam: North Holland, 1979), pp. 87–103; Galbert of Bruges, pp. 20–40; William of Apulia, *La Geste de Robert Guiscard*, M. Mathieu (ed.) (Palermo: Istituto Siciliano di Studi Byzantini e Neoellenici, 1961), p. 109; Gaufredus Malaterra, *De rebus gestis Rogerii Calabriae et Siciliae comitis et Roberti Guiscardi ducis fratris eius*, E. Pontieri (ed.) (Bologna, 1928), p. 25.

5. Prestwich, *Armies and warfare*, pp. 59–61; H. R. Loyn, *Anglo-Saxon England and the Norman Conquest* (London: Longman, 1962).

6. W. Davies, *Small worlds: the village community in early medieval Brittany* (London: Duckworth, 1988) and J. M. H. Smith, *Province and empire: Brittany and the Carolingians* (Cambridge: Cambridge University Press, 1992) emphasize the relatively limited impact of official power structures upon early medieval society, while Poly & Bournazel, *Feudal transformation*, esp. pp. 9–45, charts the tightening of seigniorial control; Reynolds, *Fiefs and vassals*, pp. 154–60.

7. France, "La guerre dans la France féodale", pp. 177–98; K. Leyser, "The battle at the Lech 955: a study in tenth century warfare", *History* **50**, 1965, pp. 1–25; J. Nelson, "Ninth century knighthood: the evidence of Nithard", in *Studies in medieval history presented to R. Allen-Brown*, C. Harper-Bill, C. J. Holdsworth, J. Nelson (eds) (Woodbridge: Boydell & Brewer, 1989), pp. 255–66.

8. Reynolds, *Fiefs and vassals*, pp. 156–7, 194–5, 425–6.

9. H. E. J. Cowdrey, "The Peace and Truce of God in the eleventh century", *Past and Present* **46**, 1970, pp. 42–67.

10. Murray, *Reason and society*, esp. pp. 90–4.

11. Otto of Freising, pp. 136–7; Gislebert, p. 197; Guillaume le Breton, *Gesta*, vol. 1, pp. 276–7.

12. J. Gillingham, "Thegns and knights in eleventh-century England: who was then the gentleman?", *Transactions of the Royal Historical Society* **5**, 1995, pp. 129–54; G. Duby, "The transformation of the aristocracy: France at the beginning of the thirteenth century", *The chivalrous society*, tr. C. Postan (London: Edward Arnold, 1977), pp. 178–85, "Les transformations sociales dans le milieu aristocratique", in *La France de Philippe Auguste*, R. H. Bautier (ed.) (Paris: CNRS, 1982), pp. 711–16; J. Flori, "Chevalerie, noblesse et luttes de classes au Moyen age: à propos d'un ouvrage récent", *Le Moyen Age* **94**, 1988, pp. 262–6, has suggested that the knights copied the nobles in adopting the chivalric code, a rather different view to that of Duby, which emphasizes the creativity of knightly aspiration; Eadmer, *Vita Sancti Anselmi*, R. W. Southern (ed.) (London: Nelson, 1962), p. 88; St Hugh in Poole, *Obligations of society*, p. 42; Contamine, *War*, p. 82 *n*37; Roger of Hovenden, vol. 4, p. 40.

13. M. R. Powicke, "Distraint of knighthood and military obligation under Henry III", *Speculum* **25**, 1950, pp. 457–70; S. L. Waugh, "Reluctant knights and jurors: respites, exemptions and public obligations in the reign of Henry III", *Speculum* **58**, 1983, pp. 937–86. The causes have been recently discussed by M. Prestwich, "*Miles in armis strenuus*: the knight at war", *Transactions of the Royal Historical Society* **5**, 1995, pp. 207–12, and P. Coss, *The knight in medieval England* (Stroud: Sutton, 1993), pp. 60–71; Prestwich, *Armies and warfare*, pp. 63–75; J. Viard & E. Déprez (eds), *Chronique de Jean le Bel* (Paris: Champion, 1904), p. 156; Contamine, *War*, pp. 80–3.

14. Duby, "Transformation of the aristocracy", p. 183; P. Coss, "Knights, esquires and the origins of social gradation in England", *Transactions of the Royal Historical Society* **5**, 1995, pp. 155–78; Galbert of Bruges, pp. 23, 23, 110, 154; Richer of Rheims, *Histoire de France 888–995*, R. Latouche (ed.), [2 vols] (Paris: Les Belles Lettres, 1937), vol. 1, p. 133; Liudprand of Cremona, *Relatio de Legatione Constantinopolitana*, B. Scott (ed.) (London: Bristol Classical Press, 1992), pp. 4, 31; OV, vol. 2, pp. 41, 127; St Bernard, vol. l, PL 182, col. 638; Hugo Farsitus, *De Miraculis B. Mariae Suessionensis*, PL 179, col. 1795.

15. According to OV, vol. 3, p. 255, Gilbert of Auffay was a "kinsman of the duke, fighting at his side surrounded by his companions in all the principal battles of the English war", while the community of the castle and landholding have been seen as important by Duby, *Mâconnaise*, pp. 161–71; R. A. Brown, "The Battle of Hastings", *Battle* **3**, 1980, p. 16;

Prestwich, *"Miles in armis strenuus"*, pp. 216–17, *Armies and warfare*, pp. 41–8; Crouch, *William Marshal*, pp. 195–204; N. Vincent, *Peter des Roches: an alien in English politics 1205–38* (Cambridge: Cambridge University Press, 1996), p. 63, argues that Peter preferred to tax his landed vassals to pay his own troops.

16. Reuter, *"Filii matris nostrae pugnant adversum nos"*, pp. 270–1; Reynolds, *Fiefs and vassals*, pp. 425–6; Arnold, *German knighthood*, pp. 225–54; K. F. Krieger, "Obligatory military service and the use of mercenaries in imperial military campaigns under the Hohenstaufen emperors", in *England and Germany in the High Middle Ages*, A. Haverkamp & H. Vollrath (eds) (Oxford: Clarendon Press, 1996), pp. 164–8; M. Mallett, *Mercenaries and their masters. Warfare in Renaissance Italy* (London: Bodley Head, 1974), pp. 6–24; D. Waley, "Chivalry and cavalry at San Gimignano: knighthood in a small Italian commune", in *Recognitions: essays presented to Edmund Fryde*; C. Richmond & I. Harvey (eds) (Aberystwyth: National Library of Wales, 1996), pp. 39–53, and see the discussion below, pp. 75, 133–4.

17. Gislebert, pp. 65, 71, 95, 99, 112, 114, 155, 209, 217, for example.

18. OV, vol. 4, p. 49, vol. 5, p. 217; R. B. Yewdale, *Bohemond I Prince of Antioch* (Princeton: Princeton University Press, 1924), pp. 36–51; P. Chaplais (ed.), *Diplomatic documents preserved in the Public Record Office 1. (1101–1272)* (London: HMSO, 1964), no. 1; Warren, *Henry II*, pp. 223–4, 537; G. Legato, "Fra ordini cavallereschi e crociata: milites ad terminum e confraternitates armate", in *Militia Christi e Crociata nei secoli XI–XII* (Milan: Vita e Pensiero, Università Cattolica del sacro Cuore, 1992), pp. 645–97; P. Edbury (ed.), "The Old French Continuation of William of Tyre", in *The conquest of Jerusalem and the Third Crusade* (Aldershot: Scolar Press, 1996), p. 38; Prestwich, *Armies and warfare*, pp. 153–4; Mallett, *Mercenaries and their masters*, pp. 6–24; S. Runciman, *The Sicilian Vespers. A history of the Mediterranean world in the later thirteenth century* (Harmondsworth: Penguin, 1960), p. 109; Salimbene de Adam, vol. 2, pp. 684, 692, 705.

19. Richer, vol. 2, p. 286; Poole, *Obligations of society*, p. 52; Contamine, *War*, pp. 91–101.

20. GF, p. 43; RA, p. 100, says that 10,000 *solidi* was offered to Godfrey de Bouillon and Robert of Normandy, 6,000 to Robert of Flanders and 5,000 to Tancred, the terms for which are reported on p. 112; Prestwich, *Armies and warfare*, pp. 90–1; K. Leyser, "Henry I and the beginnings of the German Empire", *English Historical Review* **83**, 1968, p. 14, "Early medieval warfare", in *Communications and power in medieval Europe*, T. Reuter (ed.) (London: Hambledon, 1994), p. 33; J. Prawer, *Crusader institutions* (Oxford: Clarendon Press, 1980), pp. 32–4, where it is suggested that a normal fee for one knight was worth 400–500 besants per annum.

21. Gislebert, p. 107; G. Duby, "Youth in aristocratic society", *The chivalrous society*, tr. C. Postan (London: Edward Arnold, 1977), pp. 112–22; Contamine, *War*, pp. 95–6.


## Chapter Six


1. Gislebert, p. 172, suggests that the Duke of Louvain had 400 knights and 60,000 foot in 1184 and (p. 181) that the Flemings had 400 knights and 40,000 foot in 1185.

2. Gislebert, pp. 65, 71, 95, 99, 112, 114, 155, 209, 217; *Henry II, Rotuli de Dominabus et pueris et puellis de XII comitatibus, an. 1185*, vol. 35 (London: Pipe Roll Society, 1913), p. 59; Poole, *Obligations of society*, pp. 38, 58–9; Round, *The King's Sergeants*, pp. 15, 21–34;

Round suggested that real indicator of a sergeanty in England was that it did not pay scutage, but this is contested by Poole (pp. 45–6), who points to the confusions that arose from marriage and multiple sub-infeudation.

3. D. Matthew, *The Norman Kingdom of Sicily* (Cambridge: Cambridge University Press, 1992), pp. 256–7, suggests that they numbered about 11,000 as opposed to about 8,620 knights; van Cleve, *Frederick II*, pp. 142–3, 242; see above, p. 58, *n*11; Arnold, *German knighthood*, pp. 23, 124–5; Contamine, *War*, pp. 83–4; Verbruggen, *Art of Warfare*, p. 142; John of Ibelin, *Livre des Assises de la Haute Cour*, RHC Lois 1, pp. 424–6.

4. F. M. Stenton, *Anglo-Saxon England* (Oxford: Clarendon Press, 1971), pp. 289–90; W. H. Stevenson, "Trinoda necessitas", *English Historical Review* **29**, 1914, pp. 689–703; John, "English feudalism and the structure of Anglo-Saxon society", pp. 128–53; H. G. Richardson & G. O. Sayles, *The governance of medieval England from the Conquest to Magna Carta* (Edinburgh: Edinburgh University Press, 1963), pp. 42–61, generally accepted this position, but believed (p. 51) in a general obligation to local defence. Abels, *Lordship and military obligations in Anglo-Saxon England*, has argued this case vigorously and far from accepting any universal military obligation has suggested (p. 22), that "only those nobles who were bound to the king by the tie of lordship were obliged to serve him with arms" and that the *ceorls* sometimes mentioned as owing military service were those from the king's lands who were especially obligated. Reynolds, *Fiefs and vassals*, p. 336, emphasizes that proprietors of land were the primary providers of military support to the king.

5. Reynolds, *Fiefs and vassals*, pp. 156, 426–7; Contamine, *War*, pp. 86–8, surveys the evidence, but the French and Norman examples that he mentions are all capable of a tenurial explanation, while in his *Guerre, état et société à la fin du moyen age. Etudes sur les armées des rois de France 1337–1494* (Paris: Mouton, 1972) he is drawing on material far beyond 1300; Poly & Bournazel, *Feudal transformation*, pp. 18–25, survey evidence for a universal obligation, but J. Boussard, "Services féodeaux, milices et mercenaires aux X et XI siècles", *Ordinamenti militari in Occidenti nell'Alto Medioevo: Settimane di Studio del Centro Italiano di Studi sull'Alto Medioevo XV, Spoleto 30 March – 5 April 1867* (Spoleto: C.I.S.A., 1968) pp. 140–1, is sceptical of the existence of this in the tenth century and (pp. 155–61) clearly sees the counts of Anjou operating in a quite different way: T. N. Bisson, "The organised peace in southern France and Catalonia 1140–*ca.* 1233", *American Historical Review* **82**, 1977, p. 299, *n*51, notes the continued enforcement of the universal service in the twelfth century; Reuter, *Germany in the early Middle Ages*, pp. 142–3, expresses considerable scepticism about a peasant army; Widukind, *Rerum Gestarum Saxonicarum libri tres*, G. Waitz (ed.) (Hannover: MGH, 1882), vol. I, pp. 21–2, mentions Conrad I's anxiety not to offend "the whole army of the Saxons" but never suggests that this was a mass levy, while the "whole people" addressed by Henry I at I p. 38 was clearly not an entire population, and probably was no more than the leading nobles and churchmen; *Carmen de Bello Saxonico*, MGH SS 15, p. 1231; W. Eberhard (ed.), *Vita Heinrici IV imperatoris* (Hannover: MGH, 1899), p. 19.

6. Contamine, *War*, pp. 88–9; Prestwich, *Armies and warfare*, pp. 119–23.

7. E. Hallam, *Capetian France* (London: Longman, 1980), pp. 161–3; Gaier, "Analysis of military forces", pp. 242–3; J. Riley-Smith, "A note on confraternities in the Latin Kingdom of Jerusalem", *Bulletin of the Institute of Historical Research* **44**, 1971, pp. 301–8; Prawer, *Crusader institutions*, pp. 312–3; C. Gaier, "Mentalité collective de l'infantrie communale liégeoise au Moyen Age", in *Armes et combats dans l'univers médiévale* (Brussels: De Boek-Wesmael, 1995), pp. 311–17. On Italian anti-heretic and peasant confraternities, see below, p. 70, *n*12.

8. Prestwich, *Armies and warfare*, p. 121; P. Latimer, "Henry II's campaign against the Welsh in 1165", *Welsh History Review* **14**, 1989, pp. 547–51; J. L. Nelson (ed.), *Annals of St-Bertin* (Manchester: Manchester University Press, 1991), p. 89.

9. Bradbury, Battles in England and Normandy 1066–1154, pp. 1–12, and on archery in general his *Medieval archer; Annales Pisani 1004–1175* MGH SS 19, pp. 244, 246; *Annales Sancti Iustinae Patavini* MGH SS 19, p. 189; Gerald, *Expugnatio Hibernica*, p. 230; Roger of Wendover 2, p. 176; Galbert, pp. 75, 110. The evidence for England is very well summarized by Bradbury, *Medieval archer*, pp. 76–79; Otto Morena, pp. 89–91, 114–16; for Peter of Eboli see Plate 2 and for Richard I above p. 34, *n*9; AA pp. 475, 602; Roger of Hovenden 2, p. 253; Prestwich, *Armies and warfare*, p. 129.

10. Prestwich, *Armies and warfare*, p. 127, citing Gerald of Wales, *The journey through Wales and the description of Wales*, L. Thorpe (ed.) (Harmondsworth: Penguin, 1978), vol. I, pp. 4, 113, the famous case of a knight of William de Braose pinned to his saddle by Welsh arrows. It should be noted that Gerald is not a disinterested witness to Welsh military skill. This is the main thrust of S. Davies, *Anglo-Welsh warfare and the works of Gerald of Wales* (MA Dissertation, Department of History, University of Wales Swansea, 1995) and will form an element in Davies's PhD thesis on "Anglo-Welsh warfare 1063–1272"; France, *Victory in the East*, p. 205; Potter, *Gesta Stephani*, p. 173; on the battle of Lincoln, see Davies, *Anglo-Welsh warfare*, pp. 31–2; William of Newburgh, pp. 194–6; Roger of Hovenden, vol. 2, p. 345; Prestwich, *Armies and Warfare*, pp. 123–5, 133. For a brief account of the composite armies of the Islamic East, see France, *Victory in the East*, pp. 145–6, 204–6, 359–60; on mercenaries and their origins, see below, pp. 70–5; W. Stubbs (ed.), *Select charters and other illustrations of English constitutional history*, revised H. W. C. Davis (Oxford: Clarendon Press, 1913), pp. 362–4, 463–9; F. Palgrave, *Parliamentary writs*, [2 vols] (London: Record Commissioners, 1827–34), vol. 1, p. 270.

11. Rabanus Maurus, *De procinctu Romanae miliciae*, E. Dümmler, (ed.) *Zeitschrift für Deutsches Altertum* **15**, 1872, p. 443; OV, vol. 3, p. 255; William of Poitiers, p. 150, says that the army waited a month at Dives for a fair wind, but the force had been gathering for some time; on knights making their own decisions, see p. 188. On the "feigned flights", see Brown, "Battle of Hastings', pp. 1–21; B. S. Bachrach, "The feigned retreat at Hastings", *Medieval Studies* **33**, 1971, pp. 344–7. The present writer thinks that on the first occasion William staged a desperate rally of broken troops, and on the second rally feigned a flight (pp. 190, 194); France, *Victory in the East*, pp. 367–82; Ralph of Caen, *Gesta Tancredi* RHC Oc. 3, pp. 622–3.

12. Mansi, *Concilia*, vol. 22, pp. 232–3; N. J. Housley, "Politics and heresy in Italy: anti-heretical crusades, orders and confraternities in Italy 1200–1500", *Journal of Ecclesiastical History* **33**, 1982, p. 194; Walter Map, *De nugis curialium*, M. R. James (ed.), revised C. N. L. Brooke & R. A. B. Mynors (Oxford: Clarendon Press, 1983), p. 118; H. Grundmann, "Rotten und Brabazonen, sölder-heere in 12 Jahrhundert", *Deutsches Archiv für die Erforschung des Mittelalters* **5**, 1942, p. 432, *n*2, 4.

13. Mansi, *Concilia*, vol. 19, p. 100; Richer, see above, p. 61, *n*19; on Anglo-Norman mercenaries, see J. O. Prestwich, "War and finance in the Anglo-Norman state", *Transactions of the Royal Historical Society* **4**, 1954, pp. 19–43, J. Schlight, *Monarchs and mercenaries* (Bridgeport: Bridgeport University Press, 1968), S. D. B. Brown, "The mercenary and his master: military service and monetary reward in the eleventh and twelfth century", *History* **74**, 1989, pp. 20–38 and Suger, p. 9, for his comment on William Rufus as *militum mercator et solidator*; on Henry II, see especially J. Boussard, "Les mercenaires au XII siècle. Henry de Plantagenet et les origines d'une armée de métier", Bibliothèque de l'Ecole de Chartes,

106 (1945–6), pp. 189–224, pp. 180–224; on Frederick I, Vincent of Prague, *Chronicon*, MGH SS 17, p. 683, Otto Morena, p. 124, Iohannes Codagnellus, *Annales Placentini*, O. Holder-Egger (ed.) (Hannover: MGH, 1901), p. 8; on Philip Augustus, E. Audouin, *Essai sur l'Armée royale au temps de Philippe Auguste* (Paris: Champion, 1913), pp. 73–112; for King John, see below, p. 72, *n*19; on the Latin East, see Fulcher of Chartres, *Gesta Francorum Iherusalem Peregrinantium*, RHC Oc. 3, p. 423, Ralph of Caen, p. 714, WT, pp. 596, 654, 783–4 and a charter of Amalric as Count of Ascalon of 1158, which divides the testors between *Hominibus meis* and *Stipendiariis meis* R. Röhricht (ed.), *Regesta regni hierosolymitani* (New York: Burt Franklin, 1960) p. 86; Mallett, *Mercenaries and their masters*, pp. 6–24; for a general survey of the twelfth century, see Grundmann, "Rotten und Brabazonen", pp. 419–92 and H. Géraud, "Les routiers au douzième siècle", *Bibliothèque de l'Ecole des Chartes* **3**, 1841–2, pp. 125–47.

14. Grundmann, "Rotten und Brabanzonen", pp. 424–36.

15. Grundmann, "Rotten und Brabanzonen", pp. 424–36; on the papacy and the renewed Peace Movement of the twelfth century, see Bisson, "The organised peace".

16. Quoted in A. Luchaire, *Social France at the time of Philip Augustus* (New York: Ungar, 1957), p. 261; on the date, see C. A. Knudson & J. Misrahi, "French medieval literature", *The medieval literature of Western Europe*, J. H. Fisher (ed.) (New York: New York University Press, 1966), p. 143.

17. Grundmann, "Rotten und Brabanzonen", pp. 430, *n*4, 432, *n*2, 4, 6, 433, *n*1, 2, 3; Gillingham, "War and chivalry in the history of William the Marshal", pp. 231–2; Hackett, *Girart de Roussillon*, quoted in Luchaire, *Social France*, p. 260; Géraud, "Les routiers", pp. 134–5, discusses the failure of the Archbishop of Narbonne's fulminations against such notable employers of mercenaries as the Count of Toulouse; H. E. J. Cowdrey, "Bishop Ermenfrid of Sion and the Penitential Ordinance following the battle of Hastings", *Journal of Ecclesiastical History* **20**, 1969, pp. 235–40; Gratian, *Decretum*, A. Friedberg (ed.) (Leipzig: MGH, 1879), C. 23, q. 1, c. 5, p. 893.

18. For an account of this remarkable phenomenon, see Duby, *Three Orders*, pp. 327–36; Géraud, "Les routiers", pp. 138–47, Luchaire, "Un essai de révolution sociale sous Philippe Auguste", *Grand Revue* (1900) 2, pp. 8–46, and for the context Bisson, "The organised peace"; Prestwich, *Armies and warfare*, pp. 153–4; on the Peace Movement and Archbishop Aimo, E. De Certain (ed.), *Miracula Sancti Benedicti* (Paris: Renouard, 1850), pp. 192–8, H. E. J. Cowdrey, "The Peace and Truce of God in the eleventh century", *Past and Present* **46**, 1970, pp. 42–67 and T. Head, "The Peace-League of Bourges", in *The Peace of God: social violence and religious response in France around the year 1000*, T. Head & R. Landes (eds) (Ithaca: Cornell University Press, 1992), pp. 219–38.

19. Prestwich, *Armies and warfare*, pp. 152–3.

20. On the Peace Movement of the eleventh and twelfth centuries, see above, p. 72, *n*19; on the People's Crusade, AA, p. 295; on Eudes, see N. Cohn, *The pursuit of the millennium* (London: Secker & Warburg, 1957), pp. 44–6 and W. L. Wakefield & A. P. Evans, *Heresies of the High Middle Ages* (New York: Colombia University Press, 1969), pp. 141–6; on the Second Crusade, Odo of Deuil, p. 119; on the Third Crusade, Edbury, "Old French Continuation of William of Tyre", pp. 94–5; on the Children's Crusade, N. P. Zacour, "The Childrens' Crusade", in Setton, *Crusades*, vol. 2, pp. 325–42; on the Pastoreaux, Runciman, *Crusades*, vol. 3, p. 279, and J. Riley Smith, *The crusades. A short history* (London: Athlone, 1987), p. 172, and Cohn, pp. 94–8; on Flanders, Cohn, pp. 90–3, and Gaier, "Analysis of military forces", pp. 233, 243–5.

21. Grundmann, "Rotten und Brabanzonen", pp. 420, *n*4, 421, *n*1, 2, 422, *n*1, 2, 3, 423, *n*1;

K. F. Krieger, "Obligatory military service and the use of mercenaries in imperial military campaigns under the Hohenstaufen emperors", in *England and Germany in the High Middle Ages* (Oxford: Clarendon Press, 1996), pp. 164–6.

22. See PL 143, col. 1064; PL 155, col. 825; PL 181, cols 110, 181–2; PL 187, col. 1177; PL 193, col. 963; PL 199, cols 777, 780.

23. Marianus Scotus, *Chronicon*, PL 147, col. 789; Aimo, *Historia Francorum*, PL 139, col. 700; OV, vol. 3, pp. 98–9.

24. J. F. Niermeyer, *Mediae Latinitatis Lexicon Minus* (Leiden: Brill, 1954–76), p. 991; OV, vol. 6, pp. 448, 482; Peter Cantor, *Verbum Abbreviatum*, PL 205, col. 149; WT, p. 796; Robert of Torigni, vol. 4, p. 202.

25. The earliest use is in the *Gesta Episcoporum Cameracensium*, PL 149, col. 205, see Niermeyer, *Lexicon*, p. 977. The word is used by Fulbert of Chartres in his letter to Hilderbert (PL 141, Ep. CXII, col. 255), but this is now known to be an early-twelfth-century forgery, on which see F. Behrends, *Letters and poems of Fulbert of Chartres* (Oxford: Clarendon Press, 1976), pp. lxi–ii; Gislebert, p. 100.

26. Prestwich, *Armies and warfare*, p. 153; Brown, "Military service and monetary reward", pp. 24–8, 34–5; Géraud, "Les routiers", pp. 146–7. In the agreement between Frederick Barbarossa and Louis VII, it was proposed to banish all "Brabationes vel Coterellos, equites seu pedites" (Grundmann, "Rotten und Brabanzonem" p. 450, *n*1), while a letter from Abbot Rudolf to Archbishop Stephen of Metz (1120–73) complained of a lord who quartered *solidarios suos* with a multitude of horses and palfreys on the abbey lands (PL 173, col. 212). Horses are referred to as being used by the mercenaries of King John (Grundmann, p. 429, *n*2).

27. Helmold, *Chronica Slavorum*, MGH SS 21, pp. 55–6; Gislebert, pp. 180–1; Vanderkindere, p. xxxiv, attempts to defend the huge numbers, but agrees that they were probably only indicative of large numbers.

28. Boussard, "Les mercenaires au xii siècle", pp. 189–224. In his famous article, Boussard rather exaggerates the professionalism of Henry II's mercenaries, as his full title, "Les mercenaires au xii<sup>e</sup> siècle. Henri II Plantagenet et les origines de l'armée de métier", suggests; Robert of Torigni, vol. 4, pp. 255–9; Richard of Devizes, *Chronicon de rebus gestis Ricardi primi*, J. Stevenson (ed.), [4 vols] (London: RS, 1838), vol. 2, pp. 186–8, 191, and see above, *n*18; see below, pp. 133–5; K. M. Setton, "The Catalans in Greece 1311–80", in Setton, *Crusades*, vol. 3, pp. 187–8; P. Lock, *The Franks in the Aegean 1204–1500* (London: Longman, 1995), pp. 115–16.

## Chapter Seven

1. On peripatetic kingship, see H. C. Peyer, "Das Reisekönigtum des Mittelalters", *Vierteljahrschrift für Sozial- und Wirtschaftsgeschichte* **51**, 1964, pp. 1–21; T. Charles-Edwards, "Early medieval kingship in the British Isles", in *The origins of the Anglo-Saxon kingdoms*, S. Basset (ed.) (Leicester: Leicester University Press, 1989), pp. 28–39; P. A. Stafford, "The farm of one night and the organisation of King Edward's estates in Domesday", *Economic History Review* **33**, 1980, pp. 491–502. Writers have perhaps overstated the military and somewhat neglected the domestic aspects of the castle. For a corrective view of the castle as stately home, see the very valuable C. Coulson, "Cultural realities and reappraisals in

English castle-study", *Journal of Medieval History* **22**, 1996, pp. 171–207, which has an important bibliography.

2. On this phase of Charles the Bald's rule, see J. L. Nelson, *Charles the Bald* (London: Longman, 1992), pp. 190–220, and note the high favour the monarch accorded to Egfrid (pp. 126, 135, 173); on the rise of the princes, G. Barraclough, *The crucible of Europe* (London: Thames and Hudson, 1976), pp. 84–97, provides a useful summary; R. Aubenas, "Les châteaux forts des ix et x siècles: contribution à l'étude des origines de la féodalité", *Revue de l'Histoire du Droit Français et étranger* **17**, 1938, 548–86.

3. H. Kennedy, *Crusader castles* (Cambridge: Cambridge University Press, 1994), pp. 23–5, 45–52; Bachrach, "Angevin strategy of castle-building", pp. 538, 557, 550; J. C. Andressohn, *Ancestry and life of Godfrey de Bouillon* (Bloomington: University of Indiana, 1947), p. 38; Bur, *Formation du Comté de Champagne*, pp. 148, 259–60, 318; N. J. G. Pounds, *The medieval castle in England and Wales: a social and political history* (Cambridge: Cambridge University Press, 1990), pp. 8–9, 60–63; K. S. Nicholas, "When feudal ideals failed: conflicts between lords and vassals in the Low Countries 1127–1296", in *The rusted hauberk: feudal ideas of order and their decline,* L. O. Purdon (ed.) (Gainesville: University Press of Florida, 1993), pp. 201–26.

4. N. J. G. Pounds, *The medieval castle in England and Wales: a social and political history* (Cambridge: Cambridge University Press, 1990), pp. 29–31; Bur, *Comté de Champagne*, pp. 277–9; on Anjou, see above, pp. 43–5; Adhémar de Chabannes, *Chronique*, J. Chavanon (ed.) (Paris: A. Picard, 1897), p. 60; Barlow, *William Rufus*, p. 286–7; Gislebert, pp. 181; Runciman, *Sicilian Vespers*, pp. 107–9; M. Prestwich, *Edward I* (London: Methuen, 1980), p. 174; G. T. Beech, *A rural society in medieval France: the Gâtine of Poitou in the eleventh and twelfth centuries* (Baltimore: Johns Hopkins Press, 1964), pp. 42–60; Duby, *Mâconnaise*, pp. 155–66.

5. Reuter, "*Filii matris nostrae pugnant adversus nos*", p. 249, *Early medieval Germany*, pp. 142–4; OV, vol. 2. p. 219; C. W. Hollister, *Anglo-Saxon military institutions on the eve of the Norman Conquest* (Oxford: Clarendon Press, 1962), pp. 140–4; A. Williams, "A bell-house and a burh-geat: lordly residences in England before the Norman Conquest", *Medieval Knighthood* **4**, 1992, pp. 221–40; D. Renn, "Burhgeat and Gonfanon: two sidelights from the Bayeux Tapestry", *Battle* **16**, 1994, pp. 177–98; G. Beresford, *Goltho: the development of an early medieval manor c. 850–1150* (London: English Heritage, 1987), and for a survey of early castles see R. Higham & P. Barker, *Timber castles* (London: Batsford, 1992), pp. 36–77; Pounds, *Medieval castle*, pp. 3–25.

6. Higham & Barker, *Timber castles*, pp. 100–1; D. C. Douglas, *William the Conqueror: the Norman impact upon England* (London: Eyre & Spottiswoode, 1964), pp. 53–82; D. Bates, *Normandy before 1066* (London: Longman, 1982), p. 167; O. Guillot, *Le comte d'Anjou et son entourage au xi siécle,* [2 vols] (Paris: A. & J. Picard, 1972), pp. 308–17, shows that at the start of Geoffrey Martel's reign, the count held 12–13 castles and there were 30 others within the county, of which only 12 were seigneuries in the full sense, and all of these were on the peripheries. By *c.* 1100 this latter group had grown to 44. Bur, *Comté de Champagne*, p. 279, shows similar results after the crisis of the mid-century; E. King (ed.), *The anarchy of Stephen's reign* (Oxford: Clarendon Press, 1994); Matthew, *Norman Kingdom of Sicily*, p. 258; Joinville, *Life of St Louis*, M. R. B. Shaw (ed.) (Harmondsworth: Penguin, 1970), pp. 181–90; Hampe, *Germany under the Salian and Hohenstaufen*, p. 87; A. Haverkamp, *Medieval Germany 1056–1273* (Oxford: Oxford University Press, 1988), pp. 159–69; Arnold, *German knighthood* pp. 126–31; M. Barber, *The two cities: medieval Europe 1050–1320* (London: Routledge, 1992), pp. 206–21.

7. Thompson, *Rise of the castle*, p. 19; C. Wickham, *Early medieval Italy: central power and local society* (London: Macmillan, 1981), pp. 172–81; G. Tabacco, *The struggle for power in medieval Italy: structures of political rule* (Cambridge: Cambridge University Press, 1989), pp. 193–200, 204–7; Higham & Barker, *Timber castles*, pp. 78–9; B. M. Kreutz, *Before the Normans: southern Italy in the ninth and tenth centuries* (Philadelphia: University of Pennsylvania Press, 1991), pp. 134–5; P. Partner, *The lands of St Peter: the papal state in the Middle Ages and the Renaissance* (London: Eyre Methuen, 1972), pp. 83–5; P. Toubert, *Les structures du Latium médiéval et la Sabine du IX siècle à la fin du XII siècle* (Rome: Bibliothèque des Ecoles Françaises d'Athène et de Rome, 1973), pp. 331.

8. S. Toy, *A history of fortification from 3000 BC to AD 1700* (London: Heinemann, 1955); France, "La guerre dans la France féodale", pp. 179–83; *Annales Mettensis*, MGH SS 1, an. 892; Flodoard, *Annales*, PL 135 an. 928 and 930 cols 439–41; Contamine, *War*, p. 182; B. Dearden & A. Clark, "Pont-l'Arche or Pîtres? a location and archaeomagnetic dating for Charles the Bald's fortifications on the Seine", *Antiquity* **64**, 1990, pp. 567–71; G. Fournier, *Le Château dans la France médiévale*, pp. 38, 267; Nelson, *Charles the Bald*, pp. 207–9; J. Peddie, *Alfred the good soldier: his life and campaigns* (Bath: Millstream, 1992), pp. 141–59; for possible Frankish influence on the English program of building, see J. M. Hassall & D. Hill, "Pont de l'Arche: Frankish influence on the West Saxon burh?", *Archaeological Journal* **127**, 1970, pp. 188–95; P. Stafford, *Unification and Conquest: a political and social history of England in the tenth and eleventh centuries* (London: Edward Arnold, 1989), pp. 31–3; there is a widespread belief that Henry I of Germany (918–36) built a network of fortifications against the Hungarians, as noted by M. W. Thompson, *The rise of the castle* (Cambridge: Cambridge University Press, 1991), p. 19, although this is doubted by Reuter, *Early medieval Germany*, pp. 142–4; however, see E. J. Schoenfeld, "Anglo-Saxon *burhs* and continental *burgen*: early medieval fortifications in constitutional perspective", *The Haskins Society Journal* **6**, (1994), pp. 49–66.

9. This is the general conclusion of the survey by A. Débord, "Les fortifications de terre en Europe occidentale du X au XII siècles", *Archéologie médiévale* **11**, 1981, pp. 5–123, summarized by Higham & Barker, *Timber castles*, pp. 78–113; Iohannes Codagnellus, p. 26; J. F. Verbruggen, "Note sur le sens des mots castrum, castellum et quelques autres expressions qui désignent les fortifications", *Revue Belge de Philosophie et d'Histoire* **27**, 1950, pp. 147–55; M. Fixot, *Les fortifications de terre et les origines féodales dans le Cinglais* (Caen: Centre de Recherches Archéologiques Médiévales, 1968).

10. The dating of Fulk's castles of Langeais and Montbazon has aroused considerable controversy. M. Deyres has suggested that Langeais as originally built in 993–4 was of wood, and that the present stone keep dates only from about 1020 and was a residence (*domicilium*) rather than a serious fortification, protected by a nearby wooden tower on a motte and a wooden enceinte with a gatehouse and earthworks, while Montbazon, traditionally ascribed to before 1006, was also originally of wood and its present stone structure dates only from *c.* 1050. He argues that these castles were built as part of a strategy of "lightning war", which would have precluded an immediate construction in stone and necessitated an earth and timber structure: "Les châteaux de Foulque Nerra", *Bulletin Monumental* **136**, 1974, pp. 7–28, "Le donjon de Langeais", *Bulletin Monumental* **132**, 1970, pp. 179–93, "Le château de Montbazon au XI siècle", *Cahiers de Civilisation Médiévale* **12**, 1969, pp. 158–9. This has been disputed by B. S. Bachrach, "Fortifications and military tactics: Fulk Nerra's strongholds circa 1000", *Technology and Culture* **20**, 1979, pp. 531–49. Bachrach points out that the theory that they were built quickly as part of a strategy of lightning war is uncertain, and this is very well supported by his "The Angevin strategy of castle building in the reign

of Fulk Nerra" cited above (p. 44 *n*9). However he is, as noted by Higham & Barker, *Timber castles*, p. 97, *n*53, rather dismissive of the strength of timber castles. Recent work on the sheer time that it took to construct either timber or stone castles, on which see Pounds, *The medieval castle in England and Wales*, pp. 17–20, tends to support Bachrach's dismissal of the "lightning strategy", but to support the idea that timber structures were put up first and replaced only later by stone. However, in the absence of full archaeological investigation, the matter remains unproven. M. de Bouard, "De l'aula au donjon: les fouilles de la motte de la Chapelle à Doué la Fontaine", *Archéologie Médiévale* **3–4**, 1973–4, pp. 1–110, summarized by Thompson, *Rise of the castle*, pp. 35–6; *s'Graventsteen: guide du Château des comtés de Flandre* (Gent: Archives Gent, 1980), pp. 5–7; Higham & Barker, *Timber castles*, pp. 92–107.

11. Glaber, pp. 80–2; Galbert, pp. 301–4; on Hen Domen see below, p. 87. On varieties of fortification, see C. Gaier, "La fonction stratégico-défensive du plat pays au Moyen Age dans la région de la Meuse moyenne" in *Armes et combats dans l'univers médiévale* (Brussels: De Boek-Wesmael, 1995), pp. 267–81; OV, vol. 5, p. 235; Thompson, *Rise of the castle*, pp. 110–11 for Stokesay. For Acton Burnell, see M. Wood, *The English medieval house* (London: Ferndale, 1983), p. 167, and for French parallels, J. Gardelles, *Le château féodale dans l'histoire médiévale* (Strasbourg: Publitotal, 1988), pp. 11, 56, 190; G. N. Godwin, *The civil war in Hampshire (1642–5) and the story of Basing House* (Southampton: Gilbert, 1904), pp. 80–95, 205–61, 344–64. I am grateful to my colleague Dr D. S. T. Clarke for this reference.

12. Thompson, *Rise of the castle*, pp. 28–39, is still wedded to the centrality of the motte and bailey, but reveals the wide variety of structures that exist; Stafford, *Unification and conquest*, pp. 88–9; M. W. Thompson, "Motte substructures", *Medieval Archaeology* **5**, 1961, pp. 305–6; for a survey, see Débord, Les fortifications de terre", pp. 8–11; Higham & Barker, *Timber castles*, pp. 78–111.

13. Pounds, *Medieval castle*, pp. 17–19; Powicke, *Loss of Normandy*, pp. 199–200 (citing Meyer, *Histoire de Guillaume le Maréchal*, vol. 3, p. 156), 260, 294–6; C. T. Clay (ed.), *Early Yorkshire charters. The honour of Richmond* (Wakefield: Yorkshire Archaeological Society, 1936).

14. Powicke, *Loss of Normandy*, pp. 27, 181; D. Pringle, *The Red Tower* (London: British School of Archaeology in Jerusalem, 1986), p. 13.

15. R. A. Brown, *English castles* (London: Batsford, 1976); Pounds, *Medieval castle*, pp. 3–25; Higham & Barker, *Timber castles*, pp. 36–77; Matthew, *Norman kingdom*, pp. 258–9; J. Dhondt, "Note sur les châtelains de Flandre", in *Etudes historiques dédiées à la mémoire de M. Roger Rodière* (Calais, 1947), pp. 43–51; P. Dixon & P. Marshall, "The Great Tower at Hedingham Castle: a reassessment", *Fortress* **18**, 1993, pp. 16–23; J. Prawer, *The Latin Kingdom of Jerusalem: European colonisation in the Middle Ages* (London: Weidenfeld & Nicolson, 1972), pp. 126–58; N. J. G. Pounds, *An economic history of medieval Europe* (London: Longman, 1974), pp. 242–3. Saône certainly had a strategic function, as it stood by the road from inland Syria to the coast, but its vast scale and ample accommodation suggest to me that its seigniorial function was vitally important and that this was the motor of its development, for it seems to have been grown around the original Byzantine citadel before it was in any sense a front-line structure.

16. Bachrach, "Angevin strategy of castle building", pp. 538, 557, 550; Pounds, *Medieval castle* pp. 29–31, 34–9; Davies, *The age of conquest,* pp. 28–9; Brown, *English castles*, p. 220; Gillingham, "Richard I and the science of war", p. 90, *Richard I*, pp. 262–5; Kennedy, *Crusader castles*, pp. 145–6.

17. The fathers assembled at Rheims for the Council of 1,148 complained of novel exactions for the building of castles at a time when Suger was complaining to the king about the same thing, and John of Colmieu deplored the same phenomenon in the Pas-de-Calais in about 1130: C. J. Hefele & H. LeClercq, *Histoire des Conciles*, [9 vols] (Paris: A. Le Clare, 1912), vol. 5.i, p. 826; C. Coulson, "Fortress policy in Capetian tradition and Angevin practice; aspects of the conquest of Normandy by Philip II", *Battle* **6**, 1984, pp. 13–38; Higham & Barker, *Timber castles*, pp. 96–7; Thompson, *Rise of the castle*, p. 21. On the cult of arms and chivalry, see above (pp. 58–9) and below (pp. 139–43); on fashion and the castle, see C. Coulson, "Cultural realities and reappraisals in English castle-study", "Hierarchism in conventual crenellation: an essay in the sociology and metaphysics of medieval fortification", *Medieval Archaeology* **26**, 1982, pp. 69–100; Thompson, *Rise of the castle*, p. 27, sees Castel del Monte as a castle in the military sense, but my own observation dismisses this.

18. Pounds, *Medieval castle*, p. 66; Brown, *English castles*, pp. 215–17; S. Painter, *Studies in the history of the English feudal baronage* (Baltimore: Johns Hopkins Press, 1943), pp. 170–4; J. C. Holt, *The end of the Anglo-Norman realm* (Oxford: Oxford University Press, 1975), pp. 14–5.

19. Tabacco, *Struggle for power in Medieval Italy*, pp. 193–204; *Annales Mediolanesis*, MGH SS 18. p. 365; Otto Morena, pp. 66, 128; *Annales Coloniensis maximi*, MGH SS 17, p. 768; Otto of Freising, pp. 208, 272–3.

20. Brown, *English castles*, pp. 114–5, 157–60; Pounds, *Medieval castle*, pp. 146–9; Painter, *Studies*, p. 173; N. Denholm-Young, *Seignorial Administration in England* (London: Oxford University Press, 1937), pp. 22–3; D. Crouch, *Images of aristocracy. Britain 1000–1300* (London: Routledge, 1992), p. 304; D. Greenway (ed.), *Charters of the honours of Mowbray 1107–91* (Oxford: Oxford University Press, 1972), pp. xliv–lv; C. Dyer, *Standards of living in the later Middle Ages. Social change in England 1200–1520* (Cambridge: Cambridge University Press, 1989), pp. 27–48; Bur, *La formation du Comté de Champagne*, pp. 259–60; Reuter, "Episcopi cum sua militia", p. 85; Coulson, "Fortress policy in Capetian tradition and Angevin practice", pp. 13–38; Tabacco, *Struggle for power in Medieval Italy*, pp. 222–36; D. Waley, *The papal state in the thirteenth century* (London: Macmillan, 1961), pp. 30–67; Partner, *Lands of St Peter*, pp. 248–9.

21. Pounds, *Medieval castle*, maps on pp. 28, 37, 45.

22. OV, vol. 4, pp. 74–7, is the evidence for this gift, but the editor, M. Chibnall, comments (pp. xxxii–iii) that this is unproven; for the circumstances of the rebellion, see J. Dhondt, "Une crise de pouvoir capétien 1032–4", in *Miscellanea Medievalia: in memoriam J. F. Niermeyer*, D. P. Blok et al. (eds) (Gronigen: J. B. Wolters, 1967), p. 145; Powicke, *Loss of Normandy*, pp. 185–9, 190–2, 204–8; Gillingham, "Richard I and the science of war", p. 90; Chaplais, *Diplomatic Documents*, pp. 16–18; Warren, *Henry II*, pp. 45–6, thinks unlikely the old idea that Geoffrey ever left his younger son and namesake the reversion of the Loire lands once Henry had secured England.

23. Higham & Barker, *Timber castles*, pp. 326–47; P. A. Barker, "Hen Domen", in *Five castle excavations*, A. D. Saunders (ed.) (London: Royal Archaeological Institute, 1978), pp. 101–4; M. Deyres (see above, p. 81, *n*10), has suggested that Langeais, long regarded as the earliest surviving stone castle, was actually a residence in part because of its relatively light masonry work, but it seems to the present writer that this was not a meaningful distinction, because in its day Langeais was pretty formidable, and it should not be judged by later standards of strength. Brown, *English castles*, pp. 55, 77, 78, 80–1, 84, 86; the present author has been to al-Bara, which is described by R. Burns, *Monuments of Syria* (London: I. B. Tauris, 1992), p. 57.

24. Thompson, *Rise of the castle*, pp. 43–4; Brown, *English castles*, pp. 77–9, 80–81.

25. Burns, *Monuments of Syria*, pp. 194–6; R. Fedden & J. Thomson, *Crusader castles* (London: Murray, 1957), pp. 101, 103–4; N. J. G. Edwards, *Fortifications of Armenian Cilicia* (Washington: Dumbarton Oaks, 1992); Pringle, *Red Tower*, pp. 14–15, 124–7; Kennedy, *Crusader castles*, pp. 86–9, 182–4.

26. J. Bradbury, *The medieval siege* (Woodbridge: Boydell & Brewer, 1992), pp. 132–3; Brown, *English castles*, p. 69; P. S. Fry, *Castles of Britain and Ireland* (Newton Abbot: David & Charles, 1996), p. 124, suggests, using an illustration from Matthew Paris, that Bedford, whose keep is known to have been mined in 1224, had a round tower, but Paris's illustrations are highly conventionalized and cannot be relied on for this kind of detail. W. Anderson, *Castles of Europe* (London: Elek, 1980), p. 125.

27. P. N. Jones & D. Renn, "The military effectiveness of arrow-loops: some experiments at White Castle", *Château Gaillard: Etudes de Castellogie Médiévale* **9–10**, 1982, pp. 445–56; Kennedy, *Crusader castles*, p. 179; Anderson, *Castles of Europe*, pp. 68, 86; Thompson, *Rise of the castle*, pp. 21–5; Iohannes Codagnellus, pp. 25, 45; Nicolle, *Medieval Warfare*, pp. 138–42; A. Chatelain, "Recherche sur les châteaux de Philippe Auguste", *Archéologie Médiévale* **21**, 1991, pp. 115–61.

28. Pringle, *Red Tower*, pp. 13–14.

29. P. Deschamps, *Les Châteaux des croisés en Terre Sainte III. Le défense du Comté de Tripoli et de la Principauté d'Antioche*, [2 vols] (Paris: P. Geuthner, 1973), vol. 1, pp. 259–85, 335–6, 339–40, 345–8, 349–50; R. Dussaud, *Topographie historique de la Syrie antique et médiévale* (Paris: P. Geuthner, 1927), pp. 140–1.

30. For Outrejourdan and Jacob's Ford (Chastellet), see above (p. 40) and below (p. 93); for Beit Jibrin, WT, pp. 659–60; Prawer, *Latin Kingdom*, pp. 281–4; Runciman, *Crusades*, vol. 2, pp. 339–40; Smail, *Crusading warfare*, pp. 207–8.

31. S. Tibble, *Monarchy and lordship in the Latin Kingdom of Jerusalem 1099–1291* (Oxford: Clarendon Press, 1989), pp. 20–3, 186–8; see the discussion in Prawer, *Latin Kingdom*, pp. 281–318; Edbury, *Old French continuation of William of Tyre*, p. 38.

32. Kennedy, *Crusader castles* (quoting Abu Shama), pp. 59–61; M. Benvenisti, *The crusaders in the Holy Land* (Jerusalem: Israeli Universities Press, 1970), pp. 294–300; Prawer, *The Latin Kingdom*, pp. 300–7; Thompson, *Rise of the castle*, pp. 23–4. Although Belvoir has been cleared, there is no authoritative archaeological report as yet and certainly no agreement about what might have been there originally and what Saladin might have built. For a summary, see D. Pringle, *Secular buildings in the Crusader Kingdom of Jerusalem* (Cambridge: Cambridge University Press, 1997), pp. 32–3. In these circumstances, I must say that my ideas and deductions, while drawing on those of others, are my own.

33. WT, pp. 996–1004; Pringle, *Secular Buildings*, p. 85. Runciman, *Crusades*, vol. 3, pp. 274–80. There is not much left at Beirut, where recent reconstruction of the city centre has revealed the site and a few remains, but the blockwork resembles that of Belvoir and Jacob's Ford, as does the structure of an angular tower with a sally port (author's observation).

34. M. Prestwich, *Edward I*, p. 216, and on Flint p. 212, to be compared to Chatelain, "Recherche sur les châteaux de Philippe Auguste", p. 161; Q. Hughes, *Military architecture* (London: H. Evelyn, 1974), p. 63; Brown, *English castles*, pp. 116–17, 162; Thompson, *Rise of the castle*, pp. 24, 116–17; Nicolle, *Medieval warfare*, pp. 140–1.

35. Hughes, *Military architecture*, pp. 27–30.

36. Anderson, *Castles of Europe*, pp. 24–5; Prestwich, *Edward I*, pp. 230–2.

37. Runciman, *Crusades*, vol. 2, pp. 229–31, 448–50; D. C. Douglas and G. W. Greenaway

(eds) *English Historical Documents* (London: Eyre & Spottiswoode, 1953), vol. 2, p. 492; M. Prestwich, *War, politics and finance under Edward I* (London: Faber, 1972), pp. 151–203, analyzes the king's works. A. J. Taylor, *The King's works in Wales 1277–1330* (London: HMSO, 1974) offers the best summary of the resources that Edward used to build his Welsh castles.

## Chapter Eight

1. OV, vol. 4, pp. 287–96; Suger, pp. 16–7, 36–9; Haverkamp, *Medieval Germany*, pp. 121–2; M. Chibnall, *The Empress Matilda: Queen Consort, Queen Mother and Lady of the English* (Oxford: Blackwell, 1991), pp. 118–41; Henry of Huntingdon, pp. 740–43; D. Crouch, *The Beaumont twins: roots and branches of power in the twelfth century* (Cambridge: Cambridge University Press, 1986), pp. 80–1; J. Bradbury, *Stephen and Matilda: the civil war of 1139–53* (Stroud: Sutton, 1996), pp. 113–40.

2. For the siege, see Walter of Coventry, *Memoriale fratris* W. Stubbs (ed.), [2 vols] (London: RS, 1973), *Flores Historiarum*, H. J. Hewlett (ed.) 3 vols (London: RS, 1888–9) 2, pp. 226–7; Roger of Wendover, *Flores Historiarum*, H. J. Hewlett (ed.) 3 vols (London: RS, 1888–9), 2, pp. 146–9; I. W. Rowlands, "King John, Stephen Langton and Rochester Castle, 1213–15", in *Studies in medieval history presented to R. Allen-Brown*, C. Harper-Bill, J. Holdsworth & J. Nelson (eds) (Woodbridge: Boydell & Brewer, 1989), pp. 267–79, and on the war generally, R. V. Turner, *King John* (London: Longman, 1994), pp. 225–57; on castle-building and the Capetians, see above, pp. 86–7.

3. Gislebert, pp. 168–84; *Annales Laubienses*, MGH SS 4, pp. 25–6; Aegidius Monachus Aureaevallis, *Gesta episcoporum Leodiensium*, MGH SS 25, pp. 111–12; Sigebert of Gembloux, *Continuatio Aquicinctina*, MGH SS 6, p. 423; F. R. Vegetius, *Epitome of Military Science*, N. P. Milner (ed.) (London: Liverpool University Press, 1993), p. 108; on modern ideas about the nature of medieval warfare, see above, pp. 11–12.

4. Gislebert, pp. 100–1; *Chronicon Hanoniense*, MGH SS 25, p. 446; J. Falmagne, *Baudouin V comté de Hainaut 1150–95* (Montréal: Les Presses de l'Université de Montréal, 1966), pp. 113, 116–17, 142–4, 179–81, 216–26.

5. Falmagne, *Baudouin V*, pp. 112, 129, 151–2, 155–7.

6. Gislebert, pp. 169, 175, 177, 186; Gislebert, pp. 173–5, lists Baldwin V's castles, emphasizes the speed with which he dismissed his mercenaries (p. 178) and reports his debts (p. 183).

7. Gislebert, pp. 173, 182.

8. Gislebert, p. 176.

9. Ralph of Diceto, vol. 1, p. 373; Boussard, "Les mercenaires au XIIe siècle", pp. 197–8, 201–9, 210–11, 212–13; Robert of Torigni, vol. 4, p. 232, reports Guiomar of Léon watching the burning of his castle.

10. Roger of Hovenden, vol. 2, pp. 51–2; Boussard, "Les mercenaires au XIIe siècle", pp. 201–3, 205–7; Warren, *Henry II*, p. 234; Kennedy, *Crusader castles*, pp. 83–4.

11. Smail, *Crusading warfare*, p. 214.

12. Edbury, *Old French Continuation of William of Tyre*, p. 38.

13. France, *Victory in the East*, p. 345; Crouch, *William Marshal*, pp. 121–4; S. McGlynn, *The invasion of England 1216* (Stroud: Sutton, forthcoming).

14. Kennedy, *Crusader castles*, pp. 145–79; Powicke, *Loss of Normandy*, pp. 253–6; Bradbury, *Medieval siege*, pp. 131–3; on the general reasons for the loss of Normandy, see below, pp. 45–6; Powicke, *Henry III and the Lord Edward*, vol. 2, pp. 531–9; Prestwich, *Edward I*, pp. 57–8, *Armies and warfare*, p. 300; Runciman, *Sicilian Vespers*, pp. 104–10; on the battle of Benevento, see below, pp. 178–80; Prestwich, *Edward I*, pp. 308–11.

15. OV, vol. 3, pp. 294–5, vol. 5, pp. 232–5; Prestwich, *Edward I*, pp. 182–3, mentioning attacks on Aberystwyth, Carreg Cennen, Hawarden, Llandovery and Oswestry; Kennedy, *Crusader castles*, pp. 176–7.

16. WT, p. 1003; Abu Shama, *Le livre des deux jardins*, RHC Or. 4, pp. 198, and on Belvoir, see above, pp. 92–3. Recent excavations, not yet published, reveal that Chastelleret was more incomplete than we have tended to think: I must acknowledge the kindness of Ronnie Ellenblum, who conducted the excavations and talked to me about them. However, these inferences are my own responsibility; Jacques de Vitry, *Historia Orientalis seu Hierosolymitana* in J. Bongars (ed.), *Gesta Dei per Francos* (Hanover, 1611), p. 1074; M. Barber, "Frontier warfare in the Latin Kingdom of Jerusalem: the campaign of Jacob's Ford, 1178–9", in *The Crusades and their sources: essays presented to Bernard Hamilton*, J. France & W. G. Zajac (eds) (Aldershot: Variorum, 1998), pp. 9–22.

17. Chalandon, *Histoire de la Domination Normande*, vol. 1, pp. 118–21; Prestwich, *Armies and warfare*, pp. 208–9; Taylor, *The King's works in Wales*.

## Chapter Nine

1. Pounds, *Economic history of medieval Europe*, pp. 256–69; G. A. Williams, *Medieval London: from commune to capital* (London: Athlone, 1963), pp. 315–7.

2. R. Aubenas, "Les châteaux forts des IX$^e$ et XII$^e$ siècles", *Revue de l'Histoire du Droit Français et Étranger* **17**, 1938, pp. 548–86; Verbruggen, "Note sur le sens des mots *castrum, castellum*", pp. 147–55, points to the terminological confusion, but see also efforts to suggest more consistency in individual authors by B. S. Bachrach, "Early medieval fortifications in the west of France: a revised technical vocabulary", *Technology and Culture* **16**, 1975, pp. 531–69; A. Debord, "*Castrum* et *castellum* chez Ademar de Chabannes", *Archéologie Médiévale* **9**, 1979, pp. 97–113; Pounds, *Economic history of medieval Europe*, pp. 242–4; D. Pringle, "Town defences in the Crusader Kingdom of Jerusalem", in I. A. Corfis & M. Wolfe, *The medieval city under siege* (Woodbridge: Boydell & Brewer, 1995), pp. 69–112.

3. For the attack on Hainaut, see above, pp. 97–101; Iohannes Codagnellus, p. 23; Ambroise, *The Third Crusade*, K. Fenwick (ed.) (London: Folio Society, 1958), pp. 64, 132–3; Powicke, *Loss of Normandy*, pp. 164–5; Iohannes Codagnellus, p. 25; *Annales Placentini Gibellini*, MGH SS 18, pp. 476–7.

4. Potter, *Gesta Stephani*, pp. 94–5; WT, pp. 798–9; *Annales Placentini Gibellini*, MGH SS 18, pp. 479–80, 496; Prestwich, *Armies and warfare*, pp. 284–5.

5. William of Tudela & the Anonymous, *Song of the Cathar Wars*, tr. J. Shirley (Aldershot: Scolar Press, 1996), pp. 125–6; Joinville, *Life of St Louis*, pp. 218–9.

6. France, *Victory in the East*, pp. 197–296; Otto of Freising, pp. 210–28; AA, p. 463.

7. Rogers, *Latin siege warfare*, pp. 79–83, 182–8, 212–36; Runciman, *Crusades*, vol. 3, pp. 22–53; Ambroise, pp. 72–6.

8. Munz, *Frederick Barbarossa*, pp. 146–68; Holder-Egger, *Annales Mediolanenses Maiores*,

pp. 33–4; Otto Morena, pp. 69–96. The siege of Cremona and the great campaign is reported by: Holder-Egger, *Annales Mediolanenses Maiores*, pp. 32–9; Otto Morena, pp. 69–96; Vincent of Prague, pp. 677–8; Munz, *Frederick Barbarossa*, pp. 280–307; the siege is ably described by Rogers, *Latin siege warfare*, pp. 135–43. On the battle of Carcano, see the two versions in *Ann. Med.*, pp. 41–6, and for a modern discussion, see J. France, "The Battle of Carcano: the event and its importance", *War in history* (forthcoming) and also L. M. Gaffuri, *Carcano e il Barbarossa* (Carcano: Di Tacchini, 1992); Otto Morena, p. 176.

9. William of Tudela, *Song of the Cathar Wars*, pp. 46–7, 59–62; J. Sumption, *The Albigensian Crusade* (London: Faber, 1978), pp. 136–7, 151–2.

10. William of Tudela, *Song of the Cathar Wars*, pp. 124–5, 135, 172; Sumption, *Albigensian Crusade*, pp. 192–8, 223.

11. *Annales Placentini Gibellini*, MGH SS 18, p. 481; G. Bonazzi (ed.), *Chronicon Parmense* (Citta di Castello: RIS, 1902), pp. 18–20; van Cleve, *Emperor Frederick II*, pp. 449–50, 466.

12. J. F. Powers, "Life on the cutting edge: the Luso-Hispanic frontier in the twelfth century", in *The medieval city under siege*, I. A. Corfis & M. Wolfe (eds) (Woodbridge: Boydell & Brewer, 1995), pp. 17–34, and by the same author, *A society organised for war: the Iberian Municipal Militias in the central Middle Ages 1000–1284* (Berkeley: University of California Press, 1988).

13. Stenton, *Anglo-Saxon England*, pp. 385–6, 588–60; Poole, *Domesday Book to Magna Carta*, pp. 142–4, 471; F. M. Powicke, *The thirteenth century* (Oxford: Clarendon Press, 1962), pp. 189–90; M. Toch, "The medieval German city under siege", in *The medieval city under siege* I. A. Corfis & M. Wolfe (eds) (Woodbridge: Boydell & Brewer, 1995), pp. 35–48.

14. Otto of Freising, pp. 217–8; Rogers, *Latin siege warfare*, pp. 64–90, 146–50; D. Pringle, "Town defences in the Crusader Kingdom of Jerusalem", in *The medieval city under siege* I. A. Corfis & M. Wolfe (eds) (Woodbridge: Boydell & Brewer, 1995), pp. 96–8; B. Durham, "Oxford's northern defences: archaeological studies 1971–82", *Oxoniensia* **48**, 1983, pp. 32, 35–8; J. R. Kenyon, *Medieval fortifications* (Leicester: Leicester University Press, 1990), pp. 185–7; Richard, *St Louis*, pp. 199–200; J. le Goff, *St Louis* (Paris: Gallimard, 1996), pp. 173–4; on Toulouse, see above, p. 111, *n*10; Rogers has an excellent reconstruction of the siege of Alessandria, but for the relief army see *Continuatio Sanblasiana* MGH SS 20, p. 315.

15. On castles and the birth of cities, see above, pp. 84–5; Pounds, *Medieval castle*, pp. 207–15, 220–1; C. Caple, *An interim guide to Dryslwyn Castle and its excavation* (University of Durham, Department of Archaeology: www.dur.ac.uk/Archaeology/Staff/CC/Guide.html, 1998); Kenyon, *Medieval fortifications*, pp. 189–90; Richer, vol. 1, pp. 116, 142, 280, vol. 2, pp. 133, 279; France, *Victory in the East*, pp. 221, 275–7, 340; William of Tudela, *Song of the Cathar Wars*, p. xiii; *Annales Placentini Gibellini*, p. 466; J. Riley-Smith (ed.), *The atlas of the crusades* (London: Times Books, 1991), pp. 102–3.

16. Van Cleve, *Emperor Frederick II*, pp. 398–9; E. Kantorowicz, *Frederick II*, tr. E. O. Lorimer (London: Constable, 1931); Bonazzi, *Chronicon Parmense*, p. 13.

17. "Florence" of Worcester, *Chronicon ex Chronicis*, B. Thorpe (ed.), [2 vols] (London: Sumptibus Societatis, 1848–9), vol. 2, p. 23; Potter, *Gesta Stephani*, pp. 174–5; RA, p. 293; WT, pp. 721–2; Ralph of Diceto, vol. 1, pp. 431–2.

18. GF, pp. 15, 37, 42; RA, p. 61; Edbury, *Old French Continuation of William of Tyre*, p. 33; WT, p. 799; for other examples of terror, see Bradbury, *Medieval siege*, pp. 81–2; Otto Morena, pp. 136, 141–2; Brown, *English castles*, p. 192; Prestwich, *Edward I*, p. 502.

19. Gillingham, "William the Bastard at war", pp. 149–52; J. H. & L. L. Hill, *Raymond IV de St Gilles 1041 (ou 1042)–1105* (Paris: Privat, 1959), pp. 137–8; Runciman, *Crusades*, vol. 2, p. 115; the "Castle of St Gilles", as it is now known, has been massively reconstructed in the modern period, although elements of the crusader *enceinte* remain. Its site is remarkable, for it stands on a ridge guarded by the Nahr Abou Ali to the east and north and the steep fall of the land to the west. It is about a mile away from the medieval city, which was on the El Mina peninsula. It is astonishing that this site was available, and completely understandable that the counts of Tripoli continued to use it; Bradbury, "Battles in England and Normandy", p. 8; WT, pp. 521–2; Iohannes Codagnellus, p. 14; Rolandini Patavini, *Chronica*, MGH SS 19, pp. 85–6; *Annales Sancti Iustinae Patavini*, p. 160; France, *Victory in the East*, pp. 325–55; Ambroise, p. 61.

20. On fire-throwing machines, see Rap. 299; J. France, "The text of the account of the capture of Jerusalem in the Ripoll Manuscript Bibliothèque Nationale (Latin) 5132", *English Historical Review* 53, 1988, pp. 644–5; Rogers, *Latin siege warfare*, p. 222; Ambroise, pp. 63, 67.

21. AA, pp. 321–7, 467–72, and see the comments of Rogers, *Latin siege warfare*, pp. 23–5, 223; RA, p. 239; WT, pp. 521–2; R. A. Brown, *Dover Castle* (London: HMSO, 1967), p. 12; Prestwich, *Edward I*, p. 502; William of Tudela, *Song of the Cathar Wars*, pp. 46, 166–72.

22. Bradbury, *Medieval siege,* p. 139; WT, p. 720; Brown, *English castles*, pp. 192–3; Kennedy, *Crusader castles,* pp. 148–50, 177–8; Prestwich, *Armies and warfare*, pp. 284–5; Thompson, *Rise of the castle*; Ambroise, pp. 65–8; Iohannes Codagnellus, pp. 9–10; RA, p. 44.

23. Abbon, *Siège de Paris par les Normands*, H. Waquet (ed.) (Paris: Les Belles Lettres, 1942), p. 33; Richer, vol. 2, p. 178; H. E. J. Cowdrey, "The Mahdia campaign of 1087", *English Historical Review* 92, 1977, pp. 1–29; Symeon of Durham, *Historia Regum*, T. Arnold (ed.), [2 vols] (London: RS, 1882–5), vol. 2, p. 274; Rogers, *Latin siege warfare*, pp. 64–90, 124–53, 174; Ralph of Coggeshall, *Chronicon Anglicanum*, J. Stevenson (ed.) (London: Seeleys, 1875), p. 206; *Annales Dunstaplia*, in *Annales Monastici*, H. R. Luard (ed.), [5 vols] (London: RS, 1886), vol. 3, p. 86; France, *Victory in the East*, pp. 313–4, 352–3; Prestwich, *Armies and warfare*, pp. 287–8, *Edward I*, p. 493; Bradbury, *Medieval siege*, pp. 241–50; Osbern, *De Expugnatione Lyxbonensi*, in Stubbs, *Chronicles*, vol. 2, pp. 134–6, 146–78.

24. GF, p. 91; Rogers, *Latin siege warfare*, pp. 81, 104, 179–82, 187; France, *Victory in the East*, pp. 348–54. The precise nature of "Greek Fire" has been much debated, on which see: J. Bradbury, "Greek Fire in the West", *History* vol. 64, 1979, pp. 326–1; J. Harvey & M. Byrne, "A possible solution to the problem of Greek Fire", *Byzantinische Zeitschrift* 70, 1977, pp. 91–99; E. W. Marsden, *Greek and Roman artillery*, [2 vols] (Oxford: Clarendon Press, 1969–71); J. R. Partington, *A history of Greek Fire and gunpowder* (Cambridge: Heffers, 1960). It seems likely that in its original eighth-century form this was a highly combustible liquid which was projected: it was probably a weapon with very limited value, on which see M. Whittow, *The making of Orthodox Byzantium 600–1025* (London: Macmillan, 1996), pp. 124–5. The term continued to be used and apparently applied to any form of fire which was thrown, as at the siege of Acre, on which see below, p. 121, n31.

25. GF, p. 91; Rogers, *Latin siege warfare*, pp. 179–82; WT, p. 403; Guillaume le Breton, *Philippidos*, vol. 2, pp. 54, 202; William of Tudela, *La Chanson de la Croisade Albigeoise*, E. Martin-Chabot (ed.), [3 vols] (Paris, 1931–61), vol. 1, pp. 216, 238–9, *Song of the Albigensian Crusade*, pp. 51, 54–5. These references are in D. J. Cathcart-King, "The trebuchet and other siege-engines", *Château Gaillard* 9/10, 1982, pp. 460–1 and n17.

26. Rogers, *Latin siege warfare*, Appendix III, pp. 254–73, gives the best modern account of the

state of scholarship on twelfth-century artillery and I must acknowledge my debt to his work. There is also an account in Bradbury, *Medieval siege*, pp. 250–9, useful because it mentions the many non-Latin words used for this equipment. Prestwich, *Armies and warfare*, pp. 287–96, discusses English examples across a very wide period. For *arcu-baleari*, see AA, p. 324.

27. For a late twelfth century illustration of traction-trebuchets in action see Plate 2; there is, apart from the Cathcart-King article referred to above, a considerable modern literature on trebuchets: D. R. Hill, "Trebuchets", *Viator* **4**, 1973, pp. 99–114; C. M. Gillmor, "The introduction of the traction-trebuchet into the Latin West", *Viator* **12**, 1981, pp. 1–8; J. Needham, "China's trebuchets, manned and counterweighted", in *On premodern technology and science: studies in honor of Lynn White, Jr*, B. S. Hall & D. C. West (eds) (Malibu: Udena Publications, 1976), pp. 108–9.

28. Bradbury, *Medieval siege*, pp. 256–7; Roger of Hovenden, vol. 3, p. 113; Abu Shama, p. 205.

29. In Plate 2, from a manuscript of Peter of Eboli, the defenders and the attackers of a castle use traction-trebuchets; WT, pp. 597–98; Otto Morena, pp. 54–6; France, *Victory in the East*, p. 353; Rogers, *Latin siege warfare*, pp. 82-3.

30. For the history of Saône, see G. Saadé, "Histoire du château de Saladin", *Studi Medievali* **9**, 1968, pp. 980–1017, esp. pp. 996–1003; for a useful summary, see Kennedy, *Crusader castles*, pp. 84–96.

31. Roger of Hovenden, vol. 3, pp. 116–17; Ambroise, pp. 62–6, 67; Rogers, *Latin siege warfare*, p. 222, citing Beha ed-Din's biography of Saladin.

32. H. R. Hahnloser, *Villard de Honnecourt* (Graz: Akademie Druck-und Verlagsanst, 1972), Pl. 59; Aegidii Romani, *De Regimine Principum* (Rome, 1561), pp. 357–8; Marino Sanudo, *Liber secretorum fidelium crucis*, in *Orientalis historiae*, [2 vols] (Hannover, 1611), vol. 2, pp. 79–80; P. V. Hansen, "Reconstructing a medieval Trebuchet", *Military Illustrated Past and Present* **27**, 1990, pp. 9–16. I would like to thank Peter Humphries of CADW for his information about the Caerphilly example.

33. White, *Medieval technology and social change*, pp. 102–3, cites Iohannes Codagnellus, p. 25, although says this refers to a siege of Cremona. However, according to Codagnellus, on this occasion the weapon was deployed in a hastily built camp, while in 1229 (p. 96), trebuchets are described as mounted on carts and in 1230 were carried by a small and reluctantly raised army (p. 100). Codagnellus mentions their use in 1229, 1231 (twice) and 1234 (twice) (pp. 95, 105, 108, 113, 115), always used in conjunction with other weapons such as mangonels, but never describes the weapon and never suggests that it was particularly heavy or impressive. Moreover, he quite often mentions lists of siege-equipment without trebuchets, as in the attack on Soncino in 1200 (p. 27); *Annales Ianuenses*, MGH 18, pp. 158, 326, says that trebuchets were quickly built for the attacks on Terdona in 1225 and on Sardinia in 1289. They are also mentioned in 1216, 1224 and 1227 on pp. 137, 155 and 163; Rolandini Patavini, p. 90, who mentions trebuchets elsewhere, in 1237 and 1246, pp. 65 and 84, without any indication of scale; the illustration from Bib. nat. lat. 10136, ff. 141v–142 is used in Bradbury, *Medieval siege*, p. 148.

34. William of Tudela, *Chanson de la Croisade Albigeoise*, vol. 1, pp. 216, 238–9, vol. 3, 58–63, 183, 187, 301, *Song of the Albigensian Crusade*, pp. 51, 54–5, 141, 157–8, 191; see also references in Cathcart-King, "The trebuchet and other siege-engines", p. 461, *n*17; I wish to thank Dr Alison Williams of the French Department of the University of Wales Swansea for her help in elucidating these passages; *Chronicon Sancti Martini Turonensis*,

MGH SS 26, p. 473; R. Schneider, *Die Artillerie des Mittelalters* (Berlin, 1910), p. 28, citing *Annales Marbacenses* MGH SS 17, p. 172.

35. *Annales Dunstaplia*, vol. 3, pp. 48–9, 86–8; Matthew Paris, *Chronica Majora*, H. R. Luard (ed.) (London: RS, 1876), vol. 3, pp. 85–6; J. Harvey, *English medieval architects* (London: Batsford, 1954), pp. 163–4; William de Rishanger, *Chronica*, H. R. Riley (ed.) (London: RS, 1865), pp. 222–3; R. A. Griffiths, *Conquerors and conquered in medieval Wales* (Stroud: Sutton, 1994), pp. 74–6; Matthew Paris, *Flores historiarum*, H. R. Luard (ed.), [3 vols] (London: RS, 1890), vol. 3, p. 119; Prestwich, *Armies and warfare*, pp. 289–91.

36. Cathcart-King, "The trebuchet and other siege-engines", pp. 465–9; Hill, "Trebuchets", pp. 106–16, have investigated the dynamics. It is my conclusion that operators probably did not vary ranges and weights by very much because of the complications; on Castelnaudary, see above p. 122, *n*33; Ambroise, p. 63.

37. William of Tudela, *Chanson de la Croisade Albigeoise*, vol. 3, pp. 178–9, *Song of the Albigensian Crusade*, p. 166; Bradbury, *Medieval siege*, pp. 148, 264.

38. Kennedy, *Crusader castles*, pp. 67–8; Runciman, *Crusades*, vol. 3, pp. 412–3; Hill, "Trebuchets", p. 104.

39. France, *Victory in the East*, pp. 347–54; Rogers, *Latin siege warfare*, pp. 152, 170–2, 238, 242. Gaston's special skill seems to have been siege-towers, which he built in Jerusalem in 1099 and Zaragossa in 1118; Jordan Fantosme, *Chronicle*, R. C. Johnston (ed.) (Oxford: Clarendon Press, 1981), pp. 93–4; P. Héliot, "Le Château Gaillard et les fortresses des XII–XIII siècles en Europe occidentale", *Château Gaillard*, 1, 1962, p. 68.

40. Prestwich, *Armies and warfare*, pp. 285–6; Bradbury, *Medieval siege*, pp. 245–6; *Annales Placentini Gibellini*, pp. 479; Van Cleve, *Frederick II*, p. 415. For a biography of Master Bertram, see A. Taylor, "Master Bertram, Ingeniator regis", in *Studies in medieval history presented to R. Allen-Brown*, C. Harper-Bill, J. Holdsworth, J. Nelson (eds) (Woodbridge: Boydell & Brewer, 1989), pp. 289–304. It must be said that Guiot was a conservative aristocrat who felt alienated by a changing world in which royal government and its bourgeois servants were becoming dominant, and his condemnation of mere mechanicals should be seen in this light: Guiot de Provins, *Les Oeuvres*, J. Orr (ed.) (Manchester: Manchester University Press, 1915), pp. xiv–xv, 15–16. Prestwich, pp. 284–7, has looked at the English royal accounts and shown that although such people commanded high wages they were nothing like as highly paid as the gentry; even Master James of St George never earned as much as a knight-banneret. It seems unlikely that engineers from all over Europe would have been drawn into Edward I's service if English rates were markedly below those offered elsewhere.

41. France, *Victory in the East*, pp. 44–5, 54, 160–2, 245–51; Gillingham, "Richard I and the Science of War", p. 89; Runciman, *Sicilian Vespers*, pp. 252–3; Prestwich, *Armies and warfare*, pp. 122, 299–300; on Victoria, see above, p. 115.

42. *Annales Osterhovenses 754–1433*, MGH SS 17, p. 556.

## *Chapter Ten*

1. Gaufredus, p. 71; Bachrach, "Some observations on the military administration of the Norman Conquest", pp. 1–26; Holder-Egger, *Annales Mediolanenses Maiores*, pp. 30–31; Otto of Freising, p. 211; *Annales Sancti Disibodi*, MGH SS 17, p. 29; on the siege of Crema, see above, p. 110; J. France, "The Battle of Carcano" (forthcoming); Morena, pp.

135–6: Boussard, "Les mercenaires au xiie siècle", pp. 127–9; Verbruggen, *Art of warfare*, pp. 242–7.

2. Prestwich, *Armies and warfare*, pp. 116–7; Boussard, "Les mercenaires au xii$^e$ siècle", p. 220.

3. Verbruggen, *Art of warfare*, pp. 242–7; *Annales Placentini Gibellini*, pp. 476–7; Piero della Vigna, letter of 1237, in *Petri de Vineis epistolarum*, J. R. Iselius (ed.), [2 vols] (Basle, 1740), vol. 2, p. 235; *Annales Veronenses*, MGH SS 19, p. 10; Frederick II, letter to the Holy See, *Petri de Vineis*, vol. 2, p. 302; Frederick II, letter to the Duke of Lorraine, E. Martène & U. Durand (eds), *Veterum Scriptores et Monumentorum Collectio*, [9 vols] (Paris, 1724–33), vol. 2, p. 1151; Van Cleve, *Frederick II*, p. 407, n1, relying on earlier German work suggests 25,000 imperialists and 20,000 Guelfs, but does not discuss Frederick's dispersion of his forces.

4. Saba Malaspina, *Rerum Secularum Historia* (Milan: RIS, 1726), vol. 8, col. 813; Runciman, *Sicilian Vespers*, pp. 107–11; Housley, *Italian crusades*, pp. 18–19, 145–53; Strayer, "The crusade against Aragon", pp. 107–22, *Philip the Fair*, pp. 337–9; Verbruggen, *Art of warfare*, p. 190.

5. *Annales Osterhovenses*, p. 556.

6. Prestwich, *The three Edwards*, pp. 63–6; Krieger, "Obligatory military service and the use of mercenaries in imperial military campaigns under the Hohenstaufen emperors", pp. 151–64.

7. There is an enormous literature on English administrative development, of which the following is merely a selection: Richardson & Sayles, *Governance of medieval England*; Barlow, *Feudal kingdom of England*; D. Bates, *William the Conqueror* (London: Philip, 1989); M. Chibnall, *Anglo-Norman England* (Oxford: Blackwell, 1986) and, specifically on military administration, J. C. Holt, *End of the Anglo-Norman realm*, "The end of the Anglo-Norman Realm", *Proceedings of the British Academy* **61**, 1975, pp. 223–65; Prestwich, "War and finance in the Anglo-Norman State", "Military household"; M. Prestwich, *War, politics and finance under Edward I, Edward I*, pp. 134–69; F. Lot & R. Fawtier (eds), *Le premier budget de la monarchie française* (Paris: H. Champion, 1932); M. Nortier & J. W. Baldwin, "Contribution à l'étude des finances de Philippe Auguste", *Bibliothèque de l'Ecole des Chartes* **138**, 1980, pp. 5–33; J. W. Baldwin, "La décennie décisive: les années 1190–1203 dans le règne de Philippe Auguste", *Revue Historique* **256**, 1981, pp. 311–37; T. N. Bisson, "Les domaines au temps de Philippe Auguste", in *La France de Philippe Auguste: le temps des mutations*, R. H. Bautier (ed.) (Paris: CNRS, 1982), pp. 521–38; J. W. Baldwin, *The government of Philip Augustus. Foundations of French royal power in the Middle Ages* (Berkeley: University of California Press, 1986); J. C. Holt, "The loss of Normandy and royal finances", in *War and government in the Middle Ages: essays in honour of J. O. Prestwich*, J. Gillingham & J. C. Holt (eds) (Woodbridge: Boydell & Brewer, 1984), pp. 92–105; Richard, *Saint Louis*, pp. 277–324; Le Goff, *Saint Louis*, pp. 216–50; J. R. Strayer, *The reign of Philip the Fair* (Princeton: Princeton University Press, 1980), pp. 36–236; Waley, *Italian city–republics*, pp. 32–59, "Papal armies in the thirteenth-century", pp. 1–30; Arnold, *Princes and territories*, pp. 213 (citing Gislebert of Mons, pp. 155–60), 236–7, 242–5; B. Arnold, *Medieval Germany 500–1500: a political interpretation* (London: Macmillan, 1997), p. 185, *Princes and territories*, pp. 152–85.

8. Strayer, *Philip the Fair*, pp. 392–4, "Costs and profits of war", pp. 272–5; Prestwich, *Edward I*, pp. 401–35; see above, p. 111, n11; Runciman, *Sicilian Vespers*, pp. 232–3.

9. Prestwich, *War, politics and finance*, pp. 99–100.

10. Strayer, *Philip the Fair*, pp. 372–9; Verbruggen, *Art of warfare*, pp. 149–59, 161–2, 190; Waley, *Italian city–republics*, p. 99; Mallett, *Mercenaries and their masters*, p. 12; Delbrück,

*Medieval warfare*, p. 423; N. Housley, *The Italian crusades* (Oxford: Clarendon Press, 1982), p. 150; *Annales Osterhovenses*, 556; Prestwich, *Armies and warfare*, pp. 127–9.

11. Baldwin, *Government of Philip Augustus*, pp. 166–8; Housley, *Italian crusades*, p. 153; Strayer, *Philip the Fair*, p. 374; Prestwich, *Armies and warfare*, p. 53; Verbruggen, *Art of warfare*, p. 190.

12. Waley, *Italian city-republics*, pp. 97–9; Waley, "Papal armies in the thirteenth century", pp. 1–30, "The army of the Florentine Republic from the twelfth to the fourteenth century," pp. 70–108, "*Condotte* and *Condottieri* in the thirteenth century", *Proceedings of the British Academy* **61**, 1975, pp. 337–71; Mallett, *Mercenaries and their masters*, pp. 21–2, 19–21.

13. Setton, "Catalans in Greece 1311–80", pp. 187–8; Lock, *Franks in the Aegean*, pp. 115–16; Strayer, "Costs and profits of war", p. 278; Waley, "*Condotte* and *Condottieri*", pp. 355–6.

14. Waley, "*Condotte* and *Condottieri*", pp. 547–8, "Army of the Florentine Republic", pp. 101–3; Prestwich, *Edward I*, pp. 147–9; Runciman, *Crusades*, vol. 3, p. 273; Strayer, *Philip the Fair*, pp. 372–4.

15. Prestwich, *War, politics and finance*, pp. 41–60; Baldwin, *Government of Philip Augustus*, pp. 280–1; James I, *Chronicle of James I*, p. 146; Christiansen, *Northern crusades*, pp. 79–88, 84–5; E. N. Johnson, "The German crusades in the Baltic"; Setton, *Crusades*, vol. 3, pp. 545–85.

16. Even for England, the evidence is pretty fragmentary: Prestwich, *War, politics and finance*, pp. 61–6, and see above, pp. 59–60, *n*15, on the retinues of the twelfth century. William de Nangis, *Gesta Sancti Ludovici*, pp. 422–3; J. F. Verbruggen, "La tactique militaire des armées de Chevaliers", *Revue du Nord* **29**, 1947, pp. 163–8, *Art of warfare*, pp. 73–7; Prestwich, *Armies and warfare*, pp. 13–15; William of Nangis, *Gesta Philippi Tertii*, RHGF 20, pp. 541–2.

17. France, *Victory in the East*, pp. 58, 367–73; Henry of Huntingdon, p. 235; Ambroise, pp. 79–96; Baldwin, *Government of Philip Augustus*, pp. 279–81; Housley, *Italian crusades*, p. 153.

18. Lomax, *Reconquest of Spain*, pp. 114–5; Iohannes Codagnellus, pp. 25, 60; *Annales Veronenses*, p. 15; E. Christiansen, *The northern crusades: the Baltic and the Catholic frontier 1100–1525* (London: Macmillan, 1980), pp. 163–6; Kedar, "The Battle of Hattin revisited", pp. 190–207.

19. J. Keegan & R. Holmes, *Soldiers: a history of men in battle* (London: Hamilton, 1985), pp. 143–4; Terraine, *The white heat*, p. 17; Anselm of Ribemont, letter of November 1097, in H. Hagenmeyer (ed.), *Kreuzzugsbriefe aus den Jahren 1088–1100* (Innsbruck: Olms, 1902), p. 145; GF, p. 74; Boso, *Life of Alexander III*, G. M. Ellis & P. Munz (eds) (Oxford: Blackwell, 1973), p. 74; Lomax, *Reconquest of Spain*, pp. 127–8.

20. Joinville, *Life of St Louis*, pp. 221, 233; James I King of Aragon, *Chronicle*, J. Foster (ed.), [2 vols] (London: Chapman & Hall, 1883), p. 130; Gillingham, "Unromantic death of Richard I", pp. 155–80; Lomax, *Reconquest of Spain*, p. 105.

21. *De Expugnatione Terrae Sanctae per Saladinum*, tr. J. Brundage, in *The Crusades: a documentary survey* (Milwaukee: Marquette University Press, 1962), p. 168, makes some mention of infantry, but Edbury, *Old French Continuation of William of Tyre*, pp. 46–7, ignores them; Strickland, *War and chivalry*, p. 225; Ibn al-Athir, in Gabrieli, p. 123, remarked on the huge numbers captured at Hattin, which caused a fall in the price of slaves; Lomax, *Reconquest of Spain*, pp. 105–6.

22. Strickland, *War and chivalry*, pp. 183–203; Edbury, *Old French Continuation of William of Tyre*, p. 48; OV, vol. 4, p. 272; Guillaume le Breton, *Gesta*, vol. 1, p. 292; Joinville, *Life of St Louis*, pp. 240–64.

# Chapter Eleven

1. BT, Pl. 68. There is no consensus about what happened at Hastings, but it does seem as if the initial repulse of the Norman army almost became a rout. In this, I agree with S. Morillo, "Hastings, an unusual battle", *The Haskins Society Journal* **2**, 1990, pp. 95–104, *Warfare under the Anglo-Norman kings*, pp. 163–8, and J. Bradbury, *The Battle of Hastings* (Stroud: Sutton, 1998), pp. 192–201; Ralph of Caen, pp. 622–3; Suger of St Denis, pp. 72–3; William of Malmesbury, *Historia Novella*, K. R. Potter (ed.) (Edinburgh: Nelson, 1955), p. 49; Potter, *Gesta Stephani*, p. 74; Guillaume le Breton, *Gesta*, vol. 1, pp. 281–3, 285; Joinville, *Life of St Louis*, pp. 223–4; Andrew of Hungary, *Descriptio Victoriae a Karolo Reportatae*, MGH SS 26, p. 575; *Chronica Regia Colonniensis*, MGH SS 17, p. 128; Roger of Wendover, vol. 1, p. 316, even alleged that he was too fond of staying in bed with his new wife to go out and fight.
2. See below, pp. 170, 181–4.
3. William of Poitiers, pp. 154–7, 170–1; Gillingham, "William the Bastard at war", pp. 151, 154–5; BT, Pl. 56; RA, p. 157; J. O. Prestwich, "Military intelligence under the Norman and Angevin kings", in *Law and government in medieval England and Normandy: essays presented to Sir James Holt*, G. Garnett & J. Hudson (eds) (Cambridge: Cambridge University Press, 1994), pp. 1–30; J. Deuve, *Les services secrets Normands* (Condé-sur-Noireau: C. Corlet, 1990); James I, *Chronicle*, vol. 1, pp. 294–6, 371–3.
4. Suger, p. 77; E. Edwards, *Liber Monasterii de Hyda* (London: RS, 1886), p. 317; Munz, *Frederick Barbarossa*, pp. 370–96; Pacaut, *Frederick Barbarossa*, pp. 48, 195–208; Otto of Freising, pp. 80–1; Runciman, *Crusades*, vol. 3, p. 15; Odo of Deuil, pp. 115–20; Edbury, *Old French Continuation of William of Tyre*, pp. 94–5.
5. Joinville, *Life of St Louis*, pp. 220–8.
6. Edbury, *Old French Continuation of William of Tyre*, pp. 36–40; William of Nangis, *Gesta Sancti Ludovici*, pp. 420–1.
7. OV, vol. 4, pp. 287–96; Galbert, p. 144; R. H. C. Davies, *King Stephen 1135–54* (London: Longman, 1967), pp. 69–70; J. Bradbury, *Stephen and Mathilda: the civil war of 1139–53* (Stroud: Sutton, 1996), pp. 46–7; on mercenary commanders, see above, pp. 74–5; on William Marshal, see Crouch, *William Marshal*, and on his military career Gillingham, "War and chivalry in the history of William the Marshal", pp. 227–41.
8. Baldwin, *Government of Philip Augustus*, pp. 110–11, 113–14, 115–18; Verbruggen, *Art of warfare*, p. 251, refers to him as Philip's commander-in-chief. On Bouvines, see below, pp. 235–41; William of Nangis, *Gesta Sancti Ludovici*, pp. 420, 424; Jan Van Heelu, *Rijmkronijk*, J. F. Willems (ed.) (Brussels, 1836), analyzed by Verbruggen, *Art of warfare*, pp. 260–75.
9. For more detail on Richard I, there is an enormous literature, especially by John Gillingham, whose collection of essays, *Richard Coeur de Lion: kingship, chivalry and war in the twelfth century*, is an excellent starting-point.
10. This discussion of James as a war leader draws upon his own chronicle. There is a recent study of him which is of rather limited use to historians; E. Belenguer, *Jaume I a través de la Historia*, [2 vols] (Valencia: Eliseu Climent, 1984). J. L. Shneidman, *The rise of the Aragonese–Catalan empire 1200–1350*, [2 vols] (New York: New York University Press, 1970) is very important, while F. D. Swift, *James I of Aragon* (Oxford: Clarendon Press, 1894) is very old but still useful.
11. Shneidman, *Aragonese–Catalan empire*, vol. 1, pp. 15–16; James I, *Chronicle*, pp. 122–5,

125–35, 138–42, 144–6, 149, 157–64, 176–80; Swift, *James I*, pp. 41–2, comments on the confusion of the battle.

12. James I, *Chronicle*, pp. 255–86; Shneidman, *Aragonese–Catalan empire*, vol. 1, p. 18.

13. Shneidman, *Aragonese–Catalan empire*, vol. 1, pp. 18–19, vol. 2, pp. 310–11; James I, *Chronicle*, p. 291.

14. James I, *Chronicle*, pp. 314–26, 332–4, 346–9.

15. James I, *Chronicle*, pp. 369–76, 377–9.

16. James I, *Chronicle*, pp. 383–98.

17. Abu Zakariya of Tunis emerged as the champion of Islam in North Africa, but the confusion reigning there was such that he was unable to mount a sustained war in Spain: C. A. Julien, *A history of North Africa*, tr. J. Petrie (London: Routledge & Kegan Paul, 1970), pp. 122–4.

18. James I, *Chronicle*, pp. 377–80; C. E. Dufourq, *L'Espagne Catalane et le Maghrib au XIII et XIV siècles* (Paris: Presses Universitaires de France, 1966), pp. 93–4.

19. Shneidman, *Aragonese–Catalan empire*, vol. 2, p. 310; James I, *Chronicle*, pp. 17, 146, 346, 536–7; Otto of Freising, pp. 202–4; J. M. Upton-Ward (ed.), *The Rule of the Templars* (Woodbridge: Boydell & Brewer, 1992), pp. 58–62.

20. James I, *Chronicle*, pp. 144–6, 287, 309–10, 358–9, 364–5, 392–6; Lomax, *Reconquest of Spain*, pp. 52–3.

21. On the Norman Conquest, see R. A. Brown, *The Normans and the Norman Conquest* (London: Constable, 1969); on Hastings, see above, *n*1; on the conquest of the North, see OV, vol. 2, pp. 231–3, and W. E. Kapelle, *The Norman Conquest of the North. The region and its transformation 1000–1135* (London: Croom Helm, 1979); on population in the Latin Kingdom, see below, pp. 213–14; Powers, *A society organised for war*, "Life on the cutting edge", pp. 17–34; Lomax, *Reconquest of Spain*, pp. 96–8.

22. On the army's size and the campaign of 1266, see below, pp. 181–4; Housley, *Italian crusades*, pp. 145–57; on the papal–Angevin alliance and its diplomacy, see E. Jordan, *Les origines de la domination Angevine en Italie*, [2 vols] (New York: Burt Franklin, 1960), vol. 2, pp. 536–58, 559–614; on the establishment of the Angevin kingdom, E. G. Léonard, *Les Angevins de Naples* (Paris: A. Collin, 1954), pp. 60–1, 64–73, 137–43; Runciman, *Sicilian Vespers*, pp. 237–41.

23. For 999, see H. Hoffman, "Die Anfäng die Normannen in Süditalien", *Quellen und Forschungen aus Italienischen Archivum und Bibliotek* **47**, 1967, pp. 95–144; for 1017, J. France, "The occasion of the coming of the Normans to southern Italy", *Journal of Medieval History* **17**, 1991, pp. 185–205; on the Norman character of the dominion in South Italy, see G. Loud, "*Gens Normannorum* – myth and reality", Battle **4**, 1981, pp. 104–16, and for the gradual nature of their penetration, "How Norman was the Norman Conquest of Southern Italy?", *Nottingham Medieval studies* **25**, 1981, pp. 13–34; Baldwin, *Government of Philip Augustus*, pp. 163–75, 191–5, 286–9; Holt, "The loss of Normandy and royal finance", pp. 92–105; Gillingham, "The fall of the Angevin Empire", pp. 193–200.

24. See above, pp. 129, 131–2.

## Chapter Twelve

1. Halphen, *Chroniques*, pp. 55–6, translation from Verbruggen, *Art of warfare*, p. 280.

2. See above, pp. 97–101, and below, pp. 235–41, 221–5; Halphen, *Chroniques*, p. 237, translation from Gillingham, "William the Bastard at war", p. 147.

3. William of Poitiers, pp. 170–1; for Charles of Anjou, see below, pp. 178–80; Gillingham, "William the Bastard at war", pp. 148, 151; on Mont Gisard, see above, pp. 10, 102–3; for Angevin encounters, see above, pp. 13, 49–50.

4. Iohannes Codagnellus, pp. 25, 40; *Chronicon Cremonense*, MGH SS, p. 392; *Annales Cremonenses*, MGH SS 18, p. 806; *Annales Ianuenses*, p. 132.

5. Iohannes Codagnellus, pp. 47–53, 57–60, 64–8; *Annales Parmenses*, pp. 666–7.

6. J. France, "The Battle of Carcano: the event and its importance" *War in History* (forthcoming); Bradbury, "Battles in England and Normandy", pp. 7–8; on Hattin, see below, pp. 221–5; Boso, pp. 70–1; *Annales Coloniensis Maximi*, MGH 17, pp. 779–81; *Continuatio Sanblasiana*, pp. 312–3; Ambroise, pp. 25–8, 59–71.

7. *Annales Veronenses*, pp. 8–12; Salimbene de Adam, vol. 1, pp. 131–2; *Annales Sancti Iustinae Patavini*, pp. 151–5; on the size of his army, see above, p. 129; *Annales Placentini Gibellini*, p. 476; *Annales Veronenses*, pp. 10–12.

8. *Annales Veronenses*, p. 10; Salimbene, vol. 1, pp. 132–3; *Annales Bergomates*, p. 809; *Chronicon Estense*, in Muratori 15-3 (Milan: RIS, 1723), p. 14; *Annales Placentini Gibellini*, pp. 476–7; Salimbene, vol. 1, p. 133; on the county of Cortenova, see R. Caproni, *La Battaglia di Cortenova* (Cortenova: Cassa Rurale ed Atigiana di Covo, 1987), pp. 19–25, 45–6; *Annales Bergomates*, p. 809.

9. Piero della Vigna, letter announcing the victory in *Petri de Vineis epistolarum*, vol. 2, p. 235; According to the *Annales Placentini Gibellini*, p. 477, whose very full account is generally supported by the other sources, at Soncino Frederick saw the fires lit on the citadel of Bergamo telling him that the enemy were crossing the Oglio. I am very disinclined to accept this tale for the following reasons. (a) *Annales Bergomates*, p. 809, which report the battle, do not mention it. (b) Bergamo stands high above the plain, and on a fine day its towers could undoubtedly be seen from Soncino. But to count on seeing such a signal in the murk, rain and wind of late November would have been foolish. It is far more likely that Frederick sent out scouts from Soncino, where there is a crossing of the Oglio, and they reported news of the movement of the Guelf army. This is not the only suspect element in the Piacenzan account, for it is also reported that a knight of the emperor, on a white horse, warned the Milanese of the imminent arrival of imperial forces: one wonders why they did nothing about it.

10. *Annales Placentini Gibellini*, pp. 477–8; *Chronicon Parmense*, p. 9. Caproni, *Battaglia di Cortenova*, pp. 55–9, has painstakingly examined the site, but he sees the battle as a more compact affair than the present writer; Matthew Paris, *Chronica Majora*, vol. 3, p. 443; Piero della Vigna, *Petri de Vineis epistolarum*, vol. 2, pp. 235, 302; Martène & Durand, *Veterum Scriptorum*, vol. 2, pp. 1151–3.

11. Frederick II, as noted above, and Charles of Anjou, C. Baronius and O. Raynaldi, *Annales Ecclesiastici*, [15 vols] (Lucca, 1747–56), vol. 3, pp. 242–3, both wrote accounts of their various victories, while recently a letter of Saladin's about Hattin has been discovered: C. P. Melville & M. C. Lyons, "Saladin's Hattin letter", in Kedar (ed.), *Horns of Hattin*, pp. 208–12. The literature on Hastings is enormous, and some is noted above (p. 139, *n*1).

12. On the military organization of the cities, see above, p. 33. The Courtrai chest is illustrated on the cover of Verbruggen, *Art of warfare*; for the battle see pp. 190–4 and, for Worringen, p. 267; at-Turtusi quoted by Lourie, "A society organised for war", p. 70.

13. For a very useful account of the origins of the myth, see Devries, *Medieval military technology* pp. 95–110; Oman, *Art of war*, vol. 1, pp. 149–68, 231–352, vol. 2, pp. 52–108; Delbrück, *Medieval warfare*, pp. 147–88, 225–312, 385–98, 429–52; Verbruggen, *Art of warfare*, pp. 19–110, 111–203.

14. France, "La guerre dans la France féodale", pp. 194–5, 197–8; Morillo, "Hastings, an unusual battle", pp. 95–104, which makes clear that there is now, effectively, a consensus that infantry were important at Hastings. M. Bennett, "The myth of the military supremacy of knightly cavalry", in *Armies, chivalry and warfare. Proceedings of the 1995 Harlaxton Symposium*, M. J. Strickland (ed.) (Stamford: Paul Watkins, forthcoming) has observations on the limitations of cavalry.

15. Bradbury, "Battles in England and Normandy", pp. 6–7, 8–9, 10; France, "La guerre dans la France féodale", pp. 190–1; Henry of Huntingdon, pp. 718–9; on infantry, in twelfth-century Italy, see below, pp. 160–64; on Cortenova, see above, pp. 153–5; on Bouvines, see below, pp. 235–41.

16. Lambert of Hersfeld, *Annales*, MGH SS 3, p. 136; OV, vol. 2, pp. 23–31, 357; William of Malmesbury, *Gesta Regum Anglorum*, vol. 2, p. 235; AA, p. 476; on Tinchebrai, see above, pp. 9, 159; Morillo, *Warfare under the Anglo-Norman kings*, pp. 23–5; Maciejowski, 34v; S. Lewis, *The art of Matthew Paris in the Chronica Majora* (Aldershot: Scolar Press, 1987), Fig. 227, p. 383, showing Trinity College Dublin Ms 177; Y. Harari, "The military role of the Frankish Turcopoles", *Mediterranean History Review* **12**, 1997, pp. 109–10.

17. D. J. A. Ross, "L'originalité de 'Turoldus': le maniement de lance", *Cahiers de Civilisation Médiévale* **6**, 1963, pp. 127–38; V. Cirlot, "Techniques guerrières en Catalogne féodale; le maniement de la lance", *Cahiers de Civilisation Médiévale* **28**, 1985, pp. 36–43; J. Flori, "Encore l'usage de la lance: la technique du combat chevaleresque vers l'an 1000", *Cahiers de Civilisation Médiévale* **31**, 1988, pp. 213–40; Usamah, pp. 69–70; Lewis, *Art of Matthew Paris*, Pl. XIII; M. Strickland, "Military technology and conquest: the anomaly of Anglo-Saxon England", *Battle*, vol. 19, Fig. 6.

18. Strickland, "Military technology and conquest", pp. 381–2, stresses the quality of Anglo-Saxon infantry; Suger, p. 136, OV, vol. 6, pp. 238–9; WT, pp. 937–8: Verbruggen, *Art of warfare*, pp. 73–7, gives numerous examples, but he erroneously dates the action at Darum to 1180.

19. *The Rule of the Templars*, J. M. Upton-Ward (ed.) (Woodbridge: Boydell & Brewer, 1992), pp. 59–61; M. Bennett, "La Règle du Temple as a military manual, or How to deliver a cavalry charge", in *Studies in medieval history presented to R. Allen-Brown*, C. Harper-Bill, J. Holdsworth, J. Nelson (eds) (Woodbridge: Boydell & Brewer, 1989), pp. 7–20, and reprinted by Upton-Ward as an appendix (pp. 175–88); on Muret and Bouvines, see below, pp. 167–9, 235–41.

20. On Cassel and the sources for the battle, see France, *Victory in the East*, pp. 55–6, *n*8; on Wilderen, Gaier, *Art et organisation militaires dans la principauté de Liège*, pp. 237–40, makes a very believable reconstruction on the basis of limited information; Gaier, "Le combat de Visé", pp. 11–14.

21. Lomax, *Reconquest of Spain*, pp. 70–1; B. F. Reilly, *The contest of Christian and Moslem in Spain* (Oxford: Blackwell, 1992), pp. 88–9; 'Abd-Allah, translated in C. Smith (ed.), *Christian and Muslim in Spain*, [3 vols] (Warminster: Aris & Phillips, 1988), vol. 3, p. 99.

22. Galbert, pp. 297–300; Verbruggen, *Art of warfare*, pp. 229–31, where it is referred to as the battle of Thielt, which is the name used by Oman, *History of the art of war*, vol. 1, pp. 443–5; Gillingham, "War and chivalry in the history of William the Marshal", pp. 231–2; Roger of Hovenden, vol. 4. pp. 58–9.

23. For earlier Anglo-Norman battles, see above, p. 59; Potter, *Gesta Stephani*, pp. 112–13; OV, vol. 6, p. 540. There is a good discussion of the battle in Bradbury, *Stephen and Mathilda*, pp. 90–8, and in the same author's "Battles in England and Normandy",

pp. 10–11. For a suggestion that the Welsh infantry may have been more influential, see Davies, *Anglo-Welsh warfare and the works of Gerald of Wales*, pp. 31–2.

24. France, "Battle of Carcano" (forthcoming); Holder-Egger, *Annales Mediolanenses Maiores*, pp. 62–3; *Annales Coloniensis Maximi*, MGH SS 17, p. 788; *Chronica Regia Coloniensis*, p. 126; Godfrey of Viterbo, *Pantheon*, MGH SS 22, p. 329.

25. *Annales Coloniensis Maximi*, p. 789; Holder-Egger, *Annales Mediolanenses Maiores*, p. 63; *Chronica Regia Coloniensis*, p. 128; Romoald of Salerno, *Annales*, MGH SS 19, pp. 441–2; J. B. Mittarelli (ed.), *Chronicon Tolosanus* (Venice, 1771), cols 61–4; *Continuatio Sanblasiana*, p. 316.

## Chapter Thirteen

1. Lomax, *Reconquest of Spain*, p. ix, has a very clear map showing that in the period 1210–52 the reconquered area of Spain roughly doubled; see also his account on pp. 129–59; G. Duby, *The legend of Bouvines*, tr. C. Tihanyi (Cambridge: Polity Press, 1990), pp. 139–40.

2. Alfonso VIII of Castile to the Pope, tr. in Smith, *Christians and Muslims in Spain*, vol. 2, pp. 15–25. This was a propaganda letter, but it was also unusually frank about the difficulties of the campaign.

3. Alfonso VIII of Castile to the Pope, Smith, *Christians and Muslims in Spain*, vol. 2, pp. 218–25; Lomax, *Reconquest of Spain*, pp. 124–8.

4. The most important sources for the battle are William of Tudela, *Song of the Cathar Wars*, pp. 68–71, and Peter de Vaux-de-Cernay, *Historia Albigensis*, P. Guébin & H. Maisonneuve (eds) (Paris: Librarie Philosophique J. Vrin, 1951), pp. 173–86. There is a good account in Sumption, *Albigensian Crusade*, pp. 164–9; Oman, *Art of war*, vol. 1, pp. 453–67.

5. James I, *Chronicle*, pp. 17–18.

6. Verbruggen, *Art of warfare*, pp. 156–7, gives credit to the cavalry for the victory, but I have followed the account of Gaier, *Art et organisation militaires dans la Principauté de Liège*, pp. 257–62, which seems closer to the sources; Oman, *Art of war*, vol. 1, pp. 450–3, lacks detail, especially with regard to the cavalry of Loos; on Cortenova, see above, pp. 153–6.

7. Van Cleve, *Frederick II*, pp. 72–94; Baldwin, *Government of Philip Augustus*, pp. 205–14; Rodger, *Safeguard of the sea*, p. 54.

8. Baldwin, *Government of Philip Augustus*, pp. 214–6; Verbruggen, *Art of warfare*, pp. 239–40. For an account of the battle, see Appendix I, pp. 235–41.

9. J. C. Holt, "Colonial England, 1066–1215", *Colonial England, 1066–1215* (London: Hambledon, 1997), pp. 1–24; on Lincoln, see Vincent, *Peter des Roches*, pp. 138–40; D. Carpenter, *The minority of Henry III* (London: Methuen, 1990), pp. 35–40; Crouch, *William Marshal*, pp. 121–2; F. M. Powicke, *King Henry III and the Lord Edward*, [2 vols] (Oxford: Clarendon Press, 1947), vol. 2, pp. 736–9; Prince Louis's hopes were ended when reinforcements from France were defeated in a sea-battle in the English channel – Rodger, *Safeguard of the sea*, p. 55.

10. Prestwich, *Edward I*, pp. 42–5; Powicke, *Henry III and the Lord Edward*, vol. 2, pp. 461–5,

pp. 465–6; J. R. Maddicott, *Simon de Montfort* (Cambridge: Cambridge University Press, 1994), pp. 270–2; D. A. Carpenter, *The battles of Lewes and Evesham 1264/65* (Keele: Mercia Publications, 1997); N. Hooper & M. Bennett, *Cambridge illustrated atlas of warfare: the Middle Ages* (Cambridge: Cambridge University Press, 1996), pp. 67–8; D. A. Carpenter, "Simon de Montfort and the Mise of Lewes", *Bulletin of the Institute of Historical Research* **58**, 1985, pp. 1–11.

11. Powicke, *Henry III and the Lord Edward*, vol. 2, pp. 493–502; Madicott, *Simon de Montfort*, pp. 331–45; D. C. Cox, *The Battle of Evesham: a new account* (Evesham: Vale of Evesham Historical Society, 1988).

12. On the battle of Maes Moydog, see: J. E. Morris, *The Welsh wars of Edward I. A contribution to medieval military history* (Oxford: Oxford University Press, 1901), pp. 255–7; J. G. Edwards, "The Battle of Maes Madog and the Welsh campaign of 1294–5", *English Historical Review* **39**, 1924, pp. 1–12, **46**, 1931, pp. 262–5; Davies, *Age of conquest*, p. 384.

13. Prestwich, *Edward I*, pp. 477–8; G. W. S. Barrow, *Robert Bruce and the community of the realm of Scotland* (London: Eyre & Spottiswoode, 1965), pp. 123–6.

14. Prestwich, *Edward I*, pp. 479–80; Barrow, *Robert Bruce*, pp. 142–6.

15. Ambroise, pp. 150–3.

16. Barrow, *Robert the Bruce*, pp. 203–32 has an excellent account of Bannockburn, including a learned discussion of its probable site. See also the maps in Hooper, *Cambridge illustrated atlas of warfare: the Middle Ages*, pp. 74–6.

17. Christiansen, *Northern crusades*, pp. 89–117; R. Bartlett, *The making of Europe. Conquest, colonization and cultural change 950–1350* (London: Allen Lane, 1993), pp. 60–84.

18. On the papacy and the Sicilian candidacy, see Jordan, *Les origines de la Domination Angevine*, vol. 2, pp. 370–409; Léonard, *Angevins de Naples*, pp. 37–56; Runciman, *Sicilian Vespers*, pp. 68–93; see also the forthcoming J. Dunbabin, *Charles of Anjou* (Harlow: Addison Wesley Longman, 1998).

19. *Il Libro di Montaperti*, C. Paoli (ed.) (Florence: G. P. Vieisseux, 1889) details the raising of the Florentine force and has been very clearly analysed by Waley, on which see above, p. 133, *n*11.

20. The countryside around Montaperti is pretty bare, so that for this manoeuvre to be unseen it must have been a very long detour.

21. The Florentine G. Villani, *Cronica*, G. Aquilecchia (ed.) (Turin: Giulio Einaudi, 1968), pp. 38–49, ascribes the victory to treachery in the Florentine ranks, while the Sienese sources, which are both late versions of a lost original in *Miscellanea Storica Sanese*, G. Porri (ed.) (Sienna, 1844) stress the ferocity of the Siennese army; there are accounts of the battle by R. Davidsohn, *Forschungen zur älteren Geschichte von Florenz*, [4 vols] (Berlin, 1896–1908), vol. 4, pp. 152–3; F. Schevill, *Sienna, history of a medieval commune* (London: Chapman & Hall, 1909), pp. 179–84, *History of Florence* (New York: F. Ungar, 1961), pp. 129–31; D. Waley, *Sienna and the Siennese in the thirteenth century* (Cambridge: Cambridge University Press, 1991), pp. 116–7. The battlefield is marked by a memorial in the form of a pyramid – now somewhat vandalized – on the hill of Monteapertaccio.

22. See above, p. 176; Jordan, *Domination Angevine*, vol. 2, pp. 559–602; Léonard, *Angevins de Naples*, pp. 51–9. Andrew of Hungary, *Descriptio*, pp. 567–9.

23. Andrew of Hungary, *Descriptio*, pp. 570–72; Saba Malaspina, *Rerum Sicularum Historia* (Milan: RIS, 1726), vol. 8, p. 821; C. Baronius & O. Raynaldi, *Annales Ecclesiastici*, vol. 3, pp. 188–9; Villani, *Cronica*, p. 51.

24. Andrew of Hungary, *Descriptio*, pp. 575–7; Guillaume le Breton, *Gesta*, p. 278 (Duby,

GB1, p. 42); Primatus (or Jean de Vignay), *Ex Primati Chronicis per J. de Vignay translatis*, RHGF 20, p. 28. The tactic of stabbing under the armpit recurs in Primatus's account of the Battle of Tagliacozzo of 1268, and Delbrück, *Medieval warfare*, pp. 353–7, criticized the notion as the invention of a later writer on the basis of soldiers' tales, but Delbrück did not know the sources himself: in particular, he did not know that the story is found in Andrew of Hungary, and was relying on the studies of others. Oman, *Art of war*, vol. 1, pp. 502–3, studied the battle of Benevento at length and supposed that this tactic was designed to avoid German plate armour. Runciman, *Sicilian Vespers*, pp. 109–11, follows Oman and repeats this myth. However, there is no mention of plate-armour at Benevento: the accounts stress the close order of the Germans. Moreover, although pieces of plate under the mail were in use, and knights often wore leather over their mail, there is no evidence for the use of articulated metal at this time, on which see above, pp. 18–20.

25. Villani, *Cronica*, pp. 50–6; Ricordanus Malaspina, *Historia Florentina* (Milan: RIS, 1926), vol. 8, pp. 1000–3, repeats this general account and the numbers involved, and stresses heavily the treachery of the Apulian barons, who took flight when things seemed to be going badly.

26. Saba Malaspina, *Rerum Sicularum Historia*, pp. 825–8; *Annales Sancti Iustinae Patavini*, pp. 188–9.

27. Runciman, *Sicilian Vespers*, pp. 113–26; E. G. Léonard, *Les Angevins de Naples* (Paris: Presses Universitaires de France, 1954), pp. 68–9.

28. Charles of Anjou described the movements of both armies in a letter written immediately after the battle to the pope, edited as an annex to a detailed account of the battle, by P. Herde, "Die Schlact bei Tagliacozzo. Eine historisch–topographische Studie", *Zeitschrift für Bayerische Landesgeschichte* **28**, 1962, pp. 741–44. There are older accounts of the battle by Oman, *Art of war*, vol. 1, 505–15, Delbrück, *Medieval warfare*, pp. 353–7 and Runciman, *Sicilian Vespers*, pp. 127–31, but that given by Herde is the most detailed and thorough, analyses the source exhaustively and takes topography into account. Herde returned to the battle in his "Taktiken muslimischer Heere vom ersten Kreuzzug bis 'Ayn Djalut (1260) und ihre Einwirkung auf de Schlact bei Tagliacozzo", in *Das Heilige Land im Mittelalter: Begegnungsvraum zwischen Orient und Okzident*, W. Fischer & J. Schneider (eds) (Neustadt: Verlag Degener, 1982), pp. 83–94, in which he develops the idea that Charles's tactics owed much to the presence of Alard of Saint-Valéry, a crusader veteran who advised him to employ tactics similar to those used in the East by the Muslims, on which see below, pp. 182–3. There are also accounts in T. Brogi, *La Marsica Antica e Medievale*, [2 vols] (Avezzano: Adelmo Pollo, 1981), vol. 1, pp. 214–27; A. Cantelmi, *Tagliacozzo* (Avezzano: Ferreti-Pescara, 1975), pp. 65–78.

29. Herde, "Die Schlact bei Tagliacozzo", pp. 720–5.

30. Herde, "Die Schlact bei Tagliacozzo", pp. 725–38, "Taktiken muslimischer Heere", pp. 87–9; Oman, *Art of war*, pp. 511–12, Runciman, *Sicilian Vespers*, pp. 128–30, Delbrück, *Medieval warfare*, pp. 354–5. The Valle Vacareccia at its closest is only about 100 m from the road to Avezzano, but it is very difficult to see. It presently houses a noisesome pig farm. There is an excellent view of the whole battlefield from the Avezzano junction of the new A25 motorway.

31. Herde, "Taktiken muslimischer Heere", pp. 89–91; Oman, *Art of war*, pp. 511–12, Runciman, *Sicilian Vespers*, pp. 128–30, Delbrück, *Medieval warfare*, pp. 354–5; *Annales Sancti Iustinae Patavini*, p. 190.

32. There is an account of Courtrai in Verbruggen, *Art of warfare*, pp. 190–4, but I have

followed that of K. Devries, *Infantry warfare in the early fourteenth century* (Woodbridge: Boydell & Brewer, 1996), pp. 9–22.

33. Delbrück, *Medieval warfare*, pp. 367–8, 422–4.

## Chapter Fourteen

1. Jones, "The image of the barbarian in medieval Europe", pp. 376–407; Gillingham, "Conquering the barbarians', pp. 68–84; Helmold, *Chronica Slavorum*, pp. 12, 58–9.

2. The earliest north European account of Islam is far from hostile, but makes it clear that Muslims were seen as pagans: Glaber, pp. 21–3. On the general subject, see R. W. Southern, *Western views of Islam in the Middle Ages* (Cambridge, Massachusetts: Harvard University Press, 1962), N. Daniel, *Islam and the West: the making of an image* (Edinburgh: Edinburgh University Press, 1960) and K. I. Semaan, *Islam and the medieval West* (Albany: State University of New York Press, 1980). The lay author of the *Gesta Francorum* believed the Muslims to be pagans (GF, p. 20), as did whoever wrote the *Song of Roland*, ed. and tr. D. Sayers (Harmondsworth: Penguin, 1960), as for example at the beginning of p. 55.

3. Lomax, *Reconquest of Spain*, pp. 52–3.

4. France, *Victory in the East*, pp. 252–3, 325–7; Runciman, *Crusades*, vol. 2, pp. 111–18; Lyons & Jackson, *Saladin*, p. 373; Van Cleve, *Frederick II*, pp. 213–33; on the general subject, see M. A. Köhler, *Allianzen und Verträge zwischen frankischen und islamischen Herrschern im Vorderen Orient* (Berlin: W. Gruyter, 1991); Matthew Paris portrays the Mongols as cruel and even as cannibals, and yet reports that they sent envoys to the pope, who received them well: R. Vaughan, *The illustrated chronicles of Matthew Paris* (Cambridge: Sutton, 1993), pp. 14, 77–8; B. Hamilton, "Continental drift: Prester John's progress through the Indies", *Prester John, the Mongols and the ten lost tribes*, C. F. Beckingham & B. Hamilton (eds) (Aldershot: Variorum, 1996), pp. 237–69.

5. Bartlett, *The Making of Europe*, pp. 60–84.

6. Morris, *Welsh wars of Edward I*, pp. 121–2, 178; Taylor, *King's works in Wales*, pp. 333–4; Bartlett, "Colonial aristocracies of the High Middle Ages", pp. 23–48; C. Mutafian, *Les Lusignans et l'Outre-Mer: Actes du Colloque Poitiers–Lusignan octobre 1993* (Poitiers: Université de Poitiers, 1995).

7. L. H. Nelson, *The Normans and South Wales 1070–1171* (Austin: University of Texas Press, 1966), p. 33, points to Welsh support for the rebellion of 1065.

8. For the general outline of the conquest, see Davies, *Age of conquest*, pp. 24–107; F. C. Suppe, *Military institutions on the Welsh Marches: Shropshire 1066–1300* (Woodbridge: Boydell & Brewer, 1994), pp. 154–61.

9. Nelson, *Normans in South Wales*, p. 182; Davies, *Age of Conquest*, pp. 96–101, 366–8.

10. T. Jones (ed.), *Brut y Tywysogon or The chronicle of the Princes. Peniarth Ms.20 version* (Cardiff: University of Wales Press, 1952), p. 1094; Davies, *Age of Conquest*, pp. 35–6, 45–6, 51–3; Gerald of Wales, *The journey through Wales and the description of Wales*, p. 196; T. Jones (ed.), *Brut y Tywysogon or The chronicle of the Princes. Red Book of Hergest version* (Cardiff: University of Wales Press, 1955), p. 1157; D. J. Cathcart-King, "Henry II and the fight at Coleshill", *Welsh History Review* **2**, 1964–5, pp. 367–73; J. G. Edwards, "Henry II and the fight at Coleshill: some further reflections", *Welsh History Review* **3**, 1965–6, pp. 251–63.

11. On the supposed weakness of Welsh castles see, for example, Davies, *Age of Conquest*, p. 255; for a survey, R. Avent, "Castles of the Welsh princes", *Château Gaillard* **16**, 1992, pp. 11–21, *Cestyll tywysogion/Castles of the princes of Gwynedd* (Cardiff: HMSO, 1983); J. R. Kenyon & R. Avent, *Castles in Wales and the Marches* (Cardiff: University of Wales Press, 1987). I am grateful to my colleague, I. W. Rowlands, for his comments on Welsh castles; Evans, *A medieval Prince of Wales*, p. 55; Gerald of Wales, *Journey through Wales and the description of Wales*, p. 112.

12. Gerald of Wales, *Journey through Wales and the description of Wales*, p. 148; T. Jones (ed.), *Brenhinedd y Saesson or Kings of the Saxons* (Cardiff: University of Wales Press, 1971), p. 1167; Jones, *Brut y Tywysogon 20*.

13. J. Barrow, *English Episcopal Acta VII: Hereford 1079–1234* (Oxford: Oxford University Press, 1993); R. Turvey, *The Lord Rhys, Prince of Deheubarth* (Llandysul: Gomer, 1997), p. 65; F. C. Suppe, "The cultural significance of decapitation in High Medieval Wales and the Marches", *Bulletin of the Board of Celtic Studies* **36**, 1989, pp. 147–60; Strickland, *War and chivalry* p. 309.

14. Suppe, *Military institutions of the Welsh Marches*, pp. 7–33; Davies, *Age of conquest*, pp. 323–7.

15. Davies, *Age of conquest*, pp. 333–88; on the cost of the Welsh castles and their burden, see above, pp. 94–5.

16. Gerald of Wales, *Journey through Wales and the description of Wales*, pp. 267–74; Davies, *Age of conquest*, pp. 31, 35, 45, 51–3; Nelson, *Normans in South Wales*, pp. 102, 106–8; on Gower, see above, pp. 84–5, n16; Latimer, "Henry II's campaign against the Welsh in 1165", pp. 547–1; Morris, *Welsh wars of Edward I*, p. 128.

17. Kapelle, *The Normans and the conquest of the North*; G. Ritchie, *The Normans in Scotland* (Edinburgh: Edinburgh University Press, 1954), pp. 125–226; G. W. S. Barrow, *The kingdom of Scotland: government, church and society from the 11th to 14th centuries* (London: Edward Arnold, 1973), pp. 279–336, "David I of Scotland: the balance of new and old", in his *Scotland and its neighbours in the Middle Ages* (London: Hambledon, 1992), pp. 45–66; Ritchie, *Normans in Scotland*, pp. 221–6.

18. On which, see G. W. S. Barrow, *Kingship and unity: Scotland 1000–1306* (Edinburgh: Edward Arnold, 1981); R. Mitchison, *A history of Scotland* (London: Methuen, 1970), pp. 18–31; Ritchie, *Normans in Scotland*, pp. 345–82; Barrow, "The reign of William the Lion", pp. 67–90; "The army of Alexander III's Scotland", in N. H. Reid (ed.), *Scotland under the reign of Alexander III* (Edinburgh: John Donald, 1990), pp. 132, 136–7.

19. Barrow, "The army of Alexander III's Scotland", pp. 132–47; see the comments of Aelred, *Relatio venerabilis Aelredi, abbatis Rievallensis, de Standardo*, in Howlett, *Chronicles*, vol. 3, p. 188, Henry of Huntingdon, pp. 714–6, and the discussion in Strickland, *War and chivalry*, pp. 291–329.

20. Barrow, *Kingship and unity*, pp. 153–69; Prestwich, *Armies and warfare*, pp. 196–7, is of the opinion that Edward had no strategy, but coercion and bribery of the magnates was a coherent strategy.

21. Christiansen, *Northern crusades*, pp. 18–47; Helmold, *Chronica Slavorum*, pp. 39–43, talks about Henry.

22. Helmold, *Chronica Slavorum*, pp. 25, 27, 55–6; Henry of Livonia, *Chronicle*, J. A. Brundage (ed.) (Madison: University of Wisconsin Press, 1961), p. 122.

23. F. Lotter, "The crusading idea and the conquest of the region east of the Elbe", in *Medieval frontier societies*, R. Bartlett & A. MacKay (eds) (Oxford: Clarendon Press, 1989), pp. 285–94; Helmold, pp. 59–60.

24. Lotter, "The crusading ideal and the conquest of the region east of the Elbe", pp. 294–306; Christiansen, *Northern crusades*, pp. 62–9; W. L. Urban, *The Baltic crusade* (Dekalb: Northern Illinois University Press, 1975), pp. 7–15.

25. Henry of Livonia, p. 225; Urban, *Baltic crusade*, pp. 67–159; Christiansen, *Northern crusades*, pp. 94–8.

26. Christiansen, *Northern crusades*, pp. 70–88; Urban, *Baltic crusade*, pp. 149–71.

27. Christiansen, *Northern crusades*, pp. 44–7.

28. Henry of Livonia, pp. 26–7, 48–9, 77, 110; Bartlett, *Making of Europe*, pp. 74–5.

29. Christiansen, *Northern crusades*, p. 87; Henry of Livonia, pp. 109–13.

30. Helmold, p. 60; Henry of Livonia, pp. 63, 105–6, 127–9; W. L. Urban, "The organization of the defence of the Livonian frontier in the thirteenth century", *Speculum* **48**, 1973, pp. 525–32.

31. G. Hutchinson, *Medieval ships and shipping* (Leicester: Leicester University Press, 1997), pp. 15–20; R. W. Unger, *The ship in the medieval economy 600–1600* (London: Croom Helm, 1980), pp. 136–44, 161–7. Henry of Livonia, pp. 143, 147–51, 154; Christiansen, *Northern crusades*, p. 87.

32. J. J. Saunders, *History of the Mongol Conquests* (London: Routledge & Kegan Paul, 1971), pp. 73–90; E. Pamlenyi, *History of Hungary*, tr. M. Morris & R. E. Allen (London: Collets, 1975), pp. 58–9; *Cambridge history of Poland*, [2 vols] (Cambridge: Cambridge University Press, 1950), vol. 1, p. 92; E. D. Phillips, *The Mongols* (London: Thames and Hudson, 1969), pp. 40–7; D. Morgan, *The Mongols* (Oxford: Blackwell, 1986), pp. 84–95, 90–1; J. M. Smith, "Mongol society and military in the Middle East: antecedents and adaptations", in *War and society in the eastern Mediterranean*, Y. Lev (ed.) (Leiden: Brill, 1997), pp. 250–3, establishes the effective range of the Mongol bow at about 50 m; on the limitations imposed by western European conditions on horse-peoples, see R. P. Lindner, "Nomadism, horses and Huns", *Past and Present*, **92**, 1981, pp. 3–19.

33. Christiansen, *Northern crusades*, pp. 35, 100–2; Urban, *Baltic crusade*, pp. 99–122; Henry of Livonia, pp. 48, 60–2, 73–4, 79–81, 103, 229. On the long Lithuanian Crusade, see Christiansen, *Northern crusades*, pp. 132–60, and on the general crusading movement in northern Europe in the later Middle Ages, pp. 171–218, and W. L. Urban, *The Livonian Crusade* (Washington: University Press of America, 1981).

34. Henry of Livonia, pp. 47–50, 73–4, 90–1, 134 for Lithuanian raids, pp. 144–5, 213 for raids amongst other peoples, pp. 103–4, 115–17 for Christians using similar methods; Helmold, p. 40.

35. Henry of Livonia, pp. 57, 141, 209: it is interesting, however, that he refrains from assuming that all crusaders who died fighting in battle against the pagans were martyrs, for Bishop Berthold's death in battle in 1198 is not recorded as martyrdom, while German and Livonian prisoners tortured after capture clearly are regarded as martyrs (p. 102).

## Chapter Fifteen

1. France, *Victory in the East* pp. 122–42.
2. Still the most important book for our understanding of the origins of the crusade, although first published in 1934, is C. Erdmann, *The origin of the idea of the crusade*, tr. M. W. Baldwin

& W. Goffart (Princeton: Princeton University Press, 1977); however, modern writers place Jerusalem at the heart of Urban's appeal, following H. E. J. Cowdrey, "Pope Urban's preaching of the first crusade", *History*, **55**, 1970, pp. 177–88; for an exceptionally fine modern study of the origins of the crusade and the motives of those who went, see Riley-Smith, *The First Crusade and the idea of crusading* and his *The first crusaders 1095–1131* (Cambridge: Cambridge University Press, 1997). For an examination of contemporary piety, and in particular interactions between monasteries and their patrons, bearing on the First Crusade, see M. Bull, *Knightly piety and the lay response to the First Crusade* (Oxford: Clarendon Press, 1993). For a less markedly spiritual interpretation of crusader motives, see France, *Victory in the East*, pp. 1–25, and "Patronage and the appeal of the First Crusade" in *The First Crusade*, J. Phillips (ed.) (Manchester: Manchester University Press, 1997), pp. 5–20; for a good introduction to pilgrimage and holy war in this context, see Brundage, *Medieval canon law and the crusader*, pp. 3–29, and H. E. Mayer, *The crusades* (Oxford: Oxford University Press, 1990), pp. 8–37.

3. See, for example, the accounts of Urban's speech by Robert of Rheims, *Historia Iherosolimitana*, RHC Oc. 3, pp. 727–8; Guibert of Nogent, *Gesta Dei per Francos*, RHC Oc. 4, pp. 137–40; Baldric of Dol, *Historia Jerosolimitana*, RHC Oc. 4, pp. 12–16: all these are conveniently translated in L. & J. Riley-Smith, *The Crusades: ideal and reality 1095–1274* (London: Edward Arnold, 1981), pp. 42–5, 45–9, 49–53. It is not suggested that recovery was the only theme in Urban's appeal, merely that it was a peculiarly important one; E. Hallam, *Chronicles of the Crusades* (London: Weidenfeld & Nicolson, 1989), p. 161; Baha ad-Din, in Gabrieli, *Arab historians of the Crusades*, p. 226; J. M. Powell, *The anatomy of a crusade 1213–1221* (Philadelphia: University of Pennsylvania Press, 1986), p. 17; OV, vol. 5, pp. 228–32.

4. R. Somerville (ed.), *Decreta Claromontensia*, in *The councils of Urban II* (Amsterdam: Hakkert, 1972), p. 74; Riley-Smith, *First crusaders*, pp. 7–22, sees a dichotomy between spiritual and material motives, but the spiritual and the material were bound up together and contemporary opinion, for example, never turned against Bohemond, whose exploitation of the crusade for his own ends has often appalled modern writers. On Urban's publicizing, see *Notitiae Duae Lemovicensis de praedicatione crucis in Aquitania*, RHC Oc. 5; R. Crozet, "Le voyage d'Urbain II et ses arrangements avec le clergé de France", *Revue Historique* **179**, 1937, pp. 270–310; J. France, "Les origines de la première croisade: un nouvel examen", in *Autour de la première croisade*, M. Balard (ed.) (Paris: Publications de la Sorbonne, 1996), pp. 53–5; on the financing of crusades, see Riley-Smith, *First Crusade and the idea of crusading*, pp. 31–57, and his *First crusaders*, esp. pp. 109–43.

5. For an assessment of the importance of Byzantine help to the First Crusade, see France, *Victory in the East*, pp. 298–302, 368–9, and "La stratégie arménienne de la première croisade", in *Les Lusignans et l'Outre Mer: actes du Colloque Poitiers–Lusignan, 20–24 octobre 1993*, C. Mutafian (ed.) (Poitiers, 1994), pp. 141–9; Riley-Smith, *First crusaders*, pp. 12–13, suggests that the crusaders did expect Alexius to lead them; J. France, "Anna Comnena, the Alexiad and the First Crusade", *Reading Medieval Studies* **10**, 1983, pp. 20–32; J. Phillips, *Defenders of the Holy Land: relations between the Latin East and the West 1119–1187* (Oxford: Oxford University Press, 1996), pp. 112–18, see also pp. 100–224 for the Byzantine–Crusader rapprochement.

6. M. Angold, *The Byzantine Empire 1025–1204* (London: Longman, 1984), pp. 263–83, 284–96; D. E. Queller, *The Fourth Crusade* (Leicester: Leicester University Press, 1978); J. Gill, *Byzantium and the papacy 1198–1400* (New Brunswick: Rutgers University Press, 1979).

7. On sea-power and the First Crusade, see France, *Victory in the East*, pp. 209–20, 368, "The First Crusade as a naval enterprise", *The Mariner's Mirror* **83**, 1997, pp. 389–97.

8. There is no naval history of the crusades, although there is a good chapter in J. H. Pryor, *Geography, technology and war: studies in the maritime history of the Mediterranean 649–1571* (Cambridge: Cambridge University Press, 1992), pp. 112–34. It is to be hoped that S. M. Foster, *Some aspects of maritime activity and the use of sea power in relation to the crusading states* (DPhil thesis, University of Oxford, 1978) will be expanded and published. Runciman, *Crusades*, vol. 2, pp. 247–88; C. Tyerman, *England and the Crusades 1095–1588* (Chicago: Chicago University Press, 1988), pp. 80–2; for Barbarossa and the Fourth Crusade, see above, *n*10; Powell, *Anatomy of a crusade*, pp. 123–7; Van Cleve, *Frederick II*, pp. 194–5; W. C. Jordan, *Louis IX and the challenge of crusade* (Princeton: Princeton University Press, 1979), pp. 70–71; J. H. Pryor, "Transportation of horses by sea during the era of the crusades, eighth century to AD 1285", *Mariner's Mirror* **68**, 1982, pp. 9–27, 103–22.

9. Rogers, *Latin siege warfare*, pp. 64–90; Runciman, *Crusades*, vol. 2, pp. 79–80; Prawer, *Crusader institutions*, pp. 217–49, *Latin Kingdom of Jerusalem*, pp. 391–415; Pryor, *Geography, technology and war*, pp. 116–34.

10. France, *Victory in the East*, pp. 245–6, 279–80; V. G. Berry, "The Second Crusade", in Setton, *Crusades*, vol. 1, pp. 463–512; S. Painter, "The Third Crusade", in Setton, *Crusades*, vol. 2, pp. 45–86; Johnston, "The crusades of Frederick Barbarossa and Henry VI", pp. 87–122; Gillingham, *Richard the Lionheart*, pp. 194, 300–1; Van Cleve, *Frederick II*, pp. 208–36; S. Painter, "The Crusade of Theobald of Champagne and Richard of Cornwall", in Setton, *Crusades*, vol. 2, pp. 463–86; J. R. Strayer, "The crusades of Louis IX", in Setton, *Crusades*, vol. 2, pp. 487–521.

11. France, *Victory in the East*, pp. 181–3, 325–7, 371; Berry, "Second Crusade", pp. 463–512; Villhardouin, *Capture of Constantinople*, p. 35; Powell, *Anatomy of a crusade*, pp. 137, 191.

12. France, *Victory in the East*, pp. 122–8, 143, 164, 344–5, 370–3; G. Constable, "The Second Crusade as seen by contemporaries", *Traditio* **9**, 1953, pp. 213–79; Villehardouin, *Conquest of Constantinople*, pp. 42–3; Robert of Clari, *The conquest of Constantinople*, E. H. McNeal (ed.) (New York: Columbia University Press, 1936), pp. 40–1; Queller, *Fourth Crusade*, p. 46; Powell, *Anatomy of a crusade*, pp. 125–6, 133; Painter, "The Third Crusade", pp. 455–86. The letters of the princes to the West during the First Crusade are highly critical of deserters: Hagenmeyer, *Kreuzzugsbriefe*, pp. 141–2, 146–9, 161–5; Painter, "Third Crusade", p. 71; Villehardouin, *Conquest of Constantinople*, pp. 51–2; according to Brundage, *Medieval canon law and the crusader*, pp. 127–31, failure to discharge vows was always a problem; RA, p. 52; Ralph of Caen, p. 651; Ibn al-Athir, *The collection of histories*, in Gabrieli, *Arab historians of the Crusades*, pp. 209–10; Johnson, "The crusades of Frederick Barbarossa and Henry VI", pp. 93–4, 114–16; Tyerman, *England and the Crusades*, pp. 65–6; Jordan, *Louis IX and the challenge of the crusade*, pp. 65–70; Richard, *Louis IX*, pp. 107–12.

13. Tyerman, *England and the Crusades*, pp. 64–85, shows that large numbers went with Richard, but attention is drawn to the lack of general preaching in England by P. Edbury, "Preaching the crusade in Wales", in *England and Germany in the High Middle Ages*, A. Haverkamp & H. Vollrath (eds) (Oxford, 1996), pp. 230–2; Baldwin, *Philip Augustus*, pp. 53–4; Jordan, *Louis IX and the challenge of the crusade*, pp. 65–70; Powell, *Anatomy of a crusade*, pp. 15–32; S. Schein, *Fideles crucis: the papacy, the West and the recovery of the Holy Land 1274–1314* (Oxford: Clarendon Press, 1991), pp. 15–20. On the subject as a whole, see M. Purcell, *Papal crusading policy 1244–91* (Leiden: Brill, 1975), esp. pp. 135–86.

14. Y. Lev, *State and society in Fatimid Egypt* (Leiden: Brill, 1991); W. J. Hamblin, *The Fatamid army during the early crusades* (PhD thesis, University of Michigan, 1985), esp. p. 225; France, *Victory in the East*, pp. 200–6; H. A. R. Gibb, "The armies of Saladin", *Studies in the civilization of Islam*, S. J. Shaw & W. R. Polk (eds) (Princeton: Princeton University Press, 1982), pp. 74–90; R. S. Humphreys, "The emergence of the Mamluk army", *Studia Islamica* **45**, 1977, pp. 67–99, 147–82, *From Saladin to the Mongols* (Albany: State University of New York Press, 1977), pp. 15–20; D. Ayalon, "From Ayyubids to Mamluks", *Revue des Etudes Islamiques* **49**, 1981, pp. 50–9; R. Amitai-Preiss, "The Mamluk officer class during the reign of Sultan Baybars" and A. M. Eddé, "Kurdes et Turcs dans l'armée ayyoubide de Syrie du Nord", in Y. Lev (ed.), *War and society in the eastern Mediterranean, 7th–15th centuries* (Leiden: Brill, 1996), pp. 225–36, 267–300; Ibn al-Athir, p. 120; Lyons & Jackson, *Saladin*, pp. 356–8; P. H. Newby, *Saladin in his time* (London: Faber, 1983), pp. 180–3.

15. GF, p. 49; Hamblin, *Fatimid army*, pp. 244–8; "Djash", *Encylopaedia of Islam*, vol. 2, p. 506; Nicolle, *Arms and armour*, vol. 1, p. xix.

16. GF, p. 19; RA, pp. 50–1, 56–8; Mulinder, *Crusade of 1101*; Berry, "The Second Crusade", pp. 463–512; Odo of Deuil, pp. 114–121, 125–6. The limitations of horse-archers and their need to fire at close range are stressed by Bowlus, "Tactical and strategic weaknesses of the horse archers", pp. 159–66.

17. Marshal, *Warfare in the Latin East*, pp. 177–81. The crusaders were resting in a hollow in the dunes and hills when they were surprised by the Egyptians, who had got wind of their approach. It has to be said that they were remarkably careless in not posting sentries. I would like to thank Dr Mohammed-Moain Sadek, the Director of Antiquities of the Palestine National Authority, for taking me to Bayt Hānūn in the course of a visit to sites in Gaza. See Joinville, *Life of St Louis*, pp. 218–19.

18. Runciman, *Crusades*, vol. 2, pp. 291–5; Prawer, *Crusader institutions*, pp. 102–4, 380–1, *Latin Kingdom of Jerusalem*, pp. 66–85; Benvenisti, *Crusaders in the Holy Land*, pp. 17–20. On rural settlement, see D. Pringle, *Secular buildings in the Crusader Kingdom of Jerusalem: an archaeological gazetteer* (Cambridge: Cambridge University Press, 1997) which has an excellent bibliography and R. Ellenblum's forthcoming *Frankish rural settlement in Crusader Palestine*. On Spain, see above, p. 112, *n*12.

19. See, for example, the comments of Fedden & Thompson, *Crusader castles*, pp. 14–19; on crusader castles, see above, pp. 90–3.

20. Lev, *State and society in Fatimid Egypt*, pp. 97–8, 102–3; Hamblin, *Fatimid Army*, pp. 235–94; H. S. Fink, "Foundation of the Latin states", in Setton, *Crusades*, vol. 1, pp. 368–409, esp. pp. 384–6; R. L. Nicholson, "Growth of the Latin states", in Setton, *Crusades*, vol. 1, pp. 410–48, esp. pp. 407, 410, 411–12; J. P. Phillips, "Hugh of Payns and the 1129 Damascus Crusade", in M. Barber (ed.), *The military orders. Fighting for the faith and caring for the sick* (Aldershot: Variorum, 1994), pp. 141–7; Prawer, *Crusader institutions*, pp. 471–83, argues this case, pointing out that Baldwin I claimed to rule the kingdom of Asia.

21. Runciman, *Crusades*, vol. 2, p. 281; Benvenisti, *Crusaders in the Holy Land*, p. 6; Mayer, *Crusades*, pp. 103–4, "Studies in the history of Queen Melisende of Jerusalem", *Dumbarton Oaks Papers* **21**, 1972, pp. 95–182; on the other hand, Riley-Smith, *The Crusades: a short history*, pp. 101–2, saw good reasons for it; Edessa, captured by Zengi in 1144, had been the original objective of the Second Crusade, on which see Phillips, *Defenders of the Holy Land*, pp. 82–5, 98–9; M. Hoch, "The choice of Damascus as the objective of the Second Crusade", *Autour de la Première Croisade*, M. Balard (ed.) (Paris: Publications de la Sorbonne, 1996), pp. 359–70, "The crusaders' strategy against Fatimid Ascalon and the

Ascalon project of the Second Crusade", in *The Second Crusade and the Cistercians*, M. Gervers (ed.) (New York: St Martin's Press, 1992), pp. 120–3; A. J. Forey, "The failure of the siege of Damascus in 1148", *Journal of Medieval History* **10**, 1984, pp. 13–23, has argued that the relief army was too strong, and that stories of treachery and betrayal sprang up as part of the general explanation for the failure of the whole Second Crusade, that it was due to the pride and folly of the Christians. Ibn al-Qalanisi, *Damascus Chronicle of the Crusades*, H. A. R. Gibb (ed.) (London: Luzac, 1932), pp. 286–7, speaks of "the rapid advance of the Islamic armies" causing the Franks to "retreat in disorder".

22. P. M. Holt, *The age of the Crusades* (London: Longman, 1986), pp. 44–5; D. Pringle, "Richard I and the walls of Ascalon", *Palestine Exploration Quarterly* **116**, 1984, pp. 133–47; M. W. Baldwin, "The Latin states under Baldwin III and Amalric I", and H. A. R. Gibb, "Career of Nur ad-Din", *Crusades*, vol. 1, pp. 536–8, 539–47, 516–19; Phillips, *Defenders of the Holy Land*, pp. 271–81.

23. Y. Lev, "Regime, army and society in medieval Egypt, 9th–12th centuries" in *War and society in the eastern Mediterranean 7th–15th centuries*, Y. Lev (ed.) (Leiden: Brill, 1996), pp. 115–52; Holt, *Age of the Crusades*, pp. 46–52; Baldwin, "Latin states under Baldwin III and Amalric", pp. 548–61; G. Schlumberger, *Campagnes du roi Amaury I en Egypte* (Paris, 1906). On help from the West, notably for Amalric's campaigns in Egypt, see Phillips, *Defenders of the Holy Land*, pp. 140–67.

24. On the Fifth Crusade, and those of Frederick II, Theobald and St Louis, see above, pp. 208–09; on the Mongols and the Middle East, S. Runciman, "Crusader states 1243–91", in Setton, *Crusades*, vol. 2, pp. 557–98; Holt, *Age of the Crusades*, pp. 87–9; Humphreys, *Saladin to the Mongols*, pp. 333–63; Morgan, *The Mongols*, pp. 145–57; P. Jackson, "The crisis in the Holy Land in 1260", *English Historical Review* **95**, 1980, pp. 481–513, argues that the Mongols were not as friendly to Christians as has been supposed, and that the decision of the barons of Jerusalem not to support them was, in the circumstances, sensible.

25. Fink, "The foundation of the Latin states", pp. 368–409; Nicholson, "The growth of the Latin states", pp. 410–8; WT, pp. 770–1; Usamah, pp. 42–3, 98; P. W. Edbury & J. G. Rowe, *William of Tyre, historian of the Latin East* (Cambridge: Cambridge University Press, 1988), pp. 171–4.

26. There is an excellent analysis of the general circumstances of the battle of the Field of Blood in T. S. Asbridge, "The significance and causes of the battle of the Field of Blood", *Journal of Medieval History* **23**, 1997, pp. 301–16; Walter the Chancellor, *Bella Antiochena*, RHC 5, pp. 107–9; Fulcher of Chartres, *A history of the expedition to Jerusalem*, F. R. Ryan & H. S. Fink (eds) (Knoxville: University of Tennessee Press, 1969), pp. 226–7; Matthew of Edessa, *The chronicle of Matthew of Edessa*, A. E. Dosourian (ed.) (New York: University Press of America, 1993), pp. 223–4; Ibn al-Qalanisi, *Damascus Chronicle of the Crusades*, p. 160; Kemal ed-Din, *La Chronique d'Alep*, RHC Or. 3, pp. 617–18; Ibn al-Athir, *Kamel Altevarykh*, RHC Or. 1, pp. 324–5. The site of the battlefield is described in Dussaud, *Topographie*, pp. 220–1. Smail, *Crusading warfare*, pp. 179–80, describes the battle. The reconstruction here is my own, based on looking at the site as well as the sources: while Roger was clearly surprised, his enemy could not have been very close because he was able to order his army quite elaborately. He was not in "a valley with steep wooded sides" (Smail, p. 179) but on an open plain, and evidently chose to attack rather than stand siege in Sarmada or in improvised fortifications. If he was attacking northwards, the battle could well have ended at Tell Aquibrin, whose slopes are wooded and would have been suitable for the vines amongst which, we are told, the Frankish dead lay so thickly.

27. On the "Field of Blood", see above, pp. 217–18, *n*26; Gibb, "The career of Nur ad-Din,

"The rise of Saladin, 1169–89", *Crusades*, vol. 1, pp. 515, 573; Barber, "Frontier warfare in the Latin Kingdom of Jerusalem: the campaign of Jacob's Ford, 1178–9", pp. 9–22; Smail, *Crusading warfare*, pp. 196–7; Runciman, "The crusader states, 1243–1291", pp. 563–4.

28. Smail, *Crusading warfare*, pp. 156–65; Ambroise, pp. 79–96.

29. Walter the Chancellor, p. 93; *De Expugnatione Terrae Sanctae*, p. 154; Matthew Paris, *Chronica Majora*, vol. 6, p. 206; AA, p. 434; RA, p. 55; Smail, *Crusading warfare*, pp. 111–12; Forey, *Military orders*, p. 57: the idea that they were native troops has recently been supported by A. G. C. Savvides, "Late Byzantine and crusader historiographers on Turkish mercenaries in Greek and Latin armies: the Turcopoles/Tourkopoloi", in *The making of Byzantine history: essays dedicated to D. M. Nicol*, R. Beaton & C. Roueché (eds) (Aldershot: Variorum, 1993), pp. 122–36, and H. Diament, "Can toponomastics explain the origin of the crusader lexemes *Poulain* and *Turcopole*?", *Journal of the American Name Society* **25**, 1977, pp. 183–204. Marshal, *Warfare in the Latin East*, pp. 58–9, sees them primarily as light cavalry although sometimes of mixed origin, while T. Wise, *The wars of the crusade* (London: Osprey, 1978), p. 78, sees them as auxiliary cavalrymen. Y. Harari, "The military role of the Frankish Turcopoles: a reassessment", *Mediterranean Historical Review* **12**, 1997, pp. 75–116, analyzes their role and draws attention to the very large numbers incorporated into the ranks of crusader armies – to the tune of 50 per cent of the available cavalry on occasion. Upton-Ward, *Rule of the Templars*, p. 61; Harari, pp. 114–15.

30. Ibn al-Qalanisi, *Damascus Chronicle*, pp. 175–7, 285–7, 292; Smail, *Crusading warfare*, pp. 148–54; Lyons & Jackson, *Saladin*, pp. 206–8.

31. Raynald of Châtillon has had a bad press, but a more realistic view of him in the context of his age, when he was much admired, is provided by B. Hamilton, "The elephant of Christ: Reynald of Châtillon", in *Religious motivation: biographical and sociological problems for the church historian*, D. Baker (ed.) (Oxford: Oxford University Press, 1978), pp. 97–108; Baldwin, "Decline and fall of Jerusalem", p. 606; Lyons & Jackson, *Saladin*, pp. 248–53; J. Prawer, *Crusader institutions*, p. 487. Baldwin (p. 609) probably underestimated the Muslims at 20,000 and certainly fails to note the disparity in cavalry, which was the decisive arm.

32. The best modern accounts are those of Prawer, *Crusader institutions*, pp. 484–500, which has been somewhat strengthened and deepened by Kedar, "The Battle of Hattin revisited", pp. 190–207; Lyons & Jackson, *Saladin*, pp. 255–66, use a new piece of evidence published by Melville & Lyons, "Saladin's Hattin letter", pp. 208–12. These analyses command respect by reason of their careful combination of knowledge of the sources and of the topography. I have, in general, followed the account of Kedar, because my own knowledge of the ground and the sources inclines me to do so, although as noted below, he did not treat of Guy's intentions. There are a number of older accounts. Smail, *Crusading warfare*, pp. 191–7, sets the events in the context of military development. M. W. Baldwin, *Raymond III of Tripolis and the fall of Jerusalem 1140–87* (Amsterdam: Hakkert, 1969) is very partial to Raymond, as is his account in "The decline and fall of Jerusalem", pp. 608–14. There is an account in R. L. Nicholson, *Jocelin III and the fall of the crusader states* (Leiden: Brill, 1973), pp. 157–60, that is broadly comparable to those found in outline histories of the Crusades.

33. Lyons & Jackson, *Saladin*, pp. 248–53, 258; R. C. Smail, "The predicaments of Guy of Lusignan, 1183–87", in *Outremer*, B. Z. Kedar, H. E. Mayer & R. C. Smail (eds) (Jerusalem: Yad Izhak Ben-Zvi Institute, 1982), pp. 159–76, 169–71; Barber, "Frontier warfare in the Latin Kingdom of Jerusalem", pp. 18–19, points out that as a result

of the fall of Jacob's Ford, Baisan had been abandoned; Lyons & Jackson, *Saladin*, pp. 248–53.

34. Smail, "Predicaments of Guy of Lusignan", pp. 165–6; *Crusading warfare*, p. 195; Lyons & Jackson, *Saladin*, pp. 258–9; both Prawer and Kedar avoid this question in their articles.

35. Lyons & Jackson, *Saladin*, pp. 258–9; Kedar, "Hattin revisited", pp. 195–7, agrees that Turan was the spring at which the army stopped, but argues that it had too limited a flow to serve as a base.

36. Prawer, *Crusader institutions*, p. 497; Kedar "Battle of Hattin revisited", pp. 202–3. I follow Kedar in his remark that "it is impossible to establish the exact sequence of events", although most writers, including Prawer (pp. 497–500) attempt a reconstruction.

37. Prawer, *Crusader institutions*, pp. 102–42; on colonization elsewhere, see above, pp. 187–203; D. Ayalon, "Studies on the structure of the Mamluk army – III", *Bulletin of the School of African and Oriental Studies* **16**, (1954), pp. 57–90; Bartlett, *Making of Europe*, pp. 24–59; Smail, "Predicaments of Guy of Lusignan", pp. 161–4.

38. H. Nicholson, *Templars, Hospitallers and Teutonic knights: images of the military orders 1128–1291* (Leicester: Leicester University Press, 1993); S. Schein, "The Templars: the regular army of the Holy Land and the spearhead of the army of its reconquest", in *I Templari: Mito e Storia*, G. Minucci & F. Sardi (eds) (Sienna: A. G. Viti-Ricccucci, 1989), pp. 15–28; A. J. Forey, *The military orders. From the twelfth to the early fourteenth centuries* (Basingstoke: Macmillan, 1992); M. Barber, *The new knighthood: a history of the Order of the Temple* (Cambridge: Cambridge University Press, 1994), "Supplying the crusader states: the role of the Templars", in *The Horns of Hattin*, B. Z. Kedar (ed.) (London: Variorum, 1992), pp. 314–26; J. Riley-Smith, *The Knights of St John in Jerusalem and Cyprus c. 1050–1310* (London: Macmillan, 1967).

39. M. M. Ziada, "The Mamluk sultans to 1293", in Setton, *Crusades*, vol. 2, pp. 735–58; D. Pipes, *Slave soldiers and Islam* (Yale: Yale University Press, 1981), esp. pp. 86–93; Smith, "Mongol society and the military in the Middle East", pp. 254–62; H. Rabie, "The training of the Mamluk Faris", in *War, technology and society in the Middle East*, V. J. Parry & M. E. Yapp (eds) (London: Oxford University Press, 1975), pp. 153–63; on the Mamluk capture of Crac and Marqab, see above, p. 116; M. Shatzmiller, "The crusades and Islamic warfare – a re-evaluation", *Der Islam* **69**, 1992, pp. 247–88.

40. AA, pp. 283–9; Philippe de Navarre & Gerard de Monreal, *Gestes des Chiprois*, G. Raynaud (ed.) (Geneva: J. G. Fick, 1887), pp. 807–17: the present author is fully aware that the Crusades did not end in 1291, but the fall of Acre is the last significant act in the period covered in this book. AA, pp. 284–9, 407–8; France, *Victory in the East*, pp. 312–15, 355–6.

41. Caffaro, *De Liberatione ciuitatum orientis*, RHC Oc. 5, pp. 118–19; WT, pp. 486–7, 571, 575–6, 575–7; Ibn al-Qalanisi, pp. 89–90, 99–100, 170–2; AA, pp. 542–4; WT, p. 571; Lyons & Jackson, *Saladin*, pp. 270–1; on Marqab and Crac, see above, p. 116; J. Stevenson (ed.), *Chronicon de Lanercost* (Edinburgh, 1839), pp. 128–31; Philippe de Navarre, *Gestes des Chiprois*, pp. 758–9, 764–8.

42. J. Richard, "An account of the battle of Hattin referring to the Frankish mercenaries in the Oriental Muslim States", *Speculum* **27**, 1952, pp. 168–77; Walter the Chancellor, pp. 107–8; Imad ad-Din, in Gabrieli, *Arab historians of the Crusades*, pp. 138–9; A. Forey, "The military orders and the ransoming of captives from Islam", *Studia Monastica* **33**, 1991, pp. 259–66, 267–77; Usamah, pp. 93–4; Fink, "Foundation of the Latin states", p. 389; Nicholson, "Growth of the Latin states", p. 419; Powell, *Anatomy of a crusade*, p. 190; Joinville, *Life of St Louis*, pp. 240–8; Kennedy, *Crusader castles*, p. 96.

## Chapter Sixteen

1. On the development of the *Māmluk* army, see Shatzmiller, "The Crusades and Islamic warfare – a re-evaluation", pp. 247–88. The Crusades had certainly increased the professionalism of Egyptian armies, but the real development of a standing *Māmluk* army came in the second half of the thirteenth century, in response to the Mongol threat.

## *Appendix I*

1. The sources for the battle have been collected and translated into English in Duby, *The Legend of Bouvines*, and I will make reference to that collection for convenience. However, it should be noted that in the case of Guillaume le Breton, references will be given to the main editions cited in this book and to the translations of Duby. Guillaume le Breton was present in the king's suite at the battle and wrote two accounts. The first (Duby, GB1, pp. 37–54), which has been referred to here as *Gesta*, was produced shortly after the battle and embodied in a continuation of the work of Rigord, and was probably an official version. The second (Duby, GB2, pp. 197–205) was embodied in his *Philippidos*, a Latin poem in honour of Philip Augustus, extracts from which are given by Duby. H. F. Delaborde, *Oeuvres de Rigord et Guillaume le Breton*, vol. 1, pp. lxxvii–xxxii, suggests that the *Philippidos* was first published in 1224 and revised about 10 years later. The Marchiennes account (Duby, pp. 192–3) and that of the Anonymous of Béthune (Duby, pp. 194–7) are very valuable, as is Roger of Wendover (Duby, pp. 205–8), and various other sources have something to contribute. In general, I follow the outline of events established by Verbruggen (pp. 239–60), although with some differences, as will be evident, and my conclusions are my own.
2. The Anonymous of Béthune (Duby, p. 194) says that Mortagne is 3 miles from Tournai, while Guillaume le Breton (*Gesta*, p. 267; Duby, p. 38) says it is 6 miles: 12 km is the actual distance; see below, pp. 236–7; Baldwin, *Government of Philip Augustus*, pp. 269, 276; Guillaume le Breton, *Gesta*, p. 276: Duby, GB1, p. 41; Verbruggen, *Art of warfare*, p. 246.
3. The French carts may well have resembled the ladder-sided type shown in the Maciejowski Bible, for which see Plate 4; see my comments on rates of march in France, *Victory in the East*, p. 327; and also Nesbitt, "Rate of march of crusading armies in Europe", pp. 167–82.
4. Roger of Wendover, Duby, p. 206.
5. Guillaume le Breton, *Gesta*, pp. 268–9 (Duby, GB1, pp. 38–9); stresses that the reconnaissance was not the king's idea; Guillaume le Breton, *Gesta*, pp. 270–1 (Duby, GB1, p. 39); Guillaume le Breton, *Philippidos*, pp. 313–5 (Duby, GB2, pp. 197–9); Anonymous of Béthune, Duby, p. 194.
6. For the march and deployment, see Verbruggen, *Art of warfare*, pp. 246–9; Anonymous of Béthune, Duby p. 195.
7. Guillaume le Breton, *Gesta*, pp. 267–81, *Philippidos*, pp. 320–9 (Duby, GB1, pp. 41–4, and GB2, pp. 199–200); Gislebert, pp. 97, 101–2, 103–4, 113–14, mentions Baldwin V's participation in tournaments – in 1168 involving knights, mounted sergeants and footsoldiers; in 1170 his 3,000 foot and horse were outnumbered by the forces of Godfrey

of Louvain; in 1171 he fought a sizeable battle with the Duke of Burgundy; and in 1173 took 200 knights and 1,200 foot to Soissons for a contest; Anonymous of Béthune, Duby p. 195.

8. Guillaume le Breton, *Gesta*, pp. 281–5 (Duby, GB1, pp. 44–6); Anonymous of Béthune, Duby p. 195; *Genealogiae comitum Flandriae*, MGH SS 9, p. 333.

9. Guillaume le Breton, *Gesta*, pp. 285–7, *Philippidos*, pp. 342–7; (Duby, GB1, pp. 246–9, and GB2, pp. 201–3).

10. Roger of Wendover, Duby pp. 206–7. All writers on Bouvines owe a great deal to the work of Verbruggen, *Art of warfare*, pp. 239–60, especially to his elucidation of the tactics of Guérin, and to his perception that the disorder of the allied army contributed to its defeat. My main differences are slight. (a) I would emphasize the importance of Philip's prompt action in sallying out as the allied army appeared, and his subsequent creation of a cavalry screen. (b) I would place the battle later in the afternoon, with a start at about 3 pm. (c) I can see no evidence that Philip created a third division to the north of his own position. He seems to have had time only to cobble together a single unit, of course made up of many subgroups, along a line extending from north of the Bouvines road to Gruson. Otto certainly had no time to sort out his army, and his mass charge was poorly co-ordinated. (d) I cannot place individual units in the way that Verbruggen suggests.

# Bibliography

## Primary sources

Abbon. *Siège de Paris par les Normands*, H. Waquet (ed.) (Paris: Les Belles Lettres, 1942).
Abu Shama. *Le livre des Deux Jardins*, RHC Or. 4.
Adhémar de Chabannes. *Chronique*, J. Chavanon (ed.) (Paris: A. Picard, 1897).
Aegidii Romani. *De Regimine Principum* (Rome, 1561).
Aegidius Monachus Aureaevallis. *Gesta episcoporum Leodiensium*, MGH SS 25.
Aelred. *Relatio venerabilis Aelredi, abbatis Rievallensis, de Standardo*, in Howlett, *Chronicles*, vol. 3.
Aimo. *Historia Francorum*, PL 139.
Ambroise. *The Third Crusade*, K. Fenwick (ed.) (London: Folio Society, 1958).
Andrew of Hungary. *Descriptio Victoriae a Karolo Reportatae*, MGH SS 26.
*Annales Bergomates*, MGH SS 18.
*Annales Coloniensis*, MGH SS 17.
*Annales Coloniensis Maximi*, MGH SS 17.
*Annales Cremonenses*, MHS SS 18.
*Annales Dunstaplia*, in *Annales Monastici*, H. R. Luard (ed.), [5 vols] (London: RS, 1886).
*Annales Egmundani*, MGH SS 18.
*Annales Ianuenses*, MGH 18.
*Annales Laubienses*, MGH SS 4.
*Annales Marbacenses*, MGH SS 17.
*Annales Mediolanses*, MGH SS 18.
*Annales Mettensis*, MGH SS 1.
*Annales Osterhovenses 754–1433*, MGH SS 17.
*Annales Parmenses*, MGH 18.
*Annales Pisani 1004–1175*, MGH SS 19.
*Annales Placentini Gibellini*, MGH SS 18.
*Annales Sancti Disibodi*, MGH SS 17.
*Annales Sancti Iustinae Patavini*, MGH SS 19.
*Annales Veronenses*, MGH SS 19.
Baha ad-Din in Gabrieli. *Arab historians of the Crusades*.
Baldric of Dol. *Historia Jerosolimitana*, RHC Oc. 4.
Baronius, C. & O. Raynaldi (eds). *Annales ecclesiastici*, [15 vols] (Lucca, 1747–56).

Barrow, J. *English episcopal acta VII: Hereford 1079–1234* (Oxford: Oxford University Press, 1993).

Beha ed-Din. *Anecdotes et beaux traits de la vie du Sultan Youssof (Saladin)*, RHC Or. 3.

Behrends, F. (ed.). *Letters and poems of Fulbert of Chartres* (Oxford: Clarendon Press, 1976).

St Bernard. *Letters*, PL 182.

Berhard, W. *Vita Heinrici Imperatoris* (Hannover: MGH, 1899).

Berthold of Reichenau. *Chronicon*, MGH SS 5.

Bonazzi, G. (ed.). *Chronicon Parmense* (Citta di Castello: RIS, 1902).

Boretius, A. (ed.). *Capitularia Regum Francorum*, [2 vols] (Hanover: MGH, 1883–97).

Boso. *Life of Alexander III*, G. M. Ellis & P. Munz (eds) (Oxford: Blackwell, 1973).

Brundage, J. (ed.). *The Crusades: a documentary survey* (Milwaukee: Marquette University Press, 1962).

Caffaro. *De liberatione ciuitatum orientis*, RHC Oc. 5.

*Carmen de Bello Saxonico*, MGH SS 15.

Certain, E. D. (ed.). *Miracula Sancti Benedicti* (Paris: Renouard, 1850).

Chaplais, P. (ed.). *Diplomatic documents preserved in the Public Record Office 1. (1101–1272)* (London: HMSO, 1964).

*Chronica Regia Colonniensis*, MGH SS 17.

*Chronicon Cremonense*, MGH SS 18.

*Chronicon Estense*, in Muratori 15-3 (Milan: RIS, 1723).

*Chronicon Hanoniense*, MGH SS 25.

*Chronicon Sancti Martini Turonensis*, MGH SS 26.

Clay, C. T. (ed.). *Early Yorkshire charters. The honour of Richmond* (Wakefield: Yorkshire Archaeological Society, 1936).

*Continuatio Sanblasiana*, MGH SS 20.

*De Expugnatione Terrae Sanctae*. In Brundage, J. A., *The Crusades: a documentary survey* (Milwaukee: Marquette University Press, 1962).

Douglas, D. C. & G. W. Greenaway (eds). *English historical documents*, [12 vols] (London: Eyre & Spottiswoode, 1953–77).

Duparc-Quioc, S. (ed.). *La Chanson d'Antioche*, [2 vols] (Paris: P. Geuthner, 1977–8).

Eadmer. *Vita Sancti Anselmi*, R. W. Southern (ed.) (London: Nelson, 1962).

Eberhard, W. (ed.). *Vita Heinrici IV imperatoris* (Hannover: MGH, 1899).

Edbury, P. W. (ed.). The Old French Continuation of William of Tyre. In *The conquest of Jerusalem and the Third Crusade* (Aldershot: Scolar Press, 1996).

*L'Estoire de Eracles empereur*, RHC Oc. 2.

Edwards, E. (ed.). *Liber Monasterii de Hyda* (London: RS, 1886).

Evans, D. S. (ed.). *A medieval Prince of Wales: the life of Gruffudd ap Cynan* (Llanerch: Llanerch Enterprises, 1990).

Flodoard. *Annales*, PL 135.

"Florence" of Worcester. *Chronicon ex Chronicis*, B. Thorpe (ed.), [2 vols] (London: Sumptibus Societatis, 1848–9).

Fulcher of Chartres. *A history of the expedition to Jerusalem*, F. R. Ryan & H. S. Fink (eds) (Knoxville: University of Tennessee Press, 1969).

Fulk Réchin. *Fragmentum Historiae Andegavensis, auctore Fulcone Rechin*. In Halphen, *Chroniques*.

Galbert of Bruges. *The Murder of Charles the Good*, J. B. Ross (ed.) (Toronto: Toronto University Press, 1993).

Gaufredus Malaterra. *De rebus gestis Rogerii Calabriae et Siciliae comitis et Roberti Guiscardi ducis fratris eius*, E. Pontieri (ed.) (Bologna: RIS, 1928), Chapter 4, n16.

*Genealogiae comitum Flandriae*, MGH SS 9.

Gerald of Wales. *Expugnatio Hibernica*, A. B. Scott & F. X. Martin (eds) (Dublin: Royal Irish Academy, 1978).

Gerald of Wales. *The journey through Wales and the description of Wales*, L. Thorpe (ed.) (Harmondsworth: Penguin, 1978).

Gervase of Canterbury. *Historical works of Gervase of Canterbury*, W. Stubbs (ed.), [2 vols] (London: RS, 1879–80).

Godfrey of Viterbo. *Pantheon*, MGH SS 22.

Gratian. *Decretum*, A. Friedberg (ed.) (Leipzig: MGH, 1879).

Greenway, D. (ed.). *Charters of the honours of Mowbray 1107–91* (Oxford: Oxford University Press, 1972).

Guibert of Nogent. *Gesta Dei per Francos*, RHC Oc. 4.

Guiot de Provins. *Les Oeuvres*, J. Orr (ed.) (Manchester: Presses de l'Université de Manchester, 1915).

Hackett, W. M. (ed.). *Girart de Roussillon, Chanson de Geste*, [3 vols] (Paris: A. & J. Picard, 1953–5).

Hagenmeyer, H. (ed.). *Kreuzzugsbriefe aus den Jahren 1088–1100* (Innsbruck: Olms, 1902).

Hahnloser, H. R. *Villard de Honnecourt* (Graz: Akademie Druck- und Verlagsanst, 1972).

Hefele, C. J. & H. LeClercq (eds). *Histoire des Conciles*, [9 vols] (Paris: A. Le Clare, 1912).

Helmold. *Chronica Slavorum*, MGH SS 21.

Henry of Huntingdon. *Historia Anglorum*, D. Greenway (ed.) (Oxford: Clarendon Press, 1996). Henry of Huntingdon.

Holder-Egger, O. (ed.). *Gesta Federici Imperatoris in Lombardia: Annales Mediolanenses Maiores* (Hannover: MGH, 1892). *Annales Mediolanenses Maiores*.

Hugo Farsitus. *De Miraculis B. Mariae Suessionensis*, PL 179.

Ibn al-Athir. *Kamel Altevarykh*, RHC Or. 1. Partially translated as *The collection of histories*. In Gabrieli, *Arab historians of the Crusades*.

Ibn al-Qalanisi. *Damascus chronicle of the Crusades*, H. A. R. Gibb (ed.) (London: Luzac, 1932).

Imad ad-Din. In Gabrieli, *Arab historians of the Crusades*, pp. 138–9.

Iohannes Codagnellus. *Annales Placentini*, O. Holder-Egger (ed.) (Hannover: MGH, 1901).

*Itinerarium regis Richardi*. In Stubbs, *Chronicles*, vol. 1.

Jacques de Vitry. *Historia Orientalis seu Hierosolymitana*. In *Gesta Dei per Francos*, J. Bongars (ed.) (Hannover, 1611).

James I. *Chronicle of James I king of Aragon*, J. Forster (ed.) (Farnborough: Gregg, 1968).

Jan Van Heelu. *Rijmkronijk*, J. F. Willems (ed.) (Brussels, 1836).

John of Salisbury. *The Policraticus*, C. J. Nederman (ed.) (Cambridge: Cambridge University Press, 1990).

Joinville. *Life of St Louis*, M. R. B. Shaw (ed.) (Harmondsworth: Penguin, 1970).

Jones, T. (ed.). *Brenhinedd y Saesson or Kings of the Saxons* (Cardiff: University of Wales Press, 1971).

Jones, T. (ed.). *Brut y Tywysogon or The chronicle of the Princes. Peniarth Ms. 20 version* (Cardiff: University of Wales Press, 1952).

Jones, T. (ed.). *Brut y Tywysogon or The chronicle of the Princes. Red Book of Hergest version* (Cardiff: University of Wales Press, 1955).

Jordan Fantosme. *Chronicle*, R. C. Johnston (ed.) (Oxford: Clarendon Press, 1981).

Justinian. *Leges Selectae*, PL 72.

Kemal ed-Din. *La Chronique d'Alep*, RHC Or. 3.

Lambert of Hersfeld. *Annales*, MGH SS 3.

Liudprand of Cremona. *Relatio de Legatione Constantinopolitana*, B. Scott (ed.) (London: Bristol Classical Press, 1992).

Marianus Scotus. *Chronicon*, PL 147.

Marino Sanudo. *Liber secretorum fidelium crucis*. In *Orientalis historiae*, [2 vols] (Hannover, 1611).

Martène, E. & U. Durand (eds). *Veterum scriptores et monumentorum collectio*, [9 vols] (Paris, 1724–33).

Matthew of Edessa. *The chronicle of Matthew of Edessa*, A. E. Dosourian (ed.) (New York: University Press of America, 1993).

Matthew Paris. *Chronica Majora*, H. R. Luard (ed.), [3 vols] (London: RS, 1876).

Matthew Paris. *Flores Historiarum*, H. R. Luard (ed.), [3 vols] (London: RS, 1890).

Meyer, P. (ed.). *Histoire de Guillaume le Maréchal*, [3 vols] (Paris: Société de l'Histoire de France, 1891–1901).

Mittarelli, J. B. (ed.). *Chronicon Tolosanus* (Venice, 1771).

Nelson, J. L. (ed.). *Annals of St-Bertin* (Manchester: Manchester University Press, 1991).

Nicholas, N. H. (ed.). *The siege of Carlaverock* (London: J. B. Nicols, 1828).

*Notitiae Duae Lemovicensis de praedicatione crucis in Aquitania*, RHC Oc. 5.

Odo of Deuil. *De profectione Ludovici in Orientem*, V. G. Berry (ed.) (New York: Columbia University Press, 1948).

Osbern. *De expugnatione Lyxbonensi*, in Stubbs, *Chronicles*.

Otto & Acerbus Morena. *Historia*, F. Güterbock (ed.) (Berlin: MGH, 1930).

Otto of Friesing and Rahewin. *The deeds of Frederick Barbarossa*, C. C. Mierow & R. Emery (eds) (Columbia: Columbia University Press, 1953).

Palgrave, F. *Parliamentary writs*, [2 vols] (London: Record Commissioners, 1827–34).

Paoli, C. (ed.). *Il Libro di Montaperti* (Florence: G. P. Vieisseux, 1889).

Peter Cantor. *Verbum Abbreviatum*, PL 205.

Philippe de Navarre & Gerard de Monreal. *Gestes des Chiprois*, G. Raynaud (ed.) (Geneva: J. G. Fick, 1887).

Piero della Vigna. *Petri de Vineis Judicis Cancellarii Friderici II Imperatoris epistolarum*, J. R. Iselius (ed.), [2 vols] (Basle, 1740).

Peter de Vaux-de-Cernay. *Historia Albigensis*, P. Guébin & H. Maisonneuve (eds) (Paris: Librarie Philosophique J. Vrin, 1951).

Porri, G. (ed.). *Miscellanea Storica Sanese* (Sienna, 1844).

Potter, K. R. (ed.). *Gesta Stephani* (Oxford: Clarendon Press, 1976).

Primatus (or Jean de Vignay). *Ex Primati Chronicis per J. de Vignay translatis*, RHGF 20.

Rabanus Maurus. *De procinctu Romanae miliciae*, E. Dümmler (ed.), *Zeitschrift für Deutsches Altertum* **15**, 1872, pp. 443–51.

Ralph of Caen. *Gesta Tancredi*, RHC Oc. 3.

Ralph of Coggeshall. *Chronicon Anglicanum*, J. Stevenson (ed.) (London: Seeleys, 1875).

Ralph of Diceto. *De Regibus Anglorum*, in *Opera historica*, W. Stubbs (ed.), [2 vols] (London: RS, 1876).

Richard of Devizes. *Chronicon de rebus gestis Ricardi primi*, J. Stevenson (ed.), [4 vols] (London: RS, 1838).

Richer of Rheims. *Histoire de France 888–995*, R. Latouche (ed.), [2 vols] (Paris: Les Belles Lettres, 1937).

Ricordanus Malaspina. *Historia Florentina* (Milan: RIS, 1926), vol. 8.

Robert of Clari. *The conquest of Constantinople*, E. H. McNeal (ed.) (New York: Columbia University Press, 1936).

Robert of Rheims. *Historia Iherosolimitana*, RHC Oc. 3.

Robert of Torigni. *Chronica*. In Howlett, *Chronicles*, vol. 4.

Roger of Hovenden. *Chronica Magistri Rogeris de Hovenden*, W. Stubbs (ed.), [4 vols] (London: RS, 1871).

Roger of Wendover. *Flores Historiarum*, H. J. Hewlett (ed.), [3 vols] (London: RS, 1886–9).

*Henry II, Rotuli de Dominabus et pueris et puellis de XII comitatibus, an. 1185*, vol. 35 (London: Pipe Roll Society, 1913).

Rolandini Patavini. *Chronica*, MGH SS 19.

Romoald of Salerno. *Annales*, MGH SS 19.

Saba Malaspina. *Rerum Sicularum Historia* (Milan: RIS, 1726), vol. 8.

Sayers, D. (ed.). *Song of Roland* (Harmondsworth: Penguin, 1960).

Scholz, B. W. (ed.). *Carolingian Chronicles: the Royal Frankish Annals and Nithard's Histories* (Michigan: Ann Arbor, 1972).

Salimbene de Adam. *Chronicon*, G. Scalia (ed.), [2 vols] (Bari: G. Laterza, 1966).

Schmale, F. J. & I. Schmale-Otto (eds), *Frutolfs und Ekkehards Chroniken und die Anonyme Kaiserchronik* (Darmstadt: Wissenschaft Buchgesellschaft, 1972).

Sigebert of Gembloux. *Continuatio Aquicinctina*, MGH SS 6.

Somerville, R. (ed.). *Decreta Claromontensia*, in *The councils of Urban II* (Amsterdam: Hakkert, 1972).

Stevenson, J. (ed.). *Chronicon de Lanercost* (Edinburgh, 1839).

Stubbs, W. (ed.). *Select charters and other illustrations of English constitutional history*, revised H. W. C. Davis (Oxford: Clarendon Press, 1913).

Suger of St Denis. *Vita Ludovici Grossi Regis*, H. Waquet (ed.) (Paris: H. Champion, 1929). This edition is now available in an English translation: *Deeds of Louis the Fat*, tr. R. Cusimano & J. Moorhead (Washington: Catholic University of America Press, 1992).

Symeon of Durham. *Historia Regum*, T. Arnold (ed.), [2 vols] (London: RS, 1882–5).

Theophilus. *De diversis artibus*, C. R. Dodwell (ed.) (London: Nelson, 1961).

*Triumphus Sancti Lamberti*, MGH SS 20.

Upton-Ward, J. M. (ed.). *The Rule of the Templars* (Woodbridge: Boydell & Brewer, 1992).

Vegetius, F. R. *Epitome of military science*, N. P. Milner (ed.) (Liverpool: Liverpool University Press, 1993).

Viard, J. & E. Déprez (eds). *Chronique de Jean le Bel* (Paris: Champion, 1904), p. 156.

Villani, G. *Cronica*, G. Aquilecchia (ed.) (Turin: Giulio Einaudi, 1968).

Vincent of Prague. *Chronicon*, MGH SS 17.

Wace. *Roman de Rou et des Ducs de Normandie*, H. Andresen (ed.), [2 vols] (Bonn: Henninger, 1877–9).

Wakefield, W. L. & A. P. Evans (eds). *Heresies of the High Middle Ages* (New York: Colombia University Press, 1969).

Walter the Chancellor. *Bella Antiochena*, RHC 5.

Walter of Coventry. *Memoriale Fratris*, W. Stubbs (ed.), [2 vols] (London: RS, 1973).

Walter Map. *De nugis curialium*, M. R. James (ed.), revised C. N. L. Brooke & R. A. B. Mynors (Oxford: Clarendon Press, 1983).

Whitelock, D. (ed.). *The Anglo-Saxon Chronicle* (London: Eyre and Spottiswoode, 1961).

Widukind. *Rerum Gestarum Saxonicarum libri tres*, G. Waitz (ed.) (Hannover: MGH, 1882).

William of Apulia. *La Geste de Robert Guiscard*, M. Mathieu (ed.) (Palermo: Istituto Siciliano di Studi Byzantini e Neoellenici, 1961).

William of Jumièges. *Gesta Normannorum Ducum*, J. Marx (ed.) (Rouen: Société de l'Histoire de Normandie, 1914).

William of Malmesbury. *Gesta regum Anglorum*, T. D. Hardy (ed.), [2 vols] (London: English Historical Society, 1840).

William of Malmesbury. *Historia Novella*, K. R. Potter (ed.) (Edinburgh, 1955).

William of Nangis. *Gesta Philippi Tertii*, RHGF 20.

William of Newburgh. *Historia Rerum Anglicarum*, in Howlett, *Chronicles*, vol. 2.

William of Poitiers. *Gesta Guillelmi ducis Normannorum et regis Anglorum*, R. Foreville (ed.) (Paris: Les Belles Lettres, 1952).

William of Rishanger. *Chronica*, H. R. Riley (ed.) (London: RS, 1865).

William of Tudela & the Anonymous. *La Chanson de la Croisade Albigeoise*, E. Martin-Chabot (ed.), [3 vols] (Paris, 1931–61).

William of Tudela & the Anonymous. *Song of the Cathar Wars*, tr. J. Shirley (Aldershot: Scolar Press, 1996).

## Secondary works

Abels, R. P. *Lordship and military obligation in Anglo-Saxon England* (London: British Museum Publications, 1988).

Amitai-Preiss, R. The Mamluk officer class during the reign of Sultan Baybars. In *War and society in the eastern Mediterranean, 7th–15th centuries*, Y. Lev (ed.) (Leiden: Brill, 1996), pp. 225–36.

Anderson, W. *Castles of Europe* (London: Elek, 1980).

Andressohn, J. C. *Ancestry and life of Godfrey de Bouillon* (Bloomington: University of Indiana, 1947).

Angold, M. *The Byzantine Empire 1025–1204* (London: Longman, 1984).

Arnold, B. *German knighthood 1050–1300* (Oxford: Oxford University Press, 1985).

Arnold, B. *Princes and territories in medieval Germany* (Cambridge: Cambridge University Press, 1991).

Arnold, B. *Medieval Germany 500–1500: a political interpretation* (London: Macmillan, 1997).

Asbridge, T. S. The significance and causes of the battle of the Field of Blood. *Journal of Medieval History* 23, pp. 301–16, 1997.

Aubenas, R. Les châteaux forts des IXᵉ et XIIᵉ siècles. *Revue de l'Histoire du Droit Français et Étranger* 17, pp. 548–86, 1938.

Audouin, E. *Essai sur l'armée royale au temps de Philippe Auguste* (Paris: Champion, 1913).

Avent, R. *Cestyll tywysogion/Castles of the princes of Gwynedd* (Cardiff: HMSO, 1983).

Avent, R. Castles of the Welsh princes. *Château Gaillard* 16, 1992, pp. 11–21.

Ayalon, D. Studies on the structure of the Mamluk army – III. *Bulletin of the School of African and Oriental Studies* 16, pp. 57–90, 1954.

Ayalon, D. From Ayyubids to Mamluks. *Revue des Etudes Islamiques* 49, pp. 50–9, 1981.

Bachrach, B. S. The feigned retreat at Hastings. *Medieval Studies* 33, pp. 344–7, 1971.

Bachrach, B. S. Early medieval fortifications in the west of France: a revised technical vocabulary. *Technology and Culture* 16, pp. 531–69, 1975.

Bachrach, B. S. A study in feudal politics: relations between Fulk Nerra and William the Great 995–1030. *Viator* 7, pp. 111–22, 1976.

Bachrach, B. S. Fortifications and military tactics: Fulk Nerra's strongholds *ca.* 1000. *Technology and Culture* 20, pp. 531–49, 1979.

Bachrach, B. S. The Angevin strategy of castle building in the reign of Fulk Nerra, 987–1040. *American Historical Review* **88**, pp. 533–60, 1983.

Bachrach, B. S. The cost of castle building: the case of the tower at Langeais, 992–92. In *The medieval castle: romance and reality*, K. Reyerson & F. Powe (eds) (Dubuque: Kendall-Hunt, 1984), pp. 47–62.

Bachrach, B. S. Some observations on the military administration of the Norman Conquest. *Battle* **8**, pp. 1–26, 1985.

Bachrach, B. S. The *milites* and the millennium. *The Haskins Society Journal* **6**, pp. 85–96, 1994.

Baker, D. (ed.). *Religious motivation: biographical and sociological problems for the church historian* (Oxford: Oxford University Press, 1978).

Balard, M. (ed.). *Autour de la Première Croisade* (Paris: Publications de la Sorbonne, 1996).

Baldwin, J. W. La décennie décisive: les années 1190–1203 dans le règne de Philippe Auguste. *Revue Historique* **256**, pp. 311–37, 1981.

Baldwin, J. W. *The government of Philip Augustus: foundations of French royal power in the Middle Ages* (Berkeley: University of California Press, 1986).

Baldwin, J. W. & M. Nortier. Contributions à l'étude des finances de Philippe Auguste. *Bibliothèque de l'Ecole des Chartes* **138**, pp. 5–33, 1980.

Baldwin, M. W. *Raymond III of Tripolis and the fall of Jerusalem 1140–87* (Amsterdam: Hakkert, 1969).

Baldwin, M. W. The Latin states under Baldwin III and Amalric I. In Setton, *Crusades*, vol. 1, pp. 528–62.

Barber, M. *The two cities: medieval Europe 1050–1320* (London: Routledge, 1992).

Barber, M. Supplying the crusader states: the role of the Templars. In *The Horns of Hattin*, B. Z. Kedar (ed.) (London: Variorum, 1992), pp. 314–26.

Barber, M. *The military orders. Fighting for the faith and caring for the sick* (Aldershot: Variorum, 1994).

Barber, M. *The new knighthood: a history of the Order of the Temple* (Cambridge: Cambridge University Press, 1994).

Barber, M. Frontier warfare in the Latin Kingdom of Jerusalem: the campaign of Jacob's Ford, 1178–9. In *The Crusades and their sources: essays presented to Bernard Hamilton*, J. France & W. G. Zajac (eds) (Aldershot: Variorum, 1998), pp. 9–22.

Barber, R. *The reign of chivalry* (Newton Abbot: David & Charles, 1980).

Barker, P. A. Hen Domen. In *Five castle excavations*, A. D. Saunders (ed.) (London: Royal Archaeological Institute, 1978), pp. 101–4.

Barlow, F. *The feudal kingdom of England 1042–1216* (London: Longman, 1961).

Barlow, F. *William Rufus* (London: Methuen, 1983).

Barraclough, G. *The origins of modern Germany* (Oxford: Blackwell, 1957).

Barrow, G. W. S. *Robert Bruce and the community of the realm of Scotland* (London: Eyre & Spottiswoode, 1965).

Barrow, G. W. S. *The kingdom of Scotland: government, church and society from the 11th to 14th centuries* (London: Edward Arnold, 1973).

Barrow, G. W. S. *Kingship and unity: Scotland 1000–1306* (Edinburgh: Edward Arnold, 1981).

Barrow, G. W. S. The army of Alexander III's Scotland. In *Scotland under the reign of Alexander III*, N. H. Reid (ed.) (Edinburgh: John Donald, 1990), pp. 132–48.

Barrow, G. W. S. David I of Scotland: the balance of new and old. In *Scotland and its neighbours in the Middle Ages* (London: Hambledon, 1992), pp. 45–66.

Bartlett, R. Colonial aristocracies of the High Middle Ages. In *Medieval frontier societies*, R. Bartlett & A. MacKay (eds) (Oxford: Clarendon Press, 1989), pp. 23–48.

Bartlett, R. *The making of Europe. Conquest, colonization and cultural change 950–1350* (London: Allen Lane, 1993).

Bartlett, R. & A. MacKay (eds). *Medieval Frontier Societies* (Oxford: Clarendon Press, 1989).

Basset, S. (ed.). *The origins of the Anglo-Saxon kingdoms* (Leicester: Leicester University Press, 1989).

Bates, D. *Normandy before 1066* (London: Longman, 1982).

Bates, D. *William the Conqueror* (London: Philip, 1989).

Bautier, A. M. Les plus anciennes mentions de moulins hydrauliques industriels et de moulins à vent. *Bulletin Philologique et Historique du Comité des Travaux Historiques et Scientifiques*, (1960), pp. 567–626.

Bautier, R. H. Notes sur le commerce du fer en Europe occidentale du XIII au XVI siècle. *Revue d'Histoire de la Sidérugie*, **1**, pp. 7–35, 1960; **4**, pp. 35–61, 1963.

Bautier, R. H. (ed.). *La France de Philippe Auguste: le temps des mutations* (Paris: CNRS, 1982).

Bazeley, M. L. The Forest of Dean in its relations with the crown during the twelfth and thirteenth centuries. *Transactions of the Bristol and Gloucester Archaeological Society* **33**, pp. 3–19, 1910.

Beckingham, C. F. & B. Hamilton (eds). *Prester John, the Mongols and the ten lost tribes* (Aldershot: Variorum, 1996).

Beech, G. T. *A rural society in Medieval France: the Gâtime of Poitou in the eleventh and twelfth centuries* (Baltimore: Johns Hopkins Press, 1964).

Bennett, M. Wace and warfare. *Battle* **11**, pp. 37–58, 1988.

Bennett, M. La Règle du Temple as a military manual, or How to deliver a cavalry charge. In *Studies in medieval history presented to R. Allen-Brown*, C. Harper-Bill, J. Holdsworth, J. Nelson (eds) (Woodbridge: Boydell & Brewer, 1989), pp. 7–20.

Bennett, M. The myth of the military supremacy of knightly cavalry. In *Armies, Chivalry and Warfare. Proceedings of the 1995 Harlaxton Symposium*, M. J. Strickland (ed.) (Stamford: Paul Watkins, forthcoming).

Belenguer, E. *Jaume I a través de la Historia*, [2 vols] (Valencia: Eliseu Climent, 1984).

Benvenisti, M. *The crusaders in the Holy Land* (Jerusalem: Israeli Universities Press, 1970).

Beresford, G. *Goltho: the development of an early medieval manor c. 850–1150* (London: English Heritage, 1987).

Berry, V. G. The Second Crusade. In Setton, *Crusades*, vol. 1, pp. 463–512.

Bisson, T. N. Les domaines au temps de Philippe Auguste. In *La France de Philippe Auguste: le temps des mutations*, R. H. Bautier (ed.) (Paris: CNRS, 1982), pp. 521–38.

Bisson, T. N. The organised peace in southern France and·Catalonia 1140–*ca.* 1233. *American Historical Review* **82**, pp. 290–311, 1977.

Blair, C. *European armour c. 1066–c. 1700* (London, B. T. Batsfield, 1958).

Blok, D. P. et al. (eds). *Miscellanea medievalia: in memoriam J. F. Niermeyer*, (Gronigen: J. B. Wolters, 1967).

Bouard, M. de. De l'aula au donjon: les fouilles de la motte de la Chapelle à Doué la Fontaine. *Archéologie Médiévale* 3–4, pp. 1–110, 1973–4.

Boussard, J. Les mercenaires au xii⁰ siècle. Henri II Plantagenet et les origines de l'armée de métier. *Bibliothèque de l'Ecole des Chartes* **106**, pp. 189–224, 1945–6.

Boussard, J. L'éviction des tenants de Thibault de Blois par Geoffroi Martel en 1044. *Le Moyen Age* **69**, pp. 145–7, 1963.

Boussard, J. Services féodaux, milices et mercenaires aux X et XI siècles. *Ordinamenti militari in Occidenti nell'Alto Medioevo: Settimane di Studio del Centro Italiano di Studi sull'Alto Medioevo XV, Spoleto 30 March–5 April 1967* (Spoleto: C. I. S. A., 1968), pp. 131–68.

Bowlus,C. R. Tactical and strategic weaknesses of horse archers on the eve of the First Crusade. In *Autour de la Première Croisade*, M. Balard (ed.) (Paris: Publications de la Sorbonne, 1996), pp. 159–66.

Bradbury, J. Greek Fire in the West. *History* (1979), pp. 326–1.

Bradbury, J. Battles in England and Normandy 1066–1154. *Battle* **6**, pp. 1–12, 1983.

Bradbury, J. *The medieval archer* (Woodbridge: Boydell & Brewer, 1985).

Bradbury, J. *The medieval siege* (Woodbridge: Boydell & Brewer, 1992).

Bradbury, J. *Stephen and Mathilda: the civil war of 1139–53* (Stroud: Sutton, 1996).

Bradbury, J. *The Battle of Hastings* (Stroud: Sutton, 1998).

Brogi, T. *La Marsica Antica e Medievale*, [2 vols] (Avezzano: Adelmo Pollo, 1981).

Brooke, C. N. L. The structure of medieval society. In *The flowering of the Middle Ages*, J. Evans (ed.) (London: Thames & Hudson, 1966), pp. 12–40.

Brooks, N. Medieval bridges: a window into the changing concept of state power. *The Haskins Society Journal* **7**, pp. 11–29, 1995.

Brown, R. A. *Dover Castle* (London: HMSO, 1967).

Brown, R. A. *The Normans and the Norman Conquest* (London: Constable, 1969).

Brown, R. A. *English castles* (London: Batsford, 1976).

Brown, R. A. The Battle of Hastings. *Battle* **3**, pp. 1–21, 1980.

Brown, S. D. B. The mercenary and his master: military service and monetary reward in the eleventh and twelfth century. *History* **74**, pp. 20–38, 1989.

Brundage, J. *Medieval canon law and the crusader* (Wisconsin: University of Wisconsin Press, 1969).

Bull, M. *Knightly piety and the lay response to the First Crusade* (Oxford: Clarendon Press, 1993).

Bur, M. *La formation du Comté de Champagne v. 950–v. 1150* (Nancy: Université de Nancy II, 1977).

Burgess, E. M. Further research into the construction of mail garments. *Antiquaries Journal* **33**, pp. 194–203, 1953.

Burns, J. H. (ed.). *Medieval political thought* (Cambridge: Cambridge University Press, 1988).

Burns, R. *Monuments of Syria* (London: I. B. Tauris, 1992).

Caenegem, R. van. Government, law and society. In *Medieval political thought*, J. H. Burns (ed.) (Cambridge: Cambridge University Press, 1988).

Cantelmi, A. *Tagliacozzo* (Avezzano: Ferreti-Pescara, 1975).

Caple, C. *An interim guide to Dryslwyn Castle and its excavation* (University of Durham Department of Archaeology: www.dur.ac.uk/Archaeology/Staff/CC/Guide.html, 1998).

Caproni, R. *La Battaglia di Cortenova* (Cortenova: Cassa Rurale ed Artigiana di Covo, 1987).

Carpenter, D. A. Simon de Montfort and the Mise of Lewes. *Bulletin of the Institute of Historical Research* **58**, pp. 1–11, 1985.

Carpenter, D. A. *The battles of Lewes and Evesham 1264/65* (Keele: Mercia Publications, 1987).

Carpenter, D. A. *The minority of Henry III* (London: Methuen, 1990).

Cate, J. L. The crusade of 1101. In Setton, *Crusades*, vol. 1, pp. 343–67.

Cathcart-King, D. J. Henry II and the fight at Coleshill. *Welsh History Review* **2**, pp. 367–73, 1964–5.

Cathcart-King, D. J. The trebuchet and other siege-engines. *Château Gaillard* **9/10**, pp. 456–70, 1982.

Chalandon, F. *Histoire de la domination Normande en Italie et Sicile*, [2 vols] (New York: Burt Franklin, 1969).

Charles-Edwards, T. Early medieval kingship in the British Isles. In *The origins of the Anglo-Saxon Kingdoms*, S. Basset (ed.) (Leicester: Leicester University Press, 1989), pp. 28–39.

Chatelain, A. Recherche sur les châteaux de Philippe Auguste. *Archéologie Médiévale* **21**, pp. 115–61, 1991.

Chevedden, P. E., L. Eigenbrod, V. Foley, W. Soedel. The trebuchet. *Scientific American* **272**, pp. 58–63, 1995.

Chibnall, M. Mercenaries and the *Familia Regis* under Henry I. *History* **62**, pp. 15–23, 1977.

Chibnall, M. *Anglo-Norman England* (Oxford: Blackwell, 1986).

Chibnall, M. *The Empress Mathilda: Queen Consort, Queen Mother and Lady of the English* (Oxford: Blackwell, 1991).

Christiansen, E. *The northern Crusades: the Baltic and the Catholic frontier 1100–1525* (London: Macmillan, 1980).

Cirlot, V. Techniques guerrières en Catalogne féodale; le maniement de la lance. *Cahiers de Civilisation Médiévale* **28**, pp. 36–43, 1985.

Cleve, T. C. van. *The Emperor Frederick II of Hohenstaufen, Iimmutator Mundi* (Oxford: Clarendon Press, 1972).

Cohn, N. *The pursuit of the millennium* (London: Secker & Warburg, 1957).

Constable, G. The Second Crusade as seen by contemporaries. *Traditio* **9**, pp. 213–79, 1953.

Contamine, P. *Guerre, état et société à la fin du moyen age. Etudes sur les armées des rois de France 1337–1494* (Paris: Mouton, 1972).

Corfis, I. A. & M. Wolfe (eds). *The medieval city under siege* (Woodbridge: Boydell & Brewer, 1995).

Coss, P. Knights, esquires and the origins of social gradation in England. *Transactions of the Royal Historical Society* **5**, pp. 155–78, 1995.

Coss, P. *The knight in medieval England* (Stroud: Sutton, 1993).

Coulson, C. Hierarchism in conventual crenellation: an essay in the sociology and metaphysics of medieval fortification. *Medieval Archaeology* **26**, pp. 69–100, 1982.

Coulson, C. Fortress policy in Capetian tradition and Angevin practice; aspects of the conquest of Normandy by Philip II. *Battle* **6**, pp. 13–38, 1984.

Coulson, C. Cultural realities and reappraisals in English castle-study. *Journal of Medieval History* **22**, pp. 171–207, 1996.

Cowdrey, H. E. J. Bishop Ermenfrid of Sion and the Penitential Ordinance following the battle of Hastings. *Journal of Ecclesiastical History* **20**, pp. 225–42, 1969.

Cowdrey, H. E. J. The Peace and Truce of God in the eleventh century. *Past and Present* **46**, pp. 42–67, 1970.

Cowdrey, H. E. J. Pope Urban's preaching of the First Crusade. *History* **55**, pp. 177–88, 1970.

Cowdrey, H. E. J. The Mahdia campaign of 1087. *English Historical Review* **92**, pp. 1–29, 1977.

Cox, D. C. *The Battle of Evesham: a new account* (Evesham: Vale of Evesham Historical Society, 1988).

Crouch, D. *The Beaumont twins: the roots and branches of power in the twelfth century* (Cambridge: Cambridge University Press, 1986).

Crouch, D. *William Marshal. Court, career and chivalry in the Angevin Empire* (London: Longman, 1990).

Crouch, D. *Images of aristocracy. Britain 1000–1300* (London: Routledge, 1992).

Crozet, R. Le voyage d'Urbain II et ses arrangements avec le clergé de France. *Revue Historique* **179**, pp. 270–310, 1937.

Daniel, N. *Islam and the West: the making of an image* (Edinburgh: Edinburgh University Press, 1960).

David, C. W. *Robert Curthose, Duke of Normandy* (Cambridge, Mass.: Harvard University Press, 1920).

Davidsohn, R. *Forschungen zur älteren Geschichte von Florenz*, [4 vols] (Berlin: E. S. Mittler, 1896–1908).

Davies, R. R. *The age of conquest: Wales 1063–1415* (Oxford: Oxford University Press, 1987).

Davies, S. *Anglo-Welsh warfare and the works of Gerald of Wales* (M. A. Dissertation, Department of History, University of Wales Swansea, 1995).

Davies, W. *Small worlds: the village community in early medieval Brittany* (London: Duckworth, 1988).

Davis, H. W. C. The battle of Tinchebrai. *English Historical Review* **24**, pp. 728–32, 1909; **25**, pp. 295–6, 1910.

Davis, R. H. C. Warhorses of the Normans. *Battle* **10**, pp. 67–82, 1987.

Davis, R. H. C. *The medieval warhorse* (London: Thames and Hudson, 1989).

Davis, R. H. C. *King Stephen 1135–54* (London: Longman, 1967).

Dearden, B. & A. Clark. Pont-l'Arche or Pîtres? A location and archaeomagnetic dating for Charles the Bald's fortifications on the Seine. *Antiquity* **64**, pp. 567–71, 1990.

Débord, A. *Castrum* et *castellum* chez Ademar de Chabannes. *Archéologie Médiévale* **9**, pp. 97–113, 1979.

Débord, A. Les fortifications de terre en Europe occidentale du X au XII siècles. *Archéologie Médiévale* **11**, pp. 5–123, 1981.

Delbrück, H. *Medieval warfare*, tr. W. J. Renfroe (Lincoln: University of Nebraska Press, 1982).

Denholm-Young, N. *Seignorial administration in England* (Oxford: Oxford University Press, 1937).

Deschamps, P. *Les châteaux des croisés en Terre Sainte* III. *Le défense du Comté de Tripoli et de la Principauté d'Antioche*, [2 vols] (Paris: P. Geuthner, 1973).

Deuve, J. *Les services secrets Normands* (Condé-sur-Noireau: C. Corlet, 1990).

Devries, K. *Medieval military technology* (Ontario: Broadview Press, 1992).

Devries, K. *Infantry warfare in the early fourteenth century* (Woodbridge: Boydell & Brewer, 1996).

Deyres, M. Le château de Montbazon au XI siècle. *Cahiers de Civilisation Médiévale* **12**, pp. 158–9, 1969.

Deyres, M. Le donjon de Langeais. *Bulletin Monumental* **132**, pp. 179–93, 1970.

Deyres, M. Les châteaux de Foulque Nerra. *Bulletin Monumental* **136**, pp. 7–28, 1974.

Dhondt, J. Note sur les châtelains de Flandre. In *Etudes historiques dédiées à la mémoire de M. Roger Rodière* (Calais, 1947), pp. 43–51.

Dhondt, J. *Etude sur la naissance des principautés territoriales en France (IX–X siècles)* (Bruges: De Tempel, 1948).

Dhondt, J. Une crise de pouvoir capétien 1032–4. In *Miscellanea Medievalia:* in memoriam *J. F. Niermeyer*, D. P. Blok et al. (eds) (Gronigen: J. B. Wolters, 1967), pp. 137–48.

Diament, H. Can toponomastics explain the origin of the crusader lexemes *Poulain* and *Turcopole*? *Journal of the American Name Society* **25**, pp. 183–204, 1977.

Dixon, P. & P. Marshall. The Great Tower at Hedingham Castle: a reassessment. *Fortress* **18**, pp. 16–23, 1993.

Douglas, D. C. *William the Conqueror: the Norman impact upon England* (London: Eyre & Spottiswoode, 1964).

Duby, G. *La société aux XIe et XIIe siècles dans la région mâconnaise* (Paris: S. E. V. P. E. N., 1971).

Duby, G. *The chivalrous society*, tr. C. Postan (London: Edward Arnold, 1977).

Duby, G. Youth in aristocratic society. In *The chivalrous society*, tr. C. Postan (London: Edward Arnold, 1977), pp. 112–22.

Duby, G. The transformation of the aristocracy: France at the beginning of the thirteenth century. In *The chivalrous society*, tr. C. Postan (London: Edward Arnold, 1977), pp. 178–85.

Duby, G. *The three orders: feudal society imagined*, tr. A. Goldhammer (Chicago: Chicago University Press, 1978).

Duby, G. Les transformations sociales dans le milieu aristocratique. In *La France de Philippe Auguste*, R. H. Bautier (ed.) (Paris: CNRS, 1982), pp. 711–16.

Duby, G. *The legend of Bouvines*, tr. C. Tihanyi (Cambridge: Polity Press, 1990).

Duby, G. *France in the Middle Ages, 987–1460*, tr. J. Vale (Oxford: Blackwell, 1991).

Dufourq, C. E. *L'Espagne Catalane et le Maghrib au XIII et XIV siècles* (Paris: Presses Universitaires de France, 1966).

Dunbabin, J. *France in the making, 843–1180* (Oxford: Oxford University Press, 1985).

Durham, B. Oxford's northern defences: archaeological studies 1971–82. *Oxoniensia* **48**, pp. 32–43, 1983.

Dussaud, R. *Topographie historique de la Syrie antique et médiévale* (Paris: P. Geuthner, 1927).

Dyer, C. *Standards of living in the later middle ages. Social change in England 1200–1520* (Cambridge: Cambridge University Press, 1989).

Edbury, P. Preaching the crusade in Wales. In *England and Germany in the High Middle Ages*, A. Haverkamp & H. Vollrath (eds) (Oxford: Oxford University Press, 1996), pp. 221–33.

Edbury, P. W. & J. G. Rowe. *William of Tyre, historian of the Latin East* (Cambridge: Cambridge University Press, 1988).

Eddé, A. M. Kurdes et Turcs dans l'armée ayyoubide de Syrie du Nord. In *War and society in the Eastern mediterranean, 7th–15th centuries* Y. Lev (ed.) (Leiden: Brill, 1996), pp. 267–300.

Edwards, J. G. The Battle of Maes Madog and the Welsh campaign of 1294–5. *English Historical Review* **39**, pp. 1–12, 1924; **46**, pp. 262–5, 1931.

Edwards, J. G. Henry II and the fight at Coleshill: some further reflections. *Welsh History Review* **3**, pp. 251–63, 1965–6.

Edwards, N. J. G. *Fortifications of Armenian Cilicia* (Washington: Dumbarton Oaks, 1992).

Ellenblum, R. Construction methods in Frankish rural settlements. In *The Horns of Hattin*, B. Z. Kedar (ed.) (London: Variorum, 1992), pp. 168–89.

Erdmann, C. *The origin of the idea of the crusade*, tr. M. W. Baldwin & W. Goffart (Princeton: Princeton University Press, 1977).

Evans, J. (ed.). *The flowering of the Middle Ages*, (London: Thames & Hudson, 1966).

Falmagne, J. *Baudouin V comte de Hainaut 1150–95* (Montréal: Les Presses de l'Université de Montréal, 1966).

Farmer, J. Prices and wages. In *The agrarian history of England and Wales*, vol. 2, J. Thirsk (ed.) (Cambridge: Cambridge University Press, 1988), pp. 716–817.

Fawtier, R. *The Capetian kings of France: monarchy and nation 987–1328*, tr. L. Butler (London: Macmillan, 1960).

Fedden, R. & J. Thomson, *Crusader castles* (London: John Murray, 1957).

Ffoulkes, C. *The craft of the armourer* (London: Constable, 1988).

Fink, H. S. Foundation of the Latin states. In Setton, *Crusades*, vol. 1, pp. 368–409.

Finó, J.-F. Notes sur la production de fer at la fabrication des armes en France au moyen âge. *Gladius* **3**, pp. 47–66, 1964.

Finó, J.-F. *Fortresses de la France médiévale* (Paris: A. & J. Picard, 1967).

Fischer, W. & J. Schneider (eds). *Das Heilige Land im Mittelalter: Begegnungsvraum zwischen Orient und Okzident* (Neustadt: Verlag Degener, 1982) .

Fisher, J. H. (ed.). *The medieval literature of western Europe* (New York: New York University Press, 1966).

Fixot, M. *Les fortifications de terre et les origines féodales dans le Cinglais* (Caen: Centre de Recherches Archéologiques Médiévales, 1968).

Flori, J. Sémantique et société médiévale: le verbe adouber et son évolution au XII siècle. *Annales ESC* **31**, pp. 915–40, 1976.

Flori, J. *L'idéologie du glaive: préhistoire de la chevalerie* (Geneva: Droz, 1983).

Flori, J. Chevalerie, noblesse et luttes de classes au Moyen age: à propos d'un ouvrage récent. *Le Moyen Age* **94**, pp. 262–6, 1988.

Flori, J. Encore l'usage de la lance: la technique du combat chevaleresque vers l'an 1000. *Cahiers de Civilisation Médiévale* **31**, pp. 213–40, 1988.

Folda, J. *Crusader manuscript illumination at St Jean d'Acre* (Princeton: Princeton University Press, 1976).

Foley, V., G. Palmer, W. Soedel. The crossbow. *Scientific American* (1985), pp. 104–110.

Forbes, R. J. Metallurgy. In *History of technology 2: The Mediterranean civilizations and the Middle Ages 700BC–AD1500*, C. Singer, E. J. Holmyard, A. R. Hill, T. I. Williams (eds) (Oxford: Clarendon Press, 1956), pp. 41–80.

Forey, A. J. The failure of the siege of Damascus in 1148. *Journal of Medieval History* **10**, pp. 13–23, 1984.

Forey, A. J. The military orders and the ransoming of captives from Islam. *Studia Monastica* **33**, pp. 259–66, 1991.

Forey, A. J. *The military orders. From the twelfth to the early fourteenth centuries* (Basingstoke: Macmillan, 1992).

Foster, S. M. *Some aspects of maritime activity and the use of sea power in relation to the crusading states* (DPhil thesis, University of Oxford, 1978).

Fournier, G. *Le château dans la France médiévale: essai de socologie monumentale* (Paris: A. & J. Picard, 1978) .

France, J. La guerre dans la France féodale à la fin du ix et au x siècle. *Revue Belge d'Histoire Militaire* **23**, pp. 177–98, 1979.

France, J. Anna Comnena, the Alexiad and the First Crusade. *Reading Medieval Studies* **10**, pp. 20–32, 1983.

France, J. The military history of the Carolingian period. *Revue Belge d'Histoire Militaire* **26**(2), pp. 81–99, 1985.

France, J. The text of the account of the capture of Jerusalem in the Ripoll Manuscript Bibliothèque Nationale (Latin) 5132. *English Historical Review* **53**, pp. 640–57, 1988.

France, J. Rodulfus Glaber and French politics in the early eleventh century. *Francia* **16**, pp. 101–112, 1989.

France, J. *Victory in the East: a military history of the First Crusade* (Cambridge: Cambridge University Press, 1994).

France, J. La stratégie arménienne de la première Croisade. In *Les Lusignans et l'Outre-Mer: Actes du Colloque Poitiers–Lusignan octobre 1993*, C. Mutafian (ed.) (Poitiers: Université de Poitiers, 1995).

France, J. The occasion of the coming of the Normans to southern Italy. *Journal of Medieval History* **17**, pp. 185–205, 1996.

France, J. Les origines de la première croisade: un nouvel examen. In *Autour de la première croisade*, M. Balard (ed.) (Paris: Publications de la Sorbonne, 1996), pp. 43–56.

France, J. Patronage and the appeal of the First Crusade. In *The First Crusade*, J. Phillips (ed.) (Manchester: Manchester University Press, 1997), pp. 5–20.

France, J. Technology and the success of the First Crusade. In *War and society in the eastern Mediterranean 7th–15th centuries*, Y. Lev (ed.) (Leiden: Brill, 1997), pp. 163–76.

France, J. The First Crusade as a naval enterprise. *The Mariner's Mirror* **83**, pp. 389–97, 1997.

France, J. The Battle of Carcano: the event and its importance. *War in History* (forthcoming).

France, J. & W. G. Zajac (eds). *The Crusades and their sources: essays presented to Bernard Hamilton* (Aldershot: Variorum, 1998).

French, D. H. A road problem: Roman or Byzantine. *Istanbuler Mitteilungen* **43**, pp. 445–54, 1993.

Fry, P. S. *Castles of Britain and Ireland* (Newton Abbot: David & Charles, 1996).

Gaffuri, L. M. *Carcano e il Barbarossa* (Carcano: Di Tacchini, 1992).

Gaier, C. Le problème de l'origine de l'industrie armurière liégeoise au moyen âge. *Chronique archéologique du pays de Liège* 1962), pp. 22–75.

Gaier, C. L'évolution et l'usage de l'armement personnel au pays de Liège du XII au XIV siècle. *Zeitschrift der Gesellschaft für historische Waffen-und Kostümkunde* **4**, pp. 65–86, 1962.

Gaier, C. *L'industrie et le commerce des armes dans les anciennes principautés belges du XIII à la fin du XV siècle* (Paris: Les Belles Lettres, 1973).

Gaier, C. *Armes et combats dans l'univers médiévale* (Brussels: De Boek-Wesmael, 1995).

Gaier, C. Le combat de Visé. In *Armes et Combats dans l'Univers Médiéval* (Brussels: De Boek-Wesmael, 1995), pp. 11–14.

Gaier, C. Quand l'arbalète était une nouveauté. Réflexions sur son rôle militaire du Xe au XIIIe siècle. In *Armes et combats dans l'univers médiévale* (Brussels: De Boek-Wesmael, 1995), pp. 159–82.

Gaier, C. La fonction stratégico-défensive du plat pays au Moyen Age dans la région de la Meuse moyenne. In *Armes et combats dans l'univers médiévale* (Brussels: De Boek-Wesmael, 1995), pp. 267–81.

Gaier, C. Mentalité collective de l'infantrie communale liégeoise au Moyen Age. In *Armes et combats dans l'univers médiévale* (Brussels: De Boek-Wesmael, 1995), pp. 311–17.

Gardelles, J. *Le Château féodale dans l'histoire médiévale* (Strasbourg: Publitotal, 1988).

Garnett, G. & J. Hudson (eds). *Law and government in medieval England and Normandy: essays in Honour of Sir James Holt* (Cambridge: Cambridge University Press, 1994).

Géraud, H. Les routiers au douzième siècle. *Bibliothèque de l'Ecole des Chartes* **3**, pp. 125–47, 1841–2.

Gervers, M. (ed.). *The Second Crusade and the Cistercians* (New York: St Martin's Press, 1992).

Gibb, H. A. R. Career of Nur ad-Din. In Setton, *Crusades*, vol. 1, pp. 513–27.

Gibb, H. A. R. The armies of Saladin. In *Studies in the civilization of Islam*, S. J. Shaw & W. R. Polk (eds) (Princeton: Princeton University Press, 1982), pp. 74–90.

Gillingham, J. *The kingdom of Germany in the High Middle Ages*. Historical Association Pamphlet G. 77, 1971.

Gillingham, J. *Richard the Lionheart* (London: Weidenfeld & Nicholson, 1978).

Gill, J. *Byzantium and the papacy 1198–1400* (New Brunswick: Rutgers University Press, 1979).

Gillingham, J. Introduction of knight service into England. *Battle* **4**, pp. 53–64, 1981.

Gillingham, J. Richard I and the science of war in the Middle Ages. In *War and government in the Middle Ages*, J. Gillingham & J. C. Holt (eds) (Woodbridge, 1984).

Gillingham, J. *The Angevin Empire* (New York: Holmes & Meier, 1984).

Gillingham, J. William the Bastard at war. In *Studies in medieval history presented to R. Allen-*

*Brown*, C. Harper-Bill, J. Holdsworth, J. Nelson (eds) (Woodbridge: Boydell & Brewer, 1989), pp. 41–58.

Gillingham, J. Conquering barbarians: war and chivalry in twelfth-century Britain. *The Haskins Society Journal* **4**, pp. 67–84, 1992.

Gillingham, J. *Richard Coeur de Lion: kingship, chivalry and war in the twelfth century* (London: Hambledon, 1994). The unromantic death of Richard I, pp. 155–80. The fall of the Angevin empire, pp. 193–200. War and chivalry in the history of William the Marshal, pp. 227–42.

Gillingham, J. Thegns and knights in eleventh-century England: Who was then the gentleman? *Transactions of the Royal Historical Society* **5**, pp. 129–54, 1995.

Gillingham, J. & J. C. Holt (eds). *War and government in the Middle Ages* (Woodbridge: Boydell & Brewer, 1984).

Gillmor, C. M. The introduction of the traction trebuchet into the Latin West. *Viator* **12**, pp. 1–8, 1981.

Godwin, G. N. *The civil war in Hampshire (1642–5) and the story of Basing House* (Southampton: Gilbert, 1904).

Graf, D. F. Camels, roads and wheels in late Antiquity. In *Donum Amicitiae*, E. Dąbrowa (ed.) (Krakow: Jagiellonian University Press, 1997), pp. 43–9.

*s'Graventsteen: Guide du Château des comtes de Flandre* (Gent: Archives Gent, 1980).

Griffiths, R. A. *Conquerors and conquered in medieval Wales* (Stroud: Sutton, 1994).

Grundmann, H. Rotten und Brabazonen, sölder-heere in 12 Jahrhundert. *Deutsches Archiv für die Erforschung des Mittelalters* **5**, pp. 419–92, 1942.

Guillot, O. *Le comte d'Anjou et son entourage au XIᵉ siècle*, [2 vols] (Paris: A. & J. Picard, 1972).

Hall, B. S. & D. C. West (eds). *On premodern technology and science: studies in honor of Lynn White, Jr* (Malibu: Udena, 1976).

Hallam, E. *Capetian France* (London: Longman, 1980).

Hallam, E. *Chronicles of the Crusades* (London: Weidenfeld & Nicolson, 1989).

Halphen, L. *Le comte d'Anjou au XI siècle* (Paris: Picard, 1906).

Hamblin, W. J. *The Fatamid army during the early Crusades* (PhD thesis, University of Michigan, 1985).

Hamilton, B. The elephant of Christ: Reynald of Châtillon. In *Religious motivation: biographical and sociological problems for the church historian*, D. Baker (ed.) (Oxford: Oxford University Press, 1978), pp. 97–108.

Hamilton, B. Continental drift: Prester John's progress through the Indies. In *Prester John, the Mongols and the ten lost tribes*, C. F. Beckingham & B. Hamilton (eds) (Aldershot: Variorum, 1996), 237–69.

Hampe, K. *Germany under the Salian and Hohenstaufen Emperors*, tr. R. Bennett (Oxford: Blackwell, 1973).

Hansen, P. V. Reconstructing a medieval trebuchet. *Military Illustrated Past and Present* **27**, pp. 9–16, 1990.

Harari, Y. The military role of the Frankish Turcopoles. *Mediterranean History Review* **12**, pp. 75–116, 1997.

Hardy, R. *Longbow. A social and military history* (Cambridge: P. Stephen, 1976).

Harper-Bill, C. & R. Harvey (eds). *Ideals and practice of medieval knighthood* (Woodbridge: Boydell & Brewer, 1986).

Harper-Bill, C., J. Holdsworth, J. Nelson (eds). *Studies in medieval history presented to R. Allen-Brown* (Woodbridge: Boydell & Brewer, 1989).

Harvey, J. *English medieval architects* (London: Batsford, 1954).

Harvey, J. & M. Byrne. A possible solution to the problem of Greek Fire. *Byzantinische Zeitschrift* **70**, pp. 91–9, 1977.

Harvey, S. The knight and the knight's fee in medieval England. *Past and Present* **49**, pp. 3–43, 1970.

Hassall, J. M. & D. Hill. Pont de l'Arche: Frankish influence on the West Saxon Burh? *Archaeological Journal* **127**, pp. 188–95, 1970.

Haverkamp, A. *Medieval Germany 1056–1273* (Oxford: Oxford University Press, 1988).

Haverkamp, A. & H. Vollrath (eds). *England and Germany in the High Middle Ages* (Oxford: Oxford University Press, 1996), pp. 221–33.

Head, T. The Peace-League of Bourges. In *The Peace of God: social violence and religious response in France around the year 1000*, T. Head & R. Landes (eds) (Ithaca: Cornell University Press, 1992), pp. 219–38.

Héliot, P. Le Château Gaillard et les fortresses des XII–XIII siècles en Europe occidentale. *Château Gaillard* **1**, pp. 54–75, 1962.

Herde, P. Die Schlact bei Tagliacozzo. Eine historisch–topographische Studie. *Zeitschrift fur Bayerische Landesgeschichte* **28**, pp. 679–744, 1962.

Herde, P. Taktiken muslimischer Heere vom ersten Kreuzzug bis 'Ayn Djalut (1260) und ihre Einwirkung auf de Schlact bei Tagliacozzo. In *Das Heilige Land im Mittelalter: Begegnungsvraum zwischen Orient und Okzident*, W. Fischer & J. Schneider (eds) (Neustadt: Verlag Degener, 1982), pp. 83–94.

Higham, R. & P. Baker, *Timber castles* (London: Batsford, 1992).

Hill, D. R. Trebuchets. *Viator* **4**, pp. 99–114, 1973.

Hill, J. H. & L. L. *Raymond IV de St Gilles, 1041 (ou 1042)–1105* (Paris: Privat, 1959).

Hoch, M. The choice of Damascus as the objective of the Second Crusade. In *Autour de la Première Croisade*, M. Balard (ed.) (Paris: Publications de la Sorbonne, 1996), pp. 359–70.

Hoch, M. The crusaders' strategy against Fatamid Ascalon and the Ascalon Project of the Second Crusade. In *The Second Crusade and the Cistercians*, M. Gervers (ed.) (New York: St Martin's Press, 1992), pp. 120–3.

Hoffman, H. Die Anfäng die Normannen in Süditalien. *Quellen und Forschungen aus Italienischen Archivum und Bibliotek* **47**, pp. 95–144, 1967.

Hoffmeyer, A. B. de. *An introduction to the history of the European Sword*. In *Gladius*, vol. 1 (Madrid: Instituto de Estudios sobre Armas Antiguas, 1961).

Hoffmeyer, A. B. de. *Arms and armour in Spain: a short survey* (Madrid: Instituto de Estudios sobre Armas Antiguas, 1982).

Hollister, C. W. *Anglo-Saxon military institutions on the eve of the Norman Conquest* (Oxford: Clarendon Press, 1962).

Hollister, C. W. *The military organisation of Norman England* (Oxford: Clarendon Press, 1965).

Holt, J. C. Politics and property in early medieval England. *Past and Present* **57**, pp. 3–52, (1972); **65**, pp. 130–2, 1974.

Holt, J. C. *The end of the Anglo-Norman realm* (Oxford: Oxford University Press, 1975).

Holt, J. C. The end of the Anglo-Norman Realm. *Proceedings of the British Academy* **61**, pp. 223–65, 1975.

Holt, J. C. *Robin Hood* (London: Thames and Hudson, 1982).

Holt, J. C. The loss of Normandy and royal finances. In *War and government in the Middle Ages: essays in honour of J. O. Prestwich*, J. Gillingham & J. C. Holt (eds.) (Woodbridge: Boydell & Brewer, 1984), pp. 92–105.

Holt, J. C. *Colonial England 1066–1215* (London: Hambledon, 1997).

Holt, J. C. Colonial England. In *Colonial England 1066–1215* (London: Hambledon, 1997), pp. 1–24.

Holt, P. M. *The age of the Crusades* (London: Longman, 1986).

Hooper, N. & M. Bennett, *Cambridge illustrated atlas of warfare: the Middle Ages* (Cambridge: Cambridge University Press, 1996).

Housley, N. J. Politics and heresy in Italy: anti-heretical Crusades, Orders and Confraternities in Italy 1200–1500. *Journal of Ecclesiastical History* **33**, pp. 193–208, 1982.

Housley, N. *The Italian Crusades* (Oxford: Clarendon Press, 1982).

Hughes, Q. *Military architecture* (London: H. Evelyn, 1974).

Humphreys, R. S. *From Saladin to the Mongols* (Albany: State University of New York Press, 1977).

Humphreys, R. S. The emergence of the Mamluk army. *Studia Islamica* **45**, pp. 67–99, 147–82, 1977.

Hutchinson, G. *Medieval ships and shipping* (Leicester: Leicester University Press, 1997).

Jackson, P. The crisis in the Holy Land in 1260. *English Historical Review* **95**, pp. 481–513, 1980.

Jessee, W. S. Urban violence and the *coup d'état* of Fulk le Réchin in Angers, 1067. *The Haskins Society Journal* **7**, pp. 75–82, 1995.

John, E. English feudalism and the structure of Anglo-Saxon society. In *Orbis Britanniae and other studies* (Leicester: University of Leicester Press, 1966).

Johns, C. N. *Caerphilly Castle, Mid-Glamorgan* (Cardiff: Ministry of Works, 1978).

Johnson, E. N. The Crusade of Frederick Barbarossa and Henry VI. In Setton, *Crusades*, vol. 2, pp. 87–122.

Johnson, E. N. The German crusades in the Baltic. In Setton, *Crusades*, vol. 3, pp. 545–85.

Joinville, *Life of St Louis*, M. R. B. Shaw (ed.) (Harmondsworth: Penguin, 1970).

Jones, P. N. & D. Renn. The military effectiveness of arrow-loops: some experiments at White Castle. *Château Gaillard: Etudes de Castellogie Médiévale* 9–10, pp. 445–56, 1982.

Jones, W. R. The image of the barbarian in medieval Europe. *Comparative Studies in Society and History* **13**, pp. 376–407, 1971.

Jordan, E. *Les origines de la domination Angevine en Italie*, [2 vols] (New York: Burt Franklin, 1960).

Jordan, W. C. *Louis IX and the challenge of Crusade* (Princeton: Princeton University Press, 1979).

Julien, C. A. *A history of North Africa*, tr. J. Petrie (London: Routledge & Kegan Paul, 1970).

Kantorowicz, E. *Frederick II*, tr. E. O. Lorimer (London: Constable, 1931).

Kapelle, W. E. *The Norman Conquest of the North. The region and its transformation 1000–1135* (London: Croom Helm, 1979).

Kedar, B. Z., H. E. Mayer, R. C. Smail (eds). *Outremer* (Jerusalem: Yad Izhak Ben-Zvi Institute, 1982).

Kedar, B. Z. (ed.). *The Horns of Hattin* (London: Variorum, 1992).

Kedar, B. Z. The battle of Hattin revisited. In *The Horns of Hattin*, B. Z. Kedar (ed.) (London: Variorum, 1992), pp. 190–207.

Keegan, J. & R. Holmes. *Soldiers: a history of men in battle* (London: Hamilton, 1985).

Kennedy, H. *Crusader castles* (Cambridge: Cambridge University Press, 1994).

Kenyon, J. R. *Medieval fortifications* (Leicester: Leicester University Press, 1990).

Kenyon, J. R. & R. Avent, *Castles in Wales and the Marches* (Cardiff: University of Wales Press, 1987).

Kiff, J. Images of war. *Battle* **7**, pp. 177–94, 1984.

King, E. (ed.). *The anarchy of Stephen's reign* (Oxford: Clarendon Press, 1994).

Knudson, C. A. & J. Misrahi. French medieval literature. In *The medieval literature of western Europe*, J. H. Fisher (ed.) (New York: New York University Press, 1966), pp. 110–90.

Köhler, M.A. *Allianzen und Verträge zwischen frankischen und islamischen Herrschern im Vorderen Orient* (Berlin: W. Gruyter, 1991).

Kreutz, B. M. *Before the Normans: southern Italy in the ninth and tenth centuries* (Philadelphia: University of Pennsylvania Press, 1991).

Krieger, K. F. Obligatory military service and the use of mercenaries in imperial military campaigns under the Hohenstaufen emperors. In *England and Germany in the High Middle Ages*, A. Haverkamp & H. Vollrath (eds) (Oxford: Clarendon Press, 1996), pp. 151–68.

Kuske, B. *Köln, der Rhein und das Reich* (Koln: Bohlau, 1956).

Larner, J. *Italy in the age of Dante and Petrarch 1216–1380* (London: Longman, 1980).

Latimer, P. Henry II's campaign against the Welsh in 1165. *Welsh History Review* **14**, pp. 547–51, 1989.

Legato, G. Fra ordini cavallereschi e crociata: milites ad terminum e confraternitates armate. In *Militia Christi e Crociata nei secoli XI–XII* (Milan: Vita e Pensiero, Università Cattolica del sacro Cuore, 1992), pp. 645–97.

Le Goff, J. *St Louis* (Paris: Gallimard, 1996).

Leighton, A. C. *Transport and communication in early medieval Europe AD 500–1100* (Newton Abbot: David & Charles, 1972).

Lemarignier, J. F. *Recherches sur l'homage en marche et les frontières féodales* (Lille: Bibliothèque Universitaire, 1945).

Lemarignier, J.F. *Le gouvernement royal aux premiers temps capétiens (987–1108)* (Paris: J. Picard, 1956).

Léonard, E. G. *Les Angevins de Naples* (Paris: Presses Universitaires de France, 1954).

Lev, Y. *State and society in Fatimid Egypt* (Leiden: Brill, 1991).

Lev, Y. Regime, army and society in medieval Egypt, 9th–12th centuries. In *War and society in the eastern Mediterranean 7th–15th centuries*, Y. Lev (ed.) (Leiden: Brill, 1996), pp. 115–52.

Lewis, E. *Medieval political ideas,* [2 vols] (London: Routledge & Kegan Paul, 1954).

Lewis, S. *The art of Matthew Paris in the Chronica Majora* (Aldershot: Scolar Press, 1987).

Leyser, K. The battle at the Lech 955: a study in tenth century warfare. *History* **50**, pp. 1–25, 1965.

Leyser, K. Henry I and the beginnings of the German Empire. *English Historical Review* **83**, pp. 1–32, 1968.

Leyser, K. Early medieval warfare. In *Communications and power in medieval Europe*, T. Reuter (ed.) (London: Hambledon, 1994), pp. 29–50.

Lindner, R. P. Nomadism, horses and Huns. *Past and Present* **92**, pp. 3–19, 1981.

Lock, P. *The Franks in the Aegean 1204–1500* (London: Longman, 1995).

Lomax, D. W. *The reconquest of Spain* (London: Longman 1978).

Lot, F. & R. Fawtier (eds). *Le premier budget de la monarchie française* (Paris: H. Champion, 1932).

Lotter, F. The crusading idea and the conquest of the region East of the Elbe. In *Medieval frontier societies*, R. Bartlett & A. MacKay (eds) (Oxford: Clarendon Press, 1989), pp. 285–94.

Loud, G. *Gens Normannorum* – myth and reality. *Battle* **4**, pp. 104–16, 1981.

Loud, G. How Norman was the Norman Conquest of southern Italy? *Nottingham Medieval Studies* **25**, pp. 13–34, 1981.

Lourie, E. A society organised for war – medieval Spain. *Past and Present* **36**, pp. 54–76, 1966.

Loyn, H. R. *Anglo-Saxon England and the Norman Conquest* (London: Longman, 1962).

Luchaire, A. Un essai de révolution sociale sous Philippe Auguste. *Grand Revue* **2**, pp. 8–46, 1900.

Luchaire, A. *Social France at the time of Philip Augustus* (New York: Ungar, 1957).

Lyons, M. C. & D. E. P. Jackson. *Saladin. the politics of holy war* (Cambridge: Cambridge University Press, 1982).

McGlynn, S. *The invasion of England 1216* (Stroud: Sutton, 1998).

Mallett, M. *Mercenaries and their masters. Warfare in Renaissance Italy* (London: Bodley Head, 1974).

Marsden, E. W. *Greek and Roman Artillery*, [2 vols] (Oxford: Clarendon Press, 1969–71).

Marshall, C. *Warfare in the Latin East 1192–1291* (Cambridge: Cambridge University Press, 1992).

Martindale, J. Conventum inter Guilelmum Aquitanorum comes et Hugonem Chiliarchum. *English Historical Review* **84**, pp. 528–48, 1969.

Maryon, H. Pattern welding and Damascening of sword-blades. *Conservation* **5**, pp. 25–37, 1960.

Matthew, D. *The Norman Kingdom of Sicily* (Cambridge: Cambridge University Press, 1992).

Mayer, H. E. Studies in the history of Queen Melisende of Jerusalem. *Dumbarton Oaks Papers* **21**, pp. 95–182, 1972.

Mayer, H. E. *The Crusades* (Oxford: Oxford University Press, 1990).

Melville, C. P. & M. C. Lyons. Saladin's Hattin letter. In *The horns of Hattin*, B. Z. Kedar (ed.) (London: Variorum, 1992), pp. 208–12.

Miskimin, H. A., D. Herlihy, A. L. Udovilch (eds). *The medieval city* (New Haven: Yale University Press, 1977).

Mitchison, R. *A history of Scotland* (London: Methuen, 1970).

Mitteis, H. *The state in the Middle Ages*, tr. H. F. Orton (Amsterdam: North Holland, 1975).

Morgan, D. *The Mongols* (Oxford: Blackwell, 1986).

Morillo, S. Hastings, an unusual battle. *The Haskins Society Journal* **2**, pp. 95–104, 1990.

Morillo, S. *Warfare under the Anglo-Norman Kings, 1066–1135* (Woodbridge: Boydell & Brewer, 1994).

Morris, J. E. *The Welsh wars of Edward I. A contribution to medieval military history* (Oxford: Oxford University Press, 1901).

Motta, E. Armaiuoli milanesi nel periodo visconteo-sforzesco. In *Archivio Storico Lombardo* **41**, pp. 179–80, 1914.

Mulinder, A. *The crusading expeditions of 1101* (PhD thesis, Department of History, University of Wales, Swansea, 1997).

Munz, P. *Frederick Barbarossa: a study in medieval politics* (London: Eyre & Spottiswoode, 1969).

Murray, A. *Reason and society in the Middle Ages* (Oxford: Clarendon Press, 1978).

Mutafian, C. *Les Lusignans et l'Outre-Mer: Actes du Colloque Poitiers–Lusignan octobre 1993* (Poitiers: Université de Poitiers, 1995).

Myers, H. A. & H. Wolfram (eds). *Medieval kingship* (Chicago: Nelson-Hall, 1981).

Needham, J. China's trebuchets, manned and counterweighted. In *On premodern technology and science: studies in honor of Lynn White, Jr*, B. S. Hall & D. C. West (eds) (Malibu: Udena, 1976), pp. 108–9.

Nelson, J. Ninth century knighthood: the evidence of Nithard. In *Studies in medieval history presented to R. Allen-Brown*, C. Harper-Bill, C. J. Holdsworth, J. Nelson (eds) (Woodbridge: Boydell & Brewer, 1989), pp. 255–66.

Nelson, L. H. *The Normans and South Wales 1070–1171* (Austin: University of Texas Press, 1966).

Nesbitt, J. W. Rate of march of crusading armies in Europe: a study in computation. *Traditio* **19**, pp. 167–82, 1963.

Newby, P. H. *Saladin in his time* (London: Faber, 1983).

Nicholas, K. S. When feudal ideals failed: conflicts between lords and vassals in the Low Countries 1127–1296. In *The rusted hauberk: feudal ideas of order and their decline*, L. O. Purdon (ed.) (Gainesville: University Press of Florida, 1993).

Nicolle, D. C. The impact of the European couched lance on Muslim military tradition. *The Journal of the Arms and Armour Society* **10**, pp. 6–40, 1980.

Nicolle, D. C. Arms and armour illustrated in the art of the Latin East. In *The Horns of Hattin*, B. Z. Kedar (ed.) (London: Variorum, 1992), pp. 327–40.

Nicolle, D. C. *Medieval warfare source book 1: Warfare in western Christendom* (London: Arms and Armour, 1995).

Nicholson, H. *Templars, Hospitallers and Teutonic knights: images of the military orders 1128–1291* (Leicester: Leicester University Press, 1993).

Nicholson, R. L. Growth of the Latin states. In Setton, *Crusades*, vol. 1, pp. 410–48.

Nicholson, R. L. *Jocelin III and the fall of the crusader states* (Leiden: Brill, 1973).

Niermeyer, J. F. *Mediae Latinitatis Lexicon Minus* (Leiden: Brill, 1954–76).

Norgate, K. *England under the Angevin kings*, [2 vols] (London: Eyre Methuen, 1887).

Norman, V. *Arms and armour* (London: Weidenfeld & Nicolson, 1964).

Nortier, M. & J. W. Baldwin. Contribution à l'étude des finances de Philippe Auguste. *Bibliothèque de l'Ecole des Chartes* **138**, pp. 5–336, 1980.

Oakeshott, R. E. *The sword in the age of chivalry* (London: Lutterworth Press, 1964).

Pacaut, M. *Louis VII et son royaume* (Paris: S. E. V. P. E. N., 1964).

Pacaut, M. *Frederick Barbarossa* (London: Collins, 1970).

Painter, S. *Studies in the history of the English feudal baronage* (Baltimore: Johns Hopkins Press, 1943).

Painter, S. The Crusade of Theobald of Champagne and Richard of Cornwall. In Setton, *Crusades*, vol. 2, pp. 463–86.

Painter, S. The Third Crusade. In Setton, *Crusades*, vol. 2, pp. 45–86.

Pamlenyi, E. *History of Hungary*, tr. M. Morris & R. E. Allen (London: Collets, 1975).

Parry, V. J. & M. E. Yapp (eds). *War, technology and society in the Middle East* (London: Oxford University Press, 1975).

Partington, J. R. *A history of Greek Fire and gunpowder* (Cambridge: Heffers, 1960).

Partner, P. *The lands of St Peter: the papal states in the Middle Ages and the early Renaissance* (London: Eyre Methuen, 1972).

Peddie, J. *Alfred the Good Soldier: his life and campaigns* (Bath: Millstream, 1992).

Peyer, H. C. Das Reisekönigtum des Mittelalters. *Vierteljahrschrift für Sozial- und Wirtschaftsgeschichte* **51**, pp. 1–21, 1964.

Phillips, E. D. *The Mongols* (London: Thames and Hudson, 1969).

Phillips, J. P. Hugh of Payns and the 1129 Damascus Crusade. In *The military orders. Fighting for the faith and caring for the sick*, M. Barber (ed.) (Aldershot: Variorum, 1994), pp. 141–7.

Phillips, J. P. *Defenders of the Holy Land: relations between the Latin East and the West 1119–1187* (Oxford: Oxford University Press, 1996).

Pierce, I. The knight, his arms and armour in the eleventh and twelfth centuries. In *Ideals and practice of medieval knighthood*, C. Harper-Bill & R. Harvey (eds) (Woodbridge: Boydell & Brewer, 1986).

Pierce, I. Arms, armour and warfare in the eleventh century. *Battle* **10**, pp. 237–57, 1987.

Pipes, D. *Slave soldiers and Islam* (Yale: Yale University Press, 1981).

Poly, J.-P. & E. Bournazel. *The feudal transformation 900–1200* (New York: Holmes & Meier, 1991).

Poole, A. L., *The obligations of society in the eleventh and twelfth centuries* (Oxford: Clarendon Press, 1946).

Poole, A. L. *From Domesday Book to Magna Carta 1087–1216* (Oxford: Oxford University Press, 1955).

Pounds, N. J. G. *An economic history of medieval Europe* (London: Longman, 1974).

Pounds, N. J. G. *The medieval castle in England and Wales. A social and political history* (Cambridge: Cambridge University Press, 1990).

Powell, J. M. *The anatomy of a crusade 1213–1221* (Philadelphia: University of Pennsylvania Press, 1986).

Powers, J. F. *A society organised for war: the Iberian municipal militias in the Central Middle Ages 1000–1284* (Berkeley: University of California Press, 1988).

Powers, J. F. Life on the cutting edge: the Luso-Hispanic frontier in the twelfth century. In *The medieval city under siege*, I. A. Corfis & M. Wolfe (eds) (Woodbridge: Boydell & Brewer, 1995), pp. 17–34.

Powicke, F. M. *The loss of Normandy 1189–1204* (Manchester: Manchester University Press, 1913).

Powicke, F. M. *King Henry III and the Lord Edward*, [2 vols] (Oxford: Clarendon Press, 1947).

Powicke, F. M. *The thirteenth century* (Oxford: Clarendon Press, 1962).

Powicke, M. R. Distraint of knighthood and military obligation under Henry III. *Speculum* **25**, pp. 457–70, 1950.

Prawer, J. *The Latin Kingdom of Jerusalem: European colonisation in the Middle Ages* (London: Weidenfeld & Nicolson, 1972).

Prawer, J. *Crusader institutions* (Oxford: Clarendon Press, 1980).

Prestwich, J. O. War and finance in the Anglo-Norman state. *Transactions of the Royal Historical Society* **4**, pp. 19–43, 1954.

Prestwich, J. O. Military intelligence under the Norman and Angevin kings. In *Law and government in medieval England and Normandy: essays in honour of Sir James Holt*, G. Garnett & J. Hudson (eds) (Cambridge: Cambridge University Press, 1994), pp. 1–30.

Prestwich, M. *War, politics and finance under Edward I* (London: Faber, 1972).

Prestwich, M. *Edward I* (London: Methuen, 1980).

Prestwich, M. *Miles in armis strenuus:* the knight at war. *Transactions of the Royal Historical Society* **5**, pp. 207–12, 1995.

Prestwich, M. *Armies and warfare in the Middle Ages: the English experience* (Yale: Yale University Press, 1996).

Pringle, D. Richard I and the walls of Ascalon. *Palestine Exploration Quarterly* **116**, pp. 133–47, 1984.

Pringle, D. *The Red Tower* (London: British School of Archaeology in Jerusalem, 1986).

Pringle, D. Town defences in the crusader Kingdom of Jerusalem. In *The medieval city under Siege*, I. A. Corfis & M. Wolfe (eds) (Woodbridge: Boydell & Brewer, 1995), pp. 69–112.

Pringle, D. *Secular buildings in the Crusader Kingdom of Jerusalem: an archaeological gazetteer* (Cambridge: Cambridge University Press, 1997).

Pryor, J. H. Transportation of horses by sea during the era of the Crusades, eighth century to AD 1285. *Mariner's Mirror* **68**, pp. 9–27, 103–22, 1982.

Pryor, J. H. *Geography, technology and war: studies in the maritime history of the Mediterranean 649–1571* (Cambridge: Cambridge University Press, 1992), pp. 112–34.

Purcell, M. *Papal crusading policy 1244–91* (Leiden: Brill, 1975).

Purdon, L. O. (ed.). *The rusted hauberk: feudal ideas of order and their decline* (Gainesville: University Press of Florida, 1993).

Queller, D. E. *The Fourth Crusade* (Leicester: Leicester University Press, 1978).

Rabie, H. The training of the Mamluk Faris. In *War, technology and society in the Middle East*, V. J. Parry & M. E. Yapp (eds) (London: Oxford University Press, 1975), pp. 153–63.

Reddaway, W. F., J. H. Penson, O. Halecki, R. Dyboski. *Cambridge History of Poland*, [2 vols] (Cambridge: Cambridge University Press, 1950).

Reid, N. H. *Scotland under the reign of Alexander III* (Edinburgh: John Donald, 1990).

Renn, D. F. *Norman castles in Britain* (London: Baker, 1968).

Renn, D. F. Burhgeat and Gonfanon: two sidelights from the Bayeux Tapestry. *Battle* **16**, pp. 177–98, 1994.

Renouard, Y. *Les villes d'Italie du X au début du XIV siècle*, [2 vols] (Paris: Société d'Édition d'Enseignement Supérieur, 1969).

Reuter, T. (ed.). *The medieval nobility* (Amsterdam: North Holland, 1978).

Reuter, T. Plunder and tribute in the Carolingian Empire. *Transactions of the Royal Historical Society* **35**, pp. 75–94, 1985.

Reuter, T. *Germany in the early Middle Ages, 800–1056* (London: Longman, 1991).

Reuter, T. *Episcopi cum sua militia*: the prelate as warrior in the early Staufer era. In *Warriors and churchmen in the High Middle Ages: essays presented to K. Leyser*, T. Reuter (ed.) (London: Hambledon, 1992), pp. 79–94.

Reuter, T. (ed.). *Communications and power in medieval Europe* (London: Hambledon, 1994).

Reuter, T. *Filii matris nostrae pugnant adversum nos*. Bonds and tensions between prelates and their *milites* in the German High Middle Ages. In *Chiesa e mondo feudale nei secoli x–xii* (Milan: Vita e Pensiero, Università Cattolica del sacro Cuore, 1995), pp. 247–76.

Reyerson, K. & F. Powe (eds). *The medieval castle: romance and reality* (Dubuque: Kendall-Hunt, 1984).

Reynolds, S. *Fiefs and vassals* (Oxford: Oxford University Press, 1994).

Richard, J. An account of the battle of Hattin referring to the Frankish mercenaries in the Oriental Muslim States. *Speculum* **27**, pp. 168–77, 1952.

Richard, J. *Les ducs de Bourgogne et la formation du duché du XI au XIV siècles* (Paris: Les Belles Lettres, 1954).

Richard, J. *The Latin Kingdom of Jerusalem*, tr. J. Shirley, [2 vols] (Amsterdam: North Holland, 1979).

Richard, J. *St Louis* (Paris: A. Fayard, 1983).

Richardson, H. G. & G. O. Sayles. *The governance of medieval England from the Conquest to Magna Carta* (Edinburgh: Edinburgh University Press, 1963).

Richmond, C. & I. Harvey (eds). *Recognitions: essays presented to Edmund Fryde* (Aberystwyth: National Library of Wales, 1996).

Reilly, B. F. *The contest of Christian and Moslem in Spain* (Oxford: Blackwell, 1992).

Riley-Smith, J. *The Knights of St John in Jerusalem and Cyprus c. 1050–1310* (London: Macmillan, 1967).

Riley-Smith, J. A note on confraternities in the Latin Kingdom of Jerusalem. *Bulletin of the Institute of Historical Research* **44**, pp. 301–8, 1971.

Riley-Smith, J. *The Crusades. A short history* (London: Athlone, 1987).

Riley-Smith, J. (ed.). *The atlas of the Crusades* (London: Times Books, 1991).

Riley-Smith, J. *The first crusaders 1095–1131* (Cambridge: Cambridge University Press, 1997).

Riley-Smith, L. & J. *The Crusades: ideal and reality 1095–1274* (London: Edward Arnold, 1981).

Ritchie, G. *The Normans in Scotland* (Edinburgh: Edinburgh University Press, 1954).

316

Robinson, I. S. Gregory VII and the Soldiers of Christ. *History* **58**, pp. 169–72, 1973.

Rodger, N. A. M. *The safeguard of the sea: a naval history of Britain 1660–1649* (London: HarperCollins, 1997), pp. 31–50.

Rogers, R. *Latin siege warfare in the twelfth century* (Oxford: Clarendon Press, 1992).

Röhricht, R. (ed.) *Regesta regni hierosolymitani* (New York: Burt Franklin, 1960).

Ross, D. J. A. L'originalité de "Turoldus": le maniement de lance. *Cahiers de Civilisation Médiévale* **6**, pp. 127–38, 1963.

Round, H. *The king's sergeants and offices of state* (London: Woburn, 1971).

Round, J. H. *Geoffrey de Mandeville* (London: Longman, 1892).

Rowlands, I. W. King John, Stephen Langton and Rochester Castle, 1213–15. In *Studies in medieval history presented to R. Allen-Brown,* C. Harper-Bill, J. Holdsworth, J. Nelson (eds) (Woodbridge: Boydell & Brewer, 1989), pp. 267–79.

Runciman, S. Crusader states 1243–91. In Setton, *Crusades,* vol. 2, pp. 557–98.

Runciman, S. *The Sicilian Vespers. A history of the Mediterranean world in the later thirteenth century* (Harmondsworth: Penguin, 1960).

Russell, F. H. *The just war in the Middle Ages* (Cambridge: Cambridge University Press, 1975).

Saadé, G. Histoire du Château de Saladin. *Studi Medievali* **9**, pp. 980–1017, 1968.

Saunders, A. D. (ed.). *Five castle excavations* (London: Royal Archaeological Institute, 1978).

Saunders, J. J. *History of the Mongol Conquests* (London: Routledge & Kegan Paul, 1971).

Savvides, A. G. C. Late Byzantine and crusader historiographers on Turkish mercenaries in Greek and Latin armies: the Tucopoles/Tourkopoloi. In *The making of Byzantine history: essays dedicated to D. M. Nicol,* R. Beaton & C. Roueché (eds) (Aldershot: Variorum, 1993), pp. 122–36.

Sawyer, P. H. & I. Wood. *Early medieval kingship* (Leeds: Leeds University Press, 1977).

Sayers, D. L. (ed). *The Song of Roland,* Lines 1277–9 (Harmondsworth: Penguin, 1957).

Schein, S. *Fideles crucis: the papacy, the West and the recovery of the Holy Land 1274–1314* (Oxford: Clarendon Press, 1991).

Schein, S. The Templars: the regular army of the Holy Land and the spearhead of the army of its reconquest. In *I Templari: mito e storia,* G. Minucci & F. Sardi (eds) (Sienna: A. G. Viti-Riccucci, 1989), pp. 15–28.

Schevill, F. *Siena, history of a medieval commune* (London: Chapman & Hall, 1909).

Schevill, F. *A history of Florence* (New York: F. Ungar, 1961).

Schlight, J. *Monarchs and mercenaries* (Bridgeport: Bridgeport University Press, 1968).

Schlumberger, G. *Campagnes du roi Amaury I en Egypte* (Paris: Plon, 1906).

Schneider, R. *Die Artillerie des Mittelalters* (Berlin: Weidmann, 1910).

Schoenfeld, E. J. Anglo-Saxon *burhs* and continental *burgen*: early medieval fortifications in constitutional perspective. *The Haskins Society Journal* **6**, pp. 49–66, 1994.

Semaan, K. I. (ed.). *Islam and the Medieval West* (Albany: State University of New York Press, 1980).

Setton, K. M. The Catalans in Greece 1311–80. In Setton, K. M. *Crusades,* vol. 3, pp. 167–225.

Shatzmiller, M. The Crusades and Islamic warfare – a re-evaluation. *Der Islam* **69**, pp. 247–88, 1992.

Shneidman, J. L. *The rise of the Aragonese–Catalan Empire 1200–1350,* [2 vols] (New York: New York University Press, 1970).

Singer, C., E. J. Holmyard, A. R. Hill, T. I. Williams (eds). *History of Technology* 2: *The Mediterranean civilizations and the Middle Ages 700BC–AD1500* (Oxford: Clarendon Press, 1956).

Smail, R. C. The predicaments of Guy of Lusignan, 1183–87. In *Outremer,* B. Z. Kedar,

H. E. Mayer, R. C. Smail (eds). (Jerusalem: Yad Izhak Ben-Zvi Institute, 1982), pp. 161–4.

Smail, R. C. *Crusading warfare 1097–1193* (Cambridge: Cambridge University Press, 1995).

Smith, C. (ed.). *Christian and Muslim in Spain*, [3 vols] (Warminster: Aris & Phillips, 1988).

Smith, J. M. H. *Province and Empire: Brittany and the Carolingians* (Cambridge: Cambridge University Press, 1992).

Smith, J. M. Mongol society and military in the Middle East: antecedents and adaptations. In *War and society in the eastern Mediterranean*, Y. Lev (ed.) (Leiden: Brill, 1997), pp. 250–3.

Southern, R. W. *The making of the Middle Ages* (London: Hutchinson, 1953).

Southern, R. W. *Western views of Islam in the Middle Ages* (Cambridge, Mass.: Harvard University Press, 1962).

Sprandel, R. *Das Eisengewerbe in Mittelalter* (Stuttgart: Anton Hiersemann, 1968).

Stafford, P. A. The farm of one night and the organisation of King Edward's estates in Domesday. *Economic History Review* **33**, pp. 491–502, 1980.

Stafford, P. *Unification and conquest: a political and social history of England in the tenth and eleventh centuries* (London: Edward Arnold, 1989).

Stenton, F. M. *The first century of English feudalism 1066–1166* (Oxford: Clarendon Press, 1961).

Stenton, F. M. *Anglo-Saxon England* (Oxford: Clarendon Press, 1971).

Stevenson, W. W. Trinoda necessitas. *English Historical Review* **29**, pp. 689–703, 1914.

Strayer, J. R. The crusades of Louis IX. In Setton, *Crusades*, vol. 2, pp. 487–521.

Strayer, J. R. *On the medieval origins of the modern state* (Princeton: Princeton University Press, 1970).

Strayer, J. R. The crusade against Aragon. In *Medieval statecraft and the perspectives of History* (Princeton: Princeton University Press, 1971), pp. 107–22.

Strayer, J. R. The costs and profits of war. The Anglo-French conflict 1293–1303. In *The medieval city*, H. A. Miskimin, D. Herlihy, A. L. Udovilch (eds) (New Haven: Yale University Press, 1977), pp. 272–3.

Strayer, J. R. *The reign of Philip the Fair* (Princeton: Princeton University Press, 1980).

Strickland, M. Military technology and conquest: the anomaly of Anglo-Saxon England. *Battle* **19**, pp. 353–82, 1996.

Strickland, M. *War and chivalry: the conduct and perception of war in England and Normandy 1066–1217* (Cambridge: Cambridge University Press, 1996).

Sumption, J. *The Albigensian Crusade* (London: Faber, 1978).

Suppe, F. C. The cultural significance of decapitation in high Medieval Wales and the Marches. *Bulletin of the Board of Celtic Studies* **36**, pp. 147–60, 1989.

Suppe, F. C. *Military institutions on the Welsh Marches: Shropshire 1066–1300* (Woodbridge: Boydell & Brewer, 1994).

Swift, F. D. *James I of Aragon* (Oxford: Clarendon Press, 1894).

Tabacco, G. *The struggle for power in medieval Italy* (Cambridge: Cambridge University Press, 1989).

Taylor, A. J. *The King's works in Wales 1277–1330* (London: HMSO, 1974).

Taylor, A. Master Bertram, Ingeniator regis. In *Studies in medieval history presented to R. Allen-Brown*, C. Harper-Bill, J. Holdsworth, J. Nelson (eds) (Woodbridge: Boydell & Brewer, 1989), pp. 289–304.

Tellenbach, G. *The Church in western Europe from the tenth to the early twelfth century*, tr. T. Reuter (Cambridge: Cambridge University Press, 1993).

Terraine, J. *The white heat: the new warfare 1914–18* (London: Sidgwick & Jackson, 1982).

Thirsk, J. (ed.). *The agrarian history of England and Wales*, vol. 2 (Cambridge: Cambridge University Press, 1988).

Thompson, M. W. Motte substructures. *Medieval Archaeology* **5**, pp. 305–6, 1961.

Thompson, M. W. *The rise of the castle* (Cambridge: Cambridge University Press, 1991).

Thordeman, B. *Armour from the Battle of Wisby 1361*, [2 vols] (Stockholm: Antikvitets Akademien, 1939–40).

Tibble, S. *Monarchy and lordship in the Latin Kingdom of Jerusalem 1099–1291* (Oxford: Clarendon Press, 1989).

Toch, M. The medieval German city under siege. In *The medieval city under siege*, I. A. Corfis & M. Wolfe (eds) (Woodbridge: Boydell & Brewer, 1995), pp. 35–48.

Tooke J. D. *The just war in Aquinas and Grotius* (London: S.P.C.K., 1965).

Toy, S. *A history of fortification from 3000 BC to AD 1700* (London: Heinemann, 1955).

Toubert, P. *Les structures du Latium médiéval et la Sabine du IX siècle à la fin du XII siècle* (Rome: Bibliothèque des Ecoles Françaises d'Athène et de Rome, 1973).

Turner, R. V. *King John* (London: Longman, 1994).

Turvey, R. *The Lord Rhys, Prince of Deheubarth* (Llandysul: Gomer, 1997).

Tyerman, C. *England and the Crusades 1095–1588* (Chicago: Chicago University Press, 1988).

Unger, R. W. *The ship in the medieval economy 600–1600* (London: Croom Helm, 1980).

Urban, W. L. The organization of the defense of the Livonian frontier in the thirteenth century. *Speculum* **48**, pp. 525–32, 1973.

Urban, W. L. *The Baltic Crusade* (Dekalb: Northern Illinois University Press, 1975).

Urban, W. L. *The Livonian Crusade* (Washington: University Press of America, 1981).

Verbruggen, J. F. La tactique militaire des armées de Chevaliers. *Revue du Nord* **29**, pp. 163–8, 1947.

Verbruggen, J. F. Note sur le sens des mots castrum, castellum et quelques autres expressions qui désignent les fortifications. *Revue Belge de Philosophie et d'Histoire* **27**, pp. 147–55, 1950.

Verbruggen, J. F. De Godendag. *Militaria Belgica* **1**, pp. 65–70, 1977.

Verbruggen, J. F. Het epos der Vlamme gemmentenaren. De Slag der Gulden Sporen 11 juli 1302. *Revue Belge d'Histoire Militaire* **22**, pp. 285–312, 1977.

Vercauteren, F. A kindred in northern France in the eleventh and twelfth centuries. In *The medieval nobility*, T. Reuter (ed.) (Amsterdam: North Holland, 1979), pp. 87–103.

Verlinden, C. *Robert I le Frison, comté de Flandre* (Antwerp/Paris/'S Gravenhage: De Sikkel, E. Campion, M. Nijhoff, 1935).

Vaughan, R. *The illustrated chronicles of Matthew Paris* (Cambridge: Sutton, 1993).

Vincent, N. *Peter des Roches: an alien in English politics 1205–38* (Cambridge: Cambridge University Press, 1996).

Wadsworth, J. & O. Sherby. On the Bulat–Damascus steel revisisted. *Progress in Materials* **25**, pp. 35–68, 1980.

Waley, D. Papal armies in the thirteenth century. *English Historical Review* **72**, pp. 1–30, 1957.

Waley, D. *The papal state in the thirteenth century* (London: Macmillan, 1961).

Waley, D. The army of the Florentine Republic from the twelfth to the fourteenth century. In *Florentine Studies*, N. Rubinstein (ed.) (London: Faber & Faber, 1968), pp. 109–39.

Waley, D. *The Italian City–Republics* (London: Longman, 1969).

Waley, D. *Condotte* and *Condottierri* in the thirteenth century. *Proceedings of the British Academy* **61**, pp. 337–71, 1975.

Waley, D. *Siena and the Sienese in the thirteenth century* (Cambridge: Cambridge University Press, 1991).

Waley, D. Chivalry and cavalry at San Gimignano: knighthood in a small Italian commune. In *Recognitions: essays presented to Edmund Fryde*, C. Richmond & I. Harvey (eds) (Aberystwyth: National Library of Wales, 1996).

Wallace-Hadrill, M. W. *Early Germanic kingship in England and on the continent* (Oxford: Blackwell, 1971).

Warren, W. L. *Henry II* (London: Eyre Methuen, 1973).

Waugh, S. L. Reluctant knights and jurors: respites, exemptions and public obligations in the reign of Henry III. *Speculum* **58**, pp. 937–86, 1983.

Werner, K. F. Kingdom and principality in twelfth-century France. In *The medieval nobility*, T. Reuter (ed.) (Amsterdam: North Holland, 1978), pp. 243–4.

White, L. T. *Medieval technology and social change* (Oxford: Oxford University Press, 1962).

White, L. Theophilus redivivus. *Technology and Culture* **5**, pp. 224–33, 1964.

Whittow, M. *The making of Orthodox Byzantium 600–1025* (London: Macmillan, 1996).

Wickham, C. *Early medieval Italy: central power and local society* (London: Macmillan, 1981).

Williams, A. A bell-house and a burh-geat: lordly residences in England before the Norman Conquest. *Medieval Knighthood* **4**, pp. 221–40, 1992.

Williams, G. A. *Medieval London: from commune to capital* (London: Athlone, 1963).

Wise, T. *The wars of the crusade* (London: Osprey, 1978).

Wolfram, H. *Medieval kingship* (Chicago: Nelson-Hall, 1962).

Wood, M. *The English medieval house* (London: Ferndale, 1983).

Wormald, F. (ed.). *The Winchester Psalter* (London: Harvey, Miller & Medcalf, 1993).

Yewdale, R. B. *Bohemond I Prince of Antioch* (Princeton: Princeton University Press, 1924).

Zacour, N. P. The Childrens' Crusade. In Setton, *Crusades*, vol. 2, pp. 325–42.

Ziada, M. M. The Mamluk Sultans to 1293. In Setton, *Crusades*, vol. 2, pp. 735–58.

Ziezulewicz, W. An argument for historical continuity. *Medieval Prosopography* **8**, pp. 93–105, 1985.

# Index

321